MORALITY

MORALITY

A NEW JUSTIFICATION OF
THE MORAL RULES

BERNARD GERT

OXFORD UNIVERSITY PRESS
New York   Oxford
1988

Oxford University Press

Oxford   New York   Toronto
Delhi   Bombay   Calcutta   Madras   Karachi
Petaling Jaya   Singapore   Hong Kong   Tokyo
Nairobi   Dar es Salaam   Cape Town
Melbourne   Auckland

and associated companies in
Berlin   Ibadan

Published by Oxford University Press, Inc.,
200 Madison Avenue, New York, New York 10016

Oxford is a registered trademark of Oxford University Press

Library of Congress Cataloging-in-Publication Data
Gert, Bernard, 1934-
Morality: a new justification of the Moral rules / Bernard Gert.
p.   cm.
Rev. ed. of: The moral rules. 2nd Torchbook ed. c1975.
Includes index.
ISBN-0-19-505519-5
1. Ethics. I. Gert, Bernard, 1914-   Moral rules. II. Title.
BJ1012.G45   1988   87-34850
171'.2—dc19   CIP

2 4 6 8 10 9 7 5 3 1

Printed in the United States of America
on acid-free paper

*To my mother and
to the memory of my father
in continuing gratitude for having provided me
with the understanding of morality that
this book makes explicit.*

PREFACE

It has been over twenty years since I finished the first version of *The Moral Rules* in 1966. There were three unpublished versions before the first published edition in 1970, then there were two additional published editions, in 1973 and 1975. This book is the result of two more unpublished versions and is such an extensive revision that I have actually changed the title of the book. Thanks to the extraordinary computer facilities at Dartmouth, I was able to have the entire book put on the computer and to revise it taking into consideration only philosophical concerns. This enabled me to go over each line of each page and make whatever changes I thought beneficial. It also enabled me to add material, move sections of text to new locations and, more generally, to completely rewrite the book while still retaining much of the earlier material.

All of the original 11 chapters have been revised, most of them very extensively, and I have written three new chapters. Chapter 5, Impartiality, provides an analysis of impartiality which shows why the standard tests of impartiality, reversibility, universalizability, and the veil of ignorance are inadequate. It also discusses the relationship between impartiality and morality and explains why abortion and the treatment of animals are such controversial issues. Chapter 13, Versions of Morality as Impartial Rationality, shows that the problems with Baier's *The Moral Point of View* and Rawls's *A Theory of Justice* are due to inadequacies in their accounts of rationality, impartiality, and their lack of concern with the details of a moral system. Chapter 14, Applications of the Moral System, uses the moral system to determine when paternalistic behavior is justified, and to provide a philosophical basis for the distinction between active and passive euthanasia which avoids the problems involved in all of the standard accounts.

Among the more important new material in the revised chapters is an account of a public system as a system which is known to and can be accepted by all those to whom it applies. This enables me to provide a new formal definition of morality, as a public system that applies to all rational persons, without sacrificing the view that morality must have a definite content. The explicit recognition that it is irrational to believe that we have unlimited knowledge of the future helps explain some otherwise troubling features of both rationality and morality. An examination of what counts as causing an evil, which includes a discussion of the relationship between rights and the moral rules, shows how a moral theory can yield a universal moral system which incorporates some of the points that have made ethical relativism seem attractive. More extensive development of the concept of morally relevant features, those features which determine when two violations of a moral rule count as the same kind of act, makes clear that most moral disagreements are based on disagreements about the facts. I have also more clearly identified the morally decisive question, the answer to which should be used by an impartial rational person to determine whether or not to advocate that a given kind of violation be publicly allowed.

I have tried to respond to all of the criticisms of earlier versions, to clarify what was obscure, and to add material that relates what I am doing to the work of other philosophers. I continue to believe that it is possible to write clearly and precisely without distorting the concepts that I analyze. I realize that my analysis of some concepts makes them seem clearer and more precise than many take them to be. However, I continue to believe that my analyses bring out the essential features of each concept and that what is left out is not of philosophical importance. The fact that these concepts interact so well and provide such a persuasive account of morality seems to me to confirm the essential correctness of these analyses.

I do not claim that everyone actually uses the words I analyze in accordance with the analyses that I provide. I do claim that if one does use these words in accordance with my analyses, there will be no distortion of the language. I invite the reader to see if my own use of these words conforms to my analyses. I believe that if the relevant words are used in this way it would vastly improve the quality of discussions of moral matters. But it is important to point out that nothing of significance in the moral theory, or in the moral system that is derived from it, depends on any peculiar features of the English language. What I say can be said in any language, for I have merely described the moral system that would be chosen by all impartial rational persons.

Hobbes begins his preface to the reader of *De Cive* as follows. "Reader, I promise thee here such things, which ordinarily promised do seem to challenge the greatest attention, (whether thou regard the dignity or profit of the matter treated, or the right method of handling it, or the honest motive and good advice to undertake it, or lastly the moderation of the author,) and I lay them here before thine eyes." Were such prefaces still in style I would say something very similar. I believe that I have presented a moral theory that yields a clear, coherent, and comprehensive description of the moral system that thoughtful people actually use when deciding how to act or in making moral judgments. I challenge any philosopher who holds some competing account of morality to join with me in testing our accounts by providing help to those who are engaged in trying to solve some actual moral problems.

This system may not satisfy the demands of some philosophers who want morality to provide unique answers to every moral question, but I do not believe one should try to satisfy the demands for the philosophical equivalent of squaring the circle. I have even tried to show that a moral system that provides a limit to the range of morally acceptable answers without always providing unique answers has some advantages over one that claims to always provide unique answers. I am pleased that my view that morality can be objective without always providing unique answers has now been accepted by some philosophers. However, I am aware that many philosophers still demand that a moral theory yield a moral system that provides unique answers to every moral question. It is unfortunately still fashionable for philosophers to claim that it is not possible to provide a moral theory that yields a clear, coherent, and comprehensive moral system, because they do not yet recognize that morality does not provide unique answers to every question.

My moral theory consists primarily of the analysis of three concepts, rationality, impartiality, and morality itself, together with an account of how they are related to each other. The account of rationality presented here is an elaboration of the account presented in the editions of *The Moral Rules* referred to earlier, while the account of impartiality is completely new. But the account of morality as a public system that applies to all rational persons is, for me, the most significant achievement of this book. It is not an original view; like much that I thought I had discovered on my own, I found more than merely anticipations in Baier's book. I do think I have defined the concept of a public system more precisely and so am able to make better use of it than was done previously. I may be so excited about this account of morality because it finally enables me to reply to my sister Ilene's objection that I never answer the question, What is morality? that I pose at the very beginning of the book. Also it is the final piece of the puzzle and allows everything else to fall into place. Each of the analyses of these three concepts is individually persuasive, but the interaction of the three is so impressive that it is not clear whether to consider the whole to be supported by the parts or whether, instead, to regard it as supporting them.

It is important to distinguish between a moral theory, which is an analysis and synthesis of all the relevant concepts, and a moral system, derived from that theory, which is what is actually used by people for guiding their behavior and for making judgments. The latter must not only be simple enough that it is understood and can be applied by all moral agents, there is a sense in which it must be known by all moral agents. A moral system that is significantly novel, or that can be understood or applied only by philosophers, is obviously inadequate. A moral theory may be somewhat more complex, but if it provides essential support for the moral system, it must also be understandable by and acceptable to all those who are subject to moral judgments. Otherwise one would make moral judgments of people using a moral system which one could not defend or justify to them.

My experience in talking to many groups about the moral system described in this book and in explaining the moral theory from which it is derived has convinced me that both the system and the essentials of the theory are both known and understandable to all moral agents. Further, my application of the system to actual moral problems, particularly in my role as a consultant on ethical problems in a medical center, has convinced me that the clarity that it brings to such problems has significant practical benefits. The most important benefit is that, by demonstrating the essential agreement on moral matters, it focuses greater attention on the facts of the case; it is disagreement on the facts, or on their significance, that is the source of almost all that is usually regarded as moral disagreement.

The chief philosophical problem in *The Moral Rules* was related to one technical term, "publicly advocate," that played a central role in the justification of the moral rules. I now realize that I invented this term because I did not distinguish between impartiality and morality being a public system. I combined in this one technical term features of both of these concepts. I now clearly distinguish between these two concepts, and this requires a significant restatement of my account of the justification of the moral rules. What is gratifying, however, is that the moral system is not affected by this restatement. What happened is that premises which I took to be inventions of my own, viz., the features that defined what it is to publicly advocate, turned out to be features of impartiality and of morality being a public system.

I have also come to realize the philosophically radical nature of my analysis of rationality. I had not fully realized how complete and unthinking was the acceptance of the standard formal accounts of rationality. The idea of defining a fundamental concept by means of a list is so foreign to most philosophers that, at first, they cannot even understand what I am doing. I am pleased that this idea is also finally beginning to be understood and adopted, so that those who accept some formal account will at least have to try to defend their views. Two excellent books which have sympathetic discussions of my account of rationality are *Reason and Value* by E. J. Bond (Cambridge, 1983) and *The Ideal of Rationality* by Stephen Nathanson (Humanities, 1985). In this book I have tried to take account of their discussions, to make my account of rationality fully explicit, and to show the inadequacy of all of the standard formal accounts of rationality.

The chapter on impartiality is, as far as I am aware, the first serious attempt to actually analyze the concept of impartiality rather than to provide a technical replacement for it. The realization that my own previous attempt to replace impartiality by public advocacy was due to my failure to distinguish between impartiality and morality being a public system made clear to me both the appeal of Kant's Categorical Imperative and its inadequacy. Further, explicit recognition that morality is a public system made understandable both Rousseau's general will and Hegel's account of a person willing his own punishment. As I become clearer about the nature of all the concepts involved, I realize how little of what I am saying is original. For example, Hobbes clearly states the point of morality; John Stuart Mill, especially in chapter five of *Utilitarianism,* provides an excellent account of the scope of morality; and Baier had previously insisted on the public character of morality. I am simply expressing in a language that is clearer and more precise most of what had been said before by others.

My lack of originality is most evident in the moral system that I describe. It contains nothing that is not common knowledge. This does not mean that I regard myself as having done nothing significant. The clarity and precision with which I have described both the moral theory and the moral system has enabled me to avoid the errors of those who were less clear and precise. This clarity and precision and my respect for the common moral opinions of humankind have saved me from persisting in maintaining a moral theory that results in a moral system that is in conflict with the moral judgments made by most enlightened and morally sensitive persons. Unlike the Utilitarians or the followers of Kant, I do not have to explain away any counter-intuitive results.

I realize that it is implausible to believe that I have solved all the philosophical problems concerning morality when so many great thinkers of the past, Plato, Aristotle, Aquinas, Hobbes, Kant, and John Stuart Mill, were not able to do so. In an important sense I have not solved these problems, for many of the problems that these philosophers were attempting to solve are problems which have no solution. My success is due to limiting myself to problems which can be solved. I have distinguished morality from other rational guides to conduct and have only attempted to show that impartial rational persons agree on the moral guide. Further, I have not even tried to show that such persons will agree on their answers to all moral questions, but have simply shown that they will agree on the range of morally acceptable answers. Perhaps most important, I have admitted that it is not possible to show that it is irrational to act immorally, but have contented myself with showing that it is always rational to act morally. By attempting less I believe that I have accomplished more.

Philosophy is a social, not a private endeavor. I have benefited greatly from the discussions I have had with colleagues and students. Most helpful in the preparation of this book has been my colleague Walter Sinnott-Armstrong. Several years ago he organized a faculty seminar on the last published edition of *The Moral Rules*. This seminar, which included Jack Bender and Jim Moor, while convincing me of the essential soundness of my position, showed the need for clarifying and providing further support for my views. Walter also provided constant conversation and written comments while I was working on the revisions. He used one of the photocopied versions when teaching, and provided me with detailed comments on the problems raised by his students. Our lengthy discussions of the semi-final draft of this book, while making the revisions take longer, made them seem shorter and, much more important, led to several important improvements.

Almost three decades of philosophical discussions with my very good friend and colleague Tim Duggan have influenced every part of this book. Continuing informal discusssions with the members of the philosophy department, including not only those mentioned above but also Bob Fogelin and Sally Sedgwick, were a continuing source of exasperation and encouragement. K. Danner Clouser of the Humanities Department of Hershey Medical School and a former colleague at Dartmouth continued his efforts of twenty years' standing to try and get me to clarify what I meant. Chuck Culver of the Psychiatry department, with whom I co-authored *Philosophy in Medicine* and many articles on the application of morality to medicine and psychiatry, was responsible for my rethinking of many important matters. Ron Green of the religion department and I had many interesting and valuable discussions on the differences between my views and those of Rawls. John W. Hennessey, Jr., of the Tuck School of Business not only showed me the importance of getting all the relevant facts before trying to deal with a specific moral problem, he also showed me how difficult it is to do this.

Years of teaching this material to Dartmouth undergraduates and to graduate students in the Business, Medical, and Engineering Schools helped make this book much more understandable. Working with doctors, nurses, social workers and others in dealing with particular moral issues forced me to present the material in a way that would actually be useful to non-philosophers. Dr. Robert M. Arnold, who read the entire manuscript in its most recent photocopied version and sent me extensive comments, which we then discussed on the phone, was very helpful. Several important matters are clearer because of my discussions with him. A student paper by Michael E. Bollhorst led me to clarify my account of the last two morally relevant features.

I have also been helped by many other philosophers. I had many interesting and valuable conversations with David Heyd and Igor Primoretz of the Hebrew University of Jerusalem; it was from Igor that I learned of the relationship between some of my views and some of those of Hegel and Rousseau. Carl Wellman suggested that I explain how my theory, which did not mention rights at all, can account for the discussion of rights. Hugo Bedau, by using a photocopied version of my earlier book for his class, not only encouraged me to continue revising, but also showed me how I could get comments from others which would aid in the revision. Many of those who had helped with the earlier book continued to help, especially Larry Stern and Huntington Terrell. I have also benefited from continuing discussion with two philosophers whom I first met about 20 years ago when they were both graduate students at The Johns Hopkins University, Bob Ladenson and Steve Nathanson. During that year I taught a seminar using a prepublication version of the first edition of *The Moral Rules*.

This book also contains material from articles that I have written in the last several years, many of them with Culver and/or Clouser. "Malady: A New Treatment of Disease" (*The Hastings Center Report,* June, 1981), written by the three of us, showed that the concept of rationality had a much wider application than moral theory. "Rationality in Medicine" (*The Journal of Medicine and Philosophy,* November, 1986), written by Clouser and me, dealt with some important problems in my earlier account of rationality raised by Michael Martin in his excellent article in the same issue. Two articles on paternalism, "Paternalistic Behavior" (*Philosophy and Public Affairs,* Fall 1976), and "The Justification of Paternalism" (*Ethics,* January, 1979), were written by Culver and me, as was the article "Distinguishing Between Active and Passive Euthanasia" (*Clinics in Geriatric Medicine,* February, 1986). I wrote two articles for the *Monist:* "Rationality and Sociobiology" (April, 1984) and "Moral Theory and Applied Ethics" (October, 1984); the former helped me to clarify further my account of rationality, and the latter enabled me to develop and apply the revised account of morally relevant features. The article "Virtue and Vice," written for the volume, *Virtue and Medicine* (1985), helped me to work out some problems in my account of virtues and vices.

I had the opportunity to write many of these articles because of the Sustained Development Award I received from the National Science Foundation and the National Endowment for the Humanities. This four-year award (1980–84) helped immensely by providing not only the time to develop my moral theory, but also the opportunities and incentives for applying the moral system to real moral problems. However, my views have continued to develop, and there may be discrepancies between what is said in these articles and what is said in this book. Although what I say here is what I now hold on most matters, I am now working on a book on human nature, an analysis of rationality and the emotions, and it is likely that some of the analyses that I provide of various emotions will be modified as they are developed in more detail.

A Fulbright Award to teach at the Hebrew University of Jerusalem (1985–86), together with a sabbatical leave from Dartmouth College, provided me with even more time to spend on the revisions that led to this book. I was helped by presenting an earlier version of the chapter on impartiality to the philosophy department at Hebrew University. A paper presented to the Law faculty of the Hebrew University helped me to clarify my account of both law and promises. A paper to the Israeli Philosophical Association helped me to see more clearly the relationship between my moral theory and democracy. Of course, none of these agencies or institutions is responsible in any way for the views expressed here. Nor are any of the people or groups mentioned responsible for what I have written. This is one of those unusual situations in which other people deserve some credit, but do not deserve any blame. The account of arrogance and humility that I present in this book makes clear that humility requires me to share the credit, that it would be arrogant not to, but that humility allows me to take all the blame.

Humility, on my account, does not prohibit me from claiming that this book provides a clear, coherent, comprehensive and hence useful account of morality, although prudence might require that I not state this openly. I have tried particularly hard to be clear because I agree with Hobbes that truth arises more easily from error than from confusion. This overall clarity should make it easier for philosophers to find the remaining errors and omissions and to spot any remaining obscurity. I welcome this, for I realize that philosophers are disposed not to write articles on views unless they can point out errors or clarify obscurities. I am sufficiently confident of the views presented in this book that I believe any criticism of them will result in a strengthening of my overall position.

I realize that philosophers who have already committed themselves to a view, except if it is a matter of detail, rarely admit that they are wrong and that someone else has it right. But it seems to be acknowledged by all that none of the standard accounts of morality is adequate. It has become a common practice to preface anthologies in applied ethics, e.g., medical ethics, with brief accounts of Utilitarianism, a Kantian view, etc., and to acknowledge that none of these theories is adequate. If applied ethics is intended to be anything more than consciousness raising, then this is obviously an inadequate way to proceed. My vain hope is that with the advent of applied ethics the interest in a clear, coherent, comprehensive, and useful account of morality will outweigh the traditional philosophical interest in obscure, incoherent, schematic, and useless accounts.

Hanover, N.H.   B.G.
January 1988

PREFACE

to the First Edition of *The Moral Rules*

This book is meant to make a difference, not only in one's understanding of morality, but also in the way one acts. I do not expect all those who understand this book to become morally good men; it takes more than understanding to make one morally good. But I hope to prevent those immoral actions that are a result of misunderstanding the nature of morality. There are far more of these than one realizes. I want to provide such a clear and convincing account of morality that no one who reads this book will be able to act immorally without knowing that he is doing so. Though such knowledge will not prevent all immoral action, I do think it will prevent some. A clear understanding of morality should also significantly affect one's political attitudes. I hope to make it much harder to defend immoral political policies and much easier to support morally good ones. In short, I wish to increase as much as possible the influence of moral considerations, not only in the life of each reader, but also in the life of our entire society.

This book defends traditional morality, at least as much of it as can be defended. It is not a traditional defense. In fact, some may not regard it as a defense at all, but rather as an attack. It is an attack on many traditional ways of thinking about morality, but it seems to me that the only way to defend traditional morality is to attack the traditional ways of thinking about morality. The current attacks on traditional morality are, I am convinced, due to a misunderstanding of morality. But it is a very widespread and deep-rooted misunderstanding. The proper task of moral philosophy is to clarify our thinking about morality. The goal of this book is to provide a clear understanding of the nature of morality.

One will not find in this book stirring appeals to one's emotions. The only appeal this book makes is to one's understanding. However, unlike many people, I think one's understanding can affect one's action. I hope that after I have provided a clear understanding of morality, others with greater persuasive powers than mine will be encouraged to use them to support morality. Both moral reasons and reasons of self-interest lead me to hope that this book will have a universal appeal. I hope this book is read not only in schools but also in churches and legislatures, for religion and politics affect one's attitude toward morality more than education. It is also important that it be read in the home, for the proper attitude toward morality should be taught from the very earliest age.

The key concept, the one which makes my account of morality possible, is the concept of reason. The realization that the familiar dichotomy between rational and irrational concealed an important distinction led to the introduction of the concept "allowed by reason." The recognition that hypocrisy is allowed by reason permitted the distinction between what reason requires and what reason publicly requires. And this latter distinction is necessary in order to distinguish between providing a justification of morality and giving an answer to the question "Why should one be moral?" Though there are similarities between what I say about reason and what others have said, there are also crucial differences. Insofar as the reader does not agree that everything I call irrational is irrational, he will not agree with the conclusions that I reach. It is not necessary that he agree that everything I call rational is rational. Disagreement on this point need not result in any further disagreement. It is agreement on what is irrational that is crucial.

The account of reason presented in this book has application far beyond the field of moral philosophy. Reason and the related concept of justification play a central role in almost all traditional philosophical problems. In this book, the concepts have not been developed sufficiently to make their application to other philosophical problems sufficiently clear; however, a useful beginning has been made. The application of my account of reason to the traditional philosophical problems results in a view I call "empirical rationalism." The concept of reason is also important, in varying degrees, in all of the social sciences. In psychology, especially in psychiatry, a proper account of reason would be extremely valuable. Again, only a beginning has been made in this book, but it is a beginning with possibilities.

To the professional philosopher, the most important chapters in the book will be the first four [and Chapter 5, Impartiality, of the present edition], together with the chapter on moral judgments. These chapters are primarily concerned with analyzing concepts. In Chapters 1 and 4, I am concerned with the concept of morality, in Chapter 2 with the concept of reason, and in Chapter 3 with the concepts of good and evil. I believe this book provides the first correct analyses of these concepts. Though I realize that ordinary language is vaguer and more flexible than my analyses indicate, I am confident that I have accurately described the essential features of the concepts under discussion.

To the general reader, the most important chapter will probably be the one that answers the question "Why should one be moral?" I believe that this chapter will enable parents to answer this question in a manner far superior to the way in which they now generally answer it. I think the chapters on moral ideals, on virtue and vice and on morality and society may also serve to clarify general thinking about these matters. The heart of the book, Chapters 5 and 6 [Chapters 7 and 8 in the present edition], in which I provide the justification of the moral rules, seems to me to be of equal interest to professional philosophers and to the general reader.

The primary task of this book is to provide an analysis of some important concepts and to show the relationship between them. However, an almost equally important task is to persuade the reader to take a certain attitude toward morality. Though these tasks are distinct I feel that it is important to pursue them together rather than separately. I grant it is of little general interest to determine the proper analysis of concepts, even such important ones as morality, reason, good, and evil [and impartiality]. However, it is extremely difficult to persuade people to act in a certain way if they cannot see the connection between the proposed way of acting and ways of acting to which they are accustomed. By providing an analysis of the concepts of [impartiality,] good, evil, reason, and morality, I can more effectively persuade the general reader to accept my proposals. Also, the very fact that the analyses that I offer can be useful in persuading people to act in certain ways seems to me to provide some evidence in favor of the correctness of the analyses.

Though I regard my two tasks as closely connected, I do not think that failure in one assures failure in the other. It may be that the misuse of the concepts of good, evil, reason, and morality by philosophers, psychologists, and well-intentioned moralists, both political and religious, has so degraded them that my analyses do not seem cogent. I do not think the degradation of these concepts has gone so far, but if it has, I can hope that I have done something to make possible their eventual upgrading. The lack of clear concepts of good, evil, reason, and morality is a serious matter. It makes it difficult, if not impossible, to obtain agreement on important matters even among men of good will. However, even if one does not think I have provided a correct account of good, evil, reason, and morality, I still think it possible that I may succeed in my second task. There is no doubt that all readers of this book wish to avoid what I call evils. Thus I can still hope to persuade them to take a certain public attitude toward what I call the moral rules. Further, I can still hope to provide those readers who are men of good will with a guide to conduct that will be of some value in their personal life.

Moral philosophy should be understandable to the intelligent general reader. A book on moral philosophy understandable only by professional moral philosophers is a bad book on moral philosophy. However, a book addressed only to the intelligent general reader would tend to avoid those philosophical problems that have traditionally concerned moral philosophers. While it would have an impact, it would be subject to criticism that would make it worthless in the long run. I intend this book not only to be immediately convincing, but also to stand up in the long run.

Even though I am concerned with the traditional problems of moral philosophy, it is quite likely that I will be understood more easily by the general reader than by the professional philosopher. It would not be surprising if the general reader found that I say nothing but what is obvious. He may indeed wonder what all the fuss is about. There are times when I feel this way myself. But good philosophy often seems simple after it has been done. The greater difficulty that professional philosophers may have in understanding what I say is due to their having tried to think out these problems for themselves. It is much easier to accept someone else's thinking on a matter you have not thought about than on a matter that you have thought about. Though I expect quicker acceptance from the general reader than from the professional philosopher, I consider ultimate acceptance by the latter a more important test.

Highly critical remarks about the ethical theories of previous philosophers should not be taken as evidence that I consider them worthless. On the contrary, I have learned very much from the writings of other moral philosophers, both classical and contemporary. Only philosophical accounts have been criticized because non-philosophical accounts of morality, with rare exceptions, deserve to be no more than what they usually are, topics of cocktail-party conversation. However, I would not have written this book if I did not consider all previous accounts of morality to be seriously inadequate. Usually this inadequacy is the result of oversimplification. On my account, morality is not simple. Any attempt to describe my view as a simple variation of a classical ethical theory will lead one to overlook some significant distinctions. The inadequacy of an attempt to assimilate my account of morality to a classical view should be apparent from the fact that it is equally plausible to assimilate it to the view of the utilitarians and to the view of Kant. It would be a mistake to regard my view as simply a form of negative utilitarianism (with the ultimate principle being the minimization of evil rather than the maximization of good) or as a variation on Kant (though we both regard the moral rules as those rules which rational men would will to be universal laws). Both of these accounts would oversimplify my theory and hence be inadequate.

Uncritical use of technical terms often results in the overlooking of significant distinctions. I have avoided technical terms as far as possible, but some technical terms were required. One of the most important is "publicly advocate," which replaces the term "universalize," which philosophers since Kant have employed unsuccessfully. [It turns out that I did not use my technical term successfully either, and it has been removed from the present edition.] The misuse of ordinary words is also a source of great confusion. "Principles," "obligation," and "duty" are three words commonly misused. I do not use the first two at all, and I try to distinguish my use of the third from the general philosophical use as clearly as possible. In general I have tried very hard to use words in their ordinary sense. Ordinary language when used carefully seems to me to embody most of the essential distinctions. However, I do not regard ordinary language as sacred, and when an essential distinction was not marked by the language, I have not hesitated to mark it myself. The most important of these distinctions is dividing *rational* into *required by reason* and *allowed by reason*.

Since I regard the inadequacy of all previous ethical theories to be the result of neglecting some significant distinction or of misusing language, it seemed pointless to enter into any detailed discussion of other views. My criticism of other philosophers is accordingly limited to pointing out how their misuse of language or their failure to make some significant distinction led them astray. I owe much more to other philosophers than my brief comments would indicate. My debts to John Rawls, Kurt Baier, and Marcus Singer are greater than they seem. Students of Aristotle, Kant, and Mill will realize how much I owe to these men. But by far my greatest debt is to the works of Thomas Hobbes, the great seventeenth-century English moral and political philosopher. I hope, in the not too distant future, to show that Hobbes, properly understood, is the best classical moral philosopher. [See my introduction to *Man and Citizen* by Thomas Hobbes (1972).]

I also owe much to the students at Dartmouth College, to whom I have been teaching ethics for the last eight years. Their refusal to accept the jargon that generally passes for moral philosophy forced me to think out these matters for myself. Especially valuable was an undergraduate seminar using the first version of this book, in which I received many important criticisms. This version of the book is much improved, in substance as well as in clarity and style, because of the criticisms I received from the students at The Johns Hopkins University in my graduate seminar "The Moral Rules." I have also benefited from the criticisms of Dan Clouser and his students at Carleton. Also helpful were my sister Ilene Wolosin, and my colleagues, especially Tim Duggan and Don Rosenberg. I owe a special debt of gratitude, however, to Larry Stern, the only person with whom I discussed this book while I was writing the first version. His comments, criticisms, questions, and encouragement were far more valuable than he realizes. Were it not for my discussions with him, it is very doubtful that I would have written several of the chapters.

I am grateful to the Faculty Research Committee of Dartmouth College for providing me with funds to have the first two versions of this book typed. And for additional funds to have the first version reproduced for use in my seminar. These funds removed one of those obstacles that stand in the way of those who, like myself, find it difficult to act rationally when forced to spend their own money for scholarly purposes. A Fellowship from the National Endowment for the Humanities, awarded in order to enable me to work on expanding my account of rationality and applying it to problems in the philosophy of psychology, also made it possible for me to devote more time to improving the final version of this book. Thus I owe them thanks not only for helping me to start on that future book, but also for helping me to finish the present one. I am also grateful to Mrs. Jennie Wells, who typed the first two versions of this book and who helped prepare them for reproduction. When I recall the state of the typescripts I gave her, her excellent typing seems to me to be not only a demonstration of her many skills, but also a testimony to her temperance and fortitude. Her untimely death of a heart attack was one of those natural evils that defy all attempts at justification.

It is one of the most important aims of this book to show that if morality is limited to its proper sphere, then one can expect almost complete agreement among rational men on all questions of morality. In this sense, and in this sense only, I should like to make of morality a science.

PREFACE
to the Torchbook Edition

I have used the publication of this Torchbook edition to make some changes in the text. There have been no significant philosophical changes, but I hope that I have removed some minor inconsistencies. For example, though I hold that rational action is more basic than rational belief and rational desire, I had said that irrational actions included those that were based on irrational beliefs and desires. The most significant change in the text is a new paragraph on page 37 [previous edition] in which I provide the fullest account of an irrational action. I hope, by this and other related changes, to make it clear that rational action is indeed basic.

It is usually taken as so obvious that no one ever ought to act irrationally, that it is not explicitly stated. Indeed, I did not explicitly make this statement myself in the hardcover edition. However, my entire account of reason was designed so that on the account of irrational action that I provide, no one whom we would consider responsible for his actions would ever think that he ought to act irrationally. Any account of reason that does not have this as a consequence seems to me to be clearly inadequate. For then it would be possible to show someone that a given action is irrational and yet still leave it an open question whether he ought to do it or not. The much discussed gap between "is" and "ought" resulted from the lack of an adequate concept of reason.

The other concept that needed to be clarified was that of public advocacy. Though I have made some changes in the text, I decided that it would be easier to make some remarks in this preface than to reword all of the places in the text that might otherwise require it. On page 92 [previous editions; as noted before, public advocacy has been completely removed from the present edition] I say,

"When all rational men would publicly advocate the violation I say that it is required by public reason or that reason publicly requires it. If a violation is required by public reason, then all rational men publicly advocate disobeying the rule in this situation." What is wrong with these statements is that they do not make clear that I am only talking about those rational men who accept the conditions of public advocacy. (It was also wrong to use the phrase "rational men," and in this preface I shall use "rational person" instead.) These passages can be taken in such a way so as to conclude that a rational person must take a public attitude. There were passages in the earlier edition where I seemed to draw this conclusion myself. But a rational person need not be willing to publicly advocate anything, unless, of course, he makes genuine moral judgments and not merely judgments of moral matters. For willingness to publicly advocate is essential for the kind of impartiality that one must have when making moral judgments. But a rational person need not make moral judgments, and hence need not take any public attitude.

Thus in all of those places in the text where I say that all rational men would, will, or must publicly advocate something, this means that all rational persons, *if they are publicly advocating,* would, will or must publicly advocate that thing. This reading of "all rational persons publicly advocate" does not, as far as I can see, require any other changes in the text, so that I regard it more as a clarification than as a change of meaning. However, this lack of clarity caused (and was partly caused by) my unclarity about the relationship between reason and morality. Though I was quite clear that reason did not require one to act morally, I was not completely clear that reason did not always require one to make moral judgments. I sometimes talked as if a rational person who was immoral was necessarily a hypocrite. But this is not true. In appropriate circumstances, none of the judgments of a rational person need be moral judgments and one may completely disavow even any pretence at impartiality.

Once one realizes that a rational person need not take a public attitude, the question arises "Why should one?" This was a question that should have been raised in Chapter 10. The question can be put in the following way. "Why should my judgments of moral matters be ones that I would publicly advocate?" Asking why one should be impartial in moral matters is not a senseless question, when "should" is given the appropriate sense. It certainly is not always in one's self-interest or in the interests of those one cares for to be impartial in these matters. That one's judgments will not be genuine moral judgments if one is not impartial simply prompts the question, "Why should my judgments of moral matters be moral judgments?" It is a simple matter to transform this question into "Why should I make *moral* judgments?" If we are talking about sincere judgments, viz., ones that will affect one's behavior, we can see that this question is very similar to the question "Why should I be moral?" If we do not take the judgments as sincere, then the question becomes similar to "Why should I seem moral?" I have given my answers to both of these questions in Chapter 10 [present edition, Chapter 11].

That reason does not require impartiality is contrary to the hopes of most moral philosophers, including myself. Except for the moral skeptics, all moral philosophers have tried to show that reason supports morality. But if one has an account of reason with sufficient force to result in every person responsible for his actions agreeing that no one ever ought to act irrationally, then reason will not require one to support morality except in the hypothetical way that I have described in this book. If reason is impartial in the way required by public advocacy, then it must support morality. But though it is allowed by reason to be impartial, it is not required. Further, it is doubtful that one will be impartial in moral matters unless he has sufficient concern for all involved. Public reason determines what morality is, but concern for others, not reason, determines if one acts morally.

Though I make a sharp distinction between what is required by the moral rules and what is encouraged by the moral ideals (a similar distinction is made by Mill in Chapter 5 of *Utilitarianism*), I admit that there are individual cases where it seems that we are required to act on the moral ideals. I suggest on page 123 [previous editions] that in such cases we may say that the person has a duty to act. I think we should say that a person has a duty to act, i.e., that the action is required, rather than merely encouraged, by morality, only when we think failure to do it should make him liable to punishment. This is very close to saying that whatever is required by morality should be enforced by law (ignoring the practical difficulties involved in such enforcement). Thus though I agree that we ought to help those in need, I deny that we have a general duty to do so. For a rational person would not want the moral ideals in their full generality to be enforced by law (if an enforceable law could even be formulated). Of course, it is possible to favor a law requiring positive action to prevent or relieve the suffering of evil in specific circumstances, but these circumstances would have to be carefully formulated before rational persons would publicly advocate that such action be required by morality. Only consideration of the liability to punishment makes possible the distinction between what is required by morality and what is encouraged by it.

It does not seem too much for morality to require that one have enough concern for all that one does not harm anyone. It does seem too much for it to require that one's concern for oneself and those one loves be no greater than one's concern for all others. This supports my view that one is required to obey the moral rules, but is only encouraged to follow the moral ideals. But even though I distinguish between what is required and what is encouraged by morality, anyone who finds the answers I provide for being moral, persuasive, will almost certainly be morally good as well. My fundamental answer to "Why should one be moral?" is "Because you will cause someone to suffer evil if you are not." My answer to the question "Why should one be morally good?" is "Because you will prevent someone from suffering evil if you are." Thus I do not see that anyone who accepts my account of morality will be dissuaded from doing morally good actions and content himself with merely being moral.

Though morality does not require equal concern for all, it does encourage such concern. Thus it might be useful to explain what I mean by equal concern. This may also explain why I maintain that no rational person will publicly advocate that any individual cause any significant evil simply to promote good, without the consent of the person who will suffer the evil. These topics are connected because publicly advocating is advocating an attitude like one that would be advocated by a person with equal concern for all mankind. I think of equal concern on the following model, that of parents with several children all of whom they love equally. Suppose that all but one of the children have a plan to embarrass that one in order to provide themselves with some fun and excitement. (Notice that it makes no difference how many children will enjoy the embarrassment of their sibling or how much they will enjoy it.) No parent who loves each of the children equally would allow this scheme to be carried through. Also, though such parents might allow one child to give up some of his opportunities in order to increase the already adequate opportunities of the others, they would never allow the others to force him to do so. Only if one child was considerably better off than the rest might they force him to give up something to aid his less fortunate brothers and sisters. And only if his brothers and sisters were actually suffering while he had more than he needed, would they necessarily force him to share what he had with them. My claim that no one would publicly advocate the causing of evil simply to promote good rests upon this model of public advocacy, and equal concern.

Having explained what I mean by "equal concern," and how this affects the understanding of public advocacy, I must now admit that public advocacy only requires that one have this concern for other rational persons, or those who were once rational (for a rational person must be concerned with how he will be treated if he ceases to be rational). It does not forbid concern for nonrational beings, but it does not require concern for them either. Thus one's views on the treatment of animals, on abortion, and even on infanticide, may depend on the concern that one has for animals, unborn children, and infants. Also since equal concern is not required, one may have some concern for animals, yet not enough to hold that they be fully protected by the moral rules. I would expect that in any civilized society rational persons would be fully concerned with infants, so that they would be accorded the full protection of the moral rules. With regard to unborn children, concern for them seems to increase as the time of birth comes closer.

Insofar as the abortion issue is a matter of rational disagreement, the issue turns on two considerations. One is an empirical consideration; "What effect will allowing abortion have on the way rational persons treat one another?" Insofar as one's view on abortion is determined by this consideration, it will be relevant to determine if, e.g., allowing abortion does result in less concern for all human life. The second is not an empirical matter, but turns on the degree of concern one has for unborn children. If one is as concerned with unborn children as with their prospective mothers, he will publicly advocate that no abortion be allowed, not even to save the life of the mother, just as we do not allow one innocent person to be killed in order to save another. If one is seriously concerned, but not equally concerned, he will publicly advocate that abortion be allowed only to prevent the death of the mother or where there is serious risk of her suffering other evils. As one's concern decreases he will allow abortion for less and less important reasons, until, if one has no concern at all, he will allow abortion on demand, or simply because the mother wants it. Much of the discussion of abortion involves the attempt to get people to increase or decrease their concern for the unborn child. I have nothing to add to this discussion here.

There is a temptation in writing this preface to attempt to deal with all of the issues that have been raised by readers of the hardcover edition. I have been fortunate that several people have pointed out problems in that edition which I have been able to meet by some small change in the text, plus discussion in this preface. I have been helped by my colleagues Ron Green, Victor Menza, and Jim Martin. Huntington Terrell and his students at Colgate were extremely helpful. And again I have benefited from my students here at Dartmouth. I realize that I have not answered all of their objections, but it is doubtful that I could do this even if I had unlimited time and space. Peggy Sanders was very helpful in making the corrections in the text as well as in preparing this preface. Georgina Johnston's index for this edition was also quite helpful and should enable readers of this edition to discover more easily any remaining inconsistencies.

PREFACE
to the Second Torchbook Edition

I have used the second printing of this Torchbook edition to make some more changes in the text. Almost all of these changes are related to the change in the statement of the moral attitude. Originally this attitude was formulated as follows: "Everyone is always to obey the rule except when he would publicly advocate violating it. Anyone who violates the rule when he would not publicly advocate such a violation may be punished." It has been pointed out to me by Frank Gramlich in personal correspondence that stated in this way not all rational persons would publicly take the moral attitude toward the moral rules, for it would commit a rational person to urging someone to obey a rule whenever that person would not publicly advocate violation, even if the person doing the urging would publicly advocate violation. I have therefore changed the formulation of the moral attitude by substituting "could" for "would" in both places that "would" occurred in the original formulation. I have also made other changes in the text in order to make them consistent with the revised formulation.

This change in my account of the moral attitude also eliminates the problem pointed out by Ted Bond in his critical notice of my book in *Dialogue,* vol. XII (1973), no. 3 that what is moral for one person to do is immoral for another person in exactly the same circumstances, even when they share the same beliefs. For though rational persons with the same beliefs may differ in what they *would* publicly advocate, they do not differ in what they *could* publicly advocate. What a rational person *would* publicly advocate is determined in part by his ranking of the various goods and evils, but this ranking of goods and evils plays no role in determining what he *could* publicly advocate. Thus what one rational person *would* publicly advocate, all rational persons *could* publicly advocate, for if his ranking of the goods and evils is allowed by reason then all rational persons could, consistent with their being rational, have the same rankings.

This point emphasizes the formal, as opposed to empirical, character of what I say about rational persons. When I say that *all* rational persons would do such and such, or that reason requires it, the latter expression is perhaps the less misleading expression. For I mean that not doing such and such is incompatible with the account of rationality that I have offered. Likewise, saying that *no* rational person would do such and such or that reason prohibits it, means that doing such and such is incompatible with my account of rationality. And finally, saying that *some* rational persons would do such and such, or that reason allows doing it, means that neither doing it nor not doing it is incompatible with my account of rationality. When I talk about what some, all, or no rational persons would publicly advocate, this is to be understood in the same formal fashion. All of this makes even more clear how central my account of reason is to the entire book.

Let me now point out what I think are some consequences of the new formulation. It now turns out that although it is moral, i.e., not immoral (for I use "moral" and "immoral" in a way parallel to my use of "rational" and "irrational"), for one to violate a moral rule merely if one *could* publicly advocate such a violation, it is not necessary that one *would* do so. Thus it is not necessarily immoral to go against one's conscience, i.e., act contrary to what one would publicly advocate; it is immoral only if one could not publicly advocate that violation. Given that it is not necessarily immoral to go against one's conscience, we can understand, more sympathetically, those who claim that we should not put our consciences above the law. If we limit their claim to those cases where people's consciences differ, so that some rational persons would publicly advocate obeying the law, it is a very plausible claim. I do not say that all rational persons would agree with the claim, only that some would. Furthermore, so interpreted it is compatible with the view that morality is above the law. One could hold that when all rational persons would publicly advocate violating the law then it should be disobeyed, but when some rational persons would publicly advocate obedience, then one should obey even if he himself would publicly advocate violating the law.

Since it is not necessarily immoral to go against one's conscience, we may be at a loss for the appropriate way to describe someone who violates a moral rule toward which he could publicly advocate violation, but, in fact, would publicly advocate non-violation. One is tempted to call such a man hypocritical, but if he has never made his views on the matter known to others, this seems a misuse of "hypocritical." Cases like this may provide a proper use for the term "inauthentic." But if we take "authentic" to be properly used of a man who always follows his own conscience, then, as pointed out in the previous paragraph, there will be some rational persons who prefer people to be inauthentic sometimes. Of course, in the situations where you did not want a person to follow his own conscience, you would probably not call him "authentic" if he did, but rather something like "stubborn." However, there seems to be no doubt that in general we would prefer people who were "authentic" to those who were not, for in general those who do what they *would* not publicly advocate will be more likely to do what they *could* not publicly advocate.

The fact that what is moral, i.e., not immoral, is what one could publicly advocate, not necessarily what one would publicly advocate, has as an important consequence the notion of moral tolerance. When we realize that even though the moral position taken by another is not one that we *would* publicly advocate, because we have a different ranking of the goods and evils, it is one we *could* publicly advocate, we will not ascribe to him either a lack of knowledge of the facts of the case, or a lack of moral sensitivity or insight. This does not require us to regard it as indifferent which of the two views is held, but it does limit the ways which we will regard as acceptable in trying to change the other's views or to prevent their being acted upon. It is moral intolerance as well as selfishness that Hobbes recognized as making a Leviathan necessary.

Next, a point of some theoretical interest. Many moral philosophers have held, either implicitly or explicitly, that if all the facts are known, every moral question has a unique answer. For example, the utilitarians held that which of the alternatives open to us we should take was determined by its tendency to promote the general happiness. And insofar as there was agreement on the facts, then everyone would agree that A was the right alternative or that B was or that it was indifferent which was chosen. And in saying that it was indifferent they strongly suggested that all people who looked at the issue in the appropriate way would be indifferent to which action was performed. The very strong hold this unanimity view still has on philosophers can be seen by noting that one of the strongest critics of utilitarianism, John Rawls, holds the very same position. I do not accept this position. I allow for some unresolvable moral disputes. This is a direct consequence of my position that even in moral matters not all rational men would publicly advocate the same course of action. However, at the same time, I do not accept the view that all moral disputes may be unresolvable as R.M. Hare does. This is a direct consequence of my position that, especially in moral matters, there are some courses of action that no rational person could publicly advocate. This was always the view of the matter that I had taken in the chapter on Moral Judgments, but my misstatement of the moral attitude showed that I was not as clear about it as I should have been.

One remark about reasons. On pages 33–39 [previous editions] I define reasons as beliefs which can make acting on an irrational desire rational. I still think that this definition is correct, but in the discussion of reasons I concentrate so exclusively on situations in which a reason is offered in order to justify acting on an irrational desire that my definition may be misinterpreted. It may be thought that a belief is a reason only if it is, in fact, offered in order to justify what would otherwise be an irrational action. This is not my intent at all. If a belief is such that in some situation it *can* justify what would otherwise be an irrational action, it is a reason and may with complete propriety be offered as a reason for doing something which even without that reason it would not be irrational to do. For example, I can provide a reason for going for a walk, namely, that it is good for one's health, even though there is no need for a reason to go for a walk.

I am very grateful to Ted Bond and Frank Gramlich for forcing me to reconsider the points I have discussed in this preface. The resulting changes seem to me not only to increase the consistency of my position but also to have several beneficial consequences. Some of these I have already discussed; one that I have not is an aesthetic satisfaction from seeing a fuller parallelism between rationality and morality. I do not know whether what I regard as the increased elegance of my view does anything toward increasing its adequacy, but whether it does so or not I must admit that I enjoy it simply for its own sake.

CONTENTS

MORALITY

The utility of moral and civil philosophy is to be estimated,
not so much by the commodities we have by knowing these sciences,
as by the calamities we receive from not knowing them.

Thomas Hobbes

1

MORALITY

What is morality? This question seems as if it could be answered by any intelligent person. It seems that way until one actually tries to answer it. When one does this, a funny thing happens. One finds that if one starts by saying "Morality is . . . ," nothing one says afterward seems to be quite right. Of course one can say clever things like "Morality is simply the expression of the demands of the superego." But this kind of clever remark does not enable one to understand what morality is. The superego makes many demands which are not moral demands. Which of its demands are the moral ones? If one tries to give an answer to this question, it soon becomes clear that morality cannot be equated with the demands of the superego. In fact, it eventually becomes clear that talk about the superego is completely irrelevant in determining what morality is. And so it goes with any answer that one initially proposes.

Part of the difficulty is that "morality" is an unusual word. We do not use it very much, at least not without some qualification. We do sometimes talk of "Nazi morality," "Christian morality," or of "the morality of the Greeks." But we seldom talk simply of morality all by itself. This is partly due to the widespread belief that there is no such thing as morality per se, that there is only this morality and that morality. But although this belief is widespread, it is false. In this book I shall present an analysis of morality, not of this morality or that morality, but of morality.

Definitions of Morality

I am not the first philosopher to provide such an analysis. From Plato on, moral philosophers have attempted to provide an account of morality. The widespread

3

disbelief in morality is partly due to the fact that no moral philosopher has as yet provided a satisfactory account of it. This is not, of course, the main reason; philosophers are not that influential. The main problem is that morality has not been adequately distinguished from other guides to conduct. This problem is partly the result of the fact that most people think that they know what morality is. Nazi morality is the code of conduct adopted by all true Nazis. Christian morality is the code of conduct adopted by all true Christians.

On this use of "morality," morality is simply any code of conduct adopted by a group. But it isn't. It is only a sloppy use of language that has allowed "code of conduct" to be taken as equivalent to "morality" and has allowed such monstrous phrases as "Nazi morality." The Nazi code of conduct was not a moral code; on the contrary, it was grossly immoral. Unless one enjoys talking paradoxically, as far too many people do, one should avoid the use of "morality" which forces one to talk of an immoral morality.

Some who equated morality with a code of conduct adopted by a group sought to discover whether there was a universal morality by investigating whether there were some common elements in the codes of conduct of all groups. Whether one finds a universal code of conduct depends in large part on the manner in which one looks. If, like Westermarck, one goes from society to society examining the codes of conduct that these societies actually accept, one will probably be struck more by the differences than by the similarities. Although some anthropologists have claimed that the differences often mask essential similarities, the work of anthropologists has generally been used to show that there is no universal morality.

Philosophers have not been overly concerned with the findings of anthropology. More than two thousand years ago Plato knew that there were important differences in the codes of conduct of different societies. This did not prevent him from trying to formulate a universal morality. Plato thought that an analysis of human nature could provide him with the foundation on which to build this morality. Today many philosophers try to use the findings of psychoanalysis or sociobiology in the same way. But if the facts of human nature are to provide a foundation for morality, these cannot be newly discovered facts known only by those acquainted with the relevant science, but must be facts that are known by all those whom we consider to be responsible moral agents. It cannot be that prior to psychoanalysis or sociobiology normal people did not know those facts about human nature upon which morality depends, for then normal people would not have had sufficient reason to accept morality.

Other philosophers thought that an analysis of rationality could provide the foundation for morality. For many of them, Kant is the outstanding example; morality simply became equated with a form of rationality. They tried to show not only that it was rational to be moral, but also that it was irrational to be immoral. But responsible moral agents often want to act immorally, at least, on any plausible account of morality. If rationality is to provide a secure foundation for morality then no responsible moral agent must ever want to act irrationally.

Even though all of those who have investigated the nature of morality start out with an account of morality that has a specific content, almost none of them regard that content as an essential feature of morality. Instead they define morality by means of some formula, and then try to derive the content from that formula. I call such accounts, formal accounts. As indicated previously, some define morality as the code of conduct adopted by a social group. The content of the morality is derived by investigating the codes of conduct of different groups. Others define morality as the code of conduct that would be adopted by all rational persons. They then try to derive the content of morality by determining what code of conduct all rational persons would accept. Others define morality as that code of conduct which a person takes to be overriding or most important. The content of morality is then determined by each person for himself. (It is interesting that such philosophers never discuss religion, for religion is just as plausibly defined as providing a code of conduct that a person takes to be overriding or most important.)

Morality Is a Public System

Morality is not primarily a system of conduct that a rational person decides to adopt for herself, although all rational persons are encouraged to adopt morality as a guide to their conduct. Rather, morality is a system that all rational persons advocate that other people adopt, whether or not they adopt it themselves, for morality is concerned with the behavior of people insofar as that behavior affects others. More precisely, morality is a public system that applies to all rational persons. A justified or rational morality is a public system that all impartial rational persons would advocate adopting to govern the behavior of all rational persons.

A public system is a system of conduct that is both known and understood by all those to whom it applies and one that it would not be irrational for all those to whom it applies to adopt to govern their own behavior. The rules of a game usually form a public system, they are known and understood by all those to whom they apply, the players, and it is not irrational for all the players to adopt the rules, i.e., to guide their conduct by the rules and to accept judgments made on the basis of these rules. Morality differs from other public systems by applying to all rational persons. As I use the term "morality" it has as a necessary feature that it be a public system that applies to all rational persons.

This is also what most other people, including most philosophers, regard as a necessary feature of morality. Morality is thought to apply to all rational persons. It is regarded as a system of conduct that all rational persons know and understand, as shown by the fact that ignorance of morality is never regarded as a legitimate excuse. Further, it is thought not to be irrational for any person to adopt morality as a guide, even as the overriding guide for her own conduct. However, it is recognized by almost all, even though some philosophers have tried to prove it false, that it is also not irrational not to adopt morality as a guide for one's own conduct. Although all rational persons generally want others to adopt morality as their guide to conduct, they do not necessarily want to adopt it as their own. The possibility of hypocrisy is an inevitable consequence of the nature of morality.

One can even define morality simply as a public system that applies to all rational persons. This definition, which has a very tempting simplicity, is more in accord with what Plato, Aristotle, and Kant discuss. On this definition, morality includes not only behavior that affects others but also behavior that affects only oneself. Also the promotion of good is as much a moral matter as the prevention of evil, as advocated by the Utilitarians. I shall, in fact, discuss behavior that affects only oneself as well as behavior that affects others, but I do not regard morality as applying to such behavior. I shall also discuss the promotion of good as well as the prevention of evil, though I believe that it is only the latter that is normally a moral matter. My view, which derives from Hobbes, and John Stuart Mill (see especially, Chapter Five of *Utilitarianism*), is that morality, as ordinarily thought of, is a somewhat narrower concept. However, if one prefers this wider definition of morality to the one I provide below, no important conclusions will be affected, even though there will have to be some adjustments in terminology.

The Content of Morality

Although morality has the formal features discussed above, these features do not provide a complete definition of what most people think of when they think of morality. For them, as well as for me, morality has a definite content. Morality is not merely a public system that applies to all rational persons, nor is it merely such a public system that governs that behavior that affects others. *Morality is a public system applying to all rational persons governing behavior which affects others and which has the minimization of evil as its end, and which includes what are commonly known as the moral rules as its core.* If a public system applying to all rational persons does not have this content, then even if it is justified it would not count as a justification of morality. It is only justifying a public system that has the moral rules as its core that counts as a justification of morality. Although there is not complete agreement concerning what counts as a moral rule, almost no one denies that "Don't kill," "Don't steal," and "Don't lie" are moral rules.

The central task of moral philosophy is to examine the moral rules to see if they do form the core of a public system that applies to all rational persons and then to see if this public system is such that all impartial rational persons would advocate adopting it. If the moral rules do not form the core of a public system applying to all rational persons such that all impartial rational persons would advocate adopting it, then morality as commonly conceived cannot be justified and ethical relativism, nihilism, or skepticism is the correct philosophical position. However, showing that the moral rules do form the core of a public system applying to all rational persons that all impartial rational persons would advocate adopting counts as showing that morality as commonly conceived is justified. But before one attempts to justify morality it is necessary to distinguish morality from other things and to make its content as clear, precise, and explicit as possible.

The initial task of moral philosophy is to examine the moral rules; to see if there is a unique set of characteristics which all or most, including all of the most important, moral rules have in common. If such a unique set can be found then it must be determined whether it is of such a nature as to allow the moral rules to form the core of a public system that applies to all rational persons, and then to see if that public system is such that all impartial rational persons would advocate adopting it. Some rewording of these rules is possible to make them more precise or more general; one or more of the rules may even be shown to be superfluous, or to be radically different from the rest, lacking those special characteristics which allow the moral rules to form the core of a public system applying to all rational persons. Perhaps some new rules may be discovered which have all of the characteristics of the acceptable moral rules, but if one is doing moral philosophy one must deal with these rules.

It may not seem a radical proposal to say that moral philosophy must concern itself with the nature and justification of the moral rules. Indeed it may seem to be obvious. Moral philosophers, of course, acknowledge the existence of moral rules. However, they seldom, if ever, consider their primary task to be an examination of these rules, showing their role in guiding our conduct or in making moral judgments. Rather, they have taken moral philosophy to be directly concerned with investigating (1) guides to conduct, and (2) moral judgments. This point, though subtle, is of extreme importance. By failing to recognize the central importance of moral rules in the study of moral philosophy, they were often unable to tell when they were no longer doing moral philosophy.

If one ignores the moral rules, then how is one to know which guides to conduct should be studied? A book on etiquette is a guide to conduct, yet it is not the proper subject of moral philosophy. Similarly, in making no reference to moral rules, how is one to know which judgments are moral judgments? Of course, whether they are aware of it or not, philosophers use moral rules in deciding both which guides to conduct they should study and which judgments are moral judgments. But, generally being unaware of what they are doing, they do not do it very well; they often investigate or propose guides to conduct which have nothing to do with morality and discuss judgments which are not moral judgments. And it is not unheard of to find a book, supposedly in ethics, which has almost no connection with morality.

It is not now my concern to show how the failure to distinguish morality from general guides to conduct has distorted the work of most moral philosophers; even Sidgwick equated true moral laws with rational Rules of Conduct without realizing that these true moral laws must be intimately related to the moral rules. Although it would be an interesting undertaking to examine all of the major moral philosophers and show how their failure to make this distinction leads them astray, this is not the place for it. However, I think it would be valuable to examine at least one philosopher so as to provide some detailed support for my claim.

Mill's View of Moral Philosophy

I have chosen to examine the views of John Stuart Mill. This choice is prompted by several considerations. First, all of the relevant remarks made by Mill are in the first chapter of his popular work *Utilitarianism*. Since this chapter is short (approximately six pages) and easily obtainable, it will be easy for anyone to check whether I am fair or unfair in my comments on it. Second, Mill is a well-known and increasingly respected moral philosopher, so that any confusions found in his writings are likely to be widespread. Third, Mill himself is somewhat concerned with this same problem, so that I cannot be accused of attacking someone on an issue which is not his concern. Fourth, Mill writes in English and clearly enough, so that there is no great problem in interpreting his remarks. When he is unclear, this is due to a confusion of his thought, not of his language. Fifth, utilitarianism is, and promises to remain, one of the most popular of ethical theories, and Mill is one of its principal spokesmen. Thus simply showing where Mill goes wrong at the very start of his system is itself of considerable value.

In the very first paragraph Mill maintains: "From the dawn of philosophy, the question concerning the *summum bonum,* or, what is the same thing, concerning the foundation of morality, has been accounted the main problem in speculative thought. . . ." In this seemingly innocent sentence, we can already see the seeds of confusion. In a paradigm case of a philosophical mistake, Mill has made an important philosophical claim, without even realizing that he was making any claim at all. Without any argument, Mill claims that the question concerning the *summum bonum,* or greatest good, is the same as the question concerning the foundation of morality. This claim, though it is commonly made, is quite doubtful. The same kind of mistake is sometimes made using the phrases "in other words," "that is to say," or simply "i.e."; I call it the fallacy of *assumed equivalence.*

The following passage strongly suggests that Mill correctly regards the question concerning the foundation of morality as a question of how to provide support for the moral rules.

"The intuitive, no less than what may be termed the inductive school of ethics, insists on the necessity of general laws. They both accept that the morality of an individual action is not a question of direct perception, but of the application of a law to an individual case. They recognize also, to a great extent, the same moral laws; but differ as to their evidence, and the source from which they derive their authority."

It is far from obvious that the *summum bonum* provides a foundation for moral rules. We might discover that the *summum bonum* does not provide us either with evidence or a source of authority for the moral rules. It is just as plausible that a foundation for morality is provided by discovering what helps one avoid the *summum malum,* or greatest evil, as Hobbes maintains. Hobbes denies that there is a *summum bonum,* and most contemporary philosophers agree with him. Yet Hobbes, and even philosophers who do not acknowledge either a *summum bonum* or a *summum malum,* are not thereby forced to abandon all efforts to provide a justification for the moral rules. Thus, right at the start Mill equates one of the proper tasks of moral philosophy, providing support for the moral rules, with a task, determining the *summum bonum,* whose relevance to morality is not at all clear.

Although Mill was not completely aware of it, he was not primarily doing what I call moral philosophy. Rather, he was providing a new general guide to conduct. It is interesting and important to note that Mill has been criticized precisely because his guide to conduct can conflict with the guide provided by the moral rules. It allows inflicting a significant amount of unwanted pain on one person to provide a great deal of pleasure for very many others. Yet the critics do not fully realize the significance of their criticism. Although they see that Mill's utilitarianism is inadequate, they do not see why. They do not see that utilitarianism is not primarily concerned with providing a justification for the moral rules, but offers an alternative guide to conduct.

Mill himself criticizes all previous moral philosophers for their failure to provide support for the moral rules. He says: "They either assume the ordinary precepts of morals as of *a priori* authority, or they lay down as the common groundwork of those maxims, some generality much less obviously authoritative than the maxims themselves, and which has never succeeded in gaining popular acceptance." Ironically, this seems a perfect criticism of utilitarianism.

Mill criticizes Kant for offering the categorical imperative: "So act, that the rule on which thou actest would admit of being adopted as a law by all rational beings," as "the origin and ground of moral obligation." For he holds that Kant "fails, almost grotesquely, to show that there would be any contradiction, any logical (not to say physical) impossibility, in the adoption by all rational beings of the most outrageously immoral rules of conduct." Whether Mill's criticism of Kant is warranted or not, it shows that Mill criticized previous philosophers on the same grounds that later philosophers criticized him: namely, the principle used to support the moral rules does not necessarily do so, but is, in fact, capable of supporting conduct contrary to that demanded by the moral rules.

Examination of the Moral Rules as Central to Moral Philosophy

Like Mill, most moral philosophers began by trying to see what support, if any, could be given to the moral rules. However, also like Mill, they soon lost sight of their original task. Once they found a principle, or set of principles, they forgot that the point of the principle was to provide support for the moral rules. Since their original search was initiated for a principle that would do this, it is not surprising that the application of the principle results in a guide to conduct which resembles to a greater or lesser degree the guide provided by the moral rules. Although it is barely evident in the works of some moral philosophers, what makes us regard their works as moral philosophy is the connection their principles have, or seem to have, with the moral rules. All of the major moral philosophers who offered guides to conduct thought that they were providing a justification for the moral rules. Success in this endeavor was the criterion by which they judged the systems of other moral philosophers.

Although this criterion is used by almost everyone, its significance is not appreciated. Moral philosophers continue to offer guides to conduct in the vain hope that these will coincide with the guide provided by the system of which the moral rules form the core. The task of the moral philosopher is not to offer his own guide to conduct, especially as this cannot differ in any significant way from that offered by such a system. His task is to explain and justify, if possible, the public system that contains the moral rules. The mistaken view that moral philosophers should offer general guides to conduct arises from the fact that, like Mill, most moral philosophers are not aware of the distinction between offering a general guide of their own and justifying that system of which the moral rules form the core, which is a public system applying to all rational persons. But if one strays sufficiently far from such a system, as Nietzsche does, suspicion immediately arises whether he is really doing moral philosophy. Lack of concern with a moral system is why hedonism, egoism, and stoicism are more correctly regarded as general guides to conduct or philosophies of life rather than moral philosophies.

A moral philosopher must make explicit all the features of the moral system which incorporates the moral rules. This includes making explicit the procedure for determining morally acceptable violations of these rules. Such a system should include those ways of acting that go beyond what the moral rules require, but which are still regarded as a significant aspect of morality, what I call moral ideals. It should make explicit what counts as a morally relevant feature and what features are not morally relevant. Such a moral system should be clear, coherent, comprehensive and yet easy to use. Most important, it must be a public system that applies to all rational persons, i.e., a guide to conduct that all rational persons understand and one that it would not be irrational for any one of them to adopt.

Simply providing such a moral system, though it would be extremely valuable, is not enough. A moral philosopher should justify that moral system. This is done by showing how morality is related to the concepts of rationality and impartiality, two concepts that all non-sceptical moral philosophers recognize as central to the concept of morality. Showing that a moral system, i.e., a public system that applies to all rational persons, that has the moral rules as its core, would be supported by all impartial rational persons is what I call justifying morality. A full moral theory consists of an analysis of all the relevant concepts, e.g., rationality, impartiality and morality itself, as well as an account of the moral system and its justification.

Moral Philosophy as the Study of Moral Judgments

As a consequence of many factors, but not including a realization of the points I have been making, some moral philosophers stopped offering general guides to conduct and started analyzing moral judgments. In part this was due to the sense of futility which came from looking at such a long succession of general guides to conduct, all of them inadequate in varying degrees. Since these moral philosophers did not realize that this inadequacy was due to the failure to recognize the central importance of the moral rules in moral philosophy, their analyses of moral judgments were doomed to a similar inadequacy. In fact, since moral rules are more closely connected to general guides to conduct than they are to the making of judgments, most of the analyses of moral judgments were further from an adequate moral philosophy than were the general guides to conduct. For if one does not realize the crucial importance of moral rules, it is impossible to distinguish moral judgments from other kinds of judgments, and the likelihood of even coming close is exceedingly remote. Much of the discussion of the nature of moral judgments is almost completely irrelevant to moral philosophy, though it has its own intrinsic interest.

The person who did the most to start contemporary moral philosophers on the investigation of the nature of moral judgments was G. E. Moore. His apparent clarity, at least about the task of the moral philosopher, resulted in making it almost impossible for one to distinguish moral judgments from nonmoral ones. Accepting Mill's identification of the study of the foundations of morality with the study of the nature of goodness, he stated his initial task to be an investigation of the meaning of the word "good." As a consequence of a number of considerations, including cogent criticisms of previous accounts of the meaning of "good" and a theory of meaning which he carried to fantastic lengths, he concluded that the adjective "good," in its basic sense, referred to a nonnatural property. For Moore, a statement of the form "X is good," when it does not mean "X is a means to something good," means that X has a certain nonnatural property.

Those statements which Moore says are his concern as a moral philosopher are statements attributing this nonnatural property of goodness to an object. Why Moore called goodness a nonnatural property is a complex issue which is not relevant to our discussion, for Moore's primary concern was to show that all persons agree on what things are intrinsically good. The point that was seized on by later philosophers, however, was Moore's assertion that moral judgments are statements of fact, though admittedly of a queer sort of fact. Although most disputed Moore's claim that moral judgments are statements of fact, almost no one seemed to question Moore's claim, which he never argued for, that all statements of the form "X is good" are moral judgments. Thus right at the beginning, the examination of the nature of moral judgments was presented with an insuperable obstacle by the very person who started the examination. This obstacle has not yet been overcome.

As an indication of how remote from moral philosophy these discussions of moral judgments became, one need only cite the supposedly important distinction between the emotive theory of ethics and the subjective theory. According to the emotive theory, moral judgments are merely expressions of our feelings, just as "ugh" is an expression of our feelings. It supposedly makes no more sense to ask if a moral judgment is true than if "ugh" is true. This theory was presented as a great advance over the naive subjective theory (which it is not clear that anyone ever held), viz., that moral judgments are statements about our feelings. On the subjective view, moral judgments are thought to be a disguised form of autobiographical statement, i.e., a report about our feelings toward something or somebody. The difference between these two theories is that emotivism views moral judgments as *expressions* of our feelings, subjectivism as *statements about* them.

It shows something about the state of moral philosophy that this difference was thought to be a crucial one. I admit that there are differences between these two theories. According to subjectivism moral judgments can be true or false, while according to emotivism they can be neither; but, as was rarely noted, according to emotivism moral judgments can be either sincere or insincere. The difference between the two views is as great as the difference between holding your stomach and groaning, and saying "My stomach hurts." The latter can be true or false, the former only genuine or fake.

This is not to deny that the emotive theory was important, if only in leading to the rediscovery that not all uses of language can be classified as true or false. The emotive theory paved the way for many more sophisticated attempts to describe the nature of moral judgments. The names indicate fairly clearly what the view was, e.g., "the imperative theory," "the commending theory." There were also the obvious modifications, e.g., the emotive-imperative view. No doubt a more satisfactory understanding of language has generally emerged from all this. I want to deny none of this; I am maintaining only that the connection between these theories and moral philosophy is extremely remote. Although some tried, no emotivist or subjectivist provided a plausible way of distinguishing moral judgments from other kinds of judgments. In fact, most seemed to deny that there is any significant distinction to be made. If one accepts either of these views it becomes puzzling that anyone should have ever distinguished a certain class of judgments from all others and given them a special name.

This puzzle is primarily due to the unexamined premise that moral judgments can be distinguished from other judgments by examining the words that appear in the judgment. Statements which include the words "good," "bad," "right," "wrong," "should," or "ought" are examined, as if a proper analysis of these words would clarify the nature of moral judgments. It was too obvious to be completely neglected (though many tried hard) that most statements including these words had nothing to do with morality. So there were attempts by some philosophers to distinguish moral judgments from other judgments using the same words. The most common was to stress the fact that moral judgments had some quality of universalizability. It was never completely clear what this amounted to, but insofar as one could find out what was meant, it turned out that all value judgments, e.g. aesthetic judgments, had this same quality.

All those who attempted to illuminate the nature of moral judgments by comparing them with other uses of language failed to do so, and for the same reason. They provided no way to distinguish moral judgments from nonmoral judgments. Their failure was not due to the crudity of the theories that they proposed. The most sophisticated theory, viz., that moral judgments are in some respects like statements of fact, in some respects like expressions of emotion, and in some respects like commands, is no better than its cruder predecessors in distinguishing moral judgments from nonmoral ones. All linguistic analyses of moral judgments fail because moral judgments are not distinguished from other judgments by their form, or by their function, but by their content.

The Importance of Content

The importance of content in distinguishing moral judgments from nonmoral judgments also points to the inadequacy of theories which seek to explain moral judgments by appealing to moral emotions or moral feelings. What emotions or feelings are moral? Suppose one attempts to characterize moral emotions without reference to the subject matter toward which one feels these emotions, but simply by means of introspection. The possibility arises that I could have this feeling toward anything, or perhaps toward nothing at all. When walking down the street I could all of a sudden have a moral feeling, and if I express that feeling I have made a moral judgment. This is obviously absurd. Nor if I get that feeling toward a mosquito that has just stung my child, which is more plausible, have I made a moral judgment on that mosquito when I express my emotion. It is quite possible that introspectively we sometimes have the same feelings toward a person who does an immoral action as we have toward a child or animal who does something harmful.

Substituting attitude for feeling does not help distinguish between the two cases because the word "attitude" is so vague that one cannot be sure whether it is possible to have the same attitude toward the two cases. If having an attitude toward something does not involve having certain beliefs about it, then one could have the same attitude toward a disobedient dog as toward an immoral person. If having an attitude involves having certain beliefs, then distinguishing a moral attitude from a nonmoral one will require a specification of the beliefs required for a moral attitude. Further, it will be the beliefs that will determine whether the attitude is a moral one or not.

The Scope of Moral Judgments

Moral attitudes, judgments, feelings, etc. must involve persons who count as moral agents. Some philosophers talk as if we can make moral judgments about states of affairs independent of their relationship to moral agents. It is sometimes said that a world in which there was less suffering by nonhuman animals would be a morally better world, and that this need have nothing to do with moral agents. I do not deny that such a world would be better, but to say that it would be morally better has to mean that it would be better for moral agents to act so as to bring about such a world. If there are two worlds inaccessible to moral agents and one of them has more suffering than the other, there is no moral difference between the two, though, of course, I would hope that everyone would prefer that the world with less suffering existed.

I am not claiming that moral judgments are limited to states of affairs in which the suffering of moral agents is affected, rather that they are limited to judgments in which moral agents are involved as actual or possible agents. There is considerable controversy about who has to be affected by moral agents in order for a moral judgment to be made on their actions. Everyone agrees that if another moral agent is affected, then a moral judgment is appropriate. Some think that only if moral agents are affected are moral judgments appropriate, that nothing that is done to anyone else is a matter for moral judgment.

This view must be stated more precisely in order to distinguish it from other views which sound similar. Some hold (1) only what is done to presently existing moral agents, e.g., adult human beings, is morally relevant. Others hold (2) only what is done to actual moral agents, present or future, thus including future generations, is morally relevant. Others hold (3) only what is done to actual or potential moral agents, present or future, thus including neonates and fetuses, is morally relevant. Some hold (4) that only what is done to presently existing sentient beings, thus including many animals, but excluding very early fetuses, is morally relevant. Others hold (5) that whatever is done to actual or potential sentient beings, present or future, is morally relevant; this is intended to include everyone in all of the previous categories plus future generations of animals including animal fetuses. Thus there is considerable controversy about the scope of moral judgments, from the narrowest view, (1), to the widest view, (5). But even on the widest view, the subject matter of moral judgments is limited in scope.

One cannot be clear about the nature of moral judgments without being clear about their scope. What is subject to moral judgment? This is a question that seems not to have been given sufficient weight by any of the philosophers who discuss the nature of moral judgments. It rules out any view of moral judgments which would allow moral judgments to be made of things that are not subject to moral judgments. It thus rules out almost all, if not all, of the various accounts of moral judgments that have commonly been offered; viz., that moral judgments are expressions of emotion, statements of emotion, commands, commendations, mistaken projections of internal feelings onto external objects, and so forth. None of these accounts ensures that moral judgments can be made only of things that are subject to moral judgments. This is not to deny that when we make a moral judgment we may be expressing our feelings, giving a command, commending, or condemning, or mistakenly objectifying our feelings. But when we have said this, we have done nothing to distinguish moral judgments from other kinds of judgments.

It should now be clear that no attempt to distinguish moral from nonmoral judgments can be made without taking into account the subject matter of the judgment. This is so obvious as to seem hardly worth saying. Yet it is surprising how many accounts of moral judgments have been given without mentioning the content of the judgment at all. It has already been pointed out that moral judgments are limited to judgments involving persons who are moral agents. Not all persons, however, are moral agents, only those having certain characteristics. Of a person having all of the necessary characteristics, we can make moral judgments of his actions, intentions, motives, character traits, or simply about the person in general. Of course, not all a person's actions, intentions, motives, and character traits are subject to moral judgments; some of them fall outside the limits of morality.

The two relatively distinct kinds of limitations on moral judgments are (a), moral judgments are limited to the actions, intentions, etc., of people who have certain characteristics and (b), moral judgments are limited to a rather small class of the actions, intentions, etc., of these people. A discussion of the first of these limitations largely overlaps with a discussion of what are commonly known as excuses. Excuses generally consist of showing that one either does not have, or did not have, one or more of the characteristics that are necessary before one can be subject to moral judgments.

What are the characteristics persons must have before their actions, intentions, etc., are subject to moral judgment? Since nonhuman animals are not subject to moral judgments, at least some of the characteristics that persons must have in order to be subject to moral judgments will be characteristics that these animals do not have. One of the distinguishing features of such persons is their knowledge of very general facts. It is not surprising that one of the characteristics that a person must have to be subject to moral rules is knowledge of a very general sort. One must know that persons are mortal, that they can be killed by other persons, and that they do not normally want to be killed. One must know that one person can inflict pain on or disable another person, and that persons do not normally want to be inflicted with pain or disabled. One must also know that one person can deprive another person of freedom or pleasure, and that persons do not normally want to be deprived of these things. Knowing some of these things, but not others, would subject one to some moral judgments but not others. Children are therefore not subject to some moral judgments, even though they are subject to others. A certain minimal intelligence and knowledge is required for one to be subject to moral judgment. Someone lacking this minimal knowledge lies outside the sphere of moral judgments.

The appropriateness of moral judgments is also affected by the knowledge that the person has or should have had of the particular situation. There is no dispute among philosophers, or even among nonphilosophers, that in some cases lack of knowledge renders a person totally exempt from moral judgment, but not always. For example, sometimes a person does not know, but should have made an effort to find out, e.g., driving regulations in a foreign country. Here we may feel that a tourist is responsible to some degree for an accident, though perhaps not as much as a native driver would be. And the degree of responsibility will depend, in part, on such seemingly unrelated factors as how close to the border it was, how many warnings or reminders there were, how many foreigners (the percentage) fail to find out the regulations, etc. Although we may feel that an effort should have been made to find out, the degree of responsibility will depend in part on how actual persons behave. It would be unreasonable to expect a person to know something if no one with similar knowledge and intelligence given that same opportunity knows it. Whether persons could have been expected to know the likely consequences of their action will sometimes be an undecidable question. Hence, it will also sometimes be undecidable whether or how much they should be subject to moral judgment.

One also needs some volitional ability or ability to will.[1] Persons who do not understand that there are incentives for acting and for refraining from acting, or who do not respond to any of these incentives no matter how powerful they are, are not subject to moral judgment. Such persons do not really have a will. For to have a will is to have the volitional ability to respond to the incentives for doing or refraining from doing many kinds of actions. It is not clear the degree to which nonhuman animals and very young children do have the ability to will. It is clear that moral judgments cannot be made of the actions (if this is the appropriate word) of those beings who do not have any ability to will. It is a more complex matter to determine whether a person is subject to moral judgment for an action if he simply lacks the relevant ability to will that action, and I shall not discuss it here.

Although persons must have some volitional ability to will before they are subject to moral judgment, not only actions which are willed, intentional actions, are subject to moral judgment. If people have any volitional ability, then their unintentional actions may also be subject to moral judgments. Even their failure to act, negligence, may be the proper subject of moral judgment. Some philosophers have held that it is only intentions and intentional actions which are the proper object of moral judgments. This seems to me to be a mistake fostered by not distinguishing between saying that moral judgments can only be made on those who can act intentionally and saying that moral judgments can only be made on the intentional actions of such persons. I am not limiting moral judgments to actions which are done intentionally. Also, in order to be subject to moral judgments, a person must be rational. But since rationality is the subject of the next chapter, I shall say nothing further about it here.

Excuses

Sometimes when I say "John ought not to have done X" I am making a moral judgment. If in response to my remark someone points out that, through no fault of his own, John lacked the relevant volitional ability, I do not count this remark as a moral judgment. I think this does not violate our ordinary thought about the matter. But since this judgment is incompatible with mine, it may seem odd that my statement is a moral judgement and the other is not. To avoid seeming arbitrary in excluding statements about excuses as moral judgments I propose the following. Statements about excuses concern matters presupposed by moral judgments. The response that John did not have the relevant volitional ability is not a contradiction of my judgment that John ought not to have done X, but a denial of one of its presuppositions. In making my judgment, I presupposed the person had the relevant volitional ability. By showing me that my presupposition was false, I am forced to withdraw my judgment. I do not deny the close relation between moral judgments and statements about excuses; in fact, I wish to emphasize them. I only prefer not to call these kinds of judgments moral judgments.

Excuses are generally offered when one is trying to claim exemption from moral judgment. Obviously this occurs almost invariably when the moral judgment would be unfavorable. If one claims exemption from a favorable moral judgment, this is not ordinarily called an excuse. Yet in both cases, the same kind of facts may be cited, namely that when doing the action in question, there is a lack of at least one of the characteristics necessary before one's actions are subject to moral judgment. Failure to know the consequences of one's action, either because one lacked intelligence and knowledge (which one could not have been expected to have) or because one had no reasonable opportunity, exempts one from both favorable and unfavorable moral judgments. Someone shouts, unaware that shouting will distract a child and cause an accident. If one could not have been expected to know this, one should not be subjected to moral judgment. Nor, of course, should one be subject to moral judgment if in the same circumstances shouting helps to avert a tragedy. Normally, an action that is unvoluntary, i.e., done intentionally but without the relevant volitional ability, is not subject to moral judgment, unfavorable or otherwise, e.g., a pyromaniac is not subject to moral judgment for starting fires, nor a kleptomaniac for stealing.

The Subject Matter of Moral Judgments

I have already stated that for an action to be subject to moral judgment, it must have been done by a person who had certain characteristics. If moral judgments were made only of intentional actions, showing which intentional actions were subject to moral judgments would complete the discussion of their scope. As I have already pointed out, moral judgments are also made of unintentional actions, even of the failure to act. We also make moral judgments of intentions, motives, character traits, even of the person as a whole, but these all depend ultimately on our moral judgments about actions.

We generally do not make separate moral judgments of intentions unless they have not been carried out. If people do what they intended to do, we make a moral judgment of their actions; we do not make a separate moral judgment of their intentions. Sometimes we do not carry out our intentions. Only where there is no action to make a moral judgment of, or the action is not the one intended, do we make moral judgments of intentions. Obviously, our judgment of the intention is closely related to the judgment we would have made if the action had been carried out. If the intention was not carried out because of circumstances not in the control of the agent, we may judge the intention exactly as we would have judged the action. If the failure to carry out the intention was due to the agent, we judge not only the intention, but also judge the failure to carry it out. Moral judgments of intentions are so closely connected with those of actions that there is no need to discuss them any further.

Moral judgments of motives are slightly more complex. Sometimes they are indistinguishable from judgments of intentions; sometimes they are more like judgments of character. We make favorable or unfavorable moral judgments of motives insofar as we think that the motive leads to certain kinds of action. Although a particular action is not subject to moral judgment, we may think that the motive for the action is one that is likely to lead to actions which are subject to moral judgment. Our moral judgment of a character trait also depends on the moral judgment of the actions that we think are likely to issue from it. Our general moral judgment of a person is very similar, though obviously more complex, as people have many different character traits, which do not always occur together.

I shall talk primarily about actions and the moral judgments that we make of these. I intend everything I say about our moral judgments of action to apply, with fairly obvious modifications, to the moral judgments we make of the failure to act, intentions, motives, character traits, and people as a whole. In discussing the further limitations of moral judgments, I shall only attempt to show how moral judgments are limited to certain of our actions and not attempt to show how this limits our moral judgments of intentions, motives, etc. That there are further limits to moral judgments than that they be about the actions of a person with certain characteristics should be clear. Even if I had all of the required characteristics, I would not be subject to a moral judgment for putting on my right shoe before my left, at least not in anything like normal circumstances. Not only is the scope of moral judgments limited to actions performed by persons with certain characteristics, it is also limited to a very small number of the actions done by people of this sort.

Which actions are subject to moral judgment? The simplest answer is: those that are covered by the moral system, i.e., by some moral rule or moral ideal. However, this answer, which is largely correct, is not yet of much use. It will not be of much use until we know the content of the moral system, i.e., what the moral rules and moral ideals are. But, of course, we do know some moral rules: "Don't kill," "Don't lie," "Don't steal." And we do know some moral ideals: "Aid the suffering," "Help the needy." So that the answer is not completely useless. But in order to be completely clear about the scope of moral judgments, we must have a compete and precise account of the moral system; we must know all of the basic moral rules and moral ideals and how they interact. These matters will be taken up in later chapters, but it is already clear that not all actions are covered by the moral rules or moral ideals. Thus a moral judgment cannot be adequately described as an expression of emotion, a statement about a property, a command, a statement about feelings or attitudes, or as a piece of advice. For all of these can be made of actions that are connected in no way with either moral rules or moral ideals. Simply the realization of the limited scope of moral judgments is sufficient to make clear the inadequacy of almost all previous accounts of moral judgments.

2

RATIONALITY AND
IRRATIONALITY

The concept of rationality plays a very important role not only in moral philosophy, but in almost all other areas of philosophy as well. It also plays an important role in all the social sciences, particularly political science, sociology, and psychology. It is of crucial significance in psychiatry. Although philosophers and others have generally used the concept of rationality as though this concept were understood by all, it is almost universally misdescribed. The general low esteem into which rationality has fallen in many circles is due primarily to this misdescription. Although a clear account of the concept of rationality has a value far beyond that of providing an understanding of morality, I shall generally limit myself to discussing those features of rationality which are relevant to morality.

Rationality, like morality, is primarily concerned with actions. What is basic is the distinction between rational actions and irrational ones. Understanding irrational actions is required for understanding irrational beliefs and desires, as well as the concept of an irrational person. Although it will be necessary to discuss irrational beliefs and desires, I shall have very little to say about distinguishing rational persons from irrational persons; at least since Freud it has been commonly held that this is a matter of degree. All of us act irrationally some of the time. How serious one's irrational actions have to be before he is considered irrational is a matter of responsibility standards. (See page 213.)

Irrational Actions Are Always to Be Avoided

An essential feature of the actions I classify as irrational, or rationally prohibited, is that everyone will agree that they are actions that they would never advocate to anyone for whom they were concerned; on the contrary, they would advocate that these persons always avoid performing such actions. These actions are not always called irrational, more often one uses terms like crazy, nutty, idiotic, stupid, or silly. Which of these terms one uses will depend on how serious one thinks it is, on how much it counts against the person's being rational. Philosophers who hold as diverse views of reason as Plato, Hobbes and Kant nonetheless agree that reason should always be obeyed. I agree that one ought never act against reason, that if an action is correctly described as irrational, it follows that one ought not to do it. The concept of irrationality is crucial because it is both descriptive and normative, thus allowing one to move from descriptions to prescriptions.

I used to use the phrase "prohibited by reason" as equivalent to "irrational." I have stopped using it because of the tremendous temptation it creates to think of "reason" as a faculty which issues commands and prohibitions. Plato, Hobbes, and Kant all succumb to this temptation, and except for Hobbes, there seems no way to eliminate talking of reason as a faculty without wholesale modification of the theories involved. Talk of rationality and irrationality is not talk about some faculty of human nature; it is a way of talking about the fundamental normative judgments that we make concerning human actions.

Irrationality is a more basic norma ve concept than rationality. To call an action irrational is to advocate that it not be done; however, there may be two or more rational alternatives, so that to say that an action is rational is not necessarily to advocate that it be done. Although it is true that everyone always ought to act rationally, this has to mean that no one should ever act irrationally, not that if an act is rational, it should be done. Whenever I am in doubt as to whether an action is rational or irrational, I shall call it rational. Thus it is quite likely that I shall call some actions rational which others would prefer to call irrational. This disagreement will be unimportant unless one holds that any sacrifice for others is irrational. I am primarily concerned that I call no action irrational that anyone would prefer to call rational.

Who Can Act Rationally and Irrationally?

I shall apply the term "rational" to a being only if I can also apply the term "irrational" to the same kind of being. Newborn babies do not act either rationally or irrationally, nor do most nonhuman animals. When we do consider their actions as being rational or irrational, it is only because of their similarity to actions of some as yet unspecified class of beings. It is tempting to describe this class simply as the class of all adult human beings. But this is obviously inadequate. It excludes older children, whose actions are often called rational or irrational, and it includes adults who are so severely mentally retarded that we do not regard them as acting either rationally or irrationally. Hobbes regarded the class of beings whose actions can be classified as rational or irrational as all those who can understand a language. Although this may be correct, I prefer to specify the class in a way more intimately related to the discussion of moral issues.

A person who believes that he is made of glass and can be easily shattered shows by this very belief that he is sufficiently intelligent to be labeled irrational. His belief shows that he knows that glass is the kind of substance that can be easily shattered. I regard general knowledge of this kind as necessary to show that a person is intelligent enough to be described as irrational, for this kind of general knowledge is necessary before one is subject to moral judgments. This leads to the somewhat paradoxical sounding conclusion that one must have at least a certain minimal knowledge and intelligence in order to be irrational.

Irrational Beliefs

I shall say that a person's actions can be judged rational or irrational only if that person has sufficient knowledge and intelligence to hold an irrational belief. I shall call a belief irrational if and only if (1) it is held by a person with sufficient knowledge and intelligence to know that it is false, (2) it is in conflict, either logically or empirically, with a great number of beliefs one knows to be true, and (3) this conflict is apparent to almost all people with similar intelligence and knowledge.

A belief is irrational if and only if it is held in the face of overwhelming evidence known to the person holding it. The person does not have to know that he knows things that contradict his belief, or that the overwhelming evidence would lead almost everyone with similar knowledge and intelligence to hold that it was false; all that is necessary is that almost everyone with similar knowledge and intelligence would hold the belief to be false. Except for extraordinary circumstances, irrational beliefs are false, but they are more than merely false beliefs, more than obviously false beliefs; they are obviously false beliefs held by a person who has sufficient intelligence and knowledge to know that they are false. I call such beliefs irrational because holding them generally leads to what I call irrational actions.

To say of a belief that it is irrational is to say something very strong about it, much stronger than saying that the belief is mistaken. Many beliefs are mistaken and yet not of a kind to lead one to say that they are irrational. For example, it is a mistake to believe that Oswald did not participate in the assassination of President Kennedy, but this is not an irrational belief. It would be irrational to believe that Kennedy was not assassinated. It is hard to formulate precisely the difference between the two cases. It is not sufficient to say that there is overwhelming or conclusive evidence that Kennedy was assassinated. It can be claimed, with some justification, that there is overwhelming or conclusive evidence that Oswald participated in the assassination. Nor is it sufficient to talk of our knowing the former and only believing the latter. For, again, it could be claimed that we know that Oswald participated in the assassination; that it had been proved beyond the shadow of a doubt. Nonetheless there does seem to be an important difference between the two beliefs. We feel that there can be rational disagreement about whether Oswald participated in the assassination, but that it would be irrational for anyone to deny that Kennedy was assassinated.

Of course, the above discussion has an implicit limitation; generally speaking, it is limited to those who were adults living in America in the 1960's. It would not be irrational for someone in China to believe that Kennedy was not assassinated, but that the whole thing was faked. When I talk of an irrational belief, I have in mind some limited group of people for whom it would be irrational to accept that belief. It is irrational for adults to believe in Santa Claus; it is not irrational for children to believe in him. Before one can talk simply of irrational beliefs, one must make clear what group of people one has in mind. Here there is a choice. One can try to specify some intelligent and highly educated class, e.g., readers of this book, and thereby have the opportunity of listing a great number of irrational beliefs. By specifying this class one could list as irrational beliefs the belief that the earth is flat, that the book of Genesis is literally true, that walking under a ladder brings bad luck, etc. This is a tempting choice, for I am primarily interested in persuading readers of this book that a certain attitude toward the moral rules is rationally required.

However, it is necessary to be able to speak of irrational beliefs without excluding anyone who is subject to the moral rules. It would be of little value to say that certain beliefs about the moral rules were rationally required, if this did not mean rationally required of all those who were subject to the moral rules. Thus when I talk about irrational beliefs, I shall mean beliefs which would be irrational to anyone with enough knowledge and intelligence to be subject to the moral rules. (When I say anyone from now on, I mean anyone with sufficient knowledge and intelligence to be subject to moral judgment.)

There are several beliefs or doubts or attitudes that would be considered irrational by all who make up the wide class I am considering. Prominent among these are the beliefs that are put forward by philosophical skeptics. The philosophical skeptic puts forward these beliefs in order to force us to examine more carefully the opposing or commonsense views. But someone who actually believed the propositions put forward by the skeptic would be irrational. These beliefs include the following: that we can never know, or even be reasonably sure, about what will happen in the future; that we can never know what the effects of an action will be; that we can know nothing about the world outside of our immediate sensations; that we cannot even know if there is such a world; in particular, that we cannot know if there are any other people in the world. Barring extraordinary conditions, any person with sufficient knowledge and intelligence to be subject to moral judgment would be irrational to accept any of the beliefs listed above. It is important to note that in this list of irrational beliefs, there are none that are in the slightest degree plausible as genuine beliefs, i.e., beliefs that, if relevant, would affect one's actions.

It is however, not only skeptical beliefs that are irrational, it is also irrational to believe that anyone knows everything that is going to happen. Even if one believes in determinism, whatever that comes to, it is irrational to believe that any person knows all of the consequences of any action. Any action, especially if it is at all significant, has so many consequences that it is impossible for any person to know them all. It is irrational to believe that anyone knows completely how a morally relevant action will affect himself, e.g., whether he will feel guilt, shame or remorse, or how it will affect his character. It is also irrational to believe that anyone knows completely how such an action will affect others, or even whether they will come to know about it. However, this irrational belief is often assumed by philosophers when they present moral problems for discussion. They present an action together with its consequences as if all involved knew everything that was going to happen. This is one reason why they often arrive at such weird results. It is just as irrational to believe that one can know everything as to believe that one can know nothing.

Rationally Required Beliefs

All beliefs that are not irrational to everyone with sufficient intelligence to be subject to the moral rules I shall call rational beliefs. It should be clear that not all rational beliefs are on a par. Some rational beliefs are such that anyone would be irrational not to believe them. I shall call this kind of rational belief a rationally required belief. One kind of rationally required belief is a general belief, i.e., a belief which makes no reference to any particular person, group, place, or time that is not known to all rational persons. One group of these general beliefs consists of the beliefs that the previously listed irrational beliefs are false. There is a simple logical relation between irrational beliefs, or rationally prohibited beliefs, and rationally required beliefs. If a belief is rationally required, then to hold that this belief is false is rationally prohibited or irrational. If a belief is rationally prohibited, then to hold that this belief is false is rationally required.

Another important kind of rationally required belief is a personal belief, i.e., a belief about oneself. However, even most of my beliefs about myself which I would be irrational to doubt are only rationally allowed beliefs, for other rational persons would not be irrational to deny them about themselves. I count only those personal beliefs which all rational persons must have about themselves as rationally required beliefs. The personal beliefs that are rationally required include the following: "I am mortal," "I can suffer pain," "I can be disabled," "I can be deprived of freedom," "I can be deprived of pleasure," and "I know something but not everything." Since rationally required beliefs must be beliefs that all rational persons hold, it should be clear that only a small number of rational beliefs are rationally required.

Closely related to the rationally required personal beliefs are some positive general beliefs that are rationally required. If we rule out extraordinary circumstances, we can list some general beliefs that any person intelligent enough to be subject to moral judgment would be irrational not to believe. There is no point in attempting to make a complete list of such beliefs. I shall now list only those which are immediately relevant to the present task: people are mortal, they can be killed by other persons, and they do not generally want to be killed. One person can inflict pain on or disable another; people do not generally want to have pain inflicted on them or to be disabled. People generally want to have the freedom to satisfy their desires, and it is possible for some persons to deprive others of their freedom. People do not want to be deprived of pleasure, but they can be so deprived by the actions of other persons. And finally, people have limited knowledge; they know some things, but not everything.

Since I am going to base my justification of morality on rationally required beliefs, it is important that these beliefs not involve any special knowledge, nor be peculiar to any time or place. They must be acceptable to any rational person intelligent enough to be subject to moral judgment, for we should not judge people on the basis of a moral system which is founded on beliefs they cannot hold. We can imagine circumstances in which one could come to believe that some person or group of persons was not mortal, nor subject to pain or disability. Nonetheless, in normal circumstances, it would be irrational for anyone to deny any of the beliefs listed above.

Rationally Allowed Beliefs

Not all rational beliefs are rationally required. There are some beliefs that I shall classify as rationally allowed. This class of beliefs, which are neither irrational nor rationally required, probably contains the largest number of beliefs. All those beliefs which someone intelligent enough to be subject to moral judgment could believe to be either true or false and not be considered irrational for so doing are rationally allowed beliefs. Of course, it will be irrational for some people to hold the beliefs that I call rationally allowed. Readers of this book would be irrational to believe the earth is flat. Nonetheless I call this belief rationally allowed rather than rationally prohibited because it would not be irrational for someone in the wide class I am concerned with to believe this.

The Centrality of Action

In my analysis of rationality action is central. It is primarily and basically actions that are judged rational or irrational. This does not mean that rationality and irrationality are incorrectly applied to beliefs. I have just given a fairly detailed account of what a rational belief is, and what an irrational one is. But on my analysis, these beliefs are called rational or irrational because of their connection with rational and irrational actions.

According to Aristotle, health is primarily and basically a property of persons, and all other things that are called healthy are called healthy because of their relationship to a healthy person; e.g., a healthy complexion is a sign of a healthy person. One could give a rather complete description of a healthy complexion, so that it could be recognized without ever mentioning a healthy person. But one who did not know the connection between a healthy complexion and a healthy person would not understand why such a complexion was called healthy. Those who knew of the connection but thought "healthy complexion" more fundamental than "healthy person" would be even more confused, for they would not understand why some foods were called healthy when they had no connection with one's complexion. In a similar manner, if one ignores the connection between rational beliefs and rational action, he will not understand why some beliefs are called irrational and other beliefs rational. Also if one takes rational belief to be more fundamental than rational action, he will not understand why we sometimes talk of irrational desires, when this has no connection to irrational beliefs. My account of rationality allows me to explain all of the other uses of the concept; no other account can explain why rational is used in the way I describe.

Hume's View of Reason

Hume was the philosopher who did the most to spread the confusion. He regarded rationality to be primarily and fundamentally concerned with beliefs. He held that, considered apart from beliefs, actions were neither rational nor irrational. He thought that only if actions were related to beliefs in some way could they be regarded as rational or irrational. He held that all actions based on mistaken beliefs were irrational actions and that all actions based on true beliefs were rational actions. He said: "It is not contrary to reason for me to choose my total ruin to prevent the least uneasiness of an Indian, or person wholly unknown to me. It is as little contrary to reason to prefer even my own acknowledged lesser good to my greater, and have a more ardent affection for the former than the latter." (*A Treatise of Human Nature*, Book II, Part III, Section III) According to Hume, no matter what one does, one is acting rationally if the action is not based on a mistaken belief. It should be clear that this account of rationality is not merely inadequate; it is totally false and misleading.

It is impossible to defend Hume's account of rationality as it stands, but some philosophers have attempted to defend what they consider a slightly modified Humean view. If you ask them, "Why is it rational to act on true beliefs?" they do not answer as a strict following of Hume would require, viz., "That is just what is meant by acting rationally." What they generally say is, "Acting on true beliefs generally results in maximizing satisfaction of one's desires." If you now ask, "Why is it rational to do that which generally results in maximizing satisfaction of one's desires?" you are likely to get the answer, "Everyone just does want to do that which they believe will result in maximizing satisfaction of their desires." This answer is false. Some people do not want to do that which they believe will result in maximizing satisfaction of their desires, at least if these words are used in their normal sense. Well, they might reply, "Anyone who does not want this is crazy." This is just the point. Defining rational action as action based on true beliefs is plausible only because one assumes that people always act rationally in some more basic sense. Once one recognizes that persons can act irrationally even though they have no false beliefs, then defining rational action in terms of true beliefs loses its plausibility.

The Maximum Satisfaction of Desires View

The most popular way in which Hume's account has been modified is to maintain that rational action is action compatible with the maximum satisfaction of one's desires. Note, however, that this modification completely changes Hume's view of reason. For Hume rationality has no goal, it is rational to act in any way one desires; all that rationality requires is that one act on true beliefs. It may seem only a slight revision to require that one not act in any way one desires, but limit oneself to acting in ways compatible with the maximum satisfaction of one's desires. But the change is indeed drastic, for now rationality has a goal, maximum satisfaction of one's desires, and one can act contrary to this goal even though one has no false beliefs. Thus rationality is no longer tied to beliefs, and rational action can no longer be defined in terms of true beliefs. Indeed, one now regards it as rational to have true beliefs primarily because of their connection with attaining the goal of rationality, the maximum satisfaction of one's desires.

This account of the goal of rationality leads to the view that rationality is concerned only with the means; desires are what set the ends. This is very misleading; it is rationality that requires maximum satisfaction of desires. Hume said, "Reason is, and ought only to be, the slave of the passions, and can never pretend to any other office than to serve and obey them" (Ibid.). On the modified view, rationality is not the slave of the passions, if that means it is the slave of each and every passion. Rationality is the slave of the passions only when they are considered as forming a system. Hume meant rationality to be a slave to the passions in the first sense; most followers of Hume, in the second. There is, as I have shown, an extraordinary difference between the two views. Hume's view has no plausibility; the view of his followers is extremely persuasive.

On their account, as well as on Hume's, there is no passion or desire which rationality prohibits us from attempting to satisfy simply because we want to. But unlike Hume, they maintain that rationality does prohibit us from acting so as to satisfy a desire when so acting conflicts with maximum satisfaction of our desires. If I act to satisfy one desire when I know that this conflicts with satisfying that which I regard as a greater or more important desire, then acting on that desire is irrational. Considered by itself, no desire is irrational. If there is no conflict with some more important desire, it is never irrational to act solely in order to satisfy any desire. Further, each individual decides for himself which desires he considers most important. Rationality serves only as a means for harmonizing our desires. On this view all desires, considered apart from their affect on other desires, are rationally allowed; none is either prohibited or required.

This view is extremely persuasive, primarily because the vast majority of our desires are neither rationally required nor prohibited. It is rationally allowed to desire to eat an orange or not to desire to. It is rational to want to go to a concert, and it is also rational to want to stay home. Especially when considering such a wide class of people as all those intelligent enough to be subject to moral judgment, it may seem to be impossible to find any desire that is not rationally allowed. Diversity of desires is so widespread that to classify any desire as rationally prohibited may seem completely arbitrary. Generally we do regard a desire as irrational to act on only when the person acting knows that so acting would result in the sacrifice of some more important desire. Whether a person who likes to drink but dislikes the hangover he always gets is acting irrationally or not depends on whether he considers the desire to avoid the hangover significantly more important than the desire to drink. If he does, then he is acting irrationally when he acts on his desire to drink; if he does not, he is not acting irrationally. But the desire to drink is, in either case, not an irrational desire. If it is irrational to act on it, it is because it conflicts with some more important desire. A person is not irrational if he acts simply in order to satisfy his desire to drink.

The "Cool Moment" Modification

A serious problem on this account of the rationality of desires is how to decide which of a set of desires is most important. Of course, sometimes a person may act on a desire, knowing full well at the time that it is irrational, that he is sacrificing or risking the satisfaction of much more important desires. But what of the more common case, where at the moment of action the lesser desire seems the greater? The pleasure of drinking seems to be worth the misery of the hangover. Of course, the next day one does not think so. When confronted with the same situation again, is it rational to drink? Here one can see that simply saying that the person who acts decides which is the more important desire is not enough. Is it what the person feels at the moment of acting, when in the grip of one desire? Is it later when there is a realization of what satisfaction of that desire has cost?

Faced with this problem, the most promising solution has been to talk of a considered judgment in a "cool moment." The relative weights of one's desires is judged by each person, but their weights must be judged in a moment of reflection when one is not in the grip of either desire. Only when one does not have a strong desire to drink nor is suffering from the after effects of drinking can one decide if drinking is worth the hangover it causes. What one decides then determines whether or not it is rational to drink. If on careful reflection one decides that it is worth it, it is not irrational to drink.

Of course, one may decide that there is not enough difference between the two desires to make either choice irrational. Just as with beliefs, it does not follow that in a conflict between two incompatible desires one must be irrational. There must be a significant difference between the two desires before satisfying one rather than the other can be called irrational. On this account, people decide for themselves which desire is the rational one for them to satisfy. This account leaves open the possibility that persons may often act irrationally, for they can sacrifice one desire to another when in a cool moment they consider the former significantly more important than the latter. But the final court of appeal for the rationality of acting on any desire is what that particular person would decide in a cool moment. It is not per se irrational to act so as to satisfy any desire.

For those who hold the view I have been describing, an irrational desire would be defined as follows: *A desire is irrational if and only if one knows (or should know) that acting on that desire will result in one's failing to satisfy some desire or set of desires which in a cool moment one has decided is significantly more important.* The following example should show the inadequacy of the "cool moment" definition of an irrational desire.

John Doe begins to have a slight desire to kill himself. At first it is not an important desire. From time to time he considers various ways in which he might kill himself. But he has other desires which, in a cool moment, he considers more important than this desire; so being rational, he does not act on this desire. As time passes, however, the desire to kill himself becomes more and more important. Finally there comes a time when, even in a cool moment, he decides that the desire to kill himself is more important than any of his other desires, more important even than all of them put together. At this moment, according to the "cool moment" definition, it becomes rational for him to kill himself. Since this is obviously wrong, the objection immediately comes to mind: he cannot have decided this in a cool moment. The very fact that he takes the desire to kill himself as more important than all the rest of his desires put together shows that the decision was not made in a cool moment. This objection is self-defeating. We cannot use the fact that he regards certain desires as more important than others as conclusive evidence that he cannot have done so in a cool moment. If we do, then there is no point in limiting irrational desires to those which conflict with desires we consider more important in a cool moment.

The absurdity of taking what is decided in a cool moment as decisive for the rationality of acting on a certain desire comes out even more clearly in the following example. Jane decides in a cool moment that her desire to kill herself in the most painful possible way is her most important desire. It is not her only desire, but she thinks it more important than all of her other desires put together. Among her other desires is a desire to go to a psychiatrist and see if she can be cured (notice how natural this word is) of this desire. She talks to her friend the philosopher, stating her situation, and asking for advice. The philosopher who believes what she says and who accepts the "cool moment" definition of an irrational desire should tell her that it would be irrational for her to go to a psychiatrist. For if she goes to a psychiatrist this will result in her failing to satisfy a desire which in a cool moment she considers more important. It is clear that the plausibility of the "cool moment" definition of irrational desire depends on overlooking people who suffer from mental maladies. (For an account of mental maladies see Chapter 5 of *Philosophy In Medicine*.) The "cool moment" account has no way to deal with what I shall call irrational desires.

Basic Irrational Desires

I define an irrational desire as follows: *A desire is irrational if it is always irrational to act on it simply in order to satisfy it.* It is not arbitrary to regard some desires as irrational. We do in fact do this. There are limits to what desires we consider it rational to act on. This does not mean that we can simply list a number of desires and say that it is always irrational to act on them. One can imagine reasons for acting on almost any desire which would make that action rational. Although we would consider it irrational for John to want to have his arms cut off just to see what he looked like with no arms, it would not be irrational for him to want to have his arms amputated if he thought that by so doing he would save his life. That certain desires are irrational only means that it is irrational to act simply in order to satisfy these desires. I am not claiming that to act on these desires is always irrational, nor even usually irrational, for we usually do have reasons for acting on these desires. Indeed, if we are acting rationally we must have reasons for acting on these desires. I shall, as with beliefs, provide a list of desires that it would be irrational for anyone (with sufficient intelligence to be subject to moral judgment) to act on simply in order to satisfy them.

The Desire to Die

The desire to die is irrational. Unless one has some reason, acting on this desire is irrational. Even if, in a cool moment, Jane decides that her desire to die is stronger than all of her other desires put together, we would still say she was irrational if she acted on this desire. This does not mean it is always irrational to kill oneself; one may have a reason for doing this. Being killed may be the only way to escape constant severe pain, but to do this for no reason, simply because one desires to die, is irrational. There may be some dispute as to what constitutes an adequate reason for killing oneself, that is, a reason sufficient to make the action rational; but there can be no dispute that one needs some reason. It is not enough simply to desire to do so. The desire to die is quite different from most of our desires. If we desire to wear pink shirts, we need have no reason, and acting on this desire will not be irrational. Even though we may not be able to determine precisely what counts as an adequate reason for killing oneself, we still can distinguish the desire to die from most other desires.

Although I talk about the desire to die, I am concerned with death in the normal or biological sense because of its relationship with the permanent loss of conscious life. Up until recently, there was little point in distinguishing between death and permanent loss of conscious life. Not only did the former entail the latter, but the latter almost never occurred without the former. However, due to the wonders of modern medicine it is now possible for someone to have permanently lost all consciousness and yet to be kept alive. Karen Ann Quinlan lived many years after she was no longer a person; after she had permanently lost all of her psychological features. I do not claim that it would be irrational for anyone to prefer to die rather than to live as Karen Ann Quinlan lived. My claim is that the desire to lose permanently all consciousness, to lose permanently all of one's psychological features, to lose one's personhood, is irrational.

Understood in this way, it should be clear that my claim that the desire to die is irrational is not at all controversial. If one believes that when one dies in the normal sense of that term, one's conscious life continues, but without one's body, then it is not irrational to want to die. I am not claiming that believers in Christianity or Islam have irrational desires when they look forward to dying. They are not looking forward to the permanent loss of consciousness; rather they are looking forward to a much more pleasant conscious life. On the other hand, Buddhists who do look forward to a permanent loss of conscious life are not considered irrational on my account either, for they believe that life contains much more suffering than happiness and so they have a reason for wanting to end it. I do not know how many members of these religions really hold the beliefs I have listed. Even though only a few act as if they are indifferent to death, one cannot say that only a few do hold these beliefs, for each of these religions contains provisions that lead their adherents to seek to avoid death. My own view is that if they did not have these provisions they would have far fewer living adherents. I have discussed religious beliefs primarily to make clear how uncontroversial is my claim that the desire to die, by which I mean the desire to lose permanently all consciousness, is an irrational desire.

The Desire to Suffer Pain and Other Unpleasant Feelings

I regard as equally uncontroversial the claim that the desire to suffer pain is irrational. Of course, there are reasons that can make acting on this desire rational, e.g., the belief that it is necessary to suffer pain in order to cure a disease that threatens one's life. And if the pain is mild enough or short enough, one does not need a very strong reason in order to make acting on this desire rational. This does not count against the view that to desire pain for no reason is irrational. It is not enough to make it rational simply to desire pain. The desire for pain, like the desire for death, is an irrational desire.

In the case of suffering pain, there is the troublesome case of the masochist. Is a masochist acting irrationally when seeking to suffer pain? I am not sure what to say here, but in keeping with the policy of not calling any action irrational unless there is no doubt about the matter, I shall call masochistic behavior rational if the masochist, as described by Freud, has pain inflicted on himself because it increases his sexual pleasure. This does not conflict with the view that the desire to have pain inflicted on oneself is irrational. For, as has already been noted, it is not irrational to act on an irrational desire if one has a reason. A masochist has a reason; having pain inflicted increases his sexual pleasure. If he does not believe it will increase his pleasure, if he simply has pain inflicted without a reason, then he is acting irrationally. He is also acting irrationally if the pain suffered is out of all proportion to the increase in pleasure.

Although pain is often taken to mean "physical pain" it is equally irrational to desire to suffer any of the various kinds of unpleasant feelings that are sometimes referred to as mental suffering. The desire to feel sad, anxious, or displeased is irrational. We often have reasons for wanting to have these feelings, but this is a very complex subject that I shall not go into here. Many problems in the philosophy of human nature and in aesthetics, particularly the popularity of tragedies, horror films, and works of art that cause us to feel outrage, depend for their solution on getting clear about the different feelings and the reasons that one might have for wanting to feel them.

Facial expressions, e.g., those associated with wincing, together with involuntary avoidance reactions, serve as part of the criterion of pain. Other unpleasant feelings, such as sadness, anxiety, and feeling displeased, also have facial expressions and involuntary bodily behavior as part of their criteria. People generally act so as to avoid that which causes them pain, sadness, anxiety, or displeasure, and act so as to continue feeling pleasure. Normally, this intentional behavior is perfectly correlated with these facial expressions and involuntary behavior. When, in normal contexts, there is this correspondence between the facial expressions and the intentional behavior then there is no doubt about what the person is feeling. However, if there is a discrepancy between the facial expressions, involuntary bodily reactions and behavior on the one side, and the intentional behavior on the other, then we are not certain what to think. However, in most cases I think that we are more inclined to go with the facial and bodily expressions. That there is sometimes a discrepancy between our intentional actions and our facial and bodily expressions is what gives sense to our talk of people being alienated from their feelings.

The Desire to Be Disabled

The desire to be disabled is also an irrational desire. It is irrational to desire to be blind or deaf, or to be unable to walk or talk. It is also irrational to desire to have a phobia, compulsion, addiction or any other volitional disability. As with the previous irrational desires, there are reasons, e.g., to increase the probability of being cured of a life-threatening disease, that would make it rational to want to be disabled, e.g., to have one's leg amputated. I am merely making the uncontroversial claim that desiring to be disabled for no reason is irrational. It is also irrational to desire to lose any ability that one has, either physical or mental, unless one has some reason. The desire to lose some ability, the exercise of which may cause one to suffer harm, may not be irrational, but this is because one may have an adequate reason; one wants to lose the ability because one believes that having it increases the probability of using it and thus increases the probability of one suffering some significant harm.

This does not solve the problem of what counts as an adequate reason for wanting to be disabled or to lose some ability, but simply to maintain that "I feel like it" is not enough to make it rational to act on this desire. This makes it significantly different from most of our desires, for which "I feel like it" is enough. Here again, it does not make any difference if we desire this in a cool moment. To say "I've thought it over, and what I desire to do is to have my arm cut off," is not sufficient to make it rational. On the contrary, if, in the absence of any reason for doing it, one has this desire in a cool moment, one is likely to be considered more irrational than someone who has it in a fit of anger at being so clumsy.

The Desire to Suffer Loss of Freedom

Almost identical remarks can be made about the desire to have less freedom. By freedom I do not mean merely, or even primarily, political freedom, that is, the absence of constraints against voting and engaging in other activities that are intended to affect the way one's society is governed. Total freedom would be the absence of all external constraints on one's behavior. I am not claiming that people want total freedom, for they may believe, correctly, that they could not handle such freedom, that it would turn out to be disastrous for them. I am only claiming that it would be irrational for anyone to want to have less freedom than she already has, unless she has some reason for wanting to have more constraints on her behavior. These constraints on one's behavior can be physical, as when one is tied up or locked in a cell, or they can be the result of serious threats of harm.

Sometimes one cannot engage in some behavior, not because one lacks the appropriate ability, or because there are physical constraints or threats, but because one lacks the resources, often money, to engage in that activity, e.g., spend a year doing research. On these occasions it is more customary to talk of a lack of opportunity than of a lack of freedom. I do not regard this as an important philosophical distinction, and I use the term "freedom" to include what might more commonly be called "opportunities." It is irrational for a person to want to have either more constraints on his behavior or fewer resources for engaging in some behavior unless he has some reason for this. Although it is understandable that a person angered by his failure to make anything of his opportunities might want to restrict them, that does not make it rational. And, again, were one to desire this after reflection, this would make it more irrational, not less.

There are, of course, reasons for wanting to have less freedom; it might be necessary to accept more constraints on one's behavior in order to have others accept more constraints on theirs. One might believe that one will make such bad use of one's freedom, e.g., cause oneself to die or to be severely disabled, that it would be rational to have one's freedom or opportunities restricted. Someone with insight into his character might conclude that he will never get his book written if he does not put himself in a situation which severely limits his freedom or opportunity to do anything else. But, as with the other irrational desires, one needs some reason to want to restrict one's freedom or opportunity if acting on it is not to be considered irrational.

The Desire to Suffer Loss of Pleasure

Finally, the desire to suffer loss of pleasure is irrational. Those who equate pleasure with satisfaction of desire may regard it not merely as irrational to desire to suffer loss of pleasure for oneself, but as impossible. But pleasure is not the same as satisfaction of desire and there are those who, when they find themselves experiencing pleasure, act so as to stop themselves from feeling it. If one has no reason for not experiencing pleasure, then it is irrational to act so as to lose that pleasure. As with the other irrational desires, it is usually only those who are mentally ill, or who are overcome by some strong negative emotion, who have this desire without a reason. Someone suffering from neurotic guilt or a sense of worthlessness may stop listening to music when she realizes that she is enjoying it. Of course, there are reasons that make it rational to deprive oneself of a particular pleasure. Continued enjoyment may be harmful to one's health, e.g., as smoking cigarettes or taking other drugs. Nonetheless, like other irrational desires, the desire to deprive oneself of pleasure requires a reason or acting on it is acting irrationally.

I am aware that there are important logical relations between pleasure and desires or wants. But I do not think that the relationship is as intimate as is generally maintained. The criteria for pleasure are more complex than that for desire. It is not a vast oversimplification to say that what gives one pleasure is what makes one smile. For human beings, facial expressions, e.g., some kinds of smiles, serve as one of the criteria of pleasure. It is true that intentional behavior is also one of the criteria, but it is not as central as those contemporary utilitarians who have substituted the satisfaction of desires for pleasure would have us believe. In infants, where there is at first no intentional behavior, facial expressions, together with other involuntary bodily expressions, are the most important signs of how the baby is feeling. Criteria are those features that are used to teach and test the use of psychological terms. Although they determine what these psychological terms refer to, criteria are neither necessary nor sufficient conditions for the presence or absence of the referent.

Desires Versus Wants

The basic criterion of desires and wants is intentional action; both are distinguished from wishes, which one can have without doing anything to make them come true. We generally decide what Jane desires or wants by seeing what she tries to get. Although there is no clear distinction in ordinary language between desires and wants, for purposes of clarity I shall distinguish between them; I shall say that Jane *desires* x when she has no motives for desiring x, i.e., she simply desires x or simply feels like doing or having x. I shall say that John *wants* x only when John has a motive, which may also be a reason for wanting x, e.g., he wants x because he believes it will help him satisfy his desire for y or because he believes it will help him avoid death, pain, or disability. Using this distinction, it is probably true that though most of us want money, we do not desire it. On the other hand, most of us desire to avoid pain, we do not merely want to avoid it. But some of us want to take a walk because we believe it is good for our health, and others desire to do so, that is, they simply feel like taking a walk. We can even both want and desire to take a walk, that is, though we have a motive for walking, e.g., we believe that it is healthy, we may also desire to do so, that is, we simply feel like walking.

Contrary to the popular view, the natural result of satisfaction of desire is not a feeling of pleasure, though, of course, this often happens. What satisfaction of desire usually does is to prevent displeasure. When someone fails to satisfy a desire, he is generally displeased. Watching people attempting to satisfy their desires, one will generally notice none of the criteria of pleasure when they have been successful, but if they cannot satisfy them, one will generally notice the criteria of displeasure. That Jane is sometimes displeased even after satisfying her desire is what leads us to talk of false or mistaken desires. Complete clarification of the relations between pain, pleasure, displeasure, and desire is an important and difficult task. However, it does not belong in this book, but in a book on human nature.

Other Irrational Desires

It should be clear that there are other ways of acting irrationally in addition to acting on a basic irrational desire. It is irrational to act on any desire simply because one feels like it when one believes that acting in this way will significantly increase one's chances of dying, suffering pain, being disabled, or being deprived of freedom, opportunity, or pleasure. If one knows (or should know) that satisfying a desire will result in the consequences listed above, with no compensating benefit, then such a desire must be regarded as irrational. Someone who desires to wash his hands and acts on this desire without a reason even when he knows that doing so will significantly increase his chances of suffering pain or disability, is acting irrationally.

We also regard someone who acts like the handwasher described above as suffering from a compulsion, a mental malady. That someone who suffers from a compulsion or other mental malady often acts irrationally has resulted in some blurring of the distinction between acting irrationally and suffering from a mental malady. Even though acting irrationally does count as evidence that one is suffering a mental malady, the two are quite distinct. Suppose that the handwasher described above, because of the sores caused by so much washing, had tried to stop washing his hands in order to avoid increasing the pain and disability. However, when he refrained from washing his hands he suffered such acute anxiety that he felt compelled to continue washing his hands. If he now washes his hands even though he knows that he is increasing the pain and disability, because it helps him to avoid the unbearable anxiety that comes when he refrains from washing them, then he may no longer be acting irrationally. If psychiatric help is available, then, in the absence of reasons for not using it, he is acting irrationally not to seek it, for not seeking it involves continuing to suffer anxiety or pain and disability without a reason. However, if psychiatric help is not presently available, then it may be rational for him to continue washing his hands. However, even if it is rational for him to wash his hands, he is still suffering from a compulsion, a mental malady. A person who suffers acute anxiety when he does not wash his hands is suffering from a mental malady, but it does not follow that he is acting irrationally.

Reasons for Acting

I have pointed out that it is not always irrational to act or to want to act so as to achieve the object of an irrational desire. One may often have a reason for acting or wanting to act in this way. *Reasons for acting are conscious rational beliefs that can make rational what would otherwise be an irrational action.* The belief that having my right arm cut off will save my life is a reason for having my arm cut off. In the discussion of irrational desires, several of these kinds of beliefs were mentioned. Beliefs that my action will decrease my chances of dying, of suffering pain, of being disabled, or of losing freedom or pleasure count as reasons. These beliefs are reasons because they can make rational acting to achieve the object of an irrational desire. Other reasons are beliefs that my action will increase my abilities, freedom, or pleasure. These beliefs can also make rational what would otherwise be an irrational action.

Determining what counts as a reason for acting does not solve the problem of what counts as an adequate reason. A reason adequate to make one otherwise irrational action rational may not be adequate to make some other irrational action rational. Clearly it would be irrational, in anything like normal circumstances, to act so as to suffer death, pain, or disability to win a bet of one cent.

However, I do not think it is necessary to go into this kind of detail. All that I want to make clear is that one needs some reason in order to make rational acting in any way that one believes significantly increases one's chances of suffering certain consequences. If this is granted, though there will still be practical problems in determining what will count as an adequate reason for acting in any of these ways, there should be no philosophical problems. Clearly one will need a stronger reason for wanting to be killed than for wanting to be deprived of some pleasure. This can be seen from the fact that it would be rational to deprive oneself of any pleasure in order to avoid dying, but it would be irrational to die in order to avoid being deprived of some pleasure. Thus though acting because one enjoys doing it is acting on a reason, if the consequences are serious enough, it is not an adequate reason.

Reasons as Beliefs Versus Reasons as Facts

Since reasons can make otherwise irrational acts rational, simply desiring something cannot be a reason. We have seen that merely having an irrational desire is not enough to make it rational to act on it. Although there is a sense of "reason" in which "a desire" does provide a reason, this sense of a reason has nothing to do with rationality; it simply explains one's actions. I shall always use "a reason" to mean a conscious belief that can make rational an otherwise irrational action. As long as someone has this belief whether he actually acts on it or not is irrelevant to its being a reason. Its being a reason is an objective matter, not something that is determined by the person who has the belief.

It might be thought that for reasons to be objective, they should be facts rather than conscious beliefs. One might prefer to say that it is the fact that taking an aspirin will relieve my headache that is the reason for taking the aspirin, whereas I prefer to say that it is my conscious belief that taking an aspirin will relieve my headache which is the reason for taking it. I prefer the latter way of talking because it emphasizes the close connection between reasons, the rationality of actions, and the rationality of persons. If facts were reasons, then the connection between reasons and the rationality of actions would be much too loose. There are many facts that I am not only unaware of, but that I could not be expected to be aware of. These facts do not affect the rationality of my actions when the rationality of actions counts in determining the rationality of the person acting.

Suppose I act in a way that I believe will kill me, e.g., take an overdose of some pills. If I have no conscious belief that serves as an adequate reason for committing suicide, then on my view, my action is irrational. But if reasons are facts, then if the pills were, in fact, an antidote to some poison I had unknowingly taken earlier, I would have acted rationally. This way of describing my action seems to me to be very misleading. Conversely, if I take some very unpleasant medicine because I believe that it will cure my illness, on my view, my action is rational, even though my belief is mistaken and the medicine will not cure me. However, if facts are reasons, then my action is irrational, rather than merely mistaken. Regarding facts rather than beliefs as reasons destroys the distinction between irrational and mistaken actions.

Of course, one might talk of external and internal reasons, external reasons being facts, internal reasons being beliefs. If there are external reasons to do something, then if one knows of these facts, one has an internal reason to do it. If one has an internal reason to do something, then one believes that there are external reasons to do it. External reasons determine the external rationality, sometimes misleadingly called "the objective rationality," of an action, internal reasons determine the internal rationality, sometimes misleadingly called "the subjective rationality," of an action. In the ideal case, which one hopes is also the standard or normal case, external and internal reasons coincide so that the external and internal rationality of an action are the same. However, sometimes the external and internal reasons do not coincide. If we want the rationality of actions to have some bearing on the rationality of persons, then we must regard internal rationality as the basic sense of rationality.

Once one accepts internal rationality as the basic sense of rationality, then it is clear that one ought to regard internal reasons rather than external reasons, that is, beliefs rather than facts, as the basic kind of reason. However, one cannot allow all conscious beliefs with the appropriate content as reasons; one must limit reasons to rational beliefs. One must do this because otherwise one would destroy the close connection between reasons, rational actions, and rational persons. Ruling out irrational beliefs as reasons eliminates all of the strong arguments against regarding beliefs as reasons, e.g., the argument that it allows the belief that avoiding stepping on the cracks in the sidewalk will prevent one's mother from suffering a broken back to count as a reason for not stepping on the cracks. I shall always use "a reason" to mean "an internal reason," or more precisely, a conscious rational belief. But when it is obvious that the facts are known, I shall sometimes talk of the facts as providing reasons.

Reasons Versus Motives

By "a motive," I mean a conscious belief that at the time of deliberating or acting the agent regards as, and which is part of, an acceptable explanation for his doing the action. Everything I call a reason can serve as a motive for a rational person. But some reasons may, in fact, never serve as motives for some rational persons. Further, some motives are not reasons. The belief that someone will be harmed by my action may be my motive for doing it, i.e., it may be sincerely offered and provide an acceptable explanation for my doing it. But it is not a reason; it cannot make an otherwise irrational act rational.

On my account "unconscious motives" are not motives, for at the time of acting or deliberating, the agent does not regard them as part of an acceptable explanation of his action. However, they may, in fact, be part of an acceptable explanation for the action. I do not deny the reality of unconscious motivation, however, I prefer not to call such motivation motives. This is because I want to say that an otherwise irrational action becomes rational if the person's motive for doing it is an adequate reason. If "unconscious motives" counted as motives, then this would not be true and many neurotic and compulsive actions would have to be regarded as rational.

My account of motives also rules out "rationalizations" as motives, for what one means by a rationalization is a conscious belief that the agent puts forward, sincerely or not, as part of an acceptable explanation of his action, but which is really not part of such an explanation. A motive must actually be part of the explanation of the action. Conscious beliefs often become motives, that is, explain one's action, because they are related to desires. It is the desire that makes the belief into a motive, and, in fact, we often call the whole complex of belief and desire the motive. I prefer to separate the desire and the belief, reserving the term motive for the latter because doing so allows for greater clarity and precision in describing the relationship between motives, reasons, and desires.

Philosophers have not distinguished clearly enough between beliefs which *can* make rational otherwise irrational actions (reasons) and beliefs which *do* explain them (motives). Further, they have not clearly distinguished desires from either of these. That I desire to do something is neither a reason for doing it nor my motive for doing it. Of course, I seldom need a reason for doing what I desire to, and if I desire to do something I do not normally need a motive to explain my doing it. My desire to do something may explain why I do it, but it can never make my doing it rational. But of course, acting as one desires to act is not usually irrational and so seldom needs to be made rational, even though it sometimes does. It may be that part of the confusion concerning desire is due to a failure to distinguish it from liking or enjoying. My belief that I would enjoy doing something is a reason and can be a motive for doing it.

I usually need no reason for doing those things I desire to do. If I desire to see the place where Kennedy was assassinated, I do not need a reason. If someone asks me why I desire to see it, my reply "I simply desire to" may be taken in several ways. It may explain my action by ruling out any motives for it, i.e., that I have any conscious beliefs that I would regard as explaining why I desire to see it. It may also be taken as denying that I need a reason for my desire to see it. It does not provide a reason for my desire to see the place, so it cannot make it rational to do so. But since it is not irrational to desire to see this place, there is no need to make it rational.

With very little modification, what has been said about irrational actions and the reasons that can make rational otherwise irrational actions can be said about irrationally desiring or wanting (to do) something and about the reasons that can make rational desiring or wanting (to do) that thing. Desires and wants can be treated just like actions, for purposes of assessing their rationality. This makes it even clearer why desires do not count as reasons, making rational what would otherwise be irrational. If what I want to do is irrational, it is quite clear that simply desiring to do it will not make it rational; otherwise there could be no irrational desires or wants.

Reasons for Believing

Of course, there are reasons for believing as well as reasons for acting. Although reasons for believing play no role in this book, it may be worthwhile to mention a few. The belief that I see a bird is a reason for believing that there is a bird where I see it to be. The belief that I remember taking an aspirin is a reason for believing that I took an aspirin. The belief that a proposition is entailed by something I know is a reason for believing the proposition. In normal cases reasons are beliefs that are offered in order to persuade a rational person to accept some further belief. However, since reasons for believing do not play an important role in moral philosophy, I shall limit all further discussion of reasons to reasons for acting.

The Adequacy of Reasons

Death, pain, disability, loss of freedom, and loss of pleasure cannot be compared in the abstract. Indeed, one cannot even compare different kinds of pain, disability, or loss of freedom in the abstract. Some pain is so severe that it would not be irrational to want to die in order to escape from it. However, there are lesser degrees of pain from which we would consider avoidance by death to be irrational. Death has no degrees. It seems never to be irrational to want not to die, even when it is rational to want to. Although it may sometimes be rationally allowed to want to die, it never seems rationally required. This means that it is never irrational to desire to live even though there may be circumstances, e.g., painful terminal cancer, when it would not be irrational to want to die. In general, most of our actual decisions are those in which it would be rational to act in either way.

We almost always have adequate reasons for acting in ways that would be irrational if we did not have such reasons. This accounts for some of the plausibility of the "cool moment" account of rationality. The "cool moment" account maintains that each person determines the rational way for him to act. People do differ among themselves on whether a particular reason is adequate to make rational an otherwise irrational action. It would be pointless to deny the vagueness of the notion of an adequate reason. But as we have already made clear, there are limits. A person who decides to cut off his hand in order to get rid of an irritating wart does not have an adequate reason no matter what he thinks about the matter. There are some ways of acting that are irrational no matter what the person himself thinks about it.

Definition of Irrational Action

An action is irrational in the basic sense if it is an intentional action of a person with sufficient knowledge and intelligence to know the foreseeable consequences of that action and these include significantly increased risk of his suffering death, pain, disability, loss of freedom, or loss of pleasure (including the frustration of those rational desires which he considers in a cool moment to be his more important) and the person does not have an adequate reason for the action. It is not necessary that the person actually believe the consequences to be of the kind listed above, only that almost all people with similar knowledge and intelligence would believe them to be so. On the "cool moment" account it is irrational to act on a desire only when one believes that this will significantly decrease his chances of acting on some other desires that he considers significantly more important, and it does not even require that the more important desires be rational.

There is a parasitic sense of irrational action which resembles the Humean account of an irrational action as one based on a false belief. In this sense, an irrational action is one that is based on an irrational belief. These actions are regarded as irrational because many of them meet the definition of an irrational action in the basic sense defined above, that is, many actions based on irrational beliefs result in the agent suffering an increased risk of death, pain, etc., without an adequate reason. Further, even when acting on an irrational belief does not directly increase one's risk, it seems quite likely that this is merely accidental, that if the situation were to change, the agent would not be able to react to it in a rational fashion, and so would increase his risk of suffering death etc.

Rationality and Self-Interest

I have listed five irrational desires: the desire to be killed, to be caused pain, to be disabled, to be deprived of freedom (or opportunity), and to be deprived of pleasure. Someone might ask, "Why do you call these desires irrational?" My answer is, "Because they are." We just do regard as acting irrationally anyone who acts on any one of these desires simply because he feels like doing so. This answer may seem unsatisfying. One would like an answer with a more self-evident ring to it. Thus, one might prefer to say that these desires are irrational since acting on them simply because one feels like it is acting contrary to one's self-interest for no reason. One might argue as follows: to act contrary to one's self-interest for no reason is to act irrationally. To act on certain desires simply because one feels like it is to act contrary to one's self-interest for no reason. Therefore to act on these desires simply because one feels like it is irrational. Such desires are called irrational desires.

I have also listed a number of beliefs that count as reasons. I have said that beliefs that acting in a certain way will either decrease one's chances of dying, suffering pain, being disabled, or being deprived of freedom or pleasure or will increase one's chances of obtaining more ability, freedom, or pleasure are reasons. Again one might ask, "Why are these reasons?" My answer is the same as above. They simply are. We just do believe that having one of these beliefs can make it rational to act in a way that would be irrational if one did not have such a belief.

We can, if we wish, relate all of these reasons to self-interest. We can say that the belief that acting in a certain way is in one's self-interest is a reason for acting in that way. The beliefs listed above are all beliefs that acting in a certain way are in one's self-interest. Therefore the beliefs listed above are reasons for acting in a certain way. Although some may find that the concept of self-interest makes what I say more self-evident, I do not. The concept of self-interest, if it is not to be intolerably vague, must be explained by referring to what I have called irrational desires and reasons.

On the account given so far, irrational desires are desires that are contrary to one's self-interest, and reasons are beliefs that something is in one's self-interest.

If a person is considered in isolation, as if he existed all by himself on a desert island, then this account would be adequate. Rationality is often equated with rational self-interest. This false equation is furthered by the fact that it is always rational to act in one's self-interest. But from the fact that it is always rationally allowed to act in one's self-interest, it does not follow that it is always rationally prohibited to act contrary to one's self-interest. However, if no reasons other than one's self-interest are involved, then it is rationally prohibited to act contrary to one's self-interest. When considering a person in isolation, it is irrational for her to act on any desire that results in the sacrifice of her self-interest when self-interest is interpreted in terms of the previous paragraphs.

Reasons and the Interests of Others

However, persons are generally not in isolation. They are usually found in the company of others. Considering persons in the company of others makes it clear that there are reasons in addition to reasons of self-interest. It is not irrational to deprive oneself of some pleasure, to suffer pain, etc., if one believes that one will thereby save someone else's life, relieve someone else's pain, prevent someone else being disabled, allow someone else to regain his freedom, prevent someone else being deprived of pleasure, or to increase the chances of someone obtaining more ability, freedom or pleasure.

It is thus not only the preventing of harm or the gaining of some benefit to oneself that makes it rational to deprive oneself of some pleasure, to suffer pain, etc.; it is also rational to do this in order to prevent harm to or to benefit someone else. Of course, it is also rational not to deprive oneself of pleasure or suffer pain for the sake of someone else. All that is being claimed here is that a reason is not limited to a belief that the action is in one's own interest. It is also rationally allowed to act contrary to one's self-interest in order to benefit others.

What is wrong with considering persons in isolation is that one is likely to overlook the fact that the belief that one will benefit someone else is a reason for acting. By considering persons in isolation, one is tempted to conclude that all reasons relate to one's own interest. But we do not consider a person to be acting irrationally if she gives her life in the attempt to save others, let alone one who gives her time or money for the benefit of others. Rationality cannot therefore be equated with rational self-interest.

The belief that one will benefit someone else may be as adequate a reason as the belief that one will benefit oneself. Some parents sacrifice their own interests in order to benefit their children; other parents do not. Neither choice counts against their rationality. As we have seen before, in a choice between exclusive alternatives, it often happens that both alternatives are rationally allowed; neither is rationally required. It is rational to prefer one's own interests to those of anyone else; it is also rational to prefer to benefit another at some expense to oneself. There is, as far as I can see, no warrant for saying that rationality requires benefitting others. It is, of course, rationally allowed to benefit others, but this is a much weaker and, I think, uncontroversial claim.

Basic Reasons

We have now seen that a reason for acting in a certain way need not be a belief that acting in this way will benefit oneself; it can also be a belief that acting in this way will benefit someone else. Thus rationality cannot be equated with rational self-interest. A person is not irrational if he acts in a way that he knows is contrary to his self-interest if he believes that acting in this way will benefit someone else. I have defined a reason as that which can make rational acting on an irrational desire. I am now pointing out that beliefs to the effect that acting in a certain way will benefit either oneself or someone else are reasons. Further, I think that such beliefs are the only basic reasons. Anything else that counts as a reason must be related to these basic reasons.

On this account of reasons, all reasons involve beliefs about the present or the future; a belief about the past can never be a basic reason. This means that acting in order to gain revenge, if this means having as the motive for wanting to harm another the belief that he harmed you or someone for whom you were concerned, is acting without a reason. It also means that the fact that someone intentionally, voluntarily, and freely broke a justified law, by itself, provides no reason for punishing that person. Nor does the fact that someone did you a favor provide a basic reason for your showing gratitude. This means that if any particular case of punishing a person or showing gratitude were irrational, the fact that the person "deserved" punishment or "did one a favor" would not make it rational. I realize that this sounds somewhat paradoxical, but I think that the air of paradox can be resolved upon reflection.

I shall talk about revenge and punishment somewhat later, so that I shall attempt to clarify the point here by discussing why gratitude does not provide an example of beliefs about the past, e.g., beliefs about past favors, being reasons for acting. Suppose that one way of showing gratitude involved your suffering some significant harm. If past favors provided a reason, then it would be rational to suffer that harm even if no one, neither yourself nor the person to whom you were showing gratitude were to benefit either directly or indirectly from your action. But if the person who did the favors is not going to benefit even indirectly from your action then the action cannot be one of showing gratitude. Following Hobbes, I shall define feeling gratitude as feeling like acting so as not to make the person regret that he had done you a favor. Showing gratitude must, therefore, involve benefitting that person, or at least, attempting to prevent him from feeling regret. Thus, the reason for showing gratitude is to prevent the person from feeling regret, not the fact that this person did you a favor. But this reason involves the future; it is not merely a belief about the past. That the person did you a favor may explain why you feel gratitude. It is not a belief that would make an otherwise irrational action rational, but it may motivate you to do a rational action that you would not have otherwise done.

It is also a consequence of my account of reasons that the belief that one's action is in accordance with a rule or custom is not, by itself, a reason for acting in that way. Of course, one generally needs no reason for acting in conformity with a rule or custom, but if one does need a reason, the mere fact that one's action is in accord with that rule or custom does not provide a reason. However, if one believes the rule to be a good one, then one may have a reason for acting in accordance with it, e.g., that acting contrary to the rule may erode support for it, and hence increase the probability that the benefit derived from the rule will be lost. Also, a person may follow a justified moral rule even when the circumstances indicate that no one will benefit from his following the rule in this case, because he knows that he cannot know all the consequences of his breaking the rule, including its effect on his character. So that when one knows that acting in a certain way is required by a justified moral rule, then one has a reason for acting in that way. This means that it may be rational to perform a particular act required by a justified moral rule even when doing that particular act involves some harm to oneself and does not benefit anyone. That the act is required by the rule may provide an adequate reason for acting in that way.

Even if one does not know whether the rule or custom is a good one, one may have a reason for acting in accordance with it; other people may be very upset if one goes against a commonly observed rule or custom. Also, it is often the case that one feels very uncomfortable acting contrary to a custom or rule when previously one had always acted in accordance with it. One may feel that avoiding the unpleasant feeling that would come from going against the rule is an adequate reason for undergoing the harm that comes from following it. This is very similar to the self-conscious compulsive handwasher who has a reason for washing his hands, viz., avoiding the anxiety that arises when he refrains from washing them. I admit that there are many indirect reasons for acting in accordance with a commonly accepted rule or custom; I only deny that the mere fact that there has been a rule or custom provides a reason for acting.

It is my claim that in all examples where the past, by itself, seems to provide a reason for acting, it does not really do so, but that beliefs about the future are always involved. Since reasons must be closely related to rational action, they must always involve beliefs about the present or future. Nothing else can make rational an otherwise irrational action. Further, only certain of these beliefs count as reasons; these are beliefs that one is decreasing someone's chances, either oneself or someone else, of dying, suffering pain, being disabled, or of being deprived of freedom or pleasure and beliefs that one is increasing someone's chances of obtaining more ability, freedom, or pleasure. Anything else which counts as a reason for acting does so only because it involves the basic reasons listed above. If anyone shows that there is some reason which does not involve these basic reasons, I shall have been proved wrong.

The Desire to Harm Others

Having shown that reasons include not only beliefs that one's action is in one's own self-interest, but also beliefs that it is in the interest of someone else, there is a temptation to expand the concept of an irrational desire. I have limited irrational desires to desires to act contrary to one's own self-interest. Someone may plausibly claim that it is irrational to desire to kill, inflict pain on, disable, restrict the freedom of, or deprive of pleasure, anyone, and not merely oneself, for no reason. One need not be claiming very much by calling these desires irrational. One can agree that it is not irrational to want to do any of these things if he believes that he will benefit himself, or even derive some pleasure from doing them. One need not consider a sadist, i.e., one who gets pleasure from inflicting pain on others, as irrational. Like the masochist, who gets pleasure from being inflicted with pain, the sadist is unusual, although perhaps not so unusual as we might think when we consider how many people enjoy boxing, how many laugh at accidents, etc.

We are now trying to decide whether it is irrational to act on a desire to harm others simply because one feels like it, i.e., whether the desire to harm others is an irrational desire. It is very tempting to say this, for we do talk of senseless killing. People who simply act on their desire to kill others do seem to be irrational. The student who, from the tower of the University of Texas, shot and killed all the people he could was certainly acting irrationally. And since he seems to have done this without any reason, it is tempting to conclude that anyone who acts on a desire to kill others simply because he feels like it is acting irrationally. It is not clear that we consider the student to have acted irrationally simply because he acted on his desire to harm others. He was intelligent enough to know that his action was one that significantly increased his own chances of being harmed. He may be considered irrational on the same grounds that a compulsive hand washer is considered irrational, viz., acting without a reason on a desire which he knows or should know would significantly increase his own chances of being harmed. Therefore we need not conclude that the desire to harm people is any more irrational than the desire to wash one's hands. It is irrational to act on this desire only when one believes that so acting will significantly increase his own chances of being harmed.

However, it may not seem plausible to say that the desire to harm others is like the desire to wash one's hands, both being rationally allowed except when acting on them increases one's own chances of being harmed. I think it does not seem plausible because as a matter of fact those who act on a desire to harm others simply because they want to are generally irrational. In almost any society someone who harms another increases his chances of being harmed himself. If one has no reason for harming another, one usually is acting on a desire which one knows or should know increases his own chances of being harmed. Acting in this way without a reason is acting irrationally.

As long as one takes care that he does not harm himself, it seems perfectly rational to act on a desire to harm someone, e.g., for revenge, even if one has no reason. But if the desire for revenge is so strong that it leads one to act in such a way that he seriously harms himself in order to carry out the revenge, then such action is irrational. So revenge which harms oneself is irrational, whereas revenge which does not is rationally allowed. If this is the case, then acting on the desire to harm another simply because one feels like it is not an irrational desire. To harm someone because he has made you angry is usually irrational, not because one needs a reason for harming others, but because one knows he is increasing his own chances of being harmed. Envy, at least in some mild form, is almost universal. Although we do not admire the person who seeks to harm those he envies, if he does it without harming himself, we do not regard him as acting irrationally.

There are serious objections to placing on equal footing desires to harm oneself and desires to harm others. One could be rational and be completely indifferent to other people, even though such a person would probably be suffering from a mental malady. Although it would be irrational for me to cut off my own arm just because I felt like doing it, it need not be irrational for me to cut off the arm of another just because I felt like doing it. It would, of course, be monstrous of anyone to do that, but if one were in a situation where one knew one would suffer no harm oneself it would not be irrational. I do not regard those who ran the Nazi concentration camps as acting irrationally, but as acting in a morally monstrous way. I can understand why many would like to classify pointless violence as irrational. I have no strong objection to one doing so. However, following my principle of classifying all controversial cases as rational, I prefer to regard the harming of others, when one does not increase one's own chances of suffering harm, as rationally allowed.

It may seldom be the case that anyone who is not suffering from a mental malady ever simply desires to harm another. But people have other desires, for example, the desire to feel superior to or less inferior than someone else, and this desire may lead them to act so as to harm others for no reason. Envy is exceedingly common, and it involves a desire to harm another even though one will not thereby gain anything. The desire for status seems to be one of the most prevalent desires and often leads one to harm another with no motive other than to satisfy that desire. As long as one takes care not to harm oneself, we do not usually regard such a person as acting irrationally. However, if his desire for status reaches such proportions that he harms himself, then we do regard him as acting irrationally.

Rationality, Interests, and Lists

This account of irrational desires seems to support those that want to make rationality essentially a matter of self-interest. Nonetheless, rationality does not become completely a matter of self-interest. It is still true that it is rational to sacrifice oneself to benefit others. It is irrational to sacrifice oneself to harm others. And here we can make a distinction between the sadist and the person who simply desires to harm others. For the sadist it may be rational to make some sacrifice to harm others, for he gets pleasure from so doing, and this pleasure may outweigh the sacrifice he makes. For the person who gets no pleasure from harming others, it is irrational to make any sacrifice to do so.

Causing harm to others never, by itself, makes rational an action that would otherwise be irrational, whereas helping others, by itself, can make rational an action that would otherwise be irrational. If by depriving myself of some pleasure, I enable others to enjoy themselves, what would be an irrational action becomes rational. Moreover, though it may not be irrational simply to harm others, it is irrational to do so if one thereby harms oneself and gets no pleasure or benefit. It is, however, rationally allowed for a person to harm others simply because he feels like doing so if he will not harm himself. We arrive at a concept of rational action which gives prominence to self-interest. One needs no reason to act on any desire except one which is contrary to one's self-interest, i.e., it involves suffering death, pain, etc., but this is not an essentially egoistic account of rationality because it is not irrational to help others even if one thereby harms oneself.

Although I have summarized my account of rationality and irrationality using the phrases "self-interest", "contrary to self-interest", "harm to others" and "help others", it is important to remember that these phrases are not basic to my account. It is death, pain in all of its manifestations, disabilities of all kinds, loss of freedom, and loss of pleasure that determine what counts as harm. Suffering any of these is what is contrary to one's self-interest, and if one causes others to suffer any of these one harms them. What is in one's self-interest is to avoid suffering these things and to obtain more ability, freedom and pleasure. To help others or to benefit them is to prevent their suffering death, pain, disability, loss of freedom or loss of pleasure, or to enable them to increase their abilities, freedom or pleasure.

That rationality is ultimately defined by a list rather than a formula will be, for many, a sufficient motive for rejecting my account. This preference for a formula over a list goes back at least as far as Plato. Like most such long standing preferences there is no argument in its favor. The supposed arguments against a list consist primarily of epithets like "arbitrary". A list is supposedly arbitrary in the way that a formula is not. As far as I can see the only sense in which my list is arbitrary is that it is a list rather than a formula. I have talked to no one who disputes any of the items on my list, and who does not use this list to test any formula that is put forward. If rationality is in fact the basic concept that most philosophers take it to be, then it has to be defined in terms of a list, for all basic definitions must be ostensive rather than verbal. It is surprising that this point has been so consistently overlooked.

I have admitted that rationality does not require concern for the welfare of others, especially when this conflicts with one's own welfare. It does not even seem to exclude what we generally call "senseless killing." Nonetheless it is important to see that when one's own interest conflicts with the interests of others, it is rationally allowed to act according to one's own interest or to sacrifice one's interest to others. Rationality does not offer the guide to conduct that either those who equate it with rational self-interest or those who equate it with morality assign it. This account of rationality makes clear that it does not provide the support to morality that it is sometimes claimed to do. Yet, despite appearances, it is not the enemy of morality that it has also sometimes been claimed to be.

I have attempted to provide an account of rationality such that there would be complete agreement on everything I call irrational, or rationally prohibited. I realize that many people would prefer that some of what I say is rationally allowed be classified as irrational. I do not deny that good cases can be made for calling sadism, masochism, and the desire to harm others irrational. (Although once irrationality is distinguished from suffering a mental malady, the case seems less compelling.) However, I do not want to exclude from the category of rationality anything which anyone can plausibly want to include. To call something rational, or rationally allowed, does not entail that one favors it. I realize that "rational" is often used as a word of praise, but I use it only to rule out one kind of condemnation. Only when I say that something is rationally required do I mean to commend it. It is "irrational" that has the primary normative force; to call something "irrational" is to condemn it. There are those who wish to make a sharp distinction between facts and values, between the descriptive and the prescriptive. This account of rationality shows that when dealing with rational persons such a sharp distinction cannot be made. This will become even more evident from the following discussion of good and evil.

3

GOOD AND EVIL

In most discussions of good and evil, good receives most of the attention. Indeed, sometimes evil is completely ignored, almost as if it didn't exist. Some theologians have even explicitly claimed that evil does not really exist. This view is, I believe, a central tenet of one branch of Christianity. Nonetheless, I do not think it necessary to defend the claim that there is evil in the world. Unfortunately, there is far too much evil, not all of it caused by people, though they are increasing their share consistently. In this chapter I shall provide not only a list of things which are good and of those which are evil, but also a definition of good and evil. My discussion will differ from most others in that evil rather than good will receive the most attention. This is not done from a desire to be different. Evil plays a much more important role in morality than good does.

There is little doubt about some of the things that are evil. Theologians through the centuries have recognized that there is at least a seeming inconsistency between the view that there is an all-knowing, all-powerful, and completely benevolent God and the existence of so much pain and suffering. The so-called "problem of evil" is the problem of reconciling believing in such a God with the fact that there is so much evil in the world. There is no disagreement among theologians about what counts as evil. Even those who deny the existence of evil agree about the sorts of things whose existence they are denying. They are agreed that if there really is pain, then there really is evil. Some of them are prepared to assert that there really is no pain; or that pain is not really something positive, but is a kind of privation. I shall not go into these theological subtleties. Pain is an evil. No rational person has any doubts on this matter.

47

Pain as an Evil

To say that pain is an evil is not to say that pain never serves a useful purpose. Pain sometimes provides a warning that we need medical attention. If we did not feel pain, then we might not seek the necessary medical attention, and as a result might even die. This fact about the function of pain is sometimes used in an attempt to solve the problem of evil. It is sometimes claimed that this is the best of all possible worlds, and all the evil in it is necessary evil. Even if that is so, necessary evil is evil. I am not now concerned with showing the futility of all solutions to the problem of evil. I am only providing an account of evil. Pain is an evil. To use the fact that pain helps us to avoid death as a point in favor of pain only shows that death is generally considered an even greater evil than pain.

Definition of an Evil

Everyone agrees that death and pain are evils. In the previous chapter, I pointed out that the desires for pain or death are irrational desires. Since desires for death and pain are irrational desires and since death and pain are evils, it is plausible that there is a close relationship between the objects of irrational desires and evils. In this chapter I shall attempt to show the advantages of defining an evil as the object of an irrational desire. This definition of an evil provides us with a list of evils: death, pain, disability, loss of freedom, and loss of pleasure. All of these things are generally regarded as evils. No rational person insofar as he is rational (this phrase is always to be understood when I talk of rational persons) desires any evil for himself without a reason. No rational person is indifferent to evils, either; in fact, all rational persons avoid evils for themselves unless they have an adequate reason not to. That there are circumstances in which rational people do not avoid death, pain, or disability, and may even seek them, does not count at all against the view that these things are undesirable or evils.

Some people are color blind, and there are conditions in which even normal people will not see yellow things as yellow. This does not count against the view that some things really are yellow. We determine whether a given object is really yellow or not by making sure that it is in normal conditions. Then we make sure that those who are going to decide have normal vision. Normal conditions are generally those in which we usually see that object or perhaps most things. Normal vision is determined by relatively simple tests in which, in normal conditions, a person demonstrates his ability to discriminate between yellow objects and those of another color. With appropriate provisions for those who speak a different language there is nothing wrong with defining "yellow" as the color which people with normal vision in normal conditions call "yellow."

The objectivity of yellow is maintained by the proviso "people with normal vision in normal conditions." When all of these people in these conditions call a color "yellow," it is yellow. If there is a color which these people in normal conditions cannot agree is yellow or not yellow, we then must say that the concept of yellow is to that extent vague. This color cannot be said either to be or not to be yellow. In most cases, all people with normal vision in normal conditions agree on whether or not something is yellow. The concept of yellow is a useful one, and an objective one; it contains no egocentric terms and a person can apply it sincerely but mistakenly.

The concept of evil is as objective as the concept of yellow. Further, the concept of evil is more precise than the concept of yellow. This should not be surprising. It is much more important to be precise about what is an evil than about what is yellow. All rational persons desire to avoid evils; they need have no particular concern about yellow. Defining an evil as the object of an irrational desire provides an objective account of evil, and yet not one which is independent of rational people. The definition makes it clear that a rational person seeks to avoid evils for himself, it does not require that he be concerned with avoiding evils for others. If we forget this, we create the paradoxes that have plagued philosophers from the time of Plato. No rational person chooses an evil for himself unless he has a reason, but some rational person may choose to inflict evils on others, even without a reason. Indeed, an increasing amount of evil in the world is caused by some persons inflicting evil on others. Even so, not all evil in the world is caused by the actions of persons. Floods, earthquakes, and disease still cause a significant amount.

Inadequate Definition of a Good

Having defined an evil as the object of an irrational desire, it is tempting to define a good as the object of a rational desire. If we mean by a rational desire one that is rationally allowed, we cannot expect agreement among all rational persons. For a desire that is rationally allowed need not be one that all rational persons have. Nonetheless we can see the plausibility of a definition of a good as that which is the object of a rational desire. On this account, what is good for one person need not be good for another, and indeed what is good for a person at one time need not be good for her at some later time.

No doubt, people commonly call "good" whatever is the object of their desire, and if the desire is not irrational, there is nothing wrong in doing so. I am concerned now with a concept of good such that all rational persons agree on what is good. Since agreement on what is an evil stems from the fact that no rational person desires it, we might try to reach agreement on a good by defining it as what is desired by all rational persons. We do know some things that are desired by all rational persons, but I do not think that this provides us with an adequate account of what is good. For the only things that we know are desired by all rational persons is to avoid the evils. Rational persons not only cannot desire evil, they must also desire to avoid it. They cannot be indifferent to whether or not they suffer an evil.

There is a problem in determining how much effort must be made in order to avoid an evil, but if one is rational some effort must be made to avoid suffering any significant evil, unless, of course, one has a reason for not making such an effort. Is there anything else besides the avoidance of evils that is desired by all rational persons? One might claim that there are several positive things that are desired by all rational persons: ability, freedom, and pleasure. However, if, as seems plausible, desire entails making some effort to get, at least in the absence of reasons for not making the effort, then perhaps not all rational persons do desire ability, freedom and pleasure. If one is not suffering, it is not irrational not to make an effort to gain a significant amount of additional ability, freedom or pleasure. So defining a good as the object of those desires which are rationally required might lead to the conclusion that goods are merely the absence of evils. This conclusion, although it is at least as worthwhile as defining evils as the absence of goods, is inadequate. More things are good than the absence of evil.

Personal Goods and Evils

Although the absence of evils is the only thing we are certain that all rational persons desire, we know that there are many other things which no rational person would avoid without a reason. We can therefore define *a good as that which no rational person will avoid without a reason.* Given this definition, we can list all of those things which are normally regarded as goods. Ability, freedom, and pleasure are obviously goods by this definition, for no rational person avoids these things without a reason. To do so would be equivalent to causing a loss of ability for oneself or depriving oneself of freedom or pleasure without a reason, actions which are clearly irrational. Evils are what all rational persons avoid, goods are what no rational person avoids.

This definition of a good also accounts for other goods. Health is a good, for no rational person would avoid health without a reason. To do so would be to increase one's chances of dying, suffering pain, or being disabled, which is irrational. Wealth is a good, for to avoid it without a reason would be to deprive oneself of freedom to do, or get, the things money can buy. To avoid knowledge is to avoid an ability, clearly an irrational act unless one has a reason. I do not deny that most rational persons desire health, wealth, and knowledge, but whether one desires them or not, they are goods, things which no rational person will avoid without a reason. Many other goods, such as love and friendship, could be listed if my primary purpose were to compile a complete list of all good things. This is not my primary purpose. I want to provide an understanding of the concepts of good and evil.

It should be clear that many things are neither good nor evil. Everything that is not the object of an irrational desire, but which it is also not irrational to avoid, is neither good nor evil. Sticks and stones are neither good nor evil; neither is taking a walk nor believing in God. Some people desire to collect stones; others have no interest in doing this. Some people desire to believe in God; others do not. These things are neither inherently good nor inherently evil. Only those things are inherently evil which all rational persons desire to avoid; only those things are inherently good which no rational person desires to avoid. I shall call those things that are inherently good, personal goods; and those that are inherently evil, personal evils.

I use the phrases "personal good" and "personal evil" to emphasize that a good is what no rational person desires to avoid for himself personally; an evil, what all rational persons desire to avoid for themselves personally. Although there is some connection between what I call personal goods and what philosophers have traditionally called intrinsic goods, the terms are not synonymous. Only pleasure has uniformly been considered an intrinsic good, though freedom, ability, health, knowledge, and friendship have also been considered intrinsic goods. However, wealth has always been considered an instrumental rather than an intrinsic good. Philosophers have rarely discussed intrinsic evils, although it is generally acknowledged that pain is an intrinsic evil. As I have found the concept of intrinsic goods and intrinsic evils not sufficiently clear I have abandoned it in favor of the clearer concept of personal goods and personal evils.

I have defined a personal evil as the object of an irrational desire, or that which all rational persons would avoid unless they had a reason. And I have defined a personal good as that which no rational person would avoid without a reason. Some might object to defining good and evil in terms of rationality, preferring instead either to define rationality in terms of good and evil or to define them independently. It is not crucial to my view which of these alternatives is chosen. What is crucial is what counts as goods and evils. As long as it is agreed that death, pain, disability, loss of freedom and loss of pleasure are personal evils, and that ability, freedom and pleasure are personal goods, I do not care if one claims that it is a synthetic a priori truth that all rational persons avoid the evils and no rational person avoids the goods. It is the list that is used to define both rationality and irrationality—and good and evil. I find it conceptually more elegant to use the list to define irrationality and rationality and to use these concepts to define everything else, but if someone prefers to do it differently I do not see that anything of significance turns on it.

Social Goods and Social Evils

Philosophers have called that which causes a personal good an instrumental good and that which causes a personal evil an instrumental evil. Since, depending on circumstances, the very same thing may be both an instrumental good and an instrumental evil, I have also abandoned the concepts of instrumental goods and instrumental evils, replacing them by what I call social goods and social evils. A social good is something that by its very nature increases personal good or decreases personal evil without thereby decreasing personal good or increasing personal evil. A social evil does just the opposite. Clearly the greatest social evil is war, especially nuclear war. The greatest social good is peace. Slums are a great social evil. Education and medicine are social goods. I use the phrases "social good" and "social evil" to emphasize that most of the things that by their very nature affect the personal goods and evils are social in character. To be sure, earthquakes, floods, and hurricanes often cause great personal evil, but these things do not necessarily affect people. Some hurricanes, floods, and earthquakes affect no one. This is not true of war and slums. When earthquakes, floods, or hurricanes cause great personal evil, we call it a disaster or a tragedy. War and slums always cause personal evil, so that we can say that they are evils by their very nature.

This list of personal and social goods and evils is a list of the kinds of things that by their very nature are good or evil. It is not true that nothing is good or bad but thinking makes it so. What counts as a good or an evil does not depend on the opinion of any person or particular group of persons, but is an objective matter. I am not maintaining that every use of the words "good" and "evil" is objective. As noted earlier, there is a common and correct use of "good" and "evil" by people to express their rational desires and aversions. Even this use can be best understood as parasitical on the objective use, as I shall attempt to show shortly. It is the objective sense of good and evil with which most of the major philosophers have been concerned, and this sense is also the important one in morality.

Better and Worse

We now have an account of good and evil such that though neither is defined in terms of the other, they are logically related to each other in the appropriate way. Evil is what all rational persons will avoid unless they have a reason; good is what no rational person will avoid unless he has a reason. Nothing, therefore, can be both good and evil. This account of good and evil can easily be extended to provide an account of better and worse. One alternative is better than another if all rational persons would choose it over the other, unless they had some reason for not doing so. It is better to have a thousand dollars than to have only a hundred, better to have an opportunity to choose between five alternatives than to have the opportunity to choose between only two of them. One alternative is worse than another if no rational person would choose it over the other unless he had some reason. It is worse to be disabled for two months than to be disabled for only two weeks, worse to be deprived of freedom for ten years than to be deprived of it for only five.

On this account, it is perfectly understandable how one can be confronted with a choice of two evils, one of them worse than the other. It is also understandable how one can be confronted with two goods, one of them better than the other. It also follows from these definitions that when confronted with two alternatives, one good, the other evil, the former is always better than the latter; the latter is always worse than the former. Of course, rational persons will not always agree which of two evils is worse, or which of two goods is better, e.g., when confronted with choosing between increasing wealth and increasing knowledge, rational persons will not always agree, especially since both wealth and knowledge have degrees. It is pointless to talk of knowledge being better than wealth, or vice versa. Similarly there will not be complete agreement among rational persons about which is worse, pain or loss of freedom. Obviously there are degrees of pain to escape from which all rational persons will choose some loss of freedom, but we cannot expect complete agreement where different kinds of evils are involved. Death is usually the worst evil, for all rational persons are prepared to suffer some degree of the other evils in order to avoid death. However, the other evils can become so great that death may come to be regarded by many as the lesser evil.

In a memorable phrase, John Stuart Mill maintained that "it is better to be

Socrates dissatisfied than a fool satisfied." Mill tried to support this by claiming that the pleasure of Socrates was of a higher quality than the pleasure of a fool. He made this claim only because he was committed to the view that pleasure was the only good. Having no need to make this mistaken claim, we can see that what Mill really thought was that the goods of knowledge and ability, especially mental ability, were better than pleasure. Although my personal preference is the same as Mill's, I am forced to admit that it is merely a personal preference. All rational persons need not prefer knowledge to pleasure. Indeed very few actually do. Since those who do are generally those who read philosophy, it is not surprising that Mill's view, although mistaken, has met with what seems like general approval. One must be very careful in doing philosophy not to mistake agreement among philosophers for agreement among all rational persons. That the life of the mind has been considered by philosophers as the best life shows only that philosophers prefer the life of the mind. This is not surprising; one would not expect them to be philosophers if they did not. Persons who do not prefer the life of the mind seldom write books extolling their way of life as the best. Rationality does not require emphasizing any one of the goods over the others, but allows each person to make her own choice.

This account of good and evil not only enables us to understand how one evil can be worse than another, or one good better than another, it also makes clear that there will not always be agreement about which of two evils is worse, or which of two goods is better. It should not be surprising that there may be nothing which all rational persons will agree is the worst of all possible evils, or the best of all possible goods. That there are several different kinds of goods and evils, not just pleasure and pain as the Classical Utilitarians maintained, has some important consequences. It means that two persons, both rational and both agreeing about all the facts, even when they are concerned with the same people, may advocate different courses of action. This can happen because they may rank differently the goods and evils involved. One may regard a certain amount of loss of freedom as worse than a certain amount of pain, while another person may regard the pain as worse. Within limits, it is rationally allowed to choose either way. There is not always a best decision.

The fact that when confronted with two evils or two goods it is often rationally allowed to choose either has had an extraordinary effect on some philosophers. They have concluded that presented with any two alternatives, even if one is good and the other evil, rationality never requires choosing one of them. This is obviously absurd. When confronted with a choice between a good and an evil, it is rationally required to choose the good and prohibited to choose the evil. Even in most of the cases where one is confronted with two goods or two evils, one choice is rationally required, the other rationally prohibited. It is clearly a mistake to hold that if rationality does not provide a complete guide, then it does not provide any guide at all.

Although all rational persons agree on what is good and evil, they do not always agree on what is better and worse. There is no danger that by accepting rationality as one's guide, one thereby forfeits freedom of choice. Rationality prohibits doing only those things which no rational person would choose to do.

There are no real decisions to be made in which rationality requires one alternative over the other. No rational person feels that a decision is called for when one alternative results in evil for everyone including himself, and the other results in good for everyone including himself. In those cases where rational persons genuinely feel that a decision is called for, either alternative is always rationally allowed. A person dying of terminal cancer must decide if he wants to be kept alive or not. Either choice is rationally allowed. A talented young person must choose between medical research and a well-paying private practice. Again, either choice is rationally allowed. That there is not complete agreement among all rational persons on the relative ranking of the various goods and evils does not show that there is not complete agreement on what is good and evil. Indeed, agreement concerning good and evil is presupposed in the daily lives even of those philosophers who have explicitly denied the possibility of such agreement.

Good of Its Kind

This analysis of good and evil can be extended to particular things, like tools, by specifying the interests and qualifications of rational persons. A good tool is one that all qualified rational persons would select when choosing the tool for its normal use, unless they had a reason not to. ("Qualified," "normal use" and the "unless" clause should be understood from now on.) A bad tool is one that all rational persons would try to avoid. One tool is better than another if all rational persons would prefer it. Thus two tools can be good, but one better; two tools can be bad, but one better; and naturally if one tool is good and the other bad, the former is better than the latter. This analysis works not only for tools, but also for anything that has a standard function or purpose, e.g., sports equipment. It even works for athletes, as we take their purpose to be to win. Good athletes are those who are likely to win or help their team to win.

A tool may have several characteristics that are relevant to how it performs, so it may not always be possible to decide which one of a set of tools is best. Each of them might be better in one characteristic, with no way of deciding which combination is best. All rational persons may agree that A, B, and C are good tools, and that D, E, and F are bad ones. Further even though A and B may be preferred to C, there may be no agreement on whether A or B is better. Even when judging purely functional items, there will not always be agreement among all qualified rational persons, but the lack of complete agreement does not mean that there will not be substantial agreement. Reading through an issue of *Consumer Reports* illustrates this point very clearly.

Also, that there is no right answer to the question, "Who was the best hitter in baseball?" does not mean there are no wrong answers. That there is no agreement on whether Babe Ruth, Ty Cobb, or Hank Aaron was best does not mean that there is no agreement that all three of them are better than 99 percent of all hitters, past or present. The lack of complete agreement affects the objectivity of these judgments as little as the fact that normal people sometimes disagree about whether an object is yellow affects the objectivity of judgments about color.

Aesthetic Judgments

In this regard, aesthetic judgments differ radically from judgments of functional items. I do not mean to deny the objectivity of aesthetic judgments. In judging such things as paintings, music, novels, or poems, all qualified rational persons who accept the same standards will undoubtedly reach substantial agreement. However, since works of art have no "normal function," qualified rational persons may not accept the same standards. This leads to the view that each work of art should be judged by the standards appropriate to it. This is not anarchy, for the appropriate standards will be determined by the "purpose" of the work of art. Those who believe that the only "purpose" of a work of art is to express the creativity of the artist will hold that there is a single standard for all works of art. However, if one accepts that a work of art can be designed merely to entertain, then, with some qualifications, it should be judged by how well it does that. It is also relevant for whom the work of art is intended. A children's book should not be written like a novel for intellectuals. As long as a work of art is judged on its own terms, generally determined by the intentions of the artist, I see no reason why aesthetic judgments should not be as objective as any other kind of value judgment.

However, when one says that certain kinds of paintings or music are better than others, then one reaches an area where judgment rapidly deteriorates into expression of preference. It is natural for sophisticated composers to scorn popular music as inferior. Popular music can be composed with much less knowledge of music than is required to compose serious contemporary music. It does not follow that one who can compose good serious contemporary music can also compose good popular music. Nor does it follow that because something is more difficult to do, the result should be judged superior to something less difficult to do. I realize that the designation "great" is not appropriate to those works of art designed merely to entertain, but I see no point in comparing works of art which have different purposes. Nor do I see how one can expect to reach agreement on who counts as a qualified rational person, nor on what counts as the appropriate standard by which they are all to judge.

Judgments

All judgments using the terms "good," "bad," "better," and "worse" must be made on the basis of standards. These standards will always be related to the purposes of the things being judged. Sometimes this relationship will be indirect, as in the case of judging dogs. Dogs used to have certain functions; certain forms were characteristically associated with good performance of those functions. Standards for judging dogs developed using these forms as a basis. It must, however, be admitted that many standards are now almost completely conventional, the function that originally generated the standards having long been forgotten.

Although all judgments using "good" must be made on the basis of standards, this is more a comment on the concept of judgment than on the use of the term "good," for "good" is often used not in making judgments, but in expressing one's likes, just as "bad" is often used to express one's dislikes. In calling a movie bad, I may not be making a judgment of the movie at all, but simply expressing my dislike of it. Similarly when I say that a meal was good, I may simply mean I liked it and be using no standard at all. Even this use of "good" and "bad" is best understood when related to the objective sense of these terms. Since pleasure is good, it is most natural to call that which gives me pleasure "good." This use of "good" resembles what philosophers have called "instrumentally good," a terminology I have rejected because of its misleading consequences.

It may be that it was concentration on the use of "good" and "bad" as expressing one's likes and dislikes that led philosophers to deny the objectivity of good and evil. It cannot be denied that what gives one person pleasure may not give pleasure to another. Indeed what gives pleasure to a person at one time may not give him pleasure at some future time. When we recognize that it is because a thing gives him pleasure that a person calls it good, we will see that the objectivity of good and evil underlies the seemingly subjective use of these terms. It is extraordinarily odd that though many have denied the objectivity of good and evil, these concepts play a central role in defining other concepts, e.g., reward and punishment, health and disease, whose objectivity almost no one has challenged.

Punishment

Examination of punishment and reward provides further support for the present account of good and evil. Punishment necessarily involves the infliction of an evil, though, of course, not all infliction of evil is punishment. A full account of punishment must include an account of the relationship between the person inflicting the evil and the person who suffers it. It must also include an account of the circumstances for inflicting the evil, e.g., that the evil is being inflicted on someone for having violated a moral rule. I am not here concerned with providing a complete account of punishment; I am concerned only with the relationship between punishment and the inflicting of evils.[1]

All of the evils that I have mentioned have been used as punishments. Death is usually regarded as the most severe punishment, reinforcing the view that death is usually considered the worst evil. The infliction of pain used to be a much more common punishment than it now is, and in minor form it is still used by parents. Since it admits of degrees, one cannot say that infliction of pain is more or less severe than other types of punishment. There are degrees of pain that may make death seem the lesser punishment, but some pain may be so light that one prefers it to any other punishment. Disabling has also been used as a punishment, e.g., pickpockets used to have their hands cut off. The most common punishment is deprivation of freedom. It has many advantages; there can be very precise gradations in the amount of punishment, the longer one is deprived of freedom the greater the punishment. It is fairly easy to administer and, since it can be combined with other evils, or even goods, it allows for great flexibility, a point I shall discuss in more detail later. The mildest form of punishment is generally deprivation of pleasure. This kind of punishment is usually restricted to children.

All punishments involve one or more of the evils mentioned above. If one does not think that a person has suffered one of these evils, then he does not think that the person has been punished. The suffering of these evils is so closely connected with punishment that psychologists now talk of punishment whenever a person suffers an evil contingent upon some performance of an action, even though the person may have broken no law, legal or moral. This connection between the suffering of an evil and punishment is also shown by the fact that even if a guilty person suffers an evil through natural causes he is sometimes said to have been punished.

Since being punished involves suffering some evil, and no rational person wants to suffer an evil, I must explain why some people voluntarily confess their crimes and willingly submit to punishment. Since I do not claim that all of these people are acting irrationally, I seem faced with an inconsistency. But this inconsistency is only apparent. Those people who want to be punished for their actions, if they are not irrational, have some reason for wanting this. The reasons may differ, but they fall into two broad categories. One is psychological. Due to conditions we need not investigate here, some people feel extraordinarily uncomfortable when they know they are guilty of some crime and are not punished. They submit to punishment in order to relieve themselves of these unpleasant feelings. The other reason I shall call moral. It is impossible to make this reason completely clear before the concept of morality has been clarified, all that I can say now is that some people seek to be punished because they believe it is the morally right thing to do. Generally, but not necessarily, one who has this kind of reason will also have the psychological reason.

The fact that some people seek punishment for psychological reasons shows that punishment may benefit the one being punished, it does not show that this is why we punish them. Confusion on this point may have led Plato to talk of punishment being for the benefit of the one punished. His view does not seem very plausible. It is hard to see how killing someone benefits him. Being made to suffer pain or disability benefits one only insofar as it convinces him to act in ways that will not lead to further punishment. Generally, being deprived of freedom or pleasure benefits one only in this very limited fashion. Examination of the actual administration of punishment show quite clearly that it is usually not intended for the benefit of the punished.

Although punishment itself is not for the benefit of the one punished, it is sometimes possible to benefit someone while he is being punished. This is not possible with all punishments. It is not possible with killing. It is very unlikely with inflicting pain and disabling, and is also unlikely with the deprivation of pleasure, but depriving one of freedom is perfectly compatible with doing other things for his benefit. Rehabilitation of criminals is not a replacement for punishment. It is something that can go on during punishment.

The primary reason for punishing anyone is to make it less likely that people, including the person being punished, will perform the punishable action. Killing may deter others but it does far more than this to the person who is being put to death. The same is true of other very severe punishments, such as life imprisonment. Most evils are inflicted to deter the person being punished as well as others from committing a punishable action. However, the word "deter" leads one to think that this must be done by means of threats. This is often expressed by such a saying as "This will put the fear of God in him" or "This will teach him to respect the law."

Although we talk of punishment as a deterrent, rational persons are not primarily concerned with scaring people. They wish to influence people so that they will, in fact, not perform immoral actions. Fear may deter, but it need not be the best way to prevent future punishable action. Deprivation of freedom, since it can be graduated in both duration and intensity, allows great flexibility in preventing future punishable action. Deprivation of freedom by itself serves as a deterrent, but it can be combined with rehabilitation so as to decrease further the chances of one's committing a further punishable action. I hope this is one reason that deprivation of freedom has become the most popular form of punishment.

Rewards

Rewards, like punishments, are used to influence future behavior. Whereas punishment is generally used to discourage people from performing actions, rewards are generally used to encourage people to perform them. To give people rewards is to give them goods, thus providing them with reasons for doing the kind of action being rewarded. The most common reward is money, for reasons similar to deprivation of freedom being the most common punishment: flexibility, ease of administration, and ability to make very precise gradations. It is interesting to note that being deprived of money, as in fines, is often not regarded as a punishment unless it is large enough to be regarded as causing one to suffer one of the evils. Rewards, like punishments, are often not solely or even primarily concerned with influencing the behavior of the person rewarded; they are often used to influence others who are in a position to earn such a reward later. Like punishment, reward requires some prior behavior on the part of the person rewarded, but all that I am concerned with now is the relationship between rewards and goods. A reward must be the giving of a good.

That rewards are the giving of goods, and punishments the infliction of evils affects the ways in which they can best influence future behavior. If there is a certain kind of action that I never want performed, say, stealing, it will be very difficult to discourage this kind of behavior by means of rewards. Suppose that I try to do this by offering a reward every week to everyone who does not steal. If no one steals, then, of course, there will be no further problem. But what if someone does steal, then what do I do? One certainly cannot increase the reward for the stealer, for this would have the effect of encouraging everyone to steal at least once. I can deprive him of his reward for that week. What is the difference between doing this and punishment? One might maintain that depriving of a reward is not punishing. This is normally correct, but when everyone is rewarded and only one deprived of the reward, this is not so clear. However, let us grant that depriving of a reward is not punishment and see what happens. Suppose that he does not care about the reward and continues to steal? What is to be done now? Can one raise the reward for not stealing so high that the stealer will finally prefer to get the reward rather than steal? When dealing with any large group of people in anything like normal circumstances, this seems to be impossible.

Clearly rewards are not suited for enforcing prohibitions. On the other hand, punishment is perfectly suited for this. Evil is inflicted only on the stealer, and can be increased if more discouragement is needed. Punishment can also be used to encourage those kinds of behavior that one wants everyone to perform. One can inflict an evil on anyone who does not act in the specified way—for example, make a public declaration of loyalty. However, rewards might be equally suitable for encouraging this kind of behavior. Partly, it would depend on how important it was for everyone to act in this way. If it were not critical for everyone to declare his loyalty, then rewards and punishment might be equally suitable. However, if it were important that everyone perform the specified act then punishment would be far more suitable.

Rewards are best suited for encouraging behavior that one does not require everyone to perform, for example, an act of heroism. It might be possible to encourage acts of heroism by punishing everyone who did not perform one when she had the opportunity, but this is far less suitable than rewarding those who do. There are a number of reasons why punishment is not suitable for encouraging heroic acts. First, it would lead people to avoid occasions for heroic acts. Second, it would force unnecessary action on occasions where there were several people who could perform the act. Third, given the character of most heroic acts, the punishment would have to be extremely harsh in order to encourage such action on the part of people not naturally inclined to do so. Rewards are most suitable for those kinds of action we would like to encourage but do not wish to require of everyone. For actions we require of everyone, punishment generally is more suitable than reward. For universal prohibitions, punishment is far more suitable than reward.

That punishment is more suitable than rewards for those cases in which we want universal obedience is also due, in part, to the difference between good and evil. An evil is that which all rational persons seek to avoid, so punishment will affect, at least to some degree, all rational persons. This is what is required if we seek universal obedience. A good is only that which no rational person will avoid, not that which all persons seek, hence there need be no good which will affect every rational person in the desired way. Some rational persons may be completely unmoved by the reward. Hence rewards are most suitably used only in those cases where universal obedience is not required.

This examination of punishment and reward serves to support the analysis of good and evil in several ways. It supports the objectivity of good and evil and provides empirical evidence that what I have listed as goods and evils is in accord with our normal view of the matter. That punishment is a more common way of influencing conduct than reward also supports the view that evil plays a more important role than good in the discussion of rules of conduct. That punishments are more suitable for obtaining universal obedience than rewards confirms the definitions of good and evil which show that all rational persons seek to avoid evils, but that they do not all seek goods.

Evils and Maladies

Further support for the account of evil presented in this chapter is provided by an examination of the concepts of disease, injury, and other conditions of persons that lead them to seek medical attention. To suffer any of these conditions is to suffer, or be at increased risk of suffering, an evil in the absence of a distinct sustaining cause. I call such conditions maladies, and have, together with K. Danner Clouser and Charles M. Culver, provided a precise and detailed account of a malady.[2] For our purposes here it is sufficient to note that an examination of diseases, both infectious and genetic, injuries, birth defects, headaches, etc., in order to see what they all have in common reveals that they all involve suffering, or a significantly increased risk of suffering, an evil. This is a necessary condition for a condition of a person being classified as a malady. It is not a sufficient condition; the condition must also be independent of the environment in certain ways, but here I am only concerned with the relationship between maladies and evils.

Death, pain, and disability are three evils that are intimately related to maladies. Any condition of a person that has the other necessary features of a malady, and that results in death, pain or disability is a malady. Cancer, malaria, a broken bone, and schizophrenia are all maladies because they either result in death, pain, and disability or a significantly increased risk of suffering these evils. It may be questioned whether the loss of freedom and loss of pleasure are also involved in maladies. It is certainly true that the first three evils are much more commonly involved in maladies than the last two. However, there are some maladies that involve these latter two evils, and if they were not included in the list of evils, one could not explain why the conditions that result in these evils are counted as maladies.

Someone who has an allergy has a malady. However, if he knows what he is allergic to, he may not suffer any of the first three evils, or even be at significantly increased risk of suffering them. Someone may move to Arizona to escape the severe allergic reactions he has to various kinds of pollen and be perfectly happy to stay there. Nonetheless he still has his allergy, and so still has a malady. What evil does he suffer? He suffers from a loss of freedom. He is not free to leave Arizona. Someone who is allergic to chocolate is not free to eat chocolate. This is true, even if he no longer has any desire to do so. A prisoner does not become free simply because he no longer wants to get out of jail.

Someone who suffers from a sexual dysfunction which prevents him from experiencing pleasure also has a malady. His loss of pleasure, together with the other necessary conditions, is sufficient to make his condition a malady. Someone who lost the ability to experience any pleasure, anhedonia, would certainly be suffering from a malady, even if he suffered none of the other evils. It is true that most maladies involve suffering or a significantly increased risk of suffering the first three evils, but unless one included loss of freedom and loss of pleasure as evils, one could not explain why certain conditions of a person were also classified as maladies.

Summary

The list of goods and evils provided by defining them in terms of what it is irrational to desire and what it is irrational to avoid is not arbitrary. Examination of punishment and maladies shows that this list of evils does, in fact, help to account for the unity of these concepts. We count something as a punishment or as a malady only if it involves one of these evils. Examination of rewards shows the plausibility of the list of goods. This account of goods and evils shows that it is a mistake to equate them with pleasure and pain. It is also a mistake to regard it as indifferent whether one talks of good or of evil. The discussion of moral rules will make it clear that goods are much less important than evils. It was the neglect of evil, and the concentration on good, that made it impossible for previous moral philosophers to give an adequate account of moral rules.

4

MORAL RULES

Defining Conditions of Moral Rules

In this chapter I shall try to provide the defining conditions for moral rules. I shall do this by showing that the moral rules, or at least the most important basic rules, share a set of characteristics that distinguishes them from all other rules. I shall also try to show that these characteristics enable them to form the core of a public system that applies to all rational persons, such that all impartial persons would advocate adopting that system. These defining conditions will then be tested by seeing if they adequately distinguish between basic moral rules and all other rules. These defining conditions must not exclude any obvious moral rule, nor can they allow any rule that is clearly not a moral rule to be classified as a moral one. Thus the defining conditions are tested for adequacy by seeing if they give us the results we want. It would be futile to offer as defining conditions of basic moral rules ones that either exclude "Do not kill" or include "The bishop may only move diagonally." This is why we must start with what are ordinarily regarded as moral rules in order to arrive at the set of characteristics which are the defining conditions, or definition. We must also start by accepting that some rules are not moral rules.

I am primarily concerned with the basic moral rules, and unless I explicitly say otherwise, when I talk about moral rules, I mean basic moral rules such as "Don't Kill" and "Don't Lie." Testing the adequacy of the definition of these basic moral rules is similar to the test given to axioms in mathematics or logic. We test these axioms by seeing if they allow theorems that we know to be true, and rule out theorems that we know to be false. This still leaves open the possibility that once we have a definition of moral rules it will be of some help in deciding cases of which we were previously unsure. We may, if the definition works well enough, be able to discover or formulate new moral rules, to reword some old ones, and, further, to eliminate as basic moral rules some about which we were previously unclear.

In trying to provide defining conditions of moral rules, which distinguish them from all other rules, we must discover what characteristics a rule must have in order to be a moral rule, i.e., the necessary conditions for a rule being a moral rule and what characteristics, or set of characteristics, are such that if a rule has them, it is a moral rule, i.e., the sufficient conditions for a rule being a moral rule. We must also discover what characteristics, though often associated with moral rules, are not essential characteristics. In other words, we must see what characteristics one requires a rule to have if one considers it a moral rule, and what characteristics one can deny a rule has, without being forced to deny that the rule is a moral rule. I am concerned with the logically necessary and sufficient conditions for a rule being a moral rule.

A logically necessary condition is one such that if one says that something is a moral rule and denies that it has this condition, this shows he does not understand the concepts involved. A logically sufficient condition is one such that if one says that a rule has this condition but denies that it is a moral rule, this shows that he does not understand the concepts involved.

Of course, there may be no defining conditions of moral rules, i.e., no set of characteristics which distinguish moral rules from all others. Perhaps the necessary characteristics that all moral rules share are not sufficient to make a rule a moral rule. There might be a number of different characteristics, none of them necessary, which, together with the common necessary characteristics, are sufficient to make a rule a moral rule. That there are some necessary characteristics cannot be doubted. Moral rules must be rules which rational persons can obey or disobey. I am attempting in this chapter to discover all of the necessary characteristics of moral rules, and to see if there is one set of characteristics which is both necessary and sufficient to make a rule a moral rule. To discover such a set of characteristics would be to discover the defining conditions or definition of a moral rule.

Tests of Definitions of Moral Rules

Before I set out my own definition, it will be worthwhile to investigate some of the other definitions of moral rules that have been offered. By examining these, we shall begin to see more clearly what tests a definition must meet if it is to be accepted as an adequate one. Also, it is important to show that some of the commonly offered definitions are inadequate. It will perhaps make us more willing to accept the view that the set of characteristics distinguishing moral rules from all other rules, i.e., the definition of moral rules, is not simple. Hence it may prepare us for the complexities of any definition that will prove adequate.

The Religious Definition

One of the more popular definitions offered to distinguish moral rules from others is religious. Moral rules are the rules given to us by God. This definition suffers from the obvious difficulty that different religions offer us different rules that are supposedly given to us by God. Hence even if it were an adequate definition, we might never know if it was satisfied. We can never know if the rules which are said to come from God really do so. It is also a consequence of this view that atheists cannot consider anything to be a moral rule. Further, not only atheists, but deists, or anyone who does not believe that God gave persons any rules to live by, would also be logically excluded from holding that anything is a moral rule. Also, anyone who doubted that the rule against killing came from God would necessarily have to doubt that it was a moral rule. None of these consequences seems to be true. Hence it cannot be a necessary condition for something being a moral rule that it is a command of God.

The above argument says nothing about the actual origin of moral rules, only that being God-given is not a logically necessary condition for being a moral rule. The following considerations also show that it is not a logically sufficient condition. According to all religions, God gave rules which are not moral rules. Even the so-called Ten Commandments, often called the moral laws, from which in loose fashion we take our paradigm cases of moral rules, contain rules which are not moral rules. The Commandment to remember the Sabbath day and to keep it holy is not a moral rule. Serious consideration of this rule shows that it does not have the universality we regard as a necessary feature of moral rules. All those ignorant of a particular scripture could not be expected to have a calender dividing the year into weeks consisting of seven days, much less to distinguish one day of this week from all the others.

Even if we say that moral rules are God-given, this does not provide a definition of moral rules, for God gave rules other than moral rules. We still need some further characteristics to distinguish moral rules from other rules. It is clear that a religious answer is inadequate. God-given provides us with neither a necessary nor a sufficient condition for moral rules. Again it is important to emphasize that this is not to deny that some religions may present all moral rules as God-given; it is only to deny that their being moral rules is determined by their being God-given.

The Societal Definition

Another simple definition of moral rules commonly offered is social or cultural. It has been maintained that moral rules are those rules to which a society or culture demands obedience. However, this definition, which is closely related to a view called ethical relativism, suggests that our original question, "What are the characteristics of moral rules?," should be replaced by the question, "What are the characteristics of the moral rules of such and such society?" I do not deny that some people, in fact, regard as moral rules only those rules to which their society demands obedience. I also do not deny that some people regard as moral rules those rules which they believe to have been commanded by God. Just as this latter fact does not make God-given either a necessary or a sufficient condition for a moral rule, the former fact does not make society requiring obedience a necessary or sufficient condition for a moral rule.

We now want to know whether obedience being required by one's society is either a logically necessary or a logically sufficient condition for a rule being a moral rule. Can someone maintain that a rule is a moral rule and yet deny that obedience to it is required by his society? If he can do so without our concluding that he doesn't understand what he is talking about, this shows that obedience being required by one's society is not a necessary condition for being a moral rule. Further, if one can maintain that obedience to a rule is required by his society and yet the rule is not a moral rule, this will show that obedience being required by society is not a sufficient condition.

The plausibility of regarding obedience being required by one's society as a necessary condition of a moral rule stems from the fact that all civilized societies require obedience to all the moral rules. In fact, this may be an essential feature of a civilized society. But we can easily imagine a society in which one or more of the moral rules are not enforced. To conclude from this that in this society these rules are not moral rules would simply be a misleading way of repeating that the rules are not enforced. A member of that society who criticizes his society for not enforcing certain moral rules would not show that he does not understand the concepts involved. If our own society becomes so corrupt that certain moral rules are no longer enforced, we would not show lack of understanding if we claim that the moral rules should be enforced. We think it possible that a rule can be a moral rule and yet obedience not be required by one's society. This would, in fact, serve as a basis for a criticism of one's society. Thus we do not regard being enforced by society as a necessary condition for a rule being a moral rule.

It is almost superfluous to show that obedience being required by society is not a sufficient condition for a moral rule. We are all aware that society requires us to obey rules that are not moral rules. No one maintains that all the laws of a society are moral rules, and yet obedience to laws is required. In fact, we regard some laws as immoral and use this as grounds for holding that the government should no longer enforce them. Hence even if it were a necessary condition for being a moral rule that obedience is required by the society, it would not be a sufficient one. We would still have to distinguish those rules to which society requires obedience which are moral rules from those which are not.

The Universal Obedience Definition

In addition to the two more or less popular definitions we have discussed, there are some philosophical accounts that should be considered briefly. The first of these is that a moral rule is any rule which any individual maintains should be universally obeyed. This definition does not even demand that the individual be rational. On this account "Do not walk on the cracks in sidewalks" might be one's only moral rule. Or even worse, "Kill yourself in the most painful fashion possible" might be one's only moral rule. These consequences are so absurd that the fact that moral rules could change constantly on this account seems almost a minor objection. Even if we modify this account by requiring that the individual be rational, it does not help much. "Do not speak any language but English" is a rule that a rational individual could want universally obeyed. This proposed definition, even as modified, has the effect of denying that there is any distinction between moral rules and all other rules, so it is obvious that it cannot be an adequate definition. However, when properly qualified, it does something that neither of the popular accounts does: it provides a necessary condition for a moral rule. Regarding a rule as a moral rule seems to require holding that it be universally obeyed.

The Utilitarian Definition

Probably the most well-known philosophical definition of moral rules is that provided by the utilitarians. This definition may be stated as follows: Those rules which if universally obeyed would promote the greatest happiness of the greatest number are moral rules. I have already discussed the inadequacy of Mill's utilitarian account of morality, so that there is no need to go into great detail here. I shall only note that universal obedience to the rule "Improve your sexual technique," since it would give greater pleasure to one's sexual partner, would undoubtedly increase the pleasure in the world by vast amounts. I do not think, however, that anyone regards it as a moral rule. Thus it is clear that the utilitarian definition is not a sufficient condition of moral rules and hence is not an adequate definition of moral rules. Whether, like the previous definition, it provides a necessary condition if properly qualified, is difficult to determine because it is not clear how to provide the necessary qualifications.

A Negative Rule Utilitarian Definition

A more promising definition of moral rules is the following: If the consequences of everyone disobeying the rule would be disastrous, then the rule is a moral rule. Certainly the consequences of everyone disobeying the rules against killing, stealing, or lying would be disastrous. So that this definition includes what we normally consider to be moral rules. It also excludes some rules that we do not consider to be moral rules. It would not be disastrous if no one obeyed the rule "Don't step on the cracks in sidewalks." However, though it includes all of the moral rules and excludes some non-moral rules, it does not exclude some rules which are clearly not moral rules. "Don't stand on your head all day" is a rule which if disobeyed by everyone would have disastrous consequences. Yet it is not a moral rule. Thus the proposed definition, though it provides a necessary condition for a rule being a moral rule, does not adequately distinguish moral rules from all other rules.

Properties Shared by All Moral Rules

The inadequacy of all of the simple definitions discussed above does not prove that there can be no simple adequate definition, but it does make it seem a reasonable hypothesis. Rather than offering another simple definition I shall try to find some properties shared by all of the commonly accepted moral rules. These properties will provide some of the defining conditions of moral rules. I shall also consider our attitudes toward these rules and see if I can discover that which distinguishes our attitude toward moral rules from our attitude toward all other rules. It is an essential feature of moral rules that certain attitudes are taken toward them. So it is not out of place to have these attitudes as part of the defining conditions of moral rules.

Preliminary List of Moral Rules

To talk about moral rules is to talk about kinds of actions. Certain kinds of actions are regarded as immoral unless one has a justification for doing them. Among these kinds of actions are killing, lying, stealing, committing adultery, breaking one's promise, cheating, and causing pain. Someone who kills people or lies to them, etc., and does so simply because he feels like doing so, is universally regarded as acting immorally. That a certain kind of action is immoral unless one has an adequate moral reason for doing it is what is meant by saying that there is a moral rule prohibiting that action.

Perhaps the most common moral rules, ones that would be offered by almost everyone, are the following: "Don't kill," "Don't lie," "Don't steal," and "Don't commit adultery." To this group, many would add the following: "Keep your promise," "Don't cheat," and "Don't cause pain." (I am not now maintaining that these seven rules are all justified moral rules; that will be discussed in Chapters 6 and 7.) Undoubtedly others could be added, but examination of these rules to see if they share a common set of characteristics that distinguishes them from all other rules should be sufficient, especially if these defining characteristics enable the moral rules to form the core of a public system that applies to all rational persons such that all impartial rational persons would advocate adopting it.

Formal Properties

First, I shall be concerned with what I call formal properties, those that do not specify the content of the rules. All of these rules are completely universal; they apply to all persons who can understand and follow them, i.e., to all rational persons with the relevant voluntary abilities. A rule applies to a person when it is appropriate to use a person's following or not following the rule as a basis for judging the person. This universal applicability distinguishes moral rules from the rules of a legal system, which apply only to those who fall within the jurisdiction of that legal system. Someone who completely understands a law and is perfectly capable of obeying it may still correctly say that the law does not apply to him, but someone who completely understands a moral rule and is perfectly capable of obeying it cannot correctly say that the rule does not apply to him.

From this, at least two other features of moral rules can be inferred. The first of these features is that they must be known by all rational persons. This entails that knowing the moral rules cannot depend on some specialized knowledge known only to some cultures. Any rational person who is responsible for his actions must know what the moral rules require and forbid. We do not regard ignorance of the moral rules to count as an excuse for not following them. Although we teach these rules to our children, this teaching consists more in training them to follow the rules than in providing them with some specialized knowledge. Thus the rule concerning the Sabbath cannot be considered a moral rule unless one believes that all rational persons everywhere and at all times had the concept of a week with seven days.

The second feature requires that the rule must be such that rational persons in every society, at any time, might have acted upon it or broken it. It must not concern the kind of action which rational persons in some society at some time could not have done. All who accept the seven moral rules that I have listed believe that the kinds of actions prohibited by them were real possibilities to all rational persons in all societies at all times. With the exception of adultery, and possibly stealing, there is no human society in which rational persons did not have a chance to commit the kinds of actions prohibited by these moral rules. Killing and causing pain are always possible; and given that any society demands some group activity, cooperation, etc., it is obvious that opportunities to lie, cheat, and break one's word are ubiquitous.

Although adultery and stealing depend upon the institutions of marriage and private property, these institutions are generally thought to be present in every human society. Doubt on the matter may seem to invalidate the view that actions prohibited by moral rules must be open to all rational persons in every society. For it certainly seems odd to say that if one society had no private property, then it would not be morally wrong to steal. Similarly it sounds very odd to say that if one society does not have the institution of marriage, adultery is not immoral. This is not what is being said. I am not claiming that no action is immoral if that kind of action could not have been performed by any person in any society. All that I am claiming is that a moral rule, by which I mean a basic moral rule, is one that concerns actions open to all rational persons in all societies at all times.

Driving while drunk is immoral, but obviously this kind of action was not a possibility to societies with no automobiles. Although the rule "Don't drive when drunk" is not a moral rule in the sense I am concerned with, together with some obvious facts, it is deducible that it is morally wrong to drive while drunk. One such fact is that driving while drunk significantly increases one's chances of killing or harming someone. In the same fashion, even if rules against stealing and adultery are not moral rules, this does not mean that stealing and adultery are not immoral, for an analysis of the concepts of stealing and adultery may show that their immorality is deducible from some basic moral rules.

From these formal characteristics of moral rules, it is possible to infer some other characteristics. A moral rule is unchanging or unchangeable, discovered rather than invented. A moral rule is not dependent on the will or decision of any person or group of persons. These two characteristics are obviously closely connected, for if these rules are unchangeable, they cannot be subject to the will or decision of any person or group of persons. Since we hold that moral rules applied at all times, then obviously they could not be invented or changed, or subject to the will of anyone, after the time that the first society of rational persons existed. Further, since they are known to all rational persons without special knowledge, i.e., without knowing anything more than any rational person in any society knows, knowing about them cannot depend on the will or decision of anyone.

Although a particular moral rule may have been first articulated by some one person or group at some period in history, they are regarded as having discovered the moral rule rather than having invented it. For if they had invented it, that would entail that it did not apply to persons before the time the moral rule was invented. Moral rules have a status similar to the laws of logic, or of mathematics. No one invents the laws of logic, though the articulation of them, or perhaps the discovery of them, may have taken place at some definite time or times. I do not say that moral rules are like the laws of logic in all respects; however, I do maintain that any account of moral rules which makes them subject to human decision is inadequate.

Universality, Generality, and Absoluteness

Even though moral rules are thought to be completely universal in the sense described, it would be misleading to leave it at this. To say that moral rules are universal means that they apply to all rational persons with the voluntary abilities to do the kinds of actions prohibited or required by moral rules. In discussing the scope of morality in Chapter 1, I emphasized that moral rules were limited to this class. Those who either cannot understand the rules or cannot guide their actions by them are not subject to the rules. Now I am pointing out that a moral rule cannot be limited to any group smaller than this class. If a rule applies to any group smaller than the class of all rational persons it is not a moral rule. The universality of the moral rules means that unlike almost all other rules they apply to all those who can understand them and guide their actions accordingly.

In addition to their universality, the moral rules are completely general, they simply state what kind of action is to be avoided or done, where the kind of action is one that all rational persons in any society know about. In none of these rules is there any reference to any particular person, group, place, or time. This accounts for some of the controversy that arises with regard to the scope of the moral rules. Everyone agrees that they are to be obeyed with regard to all those to whom they apply, i.e., all those who count as moral agents, but not all agree on who else is protected by the moral rules. The problem of the scope of the moral rules will be discussed in more detail in the following chapter on impartiality; here I am concerned with pointing out that the generality of the moral rules explains why all moral rules have exceptions. Even though, for all those who are protected by the moral rules, they are to be obeyed without consideration of person, group, place, or time, their generality explains why rational persons do not want them to be obeyed regardless of the circumstances.

It is the claim of some moral fanatics that one ought never to break any moral rule. This is what is claimed by those who regard the moral rules as absolute. But this claim has little support even from those who have some relevant views concerning the supernatural. Almost everyone is aware that there are circumstances when any rule can be broken without the person thereby doing anything immoral. Even killing if done in self defense is usually regarded as morally justified, and breaking a promise to save a life is not normally regarded by any rational person as being immoral. Hence one further characteristic of the moral rules must be mentioned which is often overlooked: namely, moral rules have exceptions. A person to whom a moral rule applies may in some circumstances intentionally, voluntarily and freely break it and not be acting immorally. In talking about the moral rules, neither universality, applying to all those who can understand and guide their conduct by them, nor generality, simply stating the kind of action to be done or avoided, should be confused with absoluteness. All moral rules have exceptions.

These formal features of moral rules are all compatible with the moral rules forming the core of a public system that applies to all rational persons. Their universality guarantees that the rules are understood by all rational persons; their generality guarantees that the rules concern behavior which is open to all rational persons. All that is necessary to show that the moral rules are part of a public system that applies to all rational persons is to show that it would not be irrational for any rational person to adopt this system as a guide for his own conduct. In order to show this we must go beyond talking of the formal features of moral rules and talk about their content.

The Content of Moral Rules

In the account of moral rules given so far, nothing of significance has been said about the content of the rules. From what I have said so far, "Break your promises" could be a moral rule. It is universal in the necessary sense, and it also has the necessary generality. An adequate account of the defining characteristics of moral rules must provide some limit to the content of the rules. This problem has confronted, in different forms, almost all moral philosophers. Many different answers have been given; e.g., moral rules lead to self-realization or to the greatest happiness of the greatest number. Even the most casual look at the seven moral rules listed earlier in this chapter shows that all of these accounts are inaccurate descriptions. Moral rules do not tell one to promote good, or even to prevent evil, but to avoid causing evil. It is not an accident that all moral rules are, or can be, stated as prohibitions.

The fact that moral rules tell us to avoid causing evil rather than to promote good or prevent evil has some unexpected consequences. For example, the Platonic view of a moral person as one who minds his own business can now be seen to have some plausibility. Of course, what will count as minding one's own business will depend upon the circumstances. A father who neglects his children is not minding his own business, nor is a person who fails to obey the law. Although it is sometimes contrary to our interests or desires to obey moral rules, generally obedience will not require the doing of some action which it is not one's business to do. Moral rules are therefore not quite so demanding as they are sometimes made out to be. It is not ordinarily a burden to obey them; one can generally do so by doing hardly anything at all.

That it is not ordinarily a burden to obey the moral rules does not mean that it never is. Quips such as "Everything I like is either illegal, immoral, or fattening," make clear that moral rules may, and often do, conflict with one's desires and interests. This is a characteristic which some philosophers have tried to deny by talking of true desires and real interest, but this view has never been widely accepted. A moral rule may, and for many people often does, require action contrary to their interests and their desires. Almost everyone would benefit from breaking a particular moral rule on some occasion. I am not saying that most of the time one wants to break or would benefit by breaking a moral rule. I do not think this is true. I am simply admitting what is commonly held, that there are times in the lives of almost everyone when they either want to break, or would benefit from breaking, a moral rule unjustifiably.

Acting in Accordance with a Rule Versus Following a Rule

Distinguishing between acting in accordance with a rule and following it, makes it easier to express an important difference between moral rules and most other guides to conduct. Acting in accordance with a rule simply means not violating it and does not require even being aware of the rule one is acting in accordance with. Following a rule requires that one consciously guide one's action by the rule. Leaving aside the question of justified exceptions, one ought to act in accordance with the moral rules at all times. As already noted, this is usually no great burden. In fact, it would take some considerable effort to violate moral rules more than a small fraction of the time. Most of the time we act in accordance with moral rules without thinking about them at all. One is not required to act in accordance with those precepts encouraging us to prevent or relieve evil, what I call moral ideals, at all times. Nor is one required to act in accordance with those precepts which encourage the promotion of good, what I call utilitarian ideals, all of the time. Further, when these ideals, moral and utilitarian, guide our conduct it is usually in such a way that it is more appropriate to say that we follow them rather than that we simply act in accordance with them.

"Promote Pleasure" Is Not a Moral Rule

That moral rules demand only that one avoid causing evil, not that one promote good, has another interesting consequence. It eliminates some rules which philosophers have put forward as moral rules. Consider the rule "Promote pleasure," which the utilitarians would not distinguish from the rule "Don't cause pain," or if they would, would think the distinction of little significance. Some questions that one can ask show that this rule does not have the formal characteristics of moral rules. For example, with regard to the rule "Don't cause pain" and to all other moral rules, the question "When should one obey these rules?" has no clear sense. The answer "Always," followed perhaps by a statement about justified exceptions, is not an answer about time. It would be a joke to answer this question by listing a certain time of day, or year, or even by giving a certain proportion of time, i.e., half of your waking hours. Time, per se, has no relevance to moral rules. There is no certain proportion of time when I need not obey moral rules, nor, certainly, is there any particular time of day or night at which they do not apply.

However, when one considers the rule "Promote pleasure," one sees that questions about time are relevant. The question "When should one obey the rule 'Promote pleasure'?" cannot be answered simply by "Always" even if one then adds a statement about exceptions. When this question is asked of the rule "Promote pleasure," time per se is relevant. One could answer this question quite plausibly by citing a certain proportion of one's time which should be devoted to following it. It would be less plausible, but still understandable, if one listed certain specific times of the day or year when one should obey this rule, e.g., every Sunday morning. It would be quite plausible to say that one should spend some proportion of one's life in following this rule. People have, in fact, said things strikingly like this: viz., spend one hour every day trying to make life more pleasant for those around you.

This last example suggests another important difference between moral rules and the rule "Promote pleasure." With regard to moral rules, insofar as the question "Toward whom should I obey the rule?" makes sense, it is a question about the scope of the moral rules, about what group of beings is protected by the moral rules. Within this group, one is required to obey the rules with regard to everyone. This is possible because moral rules do not generally require positive action, but only the avoidance of certain kinds of actions. If one is not killing, one is not killing anyone, and so on for all other moral rules. When one obeys these rules, there need be no specific individual with regard to whom one is doing so. (Obviously when one is keeping a promise, one is keeping it with regard to an individual, but one is not thereby breaking it with regard to anyone else.)

With the rule "Promote pleasure" the question "With regard to whom should one obey the rule?" is not so easily answered even when talking only about those protected by the moral rules. There can be genuine disagreement with regard to whom one should obey this rule. As noted above, one is sometimes advised to promote the pleasure of those around one. Some may claim that it requires obedience only with regard to those in one's local community. Others might say that it requires obedience with regard to everyone in one's country. Still others might say that it should be treated like a moral rule and obeyed with regard to everyone protected by the moral rules. Since promoting pleasure requires doing something for someone, unless I am doing something that is actually promoting the pleasure of everyone (a case almost impossible to envisage), I am not obeying the rule with regard to everyone. Whereas with most moral rules, by not acting I obey the rule with regard to everyone.

Another point, closely related to the previous one, can be raised to distinguish "Promote pleasure" from moral rules. Moral rules protect all persons equally. The question "Should you obey the rule more with regard to some than to others?" if it makes sense is obviously answered in the negative. However, when the question is asked of the rule "Promote pleasure," the answer is not obvious. As we have already noted, it could be held that this rule requires obedience only with regard to those in one's local community. It is clear that one might modify this view and hold that it should be obeyed more with regard to those in one's local community, even if some regard should be given to those outside. This rule, unlike moral rules, does not demand equal treatment of all, nor does one usually obey it equally with regard to all.

These considerations show that the rule "Promote pleasure" differs from moral rules in some significant ways. Whereas, ignoring the question of exceptions, moral rules are to be obeyed at all times, with regard to everyone equally, the rule "Promote pleasure" does not require obedience at all times with regard to everyone equally. It is not only possible, but relatively easy, for one to obey all moral rules all of the time with regard to everyone equally. It is humanly impossible to obey the rule "Promote pleasure" all of the time with regard to everyone equally. These considerations are all very closely connected to the fact that all moral rules are or can be, with no change in content, stated as prohibitions on actions. Keeping these rules at all times with regard to everyone equally is accomplished simply by not breaking them at any time with regard to anyone. The rule "Promote pleasure" demands positive action; hence, the difficulty in following it at all times with regard to everyone equally. Being required to obey the moral rules equally with regard to all those who are protected by the rules is what is meant by saying that we must obey the moral rules impartially. A rule that cannot be obeyed impartially is not a moral rule.

Moral rules require us not to cause evil for anyone; they do not require us to promote the general good. Any account of moral rules which characterizes them as leading to the greatest good for the greatest number, or even for the good of everyone alike, will be seriously misleading. It is not the promoting of good but the avoidance of causing evil which is important. Of course, if a rule is for the good of everyone alike, it cannot allow causing evil to anyone; hence the plausibility of regarding moral rules as rules that are for the good of everyone alike. But a rule that would simply promote the good of everyone alike, even one that had the formal characteristics of a moral rule, would not be a moral rule. It is not easy to think up such a rule, but the following seems to fit the description: "Greet people with a smile." This rule seems to meet all of the formal requirements of a moral rule. It is both universal and general. It applies to all rational persons. It mentions no person, group, time, or place. We would not regard it as a moral rule because of the fact that it requires the promotion of good, not merely the avoidance of causing evil. Limiting the content of moral rules to those that demand avoidance of causing evil rather than promotion of good is not a pointless limitation.

Preventing Evil Versus Promoting Good

It is a universally accepted criticism of utilitarianism that it would allow the infliction of a significant evil, e.g., great pain, on one person in order to promote a significant amount of good, e.g., great pleasure, for many others. This criticism of utilitarianism depends on there being a morally significant difference between good and evil. This can be seen from the fact that the argument does not have the same force when we substitute preventing evil for promoting good. Suppose we have a plague, which if not stopped will result in countless painful deaths. Suppose, further, that the circumstances are such that only by causing significant pain to one or more innocent people can we obtain what is necessary to stop the plague. Here, though one might cringe at taking such a step oneself, one would have to admit it was morally justifiable to cause such pain in order to prevent overwhelmingly greater evil to many others. Alyosha's answer to Ivan in *The Brothers Karamazov,* that he would not kill one innocent baby in order to produce a perfect world, is not obviously the morally right answer. If one considers the countless number of innocent babies who die in the world today, let alone the other evils suffered by almost all of humankind, it seems as if one would be a moral coward if he failed to take the opportunity offered to Alyosha.

It is extremely important to point out that such an opportunity is not a real one. Only the most unfortunate are ever in a situation where it is even plausible that they will prevent enough evil to make it justifiable to cause a significant evil to an innocent person. These rare situations should not be confused with the plans of those who advocate the sacrifice of the lives of those now living in order to promote a better world in the future. Since the prevention of evil can justify the infliction of evil when promotion of good does not, in circumstances that are otherwise the same, one must not only distinguish between promoting good and avoiding causing evil, one must also distinguish between promoting good and preventing evil. This distinction is not as obvious as the previous one. One can avoid causing evil by doing nothing, but both promoting good and preventing evil demand positive action.

Avoiding Causing Evil Versus Preventing Evil

In addition to the distinction between good and evil, it is also necessary to distinguish between avoiding causing evil and preventing evil. Since preventing evil demands positive action, it should be clear that moral rules will not demand the preventing of evil. This will be so for the same reasons advanced against considering the rule "Promote pleasure" as a moral rule; viz., one cannot, nor is one required to, obey the rule all of the time with regard to everyone equally; one cannot obey the rule impartially. The prevention of evil, however, can provide a justification for breaking a moral rule, even without the consent of the person who suffers because of the violation of the rule. In this respect the prevention of evil has a moral relevance that the promotion of good does not. Except in special circumstances, the promotion of good cannot justify the violation of a moral rule without the consent of the person who will suffer because of one's violation of the rule. Because moral rules only require that one avoid causing evil, precepts that encourage the prevention of evil cannot be classified as moral rules. That the prevention of evil is obviously a moral matter explains why I call those precepts that encourage the prevention of evil moral ideals. They will be discussed in more detail in Chapter 8.

Specifying the content of moral rules as prohibiting doing those kinds of actions which cause, or increase the probability of causing, people to suffer evils, makes it plausible that it would not be irrational for anyone to act in accordance with the moral rules. Given the universality and generality of the moral rules, which make them understood by all rational persons, we can now see that the moral rules might form the core of a public system that applies to all rational persons. This same combination of features also makes it plausible that all impartial rational persons would advocate adopting this system. By examining the moral rules we have arrived at a set of defining characteristics that enable the moral rules to form the core of a public system applying to all rational persons that all impartial rational persons would advocate adopting. The details of this system will be examined in Chapters 6 and 7; now I shall show how these defining characteristics allow one to distinguish moral rules from all other rules.

Impartial Rational Persons Advocate Acting in Accordance with Moral Rules

Since moral rules prohibit those kinds of actions which are thought to cause the suffering of evil, we can infer that all impartial rational persons generally advocate acting in accordance with them, that breaking them is generally condemned. We now have a substantial limitation on the content of moral rules, one which seems to allow us to keep all of the rules we have listed, and which excludes any rule that would obviously not be accepted as a moral rule. Not only rules which advocate the committing of evil action, such as "Kill all unbelievers," but also trivial or insignificant rules, such as "Don't cut your hair," are excluded as possible moral rules. Nonetheless, this account of the defining characteristics does allow some changes in conventional moral rules. A generally accepted moral rule may not have all of the required features, or a rule may be formulated which will have all of them even though it has not generally been listed as a moral rule. Further, it allows rewording the rules to make them more inclusive without sacrificing any of the required features of moral rules.

Most of the defining characteristics I have listed are purely formal; they simply make clear what is meant by the universality and generality of moral rules. The universality of moral rules means that they apply to all and only those who can understand and guide their actions by them, i.e., to all rational persons with the relevant voluntary abilities. This is a necessary condition for a rule to be a public rule, i.e., to be part of a public system. It also makes clear the independence of moral rules from the will or decision of any person or group of persons and entails that moral rules are unchanging. It also guarantees that persons without certain features are not subject to moral rules. The generality of moral rules, that they simply prohibit or require certain kinds of actions, means that considerations of person, place, group, or time are irrelevant, but it also explains why there are exceptions to these rules, why violating them is sometimes justified. That there are exceptions to moral rules makes clear that it is impossible to apply them mechanically in deciding what to do or in making moral judgments.

The content of moral rules is determined by the requirement that they prohibit causing evil rather than requiring the prevention of evil or the promotion of good. This leads to other characteristics of a moral rule. Although rational persons may frequently not want to act in accordance with the rule themselves, it will not be irrational for them to do so, thus satisfying another condition that public rules must have. Further, rational persons will usually want others to act in accordance with the rule with regard to themselves. It is necessary to make clear in what manner or with what qualifications all rational persons would want others to act in accordance with the moral rules with regard to themselves. Nonetheless, though vague, there is no doubt that in order to be a moral rule, all rational persons must agree in taking a certain attitude toward it, an attitude that includes the view that everyone should act in accordance with the moral rules with regard to themselves, though this is not meant to exclude exceptions.

The attitude that people should obey the moral rules with regard to oneself is not the appropriate moral attitude toward the moral rules. We believe that the appropriate moral attitude toward the moral rules is that they should be followed impartially by everyone with regard to all those protected by the rules, which includes, at least, all rational persons. We regard the moral rules as part of a public system that applies to all rational persons. This leads to the final characteristic that all moral rules have; always allowing for justified exceptions, we believe that all rational persons, if impartial, would advocate impartial obedience by all moral agents with regard to all who are protected by the moral rules. We believe that moral rules are justified. This rather vague characteristic is very important, together with the other characteristics of moral rules, it distinguishes moral rules from all other guides to conduct.

With this characteristic we have not only the necessary conditions for a rule being a moral rule, I think, we also have sufficient conditions. The usefulness of having this set of characteristics to distinguish moral rules from all other rules depends on making suitably precise this last characteristic, the attitude that impartial rational persons would take toward moral rules. This will enable us to determine if all impartial rational persons would advocate that the rules we have considered in this chapter be made part of a public system that applies to all rational persons. This will show if these rules are genuine moral rules; i.e., if they have all of the characteristics that moral rules are required to have. Making precise the attitude that all impartial rational persons would take toward the moral rules requires a precise account of rationality and impartiality. In Chapter 2 I tried to present a precise account of rationality; in the following chapter I shall try to provide a precise account of impartiality.

5

IMPARTIALITY

Moral rules require impartiality, of that there is no doubt, but there is disagreement on how or even whether the kind of impartiality that moral rules require can be achieved. Those who deny that the kind of impartiality required by the moral rules can be achieved are moral skeptics. Those who think that what passes for this kind of impartiality is simply the acceptance of the customs or mores of one's society are likely to be ethical relativists. For those philosophers who accept morality, the important problems are determining what kind of impartiality is required by the moral rules and then determining how one can achieve it. Before any of this can be done, one must provide an accurate account of the concept of impartiality.

Tests of Impartiality

The Golden Rule, "Do unto others as you would have them do unto you," is best regarded as a recommendation on how to achieve impartiality. It recommends that one act in a certain way toward someone else only if one would be willing for that person to behave in that way toward oneself. This is sometimes called the test of reversibility. (See *The Moral Point of View* by Kurt Baier.) It is regarded by some as both necessary and sufficient for achieving impartiality.

Universalizability is commonly offered as another method of achieving impartiality. Kant's Categorical Imperative, "Act only on that maxim that you would will to be a universal law," is put forward by many who do not accept any other aspect of Kant's moral philosophy. They believe that only if one is willing to universalize the maxim of one's action is one being impartial. They regard the willingness to universalize one's actions to be the test of one's impartiality: if one is willing to universalize, one is impartial; if one is not willing, then one is not acting impartially.

Another method of achieving impartiality is best exemplified by Rawls's "veil of ignorance." (See *A Theory of Justice* by John Rawls.) On this method one removes all characteristics of a person which would distinguish him/her from anyone else. He or she, for one does not know one's sex, not only knows no fact about him/herself which would differentiate him/her from anyone else, one also has no personality or character traits which are not universal. On this view, impartiality is achieved only by the total elimination of individuality. It is a consequence of this view, that all impartial persons must agree, for any features that could account for disagreement have been eliminated.

The two previous tests for impartiality do not have this consequence; on these tests it might be that two rational persons contemplating the same action would apply the test and come out with different results. John may be willing that Jane do to him what he is considering doing to her, whereas Jane would not be willing that John do to her what she is contemplating doing to him, even though both are contemplating doing the same kind of action, e.g., deceiving in order to prevent the person deceived from suffering some minor anxiety. Similarly, John may be willing that everyone perform such an action, whereas Jane would not be willing to universalize the same action. Thus John and Jane, though both impartial according to the tests of reversibility and universalizability, would come to different decisions about whether or not to perform a certain kind of action.

These different tests for impartiality are sometimes not regarded merely as tests of, or methods for achieving, impartiality, they come to be taken as replacements for it. Often it is not explicitly recognized that these tests should be regarded as providing a way of determining if one is being impartial; rather it is often simply claimed that a moral judgment must satisfy one or the other of these tests if it is to count as a legitimate or genuine moral judgment. Universalizability is sometimes put forward as if it is a necessary feature of moral judgments, not because it is required for impartiality, but because it is logically required for the correct use of such terms as "good," "wrong" and "ought." (See R. M. Hare, *The Language of Morals* and *Freedom and Reason*.)

In the predecessor of this book I invented the technical phrase "publicly advocate" and characterized public advocacy in such a way that it was intended to provide a test of impartiality. I did not completely recognize what I was doing and, in fact, used public advocacy as a replacement for impartiality. Recognition of my own mistake made clear to me that very similar mistakes were being made by those who used the other tests of impartiality that I have mentioned above. I now realize that what is necessary is an explicit characterization of impartiality and a specification of the kind of impartiality that the moral rules require. Only after that is done is it possible to determine if the various tests that are offered as tests of impartiality are satisfactory.

Impartiality Independent of Morality

On the view of morality that I am defending, an adequate system of morality must be one that would be advocated by all impartial rational persons. It is essential that the concepts of rationality and impartiality be characterized in non-moral terms. It would be worse than trivial to explain morality as a combination of rationality and impartiality if one could not provide accounts of rationality and impartiality that were independent of morality. I have already provided such an account of rationality; what I intend to do in this chapter is to provide such an account of impartiality.

Few philosophers have actually attempted an analysis of impartiality; they have generally simply replaced it by what they took to be a more adequate technical concept, e.g., universalizability. It may be thought that impartiality is simply a moral virtue, just as honesty and kindness are. If this is the case, then clearly an adequate account of impartiality will involve an account of morality, and it will be pointless to explain morality in terms of impartiality. I shall show that impartiality, though a necessary feature of morality, is not sufficient for it, that acting impartially is not always acting morally. It is an inadequate understanding of impartiality together with the assumption that impartiality necessarily involves rationality that leads one to regard impartiality as a moral virtue.

The Analysis of Impartiality

Impartiality, like simultaneity, is usually taken to be a simpler concept than it really is. Einstein made the conceptual discovery that it was inadequate to characterize the simultaneity of two events by simply talking about those two events. One is required to add something about the point of view of the observer. Einstein showed that it is inadequate to say merely "A and B occurred simultaneously;" rather one should say "A and B occurred simultaneously to an observer at C." This point was not recognized because most of the time all of the observers were at C, and so it seemed sufficient to use the simpler characterization of simultaneity. Once one realizes that observers can be at different points of view, it becomes apparent that A and B can occur simultaneously with regard to one observer, but not occur simultaneously with regard to another. There is no answer to the question, "But did A and B really occur simultaneously or not?" because this question presupposes an account of simultaneity that Einstein has shown to be inadequate.

We now often talk of a person being impartial as if that characterization were a complete one. But it is not. When one talks of impartiality, one must say something about the group toward which one is impartial and also the respects in which one is impartial with regard to this group. Often this is presupposed when one talks about impartiality, but it is worthwhile to make these presuppositions explicit. Otherwise one is very likely to make a mistake and assume that both the group and the respect in which one is impartial are always the same.

For example, we sometimes talk of an umpire or referee as being impartial.

When we say this, it is usually clear that this means that he does not favor one team over the other in making his decisions, that he makes his decisions independently of which team benefits or is harmed. If we were to make this explicit, we would say that the umpire is impartial with regard to making decisions among the competing teams. This is what was meant by the more elliptical statement that the umpire is impartial. Once this is realized then a number of other points can be made more clearly.

Suppose that the umpire has a friend playing on one of the teams. Can he be impartial? This can now be seen to be an empirical question. Stated more fully, the question becomes, "Can a person who has a friend on one team make his decisions among the competing teams in such a way that he would make the same decision regardless of which team benefits?" Most people regard this as very difficult, if not impossible to do. It is not merely that one must not consciously favor one team over the other, one must be able to detect and compensate for any unconscious tendency to favor one team. And not only this, one must be careful not to overcompensate, not to make decisions favoring the team without one's friend in order to avoid being partial toward the team with one's friend.

The difficulty of being an impartial umpire if one has some interest in or preference for one team over the other explains why one usually tries to get umpires who have no preference for one team over the other. In more important matters, judges are supposed to disqualify themselves if they have any personal interest in the outcome of a case. In these cases, it is not merely impartiality, but the appearance of impartiality, that is important, so that anything that would lead either side to suspect the judge of not being impartial is to be avoided. It is the difficulty of checking the impartiality of the judge or umpire directly that makes us want to avoid the situation which increases the likelihood of partiality. I now offer the following definition of impartiality: *A is impartial in respect R with regard to group G if and only if A's actions in respect R are not influenced at all by which member(s) of G benefit or are harmed by these actions.* Briefly, one is impartial with regard to a group in a given respect if he does not favor any member of the group over any other member in that respect.

Comparison of Two Tests of Impartiality

Is it possible to check the impartiality of an umpire or judge directly, without knowing whether he favors one side or the other? If so, what test should one use? Consider testing the impartiality of an umpire. One could make a videotape of the game, with the uniforms covered up so that one could not tell which side would benefit, and see if the umpire made the same decisions. One could present the judge with a case similar in all relevant respects, both law and fact, but without knowledge of who would benefit from the decisions, and see if he made the same decisions. One could also check for impartiality, not by taking away knowledge of who would benefit, but by reversing it. If one were to do this, e.g., by making it seem as if the other team would benefit, one could see if the person makes the same decisions.

Which of these would be the best way to guarantee impartiality? It may seem that both tests are the same, that if the same decisions are made when the knowledge of who benefits is reversed or is taken away entirely, then the decisions are made impartially. Suppose the decisions are not the same. Or suppose that two different umpires are involved and they make different decisions; how can we tell if one, both, or neither, is making his decisions impartially? It is certainly possible to believe oneself to be acting impartially when one is not doing so. One's knowledge of how the different teams will be affected by one's decisions may affect those decisions without one being aware of it. If one knows which team benefits from one's decision, it is always possible that this knowledge will affect one's decisions and therefore that one's decision will not be impartial.

It would seem that the only way to guarantee impartiality is to withhold all information about which party, from the group toward which one is supposed to be impartial, benefits from the decisions made. If this could be done it would guarantee that the decision would be impartial, for an impartial decision is one that is made regardless of who benefits or is harmed by that decision. Any decision that is made in ignorance of who will benefit or be harmed by that decision is necessarily an impartial decision. This provides us with a perfect test of impartiality. On this test of impartiality, one's decisions must be impartial with regard to members of a given group for one makes these decisions without being influenced in any way by which member of the group will benefit.

Impartiality and Consistency

Normally, one who makes impartial decisions also makes consistent decisions. Consistency, which in this context involves making the same decision whenever the circumstances are the same, is important because it allows all members of the group to make appropriate plans. Consistency does not require impartiality, because one can count as part of the *same* circumstances that certain members of the group toward which one is supposed to be impartial will be benefitted. This shows that one can consistently make decisions favoring some members of a group over others, even though one is supposed to be impartial with regard to that group. Although consistency clearly does not require impartiality, it is often thought that the latter requires the former. Although it is so uncommon as to be almost totally overlooked, it is possible to make inconsistent decisions that are completely impartial. One may simply change the way one makes decisions randomly, sometimes using one standard for making decisions, sometimes another, e.g., sometimes calling a pitch a strike if any part of the ball is as high as the kneecap, and sometimes calling a pitch a strike only if all of it is that high. If one does this without any concern, or even knowledge, of which team benefits from one's decisions, these decisions will be impartial even if inconsistent. One can make one's decisions arbitrarily, that is, for no reason at all, as long as one does not make them in order to benefit certain members of the group over others. Although inconsistency is compatible with impartiality, it is likely to cause suspicion of lack of impartiality.

If all that someone knows about members of a group is that they are members of that group, then one cannot help but act impartially toward that group. This is why justice, which is required to treat all who come before her impartially, is often symbolically portrayed with a blindfold over her eyes. This symbolic representation that justice is not aware of who it is that comes before her shows that justice is impartial, that she cannot favor any one member of the group over another.

Impartiality Is Not a Moral Virtue

Impartiality does not guarantee that the decisions made will be correct, if this requires making decisions according to the rules. All that it guarantees is that decisions will not be made because they favor one person over the other. If one does not differentiate between the members of a group toward which one is supposed to be impartial, then one is impartial with regard to that group. How one treats the members of that group is not a relevant consideration in determining one's impartiality with regard to its members.

This explains how there can be impartial enforcement of bad or unjust laws. Those enforcing the rules can be impartial with regard to all violators of the law. If they do enforce the laws in the same way regardless of who the violator is, they are enforcing the law impartially. One may prefer that they not enforce the law at all, but this has no bearing on whether or not they are enforcing the law impartially. Impartiality is often equated with justice or fairness, but this is a mistake. Both justice and fairness are moral terms, whereas impartiality is not. We do not regard someone who impartially kills everyone who walks on his lawn as acting justly or fairly. He is not in any way morally better than someone who is partial toward little children and cannot bring himself to kill them.

Until the group toward which one is impartial and the respect with which one is impartial with regard to this group are specified, it cannot be determined whether or not impartiality is desirable. It is only because we implicitly specify that a person is impartial with regard to an appropriate group and in an appropriate respect that calling people impartial is taken as praising them. Although when we say that a person is impartial these specifications are not usually made explicit they are still present implicitly. I have simply made these specifications explicit and shown their importance. If these are specified in some unexpected ways, e.g., the group is people who have refused to obey me, and the respect is seeking their ruin, then even if one is strictly impartial and discriminates against neither rich nor poor, black nor white, male nor female, then impartiality is no virtue, let alone a moral virtue.

When we think of impartiality as a moral virtue this is because the group toward which we think the person is supposed to be impartial includes himself and, at least, all other moral agents and it is impartiality with respect to obeying the moral rules. When we are dealing with this kind of impartiality, and the person is acting rationally, then impartiality can be considered to be a moral virtue. This kind of impartiality combined with rationality not only involves consistency, but also results in people acting in ways that have better results than their not acting impartially. Not all impartiality is impartiality with regard to this kind of group in this respect and it is possible to be impartial, even with regard to this kind of group in this respect and not be rational. One can easily imagine someone, perhaps due to some perverted religious belief, who inflicts great evil impartially, and it is neither rationally nor morally required to prefer such a person over one who inflicts it partially. In fact, if one were in that group toward which the person claimed impartiality, it might be rationally required to prefer the person not to be impartial as that would lessen one's chances of suffering the evil.

It is, of course, true that in the performance of many jobs, not merely umpires and judges, both impartiality and consistency are required. This is true even when the group toward which one is expected to be impartial is very small and does not include oneself, e.g., umpires and referees. I am not in any way claiming that impartiality is unimportant. Indeed, my effort in this chapter is to provide an account of impartiality which will fit all kinds of impartiality. My definition of impartiality is that one is impartial with regard to a certain group in a certain respect if and only if one's actions in that respect toward members of that group is not affected by which members of the group benefit or are harmed by those actions. This account of impartiality, by making explicit the need for further specification, allows one to distinguish impartiality proper from those other characteristics with which it is so commonly associated. Impartiality, strictly speaking, requires neither consistency nor any effort to avoid inflicting harm. As noted earlier, these characteristics of impartiality are the result of combining impartiality toward a group which includes oneself, with rationality.

The Scope of Impartiality with Respect to the Moral Rules

In talking about the scope of impartiality I am concerned now with who is in the group toward which one must act impartially in respect to following the moral rules. The question of who is to act in accordance with the moral rules was answered in the discussion of the universality of the moral rules. There, it was pointed out that the moral rules apply to all those who can understand the rules and guide their conduct by them, i.e., to all rational persons with the relevant voluntary abilities. Here, I am concerned with the group toward which all of these persons are required to act impartially when the moral rules apply to their actions. It is quite clear that to act impartially with respect to the moral rules with regard to a given group requires that one not violate the rule toward some members of that group in the same circumstances where one would not allow the rule to be violated with regard to other members of the group. It may not be so clear that it also requires that one not allow the rule to be violated because certain members of that group will benefit, when one would not allow the rule to be violated in order to benefit other members of the group.

It is the latter requirement of impartiality that makes it important to realize that the agent himself must be a member of the group toward which one must be impartial. To be appropriately impartial in respect to the moral rules requires that one not make special exceptions that benefit oneself. It is also clear that the group must include all of one's friends and relatives. One is not allowed to make special exceptions to the moral rules in order to benefit one's friends and relatives. Nor can one limit the group toward which one is impartial with regard to the moral rules to oneself and one's friends and relatives. Limiting the group in this way is clearly incompatible with the kind of impartiality required by the moral rules. Someone who obeyed the moral rules impartially only with regard to this small circle would be regarded as not taking the appropriate group as the one toward which one must be impartial.

That oneself and one's friends and relatives are part of the group toward which one must be impartial distinguishes the impartiality required by the moral rules from the impartiality required of a judge or umpire. An umpire must be impartial with regard to his decisions between the two teams, it does not even make any sense to say he must also include himself in the group toward which he must be impartial, for he is not competing in the game. Of course, an impartial umpire cannot take a bribe that would influence his decisions. This is not because he must be impartial with regard to himself, but because taking a bribe may lead him to favor one team over the other, that is, not to be impartial in making his decisions between the two teams. That it is the possibility of his being influenced by the bribe that makes us think that taking a bribe is incompatible with impartiality is shown by the fact that if it were guaranteed that the payments from the participating teams were anonymous, we would not regard them as affecting his impartiality.

The same considerations that apply to oneself and one's friends and relatives also applies to members of one's race, religion, or country. Moral impartiality does not allow one to make special exceptions to the moral rules to benefit one's race, religion, or country. Nor can one limit the group toward which one must be impartial with regard to the moral rules to members of one's race, religion, or country. It is quite clear that this is not the kind of impartiality required by the moral rules. Those who obey the moral rules impartially, but only with regard to members of their own race, we regard as racist, not moral. Those who would kill or deceive those who were not members of their religion in circumstances when they would never kill or deceive members of their religion are religious fanatics, not moral persons. Those who obey the moral rules impartially only with regard to members of their own society also are not being impartial with regard to a large enough group. For many people it will never be clear if the scope of their impartiality is appropriate with respect to the moral rules, that is, with regard to a large enough group. Confusion about the scope of impartiality required by the moral rules is an essential feature of those who hold various forms of ethical relativism. (See discussion of Toulmin and Harman, p.133.)

The scope of impartiality appropriate to the moral rules requires, at least, that one include in the group toward which one is impartial, all those to whom the moral rules apply, i.e., all rational persons with the appropriate voluntary abilities. I call such persons moral agents. Some, for quasi-aesthetic reasons, or due to confusion, limit the group toward which one must be impartial to moral agents. There is a satisfying symmetry to the view that we should act impartially in accordance with the moral rules only with regard to the same group that is required to act impartially with regard to these rules. This limitation is not an irrational limitation, but not all rational persons need accept it. Although all agree that the impartiality appropriate to the moral rules requires that this group must include, at least, all moral agents, many rational persons hold that the group includes more than moral agents.

Disagreements about the Scope of Moral Impartiality

Even though everyone agrees that the group toward which one must impartially obey the moral rules must include all moral agents, when this point is stated more precisely this agreement disappears. Some interpret "all moral agents" as all presently existing moral agents. They claim that one needs to include in the group toward which one must impartially obey the moral rules only all presently existing moral agents. Although everyone agrees that the group should include at least all presently existing moral agents, there is considerable disagreement about who else, if any others at all, also should be included in the group. Some claim that "all moral agents" means all actual present and future moral agents and the appropriate group includes all of these. Others claim that the group should include more than all moral agents, no matter how this phrase is interpreted.

No one disagrees that one must include all presently existing moral agents; those who disagree claim that the group must include more than this. The smallest change is to claim that it must include all who were ever moral agents and remain persons, that is, are still capable of any conscious awareness. This change is supported by noting that all rational persons who are moral agents would want to retain the protection of the moral rules if they were to lose their capacity to act as moral agents; at least they would want this protection as long as they could suffer from losing it. Those who put forward this argument claim that the group toward which we should be impartial includes all presently existing moral agents and all former moral agents who are still persons. Given that all presently existing moral agents know that they could become former moral agents who are still persons, it does not seem that any rational person would oppose enlarging the group in this way. I shall thus take this group as the smallest group toward which impartially following the moral rules is required and call it *The Minimal Group.*

Presently Existing Potential Moral Agents

All other enlargements of the group are controversial. The enlargement which seems to have the largest support is that which includes not only the minimal group, but also presently existing potential moral agents, especially human infants. Most readers of this book would want to include in the group toward which we should impartially follow the moral rules human infants who have not yet become moral agents. Not all rational persons would accept this. Infanticide was, and still is, very widely practiced, even by those who impartially obey the moral rules with regard to all the presently existing actual moral agents with whom they come into contact.

Even in our society there are those who accept the killing of infants whose life prospects are very poor, when they would not allow the killing of moral agents with similar prospects. It should be noted that it is primarily those human infants who do not have the prospect of ever becoming actual moral agents, e.g., severely brain damaged infants, which these people are most likely to exclude from the group toward which the moral rules require impartial obedience. If it is clear that the infants, with proper care, will become moral agents, most in our society would want to include them in the group toward which the moral rules require impartial obedience.

It is not clear what arguments can be given to prove that human infants must be included in the group toward which we should impartially obey the moral rules, nor is it clear that any argument is needed. It is simply a fact that most people in all technologically advanced societies, or those societies in which lack of enough food to live decently is not a problem, want to include in the group toward which we must impartially obey the moral rules all human infants who will become moral agents. There are, of course, sociobiological arguments, but these are not arguments why it is rationally required for persons to include human infants; they are arguments explaining why human persons do include them.

It may seem that there is substantial agreement for including presently existing potential moral agents in the group toward which we should impartially obey the moral rules. This is because we are thinking of human infants that are already born; we are not thinking of fetuses or unborn children. They are also presently existing potential moral agents. Even those who are concerned about protecting the fetus may not regard the fetuses as belonging to that group toward which the moral rules require impartiality. Those who allow for abortion for rape or incest, or even to protect the life of the mother, may not regard the fetus as having the same level of protection from the moral rules as do actual moral agents. Philosophers have already pointed out that there is no significant, relevant difference between the fetus and the neonate; neither are actual moral agents, both are potential moral agents. Yet most people feel that there is a significant, relevant difference between the two.

We can try to capture this difference by making a parallel with former moral agents. We can talk of presently existing beings capable of suffering who are potential moral agents. This does not separate fetuses from neonates, but it does distinguish fetuses in the earliest stages from neonates and fetuses in the latter stages, and many would like a distinction of this sort. However, though some rational persons may be persuaded by this argument to include infants and fetuses in the later stages in the group toward which we should impartially obey the rules, others may not be persuaded to include them. I know of no argument which is persuasive to all rational persons about whether or not to enlarge the group toward which one should impartially obey the moral rules to include all or some presently sentient but still potential moral agents, even though I suspect that most readers of this book would include them.

The Role of Emotional Involvement

Many have claimed that there is a continuum between presently existing actual moral agents and presently existing potential moral agents. They claim that it is impossible to draw a sharp line between those who are already moral agents and those who have not quite acquired the intellectual and volitional abilities to be held morally responsible for their actions. I agree with this claim, but I do not find it helpful in deciding who should be included in the group toward which the moral rules require impartial obedience, for there is no doubt that babies, even as old as a year, are not moral agents. Yet every reader of this book would want to include babies of this age in the group toward which the moral rules require impartiality. This is undoubtedly due to the fact that the interaction between moral agents and these babies is as deep and intimate as any among moral agents. Moral agents are not distinguished from those who are not moral agents by the degree of emotional involvement we have with them. Most moral agents care for these babies as much as they care for other moral agents and so want them accorded the full protection of the moral rules.

In deciding who belongs in the group toward which we should act impartially in accordance with the moral rules, the considerations that incline us one way or the other are often based on emotional considerations. It is our interaction with babies that makes us want to include them in the group that must be treated impartially. Some would claim that this interaction begins at birth and that this is why the infant or neonate is accorded the full protection of the moral rules whereas the fetus is not. I do not deny the psychological force of these considerations. Similar considerations lead us to regard killing a fetus in the very early stages of pregnancy as much less serious than killing a fetus in the very last stages. Even if the interaction is somewhat one sided, we have become more emotionally involved with the fetus in the later stages.

Our emotional involvement with others is one factor that inclines us to include them in the group accorded the impartial protection of the moral rules. The power of our emotional attachment to other beings is not necessarily affected by whether or not they are moral agents. Since all moral agents must be accorded the full protection of the moral rules, if there is any group of beings with which we are as emotionally involved as with moral agents, then we will want them to have as much protection as moral agents. Human babies are in this group for most human moral agents. (As far as we know all moral agents are human, and this undoubtedly affects the discussion of who belongs in the group toward which we should behave impartially.) Most do not have this same emotional involvement with fetuses, especially in the early stages of pregnancy.

Although our emotional involvement with those who are moral agents or potential moral agents is usually stronger than our emotional involvement with those who are not, this is not always the case. Some people are emotionally involved with animals, especially pets, in a way that equals or exceeds their emotional involvement with other moral agents. These people may want animals to be included in the group toward which we should impartially obey the moral rules. Some may even be inclined to include all presently existing sentient beings in the group to be treated impartially while not including potential moral agents who are not yet sentient beings, i.e, fetuses in the earliest stages of pregnancy.

The Role of Metaphysical, Religious, and Scientific Beliefs

Direct emotional involvement is not the only factor that influences how one determines the size and composition of the group toward which one should impartially obey the moral rules. Many are influenced by religious or metaphysical beliefs. If one believes that what is most significant about moral agents is that they have souls, then one will probably want to include in the group toward which one should be impartial all beings that one believes have a soul. If one believes that the soul enters the body at the moment of conception, then one will want fetuses from the moment of conception included in the group. If one believes that the soul enters the body at birth then one may not want to include any fetuses in the group. And if one believes that the soul enters the body at some time during pregnancy, e.g., when the fetus becomes sentient, then one will want to include all fetuses after that time in the group and may not want to include fetuses before that time. If one has some belief about transmigration of souls such that the souls of moral agents sometimes come back in the bodies of animals, then one will probably want animals to be included in the group.

Metaphysical beliefs about the nature of time and space may lead one to regard moral agents who are distant from us in time as no different from those who are distant from us in space and hence to include all actual future moral agents in the group. Other beliefs about the nature of actuality and potentiality may lead one to include all potential moral agents in the group. I shall not list all of the religious and metaphysical beliefs that may lead one to accept or reject an increase in the size of the group toward which one should impartially obey the moral rules because these beliefs, even if true, are not beliefs that are common to all rational persons. The same is true of scientific beliefs, e.g., that fetuses are members of the same biological species as all moral agents, or that there is a continuous development of a fetus from conception to birth. Since morality applies to all rational persons, all of the essential features of morality must be understood and acceptable to all rational persons, and hence no religious, metaphysical, or even scientific belief, which is not common to all rational persons can be used to determine any feature of morality.

The religious and metaphysical and scientific beliefs that incline one to accept or reject a proposed increase in the size of the group, like one's emotional involvement, only explain why one wants to increase the size of the group in a certain way; they do not provide arguments that are persuasive to all rational persons. Presenting these arguments is like showing people a picture of a fetus in order to get them emotionally involved, its success will depend in part on the skill of the presenter. Even if people become emotionally involved or are persuaded of the correctness of the argument, they may still not want to enlarge the group in the way that is being argued for. One needs no reason for refusing to enlarge the group beyond the minimal group, though, of course, there is a reason available, viz., every enlargement of the group restricts the freedom of those already in the group.

Some Possible Additions to the Minimal Group

The categories that can be used in enlarging the group toward which one must impartially obey the moral rules must be categories that are understood by all rational persons. We cannot increase the group by adding cats and dogs because there are some rational persons who have never heard of cats and dogs. We could increase the group by adding sentient beings, which would include cats and dogs, but it would also include many other animals. We might try for sentient beings which are pets of rational persons, but it may be that some rational persons have no concept of pet either. I shall list some categories which satisfy the condition that all rational persons understand that category and so are possible additions to the group toward which we must follow the moral rules impartially.

I shall start with the category that every rational person agrees must be included, all presently existing moral agents. As I have characterized moral agents, all rational persons with the appropriate volitional abilities are moral agents. If there are any rational persons without the appropriate volitional abilities the group should be enlarged to include them, for no rational person would accept being excluded from the impartial protection of the moral rules. Further, all rational persons would want to maintain the protection of the moral rules if they should cease to be rational, but remain persons, that is, remain capable of any conscious awareness. They would want to include in the group any person who had been a rational person. This group seems to me the smallest group toward which one can impartially obey the moral rules and still have the kind of impartiality that has the morally appropriate scope. It is what I called *The Minimal Group.*

Many would want to enlarge the minimal group by adding presently existing sentient beings who are potential moral agents. This would enlarge the group by adding human infants and fetuses after they had become sentient beings. I shall call this Addition 1. Others would want to enlarge the group by adding all presently existing potential moral agents, regardless of whether or not they are already sentient beings. This would enlarge the group by adding fetuses from the moment of conception or soon after. I shall call this Addition 1a.

Many would want to enlarge the group by adding actual future moral agents. They would regard doing something that one knew would kill a future moral agent two hundred years from now just as immoral as doing something one knew would kill a presently existing moral agent two thousand miles from here. Of course, there is always the uncertainty about the effects of one's actions on future moral agents, but given this uncertainty they maintain that we should be as concerned about violating moral rules with regard to future moral agents as with regard to presently existing ones. They would regard the contamination of the environment with toxic waste dumps, etc. that we know will cause serious evils to future generations as seriously immoral. I shall call this Addition 2.

Most who want to include Addition 1a and Addition 2 would enlarge the group by adding all future potential moral agents. There may be many other combinations or distinctions with regard to what moral agents should be included in the group, but it seems to me that I have already listed enough to make it clear how one might propose to add to the minimal group of presently existing moral agents. However, there are others who want to make additions to the minimal group that do not use the category of moral agent or rational person at all. Some hold that any presently existing sentient being should be included in the group toward which we should impartially obey the moral rules. I shall call this Addition 3. Others hold that any present or future sentient being should be included. This could be Addition 3a. And we could go on to include any present or future potential sentient being. As stated before, there is no addition to the minimal group that all rational persons must accept.

In determining the group toward which we are required to obey the moral rules impartially, impartiality can not be required, for this would require that the group already be specified. However, it is a valuable exercise to present situations in which members of the minimal group and members of that addition that someone wants to add to that group are paired, and see if that person is really prepared to require obeying the moral rules impartially with regard to both. If he is, then there is no argument than can be given to show that the addition should not be made to the group. Given that one includes all presently existing persons who are or were rational in the group, one may expand the group on any basis whatsoever, as long as one is prepared to have all moral agents act impartially with regard to this group whenever considering a violation of the moral rules. However, no rational person would accept any enlargement of the group beyond all actual and potential present and future sentient (conscious) beings, and most would not accept a group this large.

The group toward which the moral rules require impartiality must include all those in the minimal group, all presently existing rational persons and former rational persons, including oneself and one's friends. Impartially following the moral rules means that one does not allow anyone, including oneself, to violate a moral rule with regard to anyone in this group unless one would allow everyone to violate that same rule with regard to anyone else in that group in the same circumstances. One does not allow any violations of the moral rules that favor any one member of the group over any other member of the group. The kind of impartiality required by the moral rules is just impartiality applied to a group that includes oneself and one's friends and at least all those in the minimal group, with or without additions.

Rationality and Impartiality

A natural question to be considered is, "What is the relationship of rationality to this kind of impartiality?" Granted that we are not acting morally unless our actions with respect to the moral rules are consistent with this kind of impartiality, does rationality require this kind of impartiality? I have already pointed out in Chapter 2 that a rational person need not be concerned with anyone other than himself, or with himself and his friends and family. It follows from this that a rational person need not adopt this kind of impartiality. This conclusion goes contrary to the views of very many philosophers. Kant regarded impartiality, or at least his substitute for it, to be intimately related to rationality, and

many philosophers have followed him in this. Nonetheless, given that the concept of rationality must be such that no one ever wants to act irrationally, it
seems clear that rationality cannot require impartially obeying the moral rules
with regard to all those in the minimal group.

It is not irrational for a person to obey the moral rules impartially with regard
to the minimal group, with or without additions, but it is also not irrational for
a person not to do so. Impartiality and rationality are completely distinct concepts: that one is rational implies neither that one is impartial in the relevant
way, nor that one is not; even that one is impartial with regard to the minimal
group with respect to the moral rules does not imply either that one is rational
or that one is irrational. If one is irrational, one may simply violate the moral
rules without regard to who is hurt by one's violations and allow others to violate them in the same way. It is only if one is both rational and impartial with
respect to the moral rules with regard to the appropriate group that one will act
in a morally acceptable way. Indeed, what counts as the morally acceptable way
to act with respect to the moral rules is determined by the way that a person who
is rational and impartial in the appropriate way can advocate that one act. In
the remainder of this chapter when I talk about impartial persons I shall also
mean that they are rational.

Impartial Rational Persons Can Disagree

From what has been said about impartiality it is clear that people who are impartial with regard to the same group can disagree. Some umpires call pitches that
are at the knee strikes, while others call a pitch a strike only if it is above the
knee. Yet there is no doubt that both can be completely impartial. Indeed, as we
mentioned earlier, a single umpire, while retaining his impartiality, can sometimes call a strike according to one standard and other times according to
another. He would not be a good umpire, for a good umpire must be consistent
as well as impartial, but his failure would not be due to lack of impartiality.
Although it seems quite clear that impartial persons can disagree with each
other, it may not seem equally clear that impartial rational persons can disagree.
However, it is no less rational for an umpire to call a pitch a strike if it is at the
knee than if it is above the knee, so that adding rationality to impartiality does
not eliminate all disagreement.

Even if we add that one make one's decisions according to the rules, we will
not eliminate all disagreement. Almost all rules are vague to some degree; they
require some interpretation. As long as one's decisions are in accord with some
acceptable interpretation, then one can be rational, impartial, and acting according to the rules, and still be making different decisions than some other person
who is also rational, impartial, and acting according to the rules. Sometimes the
situation will be such that all impartial, rational persons who are acting in accordance with the rules will make the same decision; if the pitch is over the batter's
head no impartial rational person acting according to the rules will call it a
strike. But within limits, there will be many situations where impartial rational
persons acting according to the rules will disagree.

The United States Supreme Court sometimes comes down with a unanimous decision, but most often the decisions are split. There is no reason to believe that all of these split decisions require an explanation in terms of the defects in one or more of the judges as acting irrationally, partially, not acting according to the constitution, or not knowing all the relevant facts or laws. The fact that most decisions of the Supreme Court are split decisions should not lead one to the view that impartial rational persons who know all the relevant facts, laws, and the constitution will usually fail to agree. The Supreme Court does not hear the overwhelming number of cases on which they would all agree, precisely because it is known that they would agree. It only makes sense to take to the Court those issues on which it is not clear what fully knowledgeable impartial rational persons will decide.

Fully knowledgeable, impartial rational persons applying the same rules sometimes disagree even though they will usually agree. The ratio of agreement to disagreement will depend on the degree to which the facts allow for differing interpretations of the rules. In most situations where impartial decisions are required, the facts do not allow differing interpretations to result in different decisions very often. If impartial decisions were not usually in agreement, those participating could not be confident that the decisions really were impartial. The fact that disagreement can call impartiality into question has led some to characterize impartiality in such a way as to rule out any disagreement. Currently, the most prominent attempt to do this is provided by John Rawls's "veil of ignorance."

The "veil of ignorance" not only removes all knowledge of who will benefit or be harmed by one's decisions, it also removes all individuating characteristics from those who are supposed to make the impartial decisions. In this way it guarantees not only impartiality, but also unanimity. Since, by itself, the veil of ignorance eliminates the possibility of favoring any one member of the group over any other, many have taken it as the best characterization of impartiality. Since universalizability and reversibility, by themselves, do not rule out favoring any one member of the group over any others, one must also have some procedure for not allowing them to be manipulated, e.g., by using special categories or characterizations. However, universalizability and reversibility do allow for disagreement among impartial rational persons whereas the veil of ignorance does not. What is needed is a procedure that both guarantees that one cannot favor any one member of the group over any other, and yet at the same time allows for some disagreement among impartial persons.

Impartial rational persons can differ in their decisions because they may interpret the rule or standard governing their decisions differently. Some basketball referees call a foul for bodily contact between players that other referees do not call. The referees may call fouls the way they do because of their conception of how the game should be played. One may think calling a foul to discourage bodily contact results in a better game because it is a better test of the skill of the players. Another may hold that calling a foul to discourage bodily contact results in a worse game because the flow of the game is disrupted too often. Referees who call fouls or who refrain from calling them from motives like the above do not cease to be impartial. It may be that some teams do, in fact, benefit from fouls being called one way rather than the other and that other teams are hurt by this policy, but it does not follow from this that adopting one policy or the other is not impartial. Especially if one does not know who will be benefited or harmed by a given policy, it cannot be that one is not acting impartially in adopting that policy.

Removing knowledge of which members of a group will be benefited and which will be harmed guarantees that any decision made will be impartial. Once this is realized then it becomes clear that it does not matter what other knowledge people have. A referee does not cease to be impartial if he prefers a game with less physical contact. The same is true of the referee who prefers a game with minimal interference. An analogue to Rawls's veil of ignorance is not needed in order to guarantee impartiality. On the contrary, it does not even make any sense to talk of the referee having no view whatsoever on how fouls are to be called. If he had no view on this matter it would be impossible for him to interpret the rule concerning fouls in order to make any calls. One may think that he should call fouls in the way the rule intended, with no interpretation, but there is no such way. It is the mistaken view that there is one and only one correct way to apply the rules that makes one believe that to be impartial one must not have any views on the way the game should be played. Of course, there are limits on the legitimate interpretations of the rules, and most of the time during the game, these limits will determine whether or not a call should be made. It goes against all human experience to maintain that all qualified impartial rational persons will always interpret or apply a rule in exactly the same way.

What Impartiality with Respect to Moral Rules Requires

Impartiality does not require that one have no views on how to interpret the rules one is applying, only that one not be influenced in one's interpretation by how any particular person or group will be affected by that interpretation. This point holds for impartiality with respect to the moral rules as well as with regard to any other rules. Impartiality with regard to moral rules requires that one be impartial with regard to a group containing oneself, one's friends and family, and at least all rational persons. This means that when considering the violation of a moral rule with regard to a member of this group, one cannot allow it to be violated for anyone unless, in the same circumstances, one would allow it to be violated for everyone. It also means that one cannot allow it to be violated with regard to anyone unless, in the same circumstances, one would allow it to be violated with regard to everyone. Impartiality with regard to moral rules requires impartiality with regard to both those for whom the rule may be violated and those toward whom it is to be violated.

Justified Violations Must Be Publicly Allowed

To ensure impartial following of the moral rules, one must guarantee that no one will be influenced by who benefits or is hurt by what counts as the same circumstances. This requires that what counts as the same circumstances must be described using only concepts that are understandable to all rational persons.

It also requires that it not be irrational for any person to whom the moral rules apply to count these circumstances as relevant to determining when one may violate a moral rule. For the same reason it is not enough to hold that a violation is justified if everyone is allowed to violate the rule in the same circumstances; everyone must know and be able to accept the procedure by which this kind of violation is allowed. This is necessary because one cannot guarantee completely impartial following of the moral rules unless violations are allowed only when they are determined by a procedure that is known by and acceptable to all moral agents. When violations are determined by such a procedure I shall call them "publicly allowed."

That moral rules must be followed impartially requires that violations of moral rules are justified only if they can be publicly allowed. That the violations of moral rules must be determined impartially, i.e., by being publicly allowed, is not a new condition, but simply makes clear what is involved in the requirement that one must follow the moral rules impartially with regard to all members of the minimal group, with or without additions. It is impartiality that requires justified violations of moral rules to have the same characteristics that moral rules have, viz., to be known and not irrational to all whose conduct is to be governed by them. This rules out the possibility of a moral system part of which, the moral rules, are known and acceptable to all, and part of which, the procedure for determining justified exceptions, is known and acceptable only to some.

In making moral judgments on particular actions, one must, of course, know the facts of the particular case, which are not known to all rational persons. But the system of morality, itself, which one uses to make judgments once one knows these particular facts, cannot make use of any facts that are not known to, or beliefs that are not held by, all rational persons. Limiting the facts or beliefs that can be used in setting up the moral system to those that are rationally required rules out the possibility of one group using any facts known only to them in order to gain some advantage over other rational persons. This limitation on what beliefs can be used is similar to that imposed by Rawls's "veil of ignorance," but has two major differences. First, it rules out only beliefs, not desires; it does not require that all impartial rational persons have the same desires, but allows for any desires that are possible given only rationally required beliefs. This allows impartial rational persons to rank the evils differently, so they may not always advocate publicly allowing the same kind of violations. Second, it rules out many beliefs that the veil of ignorance allows, e.g., it rules out general scientific truths if these are not known to all rational persons. Thus it rules out the claim of more technologically advanced societies that their superior scientific knowledge makes their moral system superior to that developed by less advanced societies.

Impartiality not only requires universal understanding but also universal acceptability. Advocating that a violation be publicly allowed requires not only that all rational persons understand it, but also that they can accept it. Universal acceptability does not require that all rational persons advocate the same violations, only that they could do so, that it would not be incompatible with their being rational to advocate publicly allowing the violation. Using universal acceptability as a way of guaranteeing impartiality resembles the use of universalizability and reversibility as methods for determining impartiality. However, it differs from them in some important respects. First, it includes the requirement of rationality, whereas, as traditionally stated, neither universalizability nor reversibility requires that the person who is willing to universalize his judgments, or to accept the consequences if the position of victim and violator were reversed, be rational in the sense that I have provided. Universal acceptability eliminates unacceptable eccentricity because it requires that every rational person be able to advocate publicly allowing the same violation even considering that he might be a victim of this kind of violation.

Moral Impartiality

In this chapter I have taken the general definition of impartiality, *A is impartial in respect R with regard to group G if and only if A's actions in respect R are not influenced at all by which member(s) of G benefit or are harmed by these actions,* and specified what impartiality morality requires. This is impartiality with respect to acting in accordance with the moral rules with regard to a group containing oneself, one's friends and family, and at least a minimal group containing all presently existing rational persons and persons who were once rational. In order for this specification of impartiality to count as what I shall call *moral impartiality,* it must also include rationality. Moral impartiality requires that one never violate a moral rule unless one can advocate that such a violation be publicly allowed, which requires that it be understood and could be accepted by all rational persons. That moral impartiality includes rationality does not mean that impartiality, even impartiality with respect to the moral rules with regard to the minimal group, includes rationality.

In this chapter I provided an analysis of the concept of impartiality. In Chapter 2 I provided an analysis of the concept of rationality. These two concepts are not only independent of each other, they also do not depend on the concept of morality. In Chapter 1 I developed the concept of a public system which, although dependent on the concept of rationality, also does not depend on the concept of morality. In Chapter 4 I discussed several rules that are taken to be paradigm cases of moral rules. In the following two chapters I shall show how these three concepts are related to these rules. I want to show what attitude impartial rational persons would take toward certain rules considered as part of a public system that applies to all rational persons. If I can show that all impartial rational persons would advocate adopting a public system that contains most of what are taken to be the moral rules, I will consider myself to have justified morality and to have shown that all of the rules contained in this public system are genuine or justified moral rules.

6

JUSTIFICATION
OF THE MORAL RULES—
THE FIRST FIVE

In this chapter I shall examine the attitude that rational persons would adopt toward certain rules. First I shall examine the attitude that they would adopt toward these rules simply in virtue of their being rational. Then I shall examine the attitude that rational persons would adopt toward these rules if they were also what I characterized in the previous chapter as morally impartial. When I talk about impartiality in this and all subsequent chapters I shall always mean moral impartiality, so that by impartial rational persons I shall always mean those who are morally impartial. I shall also examine the attitude of rational persons toward these rules considered as moral rules, i.e., as public rules applying to all rational persons. Finally, I shall examine the attitude of impartial rational persons toward these rules considered as moral rules.

I shall, in these discussions, also examine the relationship between the attitude that all impartial rational persons would adopt toward these rules and the attitude that all rational persons, whether or not they are impartial, would adopt toward these rules when considering them as public rules. However, the most important task is to show that the attitude that all impartial rational persons would adopt toward these rules considered as moral rules is what I shall call "the moral attitude." This attitude, which requires impartial obedience, is what I take to be the appropriate attitude to take toward the moral rules. This is sufficient for what I call a justification of the moral rules. This discussion will not depend in any way on the meaning of any so-called ethical term, e.g., "good," "bad," "right," "wrong," "ought," or "should."

Although I am interested in providing a justification of the moral rules, it may turn out that some commonly accepted moral rules will not be justifiable. Further, some new rules may be formulated, which will be justifiable in the same way as most of the justified rules of common or ordinary morality. This may lead to some revision of the list of ordinary or commonly accepted moral rules, but most of the rules will be the same and there should be no surprises. An important task in this chapter and the next is to provide precise formulations of those rules toward which all impartial rational persons would adopt the moral attitude. I regard all and only those rules toward which all impartial rational persons adopt the moral attitude as justified moral rules, I also regard them as the basic rules of a rational morality. I shall sometimes simply call these rules the moral rules; nothing turns on which alternative is used.

Since I have not performed an empirical investigation involving all the rational persons in the world, it would seem that I could not reach any significant conclusions about the attitudes of all rational persons on any topic, including their attitudes toward certain rules. However, I am concerned with rational persons only insofar as they are rational. (If I were concerned with the irrational aspect of rational persons, I might as well be concerned with irrational persons.) Thus I can employ the conclusions of chapter two on the nature of rationality. However, nothing in that chapter makes it obvious that there are any rules toward which *all* rational persons will agree to take a certain attitude. Indeed, if we do not specify the beliefs that these rational persons can use, then there may not be any attitude toward anything on which all rational persons will agree. One's attitude is usually determined by one's beliefs; and since rationally allowed beliefs can vary so much, unless we restrict beliefs to those that are rationally required, it is most likely that all rational persons will have no significant agreement in attitude.

Justifying a moral system requires providing a public system that incorporates the moral rules and that applies to all rational persons and then showing that all impartial rational persons would advocate adopting that system as the public system that all rational persons should use as a guide for their conduct and a basis for their judgments. Of course, in deciding how to act, or in making judgments about the actions of others, one must make use of information about the circumstances that is not common knowledge, but in formulating and justifying the moral system that one applies to these circumstances one can use only beliefs that are rationally required. This limitation is necessary since a moral system must be such that it is understood and can be accepted by all rational persons. Although we acknowledge that moral agents are sometimes ignorant of the consequences of their actions or of morally relevant circumstances and that this ignorance sometimes totally excuses them from moral judgments, we do not acknowledge that a moral agent can ever be totally excused because of ignorance of the moral system.

It is appropriate to limit the beliefs used in formulating and justifying the moral rules to those which are rationally required since only rationally required beliefs are held by all those to whom the moral rules apply, i.e., all moral agents. Accepting this limitation to rationally required beliefs, I shall examine the conceptual or analytic relationship between being rational, both when one is not impartial and when one is, and advocating a certain attitude toward a particular set of rules considered as moral rules. I have specified what it is to be both rational and impartial independently of showing anything about one's attitudes toward any rules; therefore it is of some significance to show that all impartial rational persons will take an attitude that is just the attitude we think ought to be taken toward a particular set of rules considered as moral rules. How significant the conclusion is depends on the adequacy of the concepts of rationality, morality, and impartiality presented in prior chapters. Insofar as one regards those analyses as correct, just so far will one acknowledge the significance of the relationship among rationality, impartiality and taking a certain attitude toward a certain set of rules, considered as moral rules.

Do Not Kill

The rules toward which all rational persons will share a certain attitude are closely related to the commonly accepted moral rules. Therefore I shall start by considering what attitude all rational persons would take toward the most important moral rule, "Don't kill." We know one attitude which they need not hold; not all rational persons would want to obey the rule themselves. This is not to deny that some rational persons might want to obey it; it is only to affirm that some rational persons might not want to obey it themselves.

At first glance it would seem that they all would want all other people to obey the rule. But, to say this simply, as if all rational persons never wish anyone to be killed, at least not by anyone other than themselves, does not seem correct. One can be perfectly rational and not be concerned with the killing of persons of whom one has no knowledge; one can even be unconcerned with the killing of people of whom one does have knowledge. By concern for persons, or caring for them, I mean simply that the belief that doing something will help them avoid suffering some evil is a motive for doing that thing. If all rational persons are to hold an attitude toward the rule, it will not be simply that they want all other people to obey the rule.

Consider the following attitude that all rational persons might adopt: "I want all other people to obey the rule with regard to me." This seems quite plausible. Rational persons are necessarily concerned with their own preservation. However, as we pointed out in Chapter 2, rationality and self-interest are not synonymous. A rational person might be as concerned with the preservation of some others as with his own preservation. A person is not irrational if he sacrifices his life to save others, though, of course, he is not irrational if he does not. Nonetheless, though a rational person can sacrifice his life for others, he must also want to preserve his own life. Hence it seems that all rational persons would hold this attitude toward the rule.

It is possible to modify the attitude in a way which does not suggest that a rational person must be concerned only with his own preservation. All rational persons might hold this formulation: "I want all other people to obey the rule with regard to anyone for whom I am concerned, including, of course, myself." If a rational person were concerned only with himself, he would want the rule obeyed only with regard to himself; if he were concerned with his family as well, he would want the rule obeyed with regard to them; if he were concerned with all rational persons, he would want it obeyed with regard to everyone. Even though rational persons can differ in the breadth of their concern for people, they would all want the rule to be obeyed by all others with regard to those for whom they were concerned. This is not to say that all would want it not to be obeyed by themselves or with regard to those for whom they were not concerned; it is only to say that some might not want this.

It now seems as if we have an attitude toward the rule "Don't kill" which all rational persons would hold; "I want all other people to obey the rule with regard to all persons for whom I am concerned, including, of course, myself." Although it may seem that all rational persons would hold this attitude, some might not. As we pointed out in Chapter 2, there are circumstances in which it is not irrational to want to die, or even to be killed, e.g., when faced with torture or some incurable and extremely painful disease. A rational person may, therefore, not take such an absolute attitude toward the rule. Let us modify the attitude as follows: *"I want all other people to obey the rule 'Don't kill' with regard to all for whom I am concerned, including myself, except when those people have (or would have if they knew the facts) a rational desire not to have the rule obeyed with regard to themselves."*

Again it must be emphasized that to say that all rational persons would take this attitude toward the rule does not mean that there is not some further attitude that some or most rational persons might take toward the rule. I am only trying to formulate an attitude that a rational person must take toward the rule, and so I must be extremely careful not to include anything on which rational persons might disagree. It seems that a rational person must want all other people to obey the rule "Don't kill" with regard to anyone for whom he is concerned, except when that person has a rational desire not to have the rule obeyed with regard to himself. This does not mean that a rational person would necessarily want someone to kill a person for whom he was concerned (including himself) if that person had a rational desire to be killed. It means simply that when someone he cares for has a rational desire to be killed, rational persons might differ on whether or not he should be killed. The "except" clause does not mean that all rational persons want the rule not to be obeyed in these cases, but only that they need not want it to be obeyed.

It may now seem that we have an attitude which all rational persons would take. Although it is hard to think of a situation in which a rational person would not want to take this attitude, I think some situations can be found. Suppose someone for whom I am concerned is not concerned for me; in fact, he is going to kill me. I would not want someone to obey the rule "Don't kill" with regard to him, if killing him was the only way to keep him from killing me. To avoid the objection that I should not be concerned for someone who is going to kill me, I present the following example. I am suffering from some disease. I need a transplanted vital organ in order to survive. Someone for whom I am concerned is the only one who has a suitable organ, but to remove it from him would kill him. If I could not kill him, to take the proposed attitude would commit me to wanting no one else to do something that is necessary to prevent my dying. For it says that I want no one else to break the rule with regard to those for whom I am concerned unless they have a rational desire not to have the rule obeyed with regard to them. But it certainly is rational for me to want someone to break the rule with regard to this person, even though he may have no rational desire to have the rule broken with regard to himself. A further objection: it may be that some person for whom I am concerned has a rational desire that the rule be broken with regard to himself, but that I have a rational desire that it not be broken with regard to him. In order to meet these objections let us substitute the word "I" for the words "those people" in the except clause and make the other changes required by this substitution. We have now made the attitude one that all rational persons would take.

The Egocentric Attitude

I conclude that *all* rational persons would take the following attitude toward the rule "Don't kill": *"I want all other people to obey the rule 'Don't kill' with regard to all for whom I am concerned (including myself), except when I have (or would have if I knew the facts) a rational desire that the rule not be obeyed with regard to them."* I call this attitude *The Egocentric Attitude.* It is extremely important to note that I am not maintaining that there is no other attitude that a rational person would take toward this rule. In fact, I have insisted that there are any number of attitudes that a rational person could take. All that I am maintaining here is that every rational person must take this attitude, not that he would not enlarge upon it. I am not even maintaining that there is no other attitude which all rational persons would take (I shall provide one); I am only maintaining that none would refuse to take the attitude as I have formulated it.

Do Not Cause Pain

Having formulated an attitude that all rational persons would take toward the rule "Don't kill," let us examine some other rules toward which the same attitude would be taken. It seems plain that the rule "Don't cause pain" is also a rule toward which all rational persons would take the same attitude. I use the term "pain" to include not only physical pain but also all kinds of mental suffering. One may object that I have forgotten about sadists and masochists. I admitted in Chapter 2 that sadism and masochism need not be irrational. If one genuinely enjoys inflicting pain on others or in having others inflict pain on oneself, one may be suffering from a mental disorder, but one need not be irrational. Having admitted this, how can I affirm that all rational persons, which includes sadists and masochists, would take the required attitude toward the rule "Don't cause pain"? With the sadist, of course, there is no trouble. A rational sadist would want all other people to obey the rule with regard to himself and those people for whom he is concerned except when he did not want them to. Thus a sadist, if rational, would take the same attitude toward the rule "Don't cause pain" that all rational persons take toward the rule "Don't kill."

The difficulty with the masochist, the person who enjoys pain, is that since he enjoys pain, he would not seem to want others to obey the rule "Don't cause pain" with regard to himself. However, a masochist may have nonmasochistic friends and would take the attitude for their sake. More importantly, masochists do not enjoy all pain, nor do they enjoy pain in all circumstances. Hence, if rational, he would accept the stated attitude toward the rule "Don't cause pain," for it includes the "except" clause. Thus others need not obey the rule toward him when he has a rational desire for them not to obey it. If they know in a particular circumstance that he would enjoy pain, then he is not committed to wanting that they not cause him pain. The masochist can make much greater use of the "except" clause.

It may seem absurd to worry about sadists and masochists. It could be held that one need not provide an attitude that everyone, including those with mental maladies would take. But my aim is to provide an attitude that *all* rational persons could take, and though sadists and masochists may be mentally ill, they need not be irrational. As long as they are aware that most people do not generally enjoy being inflicted with pain, then being rational, they should take the same attitude as more normal rational persons. The importance of seeing this is that it shows that by rational persons I do not mean persons with a certain basic goodness, or normalcy, or any other vague but suspicious characteristic. Even masochists and sadists, without giving up their sadism or masochism, will, if rational, take the same attitude toward certain rules as more ordinary rational persons. This shows that the connection I am making between rationality and certain rules is not one that simply takes the traditional moral problems and makes them problems of rationality.

Although I formulate this rule as "Don't cause pain," and in my discussion of it have concentrated on physical pain, I should repeat here that I regard this rule as prohibiting not only the causing of physical pain, but also mental pain or suffering, as discussed in Chapter 2. This mental suffering need not even be of the kind that is normally called mental pain, e.g., the kind that comes from being subjected to sudden verbal abuse. I include in mental suffering any feeling or emotion that involves the feelings of sadness, displeasure, or anxiety; it is only for the sake of simplicity that I formulate the rule as I do.

Do Not Disable

We have seen that all rational persons would take the same attitude toward the rules "Don't kill" and "Don't cause pain." It requires no additional argument to show that all rational persons would take this same attitude toward the rule "Don't disable." What is required is to make clear what disabling involves. As I use the term, to disable someone is to take away or diminish any of his voluntary abilities, which are composed of physical abilities, mental abilities, and volitional abilities. A voluntary ability is an ability to do a kind of voluntary act. Cutting off a person's hands takes away the ability to do many kinds of voluntary acts by causing a serious physical disability. Destroying certain parts of a person's brain takes away the ability to do many kinds of voluntary acts, e.g., adding and subtracting numbers, by causing a mental disability. Causing someone to have a phobia, e.g., claustrophobia, takes away the ability to do some kinds of voluntary acts, e.g., entering an elevator, by causing a volitional disability. To take away someone's ability to do any kind of voluntary act is to disable him. As with pain, there are degrees of disability, but no rational person wants to be disabled in any degree unless he has some reason. All rational persons would take the same attitude toward the rule "Don't disable" as they took toward the two previous rules. (For a further account of voluntary abilities and volitional disabilities see "Voluntary Abilities" and "Free Will as the Ability to Will," by Timothy Duggan and Bernard Gert, and Chapter 6 of *Philosophy in Medicine* by Charles M. Culver and Bernard Gert.)

Do Not Deprive of Freedom

Once one has accepted the rule against disabling, it immediately becomes apparent that there is another rule toward which all rational persons would take the same attitude: namely, a rule prohibiting the limiting of the exercise of one's abilities. In fact, it may often be impossible to decide whether one is being disabled or simply being prevented from exercising one's ability. This is especially true when the disabling, if it is to be called that, is temporary. This is the old question of deciding when one's power is being taken away, and when one's liberty. It is often an undecidable issue, although most cases are clear-cut. That there are many borderline cases, e.g., giving a person drugs in order to prevent his doing something, is not important because we have both rules. Even if it can't be decided whether one is being disabled or simply being prevented from exercising one's abilities, it will always be clear that it is one of the two. Hence no ambiguous act will unacceptably be allowed. A rational person will take the same attitude toward the limiting of his exercise of his abilities as he would toward the diminishing or removing of them. It is not necessary for him to decide if a given act fits under one or the other of these rules; all that is necessary is that it is clear that it falls under one or the other. A rational person need make no important distinction between someone who intends to cut off his arm and someone who intends to tie it in such a way as to make it permanently unusable.

Although it is clear that all rational persons will take the same attitude toward this fourth rule as they did toward the previous three, it is not so clear how to formulate it simply using traditional and easily understood terms. The rule is meant to prohibit interference with the exercise of one's voluntary abilities, i.e., performing voluntary actions, and no matter how formulated this is what is meant by the rule. In the past I formulated this rule as "Don't deprive of freedom or opportunity," because freedom and opportunity are so closely related. Being deprived of freedom is simply being deprived of an indefinite number of opportunities. Being deprived of an opportunity is usually simply being deprived of the freedom to do some particular thing. However, when the deprivation is due to coercion, we usually say that the person has been deprived of freedom rather than opportunity. Thus I regarded it as pointless to have two separate rules concerning freedom and opportunity. (I am probably also influenced by the desire to end up with ten rules.) To deprive someone of freedom, as when you put him in a cell or tie him to a chair, prevents him from doing an indefinite number of things. To deprive someone of an opportunity, as when you do not allow him to participate in a game, prevents him from doing some specific things.

How many opportunities one must deprive a person of before it is appropriate to talk of depriving him of his freedom is more a problem of language than of morality. (The distinction between freedom and opportunity may not even be present in languages other than English.) I do not claim that my account of freedom and opportunity captures exactly what is ordinarily meant by these terms, but since I used these terms to formulate a rule that prohibits interference with the exercise of one's voluntary abilities there is no doubt that all rational persons will take the same attitude toward being deprived of freedom or opportunity as they did toward being disabled. It is simply for aesthetic reasons that I now formulate the fourth rule simply as "Don't deprive of freedom," for I mean by it exactly what I meant by the earlier formulation which included opportunity; I intend it to prohibit any interference with the exercise of one's voluntary abilities.

Do Not Deprive of Pleasure

The final rule toward which all rational persons can immediately be seen to take the same attitude as they did toward the previous four rules has often not been distinguished from the second rule, "Don't cause pain." I formulate it as, "Don't deprive of pleasure." This makes clear that causing pain is not depriving of pleasure or vice versa. To build a wall in order to prevent someone from enjoying the sight of flowers is to deprive of pleasure; it is not to inflict pain. To torture someone, physically or mentally, is not to deprive of pleasure, but to inflict pain and suffering. This makes clear the greater significance of pain; inflicting pain is generally worse than depriving of pleasure. Yet a rational person would take the same attitude toward the rule "Don't deprive of pleasure" as he did toward the previous four rules.

This rule seems somewhat vaguer than the rest, for what gives pleasure to one person may not give pleasure to another. Indeed, what gives pleasure to a person at one time may not give pleasure to him at some other time. But as we pointed out earlier (Chapter 2, pp. 32–33), smiling, together with other facial and bodily expressions, provides us with a criterion of pleasure, so that there is usually no difficulty in knowing what gives a person pleasure, or what he enjoys doing or having done to him. The rule against depriving someone of pleasure tells one not to do that which will make a person stop feeling like smiling, unless, of course, the person wants you to.

Many philosophers have been tempted to regard "pleasure" as a word that each person discovers the meaning of by introspection. But though this may sound plausible for pleasure, and even more plausible for pain, it has the absurd consequence that no one knows what anyone else means when he talks of pleasure or pain. I shall talk of smiling as the criterion of pleasure, even though I am aware there are many different kinds of smiles and that it is only certain kinds of smiles together with other facial and bodily characteristics that serve as criteria of pleasure. Similarly, I shall talk of wincing as the criterion of pain, even though this involves a vast oversimplification. It is only by employing these criteria that we can account for people understanding what others mean by pleasure and pain. To feel pleasure is to feel like smiling; to feel pain is to feel like wincing. It is no accident that pleasure and pain are sometimes called feelings. This account of pleasure and pain also makes understandable how so many diverse things can be pleasing as well as painful, for many different things make us feel like smiling and many make us wince. An ice cream cone, a job well done, the easing of a pain, and a smile from one we love, all give pleasure. And an unexpected insult may make us wince as much as a slap in the face.

Contrasting pleasure with pain is slightly misleading. Although smiling and wincing are usually incompatible, the case of the masochist shows that they are not necessarily so. An equally valid contrast is that between smiling and crying. This contrast lies behind our contrasting happy with sad. However, smiling and crying, like smiling and wincing, can occur together, so that sadness should not be regarded as the best contrast with pleasure. Not surprisingly, the opposite of being pleased is being displeased. Smiling and frowning, which is the most salient criterion of being displeased, cannot occur together. The second rule, prohibiting causing pain, should be regarded not only as prohibiting making someone feel like wincing, but also making her feel like crying or frowning. Anxiety, an extremely unpleasant feeling, is also a part of the list of things prohibited by the second rule, but I shall not even try to describe its most salient behavioral criterion, because even more than the other feelings its behavioral criteria are more easily recognized than described.

Even this brief account of pleasure, pain, sadness, displeasure and anxiety makes it clear that one need be feeling none of these. One need not feel like smiling, wincing, crying, frowning, nor have any closely related feeling. In fact, even the most casual examination of people around one leads to the view that most people most of the time are feeling neither pleasure, pain, sadness, displeasure, nor anxiety. This is not to say that they are not in some state which may lead to their having one of the feelings mentioned above. If they are uninterested in what they are doing they are very likely to become bored, which is a form of displeasure that is extremely annoying. If they are absorbed in some activity so that they are likely to be pleased by their recollection of it, we even say that they are enjoying themselves while they are so absorbed. I realize much more must be said in order to provide an adequately precise account of these feelings. But I think that these concepts are sufficiently clear to make the rules in which they are contained understandable enough to be useful.

Final Statement of The Egocentric Attitude

We now have five rules toward which all rational persons would take a certain attitude. The five rules are:

1. Don't kill.
2. Don't cause pain.
3. Don't disable.
4. Don't deprive of freedom.
5. Don't deprive of pleasure.

The egocentric attitude that all rational persons would take toward these five rules, stated with its final modifications, is: "I want all other people to obey the rule with regard to all for whom I am concerned (including myself) except when I have (or would have if I knew the facts) a rational desire not to have the rule obeyed with regard to them." The "except" clause does not imply that all rational persons want the rule not to be obeyed when the clause applies, but only that they need not want it to be obeyed.

A rational person takes the egocentric attitude toward the five rules because he wants to protect himself and those he cares for from certain consequences. These consequences: death, pain, disability, loss of freedom, and loss of pleasure, are the five evils discussed in Chapter 3. All rational persons want to avoid these consequences. The rules can be formulated in order to make this point more obvious:

1. Don't cause death.
2. Don't cause pain.
3. Don't cause loss of ability.
4. Don't cause loss of freedom.
5. Don't cause loss of pleasure.

Stated in this way it becomes clear why a rational person takes the egocentric attitude toward the rules. All rational persons take this attitude toward the rules because they all want to protect themselves and those they care about from suffering any evil. Realizing that evils can be suffered because of the actions of others, they take the egocentric attitude toward the rules. This is why it is rationally required to take the egocentric attitude toward the five rules under discussion (no matter how stated), not because rational persons somehow simply want others to act according to certain rules. This attitude toward these rules is rationally required because it is an attitude required of those who want to avoid the consequences that all rational persons want to avoid.

Rationality does not contain a queer implicit notion that requires rational persons to want all others to act according to moral rules. Moral rules, at least the ones under discussion, are rules that prohibit causing the kinds of consequences that rational persons want to avoid. A rational person wants to avoid these consequences as much when they are brought about by natural causes as when they are brought about by the actions of persons. A rational person wants to avoid death, pain, disability, loss of freedom and loss of pleasure, whether these are caused by an avalanche, or a person, or a mosquito. (It is not surprising that in theology the problem of evil arises in those cases where these evils are brought about, not through the voluntary actions of persons, but simply in the course of nature.)

All of these rules can be broken unintentionally; i.e., a person can bring about the consequences that the rules prohibit causing without intending to do so. A drunken driver can break all five rules, even though he has no intention of doing so. Rational persons are primarily concerned with avoiding suffering evils, not with prohibiting certain kinds of intentional actions. They intend the moral rules not only to prohibit intentional violations, but also to prohibit those kinds of thoughtless actions which would lead to the same undesirable consequences. They not only want others to refrain from intentionally disobeying these rules, they also want them to take care not to break them unintentionally. But since they know that people usually do what they intentionally set out to do, they also want to discourage intentional actions undertaken to violate the rules even if the intention is, without the agent changing his mind, not successfully carried out, e.g., they will count it as a violation of the rule against killing if a person shoots to kill, but misses.

Replacement of the Egocentric Attitude

Although the attitude described above is one that would be taken by all rational persons, it is not the attitude we think should be taken toward the moral rules. The egocentricity of the attitude must be eliminated. We do not normally say that a moral rule ought to be obeyed only toward those for whom one is concerned. I pointed out in the preceding chapter that the moral rules must be obeyed impartially with regard to a group that includes oneself, one's friends and at least all presently existing moral agents. The problem we now face is replacing the egocentric attitude toward the five rules under discussion with an impartial attitude while at the same time keeping it an attitude that would be taken by all rational persons.

In a very important sense, this problem cannot be solved. No adequate account of rationality, according to which no rational person ever wants to do anything irrational, can require all rational persons to favor impartial obedience to these five rules. Rational persons may have rationally allowed beliefs, perhaps based upon the circumstances they are in, or the training or education they have received, such that it would not be irrational for them not to favor impartial obedience to these moral rules. Or they may be so unconcerned with some members of the minimal group that it is rationally allowed for them not to favor impartial obedience to the moral rules.

We have already eliminated the problem caused by rationally allowed beliefs by restricting the beliefs that rational persons can use to those that are rationally required. We can eliminate the problem caused by advocating to too small an audience by requiring that the attitude one adopts toward the rules be such that it would be rational for all persons to accept. The first requirement, restriction to rationally required beliefs, is intimately related to both impartiality and the public character of morality, and the second requirement, that the attitude be one that it would be rational for all rational persons to accept, is also intimately related to morality being a public system that applies to all rational persons. Since I am primarily concerned with showing what attitude all impartial rational persons would take toward these five rules when considered as a part of a public system that applies to all rational persons, these requirements are not arbitrary constraints.

Ensuring that one has the appropriately moral attitude toward the rules requires more than merely limiting the beliefs one uses to those that are shared with all rational persons, i.e., rationally required beliefs. The appropriate attitude also cannot involve, either explicitly or implicitly, any egocentric references. The attitude that everyone obey the rule toward me and those for whom I am concerned is clearly not the appropriately moral attitude toward the rules. However, we do not need to add a new constraint on the appropriate attitude because an attitude that contains either explicitly or implicitly egocentric references is not one that it would be rational for all rational persons to accept.

In one sense, an egocentric attitude is one that it would be rational for all rational persons to accept, i.e., they all want the rules obeyed with regard to themselves and those for whom they are concerned. But in a more important sense, they do not accept the same attitude, for most persons are concerned with different groups of people. Although we may express our attitudes in the same words, your attitude toward the rules is not the same as mine if we are concerned with different groups of people. This being the case, it will be irrational for someone for whom I am not concerned and who is not concerned with me to accept my egocentric attitude toward the rules. It will be irrational for such persons to accept my egocentric attitude because doing so restricts their freedom and increases their chances of suffering the other evils in order to benefit those for whom they are not concerned, when the evils they will suffer, or their chances of suffering these evils, are greater than the evils they will avoid causing or prevent.

Unless she had an impartial concern for all rational persons, the egocentric attitude that a rational person accepted would be one that it would be irrational for some other rational person to accept. Each rational person will at least demand that the attitude be modified so as to include herself and those for whom she cares. Thus if one requires that the attitude be one that it would be rational for all persons to accept, the attitude that must be adopted is that the rules be obeyed with regard to, at least, all rational persons. A rational person also knows that all other rational persons want her to obey the rules. Thus insofar as the attitude adopted must be one that it would not be irrational for all other rational persons to accept, one must advocate that the rules be obeyed by everyone, including oneself. Adding the condition that all other rational persons could accept the same attitude, a rational person cannot adopt any attitude toward the rules except one like that which would be adopted by a rational person who has an impartial concern for all rational persons. Thus it seems that we can have all rational persons adopt the appropriate attitude toward the moral rules by adding the feature that the attitude they adopt be one that could be accepted by all rational persons.

Considering These Rules as Public Rules Applying to All Rational Persons

We now have two constraints limiting the attitude that rational persons must take toward the rules: they can use only rationally required beliefs, and the attitude they accept must be one that could be accepted by all rational persons. These two constraints are also the constraints that must be accepted when one considers any rule as a public rule that applies to all rational persons, i.e., as a moral rule. When one considers these rules as moral rules in this sense, then one is taking what I call "a moral attitude" toward the rules. This allows for a conflict between the moral attitude a rational person takes toward these rules and the attitude that one really holds toward them. It is this latter attitude that is most likely to serve as a guide to one's actions. The attitude one adopts toward these rules considered as moral rules is not necessarily the attitude that one actually takes toward these rules or wants others to take toward these rules. The moral attitude that one takes toward these rules need not be sincere, though of course it may be.

I have now shown that if a person is considering these rules as moral rules, she must adopt an attitude that could be agreed upon by all rational persons. Thus the attitude that will be adopted will be an impartial rather than an egocentric attitude. Since what I wished to do was to replace the egocentric attitude with an impartial one, I may now claim to have accomplished this task. However, it may be interesting to consider whether one can accomplish this task using only the condition that one can use only those beliefs that are rationally required. This means that one does not use any beliefs about her gender, social position, abilities, wealth, race, religion, nationality, whom she cares for, or who cares for her. Every personal and general belief that she holds is one that is held by every other rational person; she differs from other rational persons only in her desires, for I have not added the condition that a rational person have only rationally required desires, but allow any rational desire that is possible using only rationally required beliefs. No rational person will desire to avoid the goods, and all will desire to avoid the evils, but they will not rank them in the same way. When faced with a choice between two evils or between two goods, rational persons, having only rationally required beliefs, may sometimes make different choices.

I am now examining whether the constraint that one use only rationally required beliefs, by itself, has the result that all rational persons will adopt the attitude that the rules under consideration be obeyed by all with regard to all with no egocentric exceptions. Is this constraint sufficient to make rational persons replace their egocentric attitude with a more appropriate attitude toward these rules? Rational persons not only desire to avoid the evils caused by violations of these rules, they also desire everyone for whom they are concerned to avoid these evils. Since they may be concerned with all rational persons, it seems that the attitude they would take toward these rules is that they be obeyed impartially with regard to all. It seems as if at least part of the egocentricity of the attitude would be eliminated.

Would a rational person also take the attitude that the rules be obeyed by all, including herself? She knows that all rational persons desire to avoid the evils that the moral rules prohibit causing, so she knows that rational persons do not want her to inflict unwanted evil on them. She is aware that taking any attitude toward the moral rules other than that they be obeyed by all rational persons, including herself, with regard to all, is not going to be accepted by all rational persons. If she does not care whether or not her attitude would be accepted by all rational persons, then this need not determine what attitude she takes. However, if she were truly impartial, then she would take an attitude that these rules be obeyed by all with regard to all. I conclude that simply limiting a person's beliefs to those that are rationally required is not sufficient to guarantee that she will take the appropriate attitude toward these rules. However, adding that the person is impartial does result in her taking the appropriate attitude.

Given the constraint that one use only rationally required beliefs we can now see the close connection between being impartial and the condition that one's attitude be acceptable to all rational persons. I have tried to show that, given the limitation to rationally required beliefs, if one is impartial, one will adopt the same attitude as one who is considering these rules as moral rules. One might even adopt as the test of one's considering a rule as a moral rule that one is using only rationally required beliefs and is impartial with regard to all persons to whose behavior the rule applies. Conversely, one can adopt as a test of one's impartiality with regard to the rules that one is considering them as moral rules, that is, as public rules that are understood and could be accepted by all rational persons.

If the argument of the previous paragraphs is correct, when one is limited to rationally required beliefs, then impartiality toward the moral rules and considering them as moral rules are very intimately related. Also it is interesting that simply by accepting the limitations that one use only rationally required beliefs and that one adopt an attitude toward the rules that is acceptable to all rational persons, one necessarily considers these rules as moral rules. This shows that there is more in the writings of those who regard the moral law as the natural law than they are usually given credit for. For natural law is regarded as that law which is known and agreeable to all rational persons. What the defenders of the natural law account of morality were missing was an adequate account of rationality.

I have now shown that once one has limited rational persons to using only rationally required beliefs, one can replace the egocentric attitude toward the rules by an appropriately moral attitude, either by adding the constraint that the person also be impartial, or the constraint that the attitude be one that would be acceptable to all rational persons. I have argued that it does not make any difference which of these constraints one chooses, as both of them, independently, would result in all rational persons taking the appropriately moral attitude toward these rules. However, I admitted that a rational person need not accept either the limitation to rationally required beliefs or to either one of the added constraints. However, the limitation to rationally required beliefs was shown to be necessary to provide any agreement at all among all rational persons, even on the egocentric attitude. Further, since morality must be understandable to all rational persons, this limitation is necessary in order to ensure that the moral system will be understandable to all rational persons.

The constraint that one's attitude be one that is acceptable to all rational persons is also necessary in order for one to consider these rules as moral rules. For as we have pointed out, morality is a public system that applies to all rational persons, and this requires not only that all rational persons understand it, but also that it not be irrational for them to accept it. These two constraints, the limitation to rationally required beliefs and that the attitude be acceptable to all rational persons, guarantee that one regards these rules as moral rules. The constraint that one be impartial is also a natural constraint when talking about morality, for it is universally acknowledged that the moral rules require impartial obedience. This constraint together with the limitation to rationally required beliefs also seems to result in every rational person taking the appropriately moral attitude toward these rules.

If one accepts either of the combination of constraints discussed above, then one will consider these rules as moral rules, i.e., will take the appropriately moral attitude toward these rules. Whether one describes this attitude as regarding these rules as public rules that apply to all rational persons or as taking an attitude toward these rules with the kind of impartiality that moral rules require makes little difference. The important point is to determine the features of the attitude that impartial rational persons would take with respect to the rules discussed so far when considering them as moral rules. One can do this by seeing what follows from moral impartiality, or what follows from considering these rules as public rules applying to all rational persons, or what follows from the two of them together. It would probably be more elegant to use only one of these, but since morality involves both impartiality and publicity, I shall use both of them.

The Attitude of Impartial Rational Persons Toward Violations of the Rules

An impartial rational person's attitude toward these rules considered as public rules applying to all rational persons does not encourage blind obedience to them. On the contrary, it allows that quite often they need not be obeyed. Less often, all impartial rational persons may even advocate that they should not be obeyed. Not only are there justified violations of the moral rules, there is even unjustified keeping of them. For an impartial rational person does not have a fetish for neat, uncluttered obedience to rules, but desires, insofar as possible, to avoid the unwanted evil consequences that usually result from violation of the moral rules. Sometimes, violation of a moral rule may result in preventing significantly more evil than is caused by the violation. This possibility must be taken into account in formulating an attitude toward the rules that would be taken by an impartial rational person. Since these rules are being considered as part of a public system applying to all rational persons, all violations must be such that they can be publicly allowed. A publicly allowed violation is a violation that is understood and can be accepted by all rational persons.

In Chapter 2 we saw that only those actions which would be irrational if one did not have a reason for them needed to be justified. By providing reasons which showed either that the action was rationally allowed or, less frequently, rationally required, such actions could be justified. Rational justification simply consists in providing reasons which are adequate to make an otherwise irrational action rational. In a similar manner, only those actions which would be immoral if one did not have a reason need to be morally justified. These are violations of the moral rules. A violation can be justified by providing reasons which would result in either some impartial rational persons advocating that that kind of violation be publicly allowed, or less frequently, all impartial rational persons advocating that such a violation be publicly allowed.

When all impartial rational persons would advocate that a violation be publicly allowed, no impartial rational person would condemn or punish such a violation, and I call it a strongly justified violation, e.g., breaking a trivial promise in order to save a life. Not only are such violations not immoral, obeying the rule in these circumstances would be morally wrong, i.e., no impartial rational person would advocate obeying the rule. When impartial rational persons differ on whether or not they would advocate that a violation be publicly allowed, I call it a weakly justified violation, e.g., breaking a bad law in order to get it changed. All impartial rational persons advocate liability to punishment for some weakly justified violations and some impartial rational persons advocate liability to punishment for all weakly justified violations. Most genuine moral perplexities arise when considering whether to advocate performing one of these kinds of violations, or deciding what to do when someone else performs one of them. When no impartial rational person would advocate that a violation be publicly allowed it is a morally unjustified violation, e.g., killing people in order to get their money. All impartial rational persons would advocate that such violations may be punished.

One kind of strongly justified violation occurs when, with her consent, one inflicts an evil on a rational person in order to prevent her suffering a significantly greater evil. This is an extremely common occurrence in medicine; most doctors do this daily. A kind of weakly justified violation sometimes occurs when significantly greater evil is prevented by breaking the rule than is caused by the violation, though not for the same persons. This kind of violation is often involved in government regulation of companies who are causing health problems by polluting the atmosphere. Since much government regulation involves a deprivation of freedom which is only weakly justified, it is not surprising that there is so much controversy concerning it. Morally unjustified violations include most criminal actions; the rule is broken simply in order to promote good for oneself or for someone for whom one is concerned.

An impartial rational person's attitude toward the moral rules must take account of the different kinds of violations. The following is the first formulation of what counts as the morally appropriate attitude, I shall call it the "moral attitude": "Everyone is to obey the rule with regard to everyone except when an impartial rational person can advocate that the violation be publicly allowed." The "except" clause does not mean that all impartial rational persons agree that one is not to obey the moral rule when an impartial rational person could advocate that the violation be publicly allowed, but only that they do not agree that one should obey the rule in this situation.

What Counts as Depriving?

In order to fully understand the moral attitude, one must understand what counts as obeying a rule and what counts as violating it. It is not as obvious as it seems, what counts as depriving someone of freedom or pleasure, so that the

rules against depriving someone of pleasure and freedom need some further clarification. Doing something which causes a person to have less freedom or pleasure counts as depriving him of freedom or pleasure. The action may be done
intentionally or knowingly, but it may also be done thoughtlessly. Someone who
talks loudly during a concert with the result that I can no longer enjoy it is
depriving me of pleasure, independently of whether that was his intention or
even whether he was aware of that consequence. Failing to act does not count
as depriving someone of pleasure or freedom unless that failure to act is a violation of one of the second five moral rules (to be discussed in the following
chapter). If someone does not give me a ride to the concert, he is not depriving
me of the opportunity to hear it unless by not doing so he has violated a moral
rule; e.g., he has broken his promise to give me a ride. Failing to act does not
count as violating either the rule against depriving of freedom or the rule against
depriving of pleasure unless such failure violates one of the second five moral
rules.

Further, even some actions that result in someone having less freedom or
pleasure than they would have if I had not performed that action do not count
as depriving that person of freedom or pleasure. For example, if I am waiting in
line to buy some tickets for a football game, I am not violating the rule against
depriving of freedom (opportunity) if I buy the last ticket and no one else standing behind me in the line can go to the game. Nor am I depriving someone of
pleasure if I buy the last bag of popcorn. But am I not doing something that
causes others to have less freedom or opportunity? I claim that I am not. If I
were, I would need a justification or excuse for buying the last ticket or the last
bag of popcorn in order to avoid moral condemnation of my action. But I do
not need any such justification or excuse; I can buy the last ticket or the popcorn
simply because I want to and not thereby be doing anything immoral.

If I intentionally act in order to make it impossible for someone to see the
football game, e.g. buy up all the remaining tickets, I am acting immorally. Now
suppose my action results in someone having less freedom or pleasure, but is
not intentionally done in order to deprive someone of freedom or pleasure and
is not a violation of one of the second five moral rules. Should my action be
taken as violating a moral rule, e.g., as in the case of talking too loudly at a
concert, or as not violating the rule, e.g., as in buying the last ticket? It may seem
as if deciding this is determined by whether we count my action as causing the
person to have less freedom or pleasure. However, I think that the opposite is
true, that what counts as causing a person to have less freedom or pleasure is
determined by what counts as depriving someone of freedom or pleasure, and
that this is determined by how one interprets the moral rules against depriving
of freedom or pleasure.

What Counts as Causing an Evil?

The problems that arise in determining what counts as causing death, pain, and
disability are the same problems that arise in determining what counts as depriving of freedom and pleasure. As with the rules against depriving of freedom and

pleasure, the failure to act does not count as a violation of the rules against killing, causing pain, and disabling, unless such failure is also a violation of one of the second five rules. When the failure to act is a violation of one of the second five rules and the result is that some person suffers an evil, then it is also a violation of one of the first five rules and counts as causing an evil. It is only in these circumstances that failing to act counts as causing an evil. However, as indicated by the previous discussion, this does not mean that all actions which result in some person suffering one of the evils is a violation of one of the first five rules and counts as causing the evil.

In the morally relevant sense, I cause an evil by my action only when I can correctly be said to have violated one of these moral rules by my action. This is just the reverse of what one might have expected to be the case, i.e., that I can be said to have violated one of these rules only when my action causes someone to suffer an evil. In most problematic cases, we determine what counts as causing an evil by determining whether or not we want to say that one of these rules has been broken rather than the reverse. It is our view on whether or not the person needs an excuse or a justification in order to avoid moral condemnation that determines whether or not we say that he caused the evil. There is no scientific sense of cause that can be used to settle whether or not some particular act counts as causing an evil. This accounts for some of the disagreement that is so common about whether people in the rich countries are causing the misery of those in the poor ones.

This does not mean that it is an entirely arbitrary matter whether or not one is violating one of these moral rules. First, intentionally causing an evil is the same thing as intentionally violating one of these rules. Second, there are some cases where, even if unintentional, one's action counts as a violation of one of these rules. For example, driving a car and skidding on a slippery patch of road and thereby hitting someone, counts as causing the evil that the person hit suffers. This is true even if one's hitting the person was not only unintentional, but was also unforeseeable and not due to any negligence on one's part. If the latter is true, then one is totally excused, but one still violated the relevant rule. What counts as a totally excusable violation of a moral rule and what counts as no violation of it at all are determined by the interpretation of the rule. It is this interpretation which determines whether or not one has caused the evil and thus needs an excuse or justification, or has not done anything which even needs an excuse or justification. What is sometimes discussed under the topic of rights is best understood as a way of discussing the interpretation of these rules.

Rights

It is commonly said that everyone has the right not to be killed. The same seems to be true of the right not to be caused pain, not to be disabled, not to be deprived of freedom, and not to be deprived of pleasure. These rights are claimed to be not merely legal rights, they are said to be moral rights. One of the clearest ways to see the intimate relationship, perhaps even one of identity, between violating one of these basic rights and breaking a basic moral rule, is to consider the question, "Who can violate rights?" (My daughter, Heather, is the one who led me to consider this question.) It then becomes obvious that only moral agents can violate rights. Your rights are violated when a moral agent breaks the relevant moral rule with regard to you, e.g., she violates your right not to be killed by breaking the moral rule against killing with regard to you. With regard to the rights mentioned above, it seems to me that talking about rights and my way of talking about moral rules may simply be two ways of talking about the same thing.

On my account of the moral rules, they are not merely useful rules that indicate what way of acting will result in the least amount of evil being suffered, they provide strong protection to the individual against violations done in order to benefit others. The moral attitude toward the moral rules does allow for some justified violations, viz., when impartial rational persons can advocate that such a violation be publicly allowed. These cases will coincide with those cases where some impartial rational persons will hold that it is morally justifiable to violate or override a person's rights. When John kills Jane, either we can say that John has violated Jane's moral right not to be killed or we can say that John violated the moral rule against killing with regard to Jane. I prefer the latter way of talking because it seems to me to allow a conceptually clearer, more precise, and more fruitful way of discussing the moral aspects of killing and of causing any other evil.

Although I do not see the usefulness of talking about rights not to suffer the evils that the moral rules prohibit causing, it does seem to me that other rights may play a useful role in explaining how the first five rules should be interpreted. As mentioned in the last section, there are sometimes disagreements as to whether an action that results in someone suffering an evil counts as breaking a moral rule. I have already pointed out that if one violates one of the second five moral rules (to be discussed in the next chapter) then if an evil results, this counts as violating one of the first five. Since one of these second five moral rules prohibits breaking the law, the law can determine whether or not one has violated one of the first five moral rules, and can therefore determine whether or not one has caused someone to suffer an evil. Thus the law can determine whether someone's right not to suffer one of the evils has been violated even when we are talking about moral rights and not merely legal ones, assuming of course, that the law itself is morally acceptable.

Sometimes when no law is violated and none of the other second five rules violated, we still have to decide whether the evil suffered by John has been caused by Jane, that is, we have to decide whether or not Jane has violated one of the first five moral rules with regard to John. It is in these situations that rights are useful. Consider the situation mentioned earlier where one person in a concert talks very loudly with the result that someone else is deprived of pleasure. In this situation we regard the first person as having broken the moral rule against depriving of pleasure because we hold that the first person did not have the right to talk loudly during the concert and the second person did have the right to listen to the concert. Now consider the situation where I buy the last ticket to the game with the result that the other people behind me in line cannot see the game. In this situation, I have the right to buy the ticket and they do not have any right to see the game. In this situation, we say that I did not break the rule against depriving people of freedom or pleasure. If I am acting within my rights and not violating others' rights, then even if what I do results in their suffering some evil, I have still not violated a moral rule with regard to them unless I intentionally acted in order to bring about this result.

Suppose we are wondering about whether or not Jane, who is annoyed by John's looking at her, has been caused to suffer this evil by John, that is, whether John has violated the moral rule against causing pain with regard to Jane. If we hold that people have a right to privacy, then it will be relevant to determine the circumstances in which John looked at Jane. If John is standing on a street corner looking at all the women who pass without making any overt moves to approach the women, then even if Jane is annoyed at being looked at, it would not be correct to say that John had broken a moral rule with regard to Jane. John has the right to look wherever he wants in public and Jane has no right to walk on the street unlooked at. However, if John is peering through Jane's window, then by invoking the right to privacy, we can say that Jane's annoyance at being looked at is caused by John, that John has violated a moral rule with regard to Jane. John has no right to look in Jane's window and Jane has a right to be in her room unlooked at. The right to privacy helps us to determine when to say that a given moral rule is being violated.

Another example. Suppose a photographer is following a famous person around, constantly taking pictures of him. He is annoyed and asks her to stop. She claims that his annoyance is his own problem, that she has the right to take any pictures she wants as long as he is in a public place and that he has no right to be in a public place unphotographed. He claims that he has a right to be left alone, even in public places, and that she has no right to photograph him whenever she wants. He claims a right to privacy and denies her right to photograph him. She claims a right to photograph and denies his right to privacy. She is claiming that she is not violating the moral rule against causing pain (annoyance), and he is claiming that she is. Who is correct? This depends upon the society. It is a particular society that determines that one has no right to talk loudly in a concert and that one does have a right to listen to a concert. It is a particular society that determines whether one has the right to look at people in public or in private. It is also a particular society that determines how much one has a right to be left alone and how much of a right one has to photograph people.

Sometimes these rights are determined by courts of law, but often there is simply a general understanding which has no formal legal standing. In a particular society it is just generally understood that when John suffers an evil as a result of Jane's action, Jane is sometimes regarded as having caused John to suffer that evil and sometimes not; that is, sometimes Jane is regarded as having violated the relevant moral rule with regard to John and sometimes not. In our society that is often expressed in terms of rights. I do not claim that there are universal rights. On my view, rights, like the right to privacy, are introduced by a society as an aid in determining what counts as a violation of one of the first five moral rules. But since each society introduces its own right to privacy, even if a society has a right to privacy, it may not have the same scope as another society with a similar right; that is, it may not result in the same interpretation of the moral rules.

Talk about fundamental rights, such as the right not to be killed, involves issues that are more clearly discussed by talk about moral rules. Saying that one has a right not to be killed is more clearly said by saying that there is a moral rule against killing. Saying that one's rights should be protected says no more than saying that the moral rules should be enforced. To say that one is justified in violating someone's right not to suffer a particular evil is to say that one is justified in violating the relevant moral rule with regard to him. Sometimes, we say that a person has a right, e.g., a child has the right to be fed, when it would be clearer to say that someone else would be violating his duty if he did not feed her. I do not claim that the simple translations that I have offered are completely adequate, but I do claim that with regard to these fundamental rights, nothing is involved that cannot be dealt with by talking only of the corresponding moral rules.

However, I do not regard what I call non-fundamental rights, such as the right to privacy, or the right to a clean environment, as being similarly superfluous. They are useful as aids in determining, for a given society, what is regarded as a violation of one of the first five moral rules. They account for the ounce of truth in the ethical relativist's claim that different societies have different moral rules. The moral rules are completely universal but, when they are not intentionally violated and there is no violation of any of the second five rules, what counts as a violation is interpreted differently by different societies. Some of this interpretation is expressed by talking about rights. Thus, unlike the moral rules which are unchanging, rights can change and develop as we come to interpret the moral rules differently. When I talk of the moral rules in what follows, it must be kept in mind that I recognize that there may be some differences in determining what counts as a violation of one of these rules.

Punishment Is Part of a Moral System

Although all rational persons, if impartial, will adopt the moral attitude toward the moral rules, not all rational persons are impartial, and hence not all will obey the rules as the moral attitude requires. Although impartial rationality requires adopting the moral attitude, rationality does not require acting on this attitude. Rationality always allows, but it does not always require, acting morally. It is the mark of a false theory to "prove" that it is irrational to act immorally. The most that one can hope to show is that all impartial rational persons will take the moral attitude toward all of the justified moral rules. But all impartial rational persons are aware that their agreement on the moral attitude does not guarantee that no one will violate a moral rule except when an impartial rational person could advocate that violating it be publicly allowed. A rational person need not be a hypocrite, but all rational persons are aware of the possibility of hypocrisy. Awareness of the possibility of unjustified violation of the rules requires us to consider an impartial rational person's attitude toward such violations.

It is clear that all rational persons wish to discourage the breaking of these rules, at least with regard to those for whom they are concerned. They know, however, that the morally appropriate attitude toward the rules requires impartial treatment of all those who unjustifiably break the rules with regard to anyone. A rational person, insofar as she is impartially concerned with protecting everyone from suffering the evils caused by violations of the moral rules, will support measures which will discourage anyone from unjustifiably breaking these rules. If this were her only consideration, she might recommend the harshest measures to be used against anyone unjustifiably breaking the rules. However, she has another consideration: namely, what will happen to those who unjustifiably break any of the rules. To adopt as part of the public system the harshest possible measures against anyone who breaks the rule might result in excessively harsh measures toward those who break the law. They would be excessive because much greater evil would be inflicted on violators than would be prevented by such infliction of evil. An impartial rational person must be as concerned with those who violate the rules as with those who are victims of the violation.

The measures adopted must be harsh enough to discourage most serious unjustified violations of the rules, not only intentional ones, but also those done thoughtlessly. An impartial rational person will be prepared to do more to prevent those violations of the rules which cause the greatest amount of evil consequences. Hence he will, as an impartial rational person, adopt harsher measures for the violation of the rule against killing than for violation of the rule against the deprivation of pleasure. The harshness of the measures for violations of rules against causing pain, disabling, and deprivation of freedom will vary according to the degree of pain, disability, and loss of freedom. In some cases, the amount of pain, disability, or loss of freedom may demand measures as harsh as that against killing; in others, as little as that against the deprivation of pleasure.

Since the public system must discourage everyone from unjustifiably breaking the rules, the kinds of measures adopted to discourage violations of the rules must be those that will in fact serve to discourage all rational persons from unjustifiably breaking the rules. Only the infliction of evil on the violator is this kind of measure, for we saw in Chapter 3 that only the infliction of an evil serves to discourage all from performing an unwanted act. The question arises, "What evil?" Perhaps the same one that the violator inflicted on some person. If he killed, let him be killed; if he caused pain, let him have pain inflicted upon him; if he disabled, let him be disabled, etc. Although this formula might appeal to some rational person's aesthetic sense, or sense of fitness of things, it does not seem supported by the best reasons.

The point of inflicting evil on violators is not to establish some fitness, but to prevent further violation of the rules. An eye for an eye may have some appeal, but unless it can be shown that a public system that includes such retribution prevents violations better than a more lenient public system, no impartial rational person will accept it. Of two public systems that inflict evil on violators and are equally good at discouraging violations, an impartial rational person will choose that which inflicts the lesser evil, for his goal is to have the least amount of evil suffered overall. A rational person who is not impartial wants those he cares about protected as much as possible from those he does not care about, and to have as little evil as possible inflicted on those he cares about when they break the rules with regard to those he does not care about. An impartial rational person is equally concerned with all.

Given his goal, an impartial rational person can decide between public systems which discourage violators equally well by picking that which is most lenient, i.e., inflicts the least evil; and of all those public systems which are equally lenient, by picking that which most discourages violations. Here, of course, rationality requires trying to find out what effect adopting public systems with different sets of evils would, in fact, have in discouraging future violations. This cannot be known *a priori*. Further, between a public system which includes as punishments a set of evils which is harsher and better at discouraging violations and one which is less harsh and not as good at discouraging violations, impartial rationality allows either choice. One impartial rational person may prefer the balance one way; another, the other way. One impartial rational person may be prepared to allow more evil to be inflicted on violators to prevent a given amount of evil for victims than some other impartial rational person because she gives greater weight to the morally relevant consideration that the evil is a punishment for violating a moral rule. Some rational persons may prefer a public system that results in the least number of people suffering the most serious evils, without even considering whether it is victims or violators that will be suffering. But even here there may not always be agreement on what counts as the most serious evils.

A moral system allows evils to be inflicted on those who unjustifiably violate the rules in order to discourage future violation of the rules. Thus the public system will allow punishment only for those violators who are capable of guiding their actions by the rules. It will not, except under special circumstances, allow inflicting evil on those who violate the rules through no fault of their own, either through excusable ignorance of the consequences of their actions or through inability to act according to their knowledge. These special circumstances are those where knowing that evil will be inflicted if one causes evil, no matter what, results in significantly less evil being caused. Absent these special circumstances, the public system will not allow inflicting evil in these cases because, by hypothesis, allowing such infliction of evils will do nothing to discourage violations and will allow inflicting evil on those who violate the rules through excusable ignorance or inability to act. This is simply a special case of choosing between two systems which equally discourage violations when one of them is more lenient than the other.

Using the Moral Attitude to Distinguish Moral from Non-Moral Rules

This seeming digression on an impartial rational person's attitude toward those who unjustifiably violate the rules provides an important feature of an impartial rational person's attitude toward the moral rules. I count as a moral rule any rule toward which all impartial rational persons adopt the appropriate moral attitude. If we accept "Everyone is to obey the rule with regard to everyone except when an impartial rational person could advocate that the violation be publicly allowed," as the appropriate moral attitude, then a number of obviously non-moral rules might be regarded as moral rules. For example, the rule "Promote pleasure" might be considered a moral rule, for it may seem that all impartial rational persons would favor adopting this attitude toward this rule. In order to more clearly distinguish this rule from the moral rules, one must include in the appropriate moral attitude an impartial rational person's attitude toward those who unjustifiably violate a moral rule. All impartial rational persons would adopt the attitude that all those who unjustifiably violate the moral rules be liable to punishment. Failure to include this feature as part of the public system would lessen the protection from violations that all impartial rational persons desire.

An impartial rational person's attitude toward each of the moral rules can now be stated as follows: "Everyone is to obey the rule with regard to everyone except when an impartial rational person can advocate that the violation be publicly allowed. Anyone who violates the rule when no impartial rational person can advocate that such a violation be publicly allowed may be punished." This is the second formulation of what I call the moral attitude. Only those rules toward which all impartial rational persons would adopt this attitude count as genuine or basic or justifiable moral rules. It is clear that all impartial rational persons would adopt the moral attitude toward the five rules discussed in this chapter. Thus we may now be said to have justified five moral rules, or to have shown that at least five rules are justifiable or genuine or basic moral rules.

One of the reasons for including an impartial rational person's attitude toward unjustified violations into the moral attitude was to make clear that "Promote pleasure" is not a moral rule. Thus it should be no surprise that not all impartial rational persons would adopt the newly stated moral attitude toward the rule "Promote pleasure." Indeed it is doubtful if any impartial rational person would adopt this attitude. Unlike the five moral rules, this rule cannot possibly be obeyed all of the time. Nor is it likely that it can ever be obeyed with regard to everyone. This requires an impartial rational person either to adopt the attitude that anyone be allowed to violate the rule with regard to most people whenever he feels like doing so or else to adopt the attitude that everyone be liable to punishment all or almost all of the time. To do the former would make it pointless to adopt the moral attitude toward the rule; to do the latter would be to increase everyone's chances of suffering evil. I see little likelihood of any impartial rational person adopting the moral attitude toward the rule "Promote pleasure."

The same arguments show that "Prevent evil" is also not a moral rule. It might seem more plausible that some impartial rational persons might adopt the moral attitude toward this rule. However, the impossibility of obeying the rule all of the time with regard to everyone makes it quite clear that no impartial rational person would adopt the moral attitude toward it. The addition of the impartial rational person's attitude toward unjustified violations even eliminates as moral rules modifications of the above rules that can be obeyed all of the time. Consider the rule "Offer to promote pleasure for the first person you see each day." This rule may not have the generality required of moral rules, but even ignoring this, not all impartial rational persons would adopt the moral attitude toward it. An impartial rational person need not hold that the increase in the chances of having one's pleasure promoted is greater than the risk of suffering punishment. The same kind of point holds even when we substitute "prevent pain" for "promote pleasure" in the rule, for unless the rule is pointless because all impartial rational persons would advocate publicly allowing violating it whenever one felt like doing so, an impartial rational person need not hold that it decreases the chances of people suffering evils.

The Punishment Provision

Including in the moral attitude the provision that unjustified violations may be punished has made the moral attitude into a test which excludes the rules that we want excluded and includes the rules we want included. Since this provision serves such an important task, it merits examination in some more detail. I have said that an impartial rational person adopts as part of his moral attitude that unjustified violations *may* be punished. What is the point of the "may"? Why didn't I say that unjustified violations are to be punished? I could indeed have said this. But then I would have needed to qualify this. There may be situations in which punishing unjustified violations would cause significantly more evil than would result from failure to punish. This could be true even if it were part of the public system that such violations are not to be punished. In these cases, impartial rational persons would not advocate punishment even if punishment is determined in the way that we outlined earlier in the chapter.

An impartial rational person does not advocate that unjustified violations be punished in order to achieve some metaphysical fitness in the nature of things. His goal is to minimize the amount of evil suffered, which is generally best served by punishing unjustified violations. But if it is not, an impartial rational person is not committed to punishment. That is why impartial rational persons advocate only that those who unjustifiably violate the rules *may* be punished rather than simply say that they are to be punished. There are also further reasons. To advocate punishment requires someone to do the punishing. Who this someone should be and how he should go about his job is more properly a subject for political philosophy than for moral philosophy. Some things, however, should be said. First, it usually will be the responsibility of the government to punish. However, setting up a system that results in punishing all unjustified violations may cost more than it is worth.

On a more personal level parents are generally considered to have the responsibility to punish their children for less serious violations. A parent may know that punishing his child for an unjustified violation will do more harm than good. Thus though the child has put himself in a position where he may be punished, I do not want to assert categorically that he should be. If punishment is the best way to discourage future violations, I think that children should usually be punished for unjustified violations, but one must admit that there are times when they should not be. To insist that unjustified violations demand punishment, regardless of the consequences, is to allow one's desire for retribution to overwhelm what one knows is the rational way to behave.

Advocating That Violations Be Publicly Allowed

Since the moral attitude allows breaking the rule only when an impartial rational person could advocate that breaking it be publicly allowed, it is important to examine what is involved in advocating that a violation be publicly allowed. An impartial rational person can advocate that a violation be publicly allowed only if all rational persons understand and are able to accept what he is advocating. This means that an impartial rational person who advocates that a violation of a rule be publicly allowed must provide a description of the violation that is understood and can be accepted by all rational persons. Suppose it is correct to describe a violation as one in which the person toward whom one is violating the rule has made a rational request that the rule be violated with regard to him because the violation will prevent significantly more evil than it causes. This description is such that all impartial rational persons would advocate that a violation of the rule be publicly allowed.

A clear example of this kind is one in which a person requests that his doctor give him a painful rabies shot because he knows that failure to have it will result in significantly greater pain and death. In fact, in this example, given the extremely horrible nature of death by rabies, even if the person, solely because of his irrational fear of present pain, refuses the rabies shot, still all fully informed impartial rational persons would advocate that giving it to him be publicly allowed. However, when the evil that a person would suffer if you did not break the rule with regard to him is not of this magnitude, even if it is indisputably significantly greater than the evil he would suffer if you did break the rule, then impartial rational persons may disagree on whether they would advocate that breaking the rule with regard to him when he does not consent to it be publicly allowed. If it is not indisputably significantly greater then no impartial rational person would advocate that such a violation be publicly allowed. (This is why informed consent is so important in medicine.)

Impartial rational persons may also advocate that violating a moral rule whenever this results in significantly less evil being suffered be publicly allowed, even when the evil is shifted from one person to another. However, it must be indisputable that the evil being prevented by the violation is significantly greater than the evil caused. But even when this is the case, impartial rational persons may still disagree on what violations they advocate publicly allowing. One impartial rational person might advocate that killing one person in order to save fifty others be publicly allowed. He might feel that this will decrease the future possibilities of rational persons suffering preventable deaths. Another might not advocate that a violation be publicly allowed in this situation unless the first person was the one who was going to kill the other fifty. He might feel that publicly allowing this kind of killing of the innocent would result in such a significant decrease in the protection from violations of the rule for the innocent, plus general anxiety due to added uncertainty, that it more than offsets the possible benefit. Thus we can see that even when the evil being caused by violation of the rule is significantly less than that which one believes will be prevented by the violation, there will be some impartial rational persons who will not advocate that a violation of the rule be publicly allowed.

Nonetheless, there are extreme cases in which all impartial rational persons would advocate that a violation be publicly allowed even if the evil is to be switched from one person to another. There is a point at which the amount of evil to be prevented by breaking the rule is so much greater than the amount of evil caused by breaking it, that one ought to break it. For example, if an innocent child contracts some highly dangerous and infectious disease, similar to that which causes plagues, it will be justifiable to deprive him of his liberty in order to keep the plague from spreading. An impartial rational person would advocate that some violation of the rules be publicly allowed even if not for the benefit of the person with regard to whom the rule is violated. However, she would not do this lightly, and some impartial rational persons will demand an extremely high proportion of evil prevented to evil caused before they would advocate that a violation be publicly allowed. Further, all impartial rational persons will demand good specific reasons for believing that significantly more evil is being prevented by violating than by obeying the rule before advocating that it be publicly allowed.

Punishment is also a violation of the moral rules which is sometimes justifiable. Of course, one must be the appropriate person to administer the punishment. There also is a further limitation: namely, more evil should not be inflicted than an impartial rational person could advocate be publicly allowed for this kind of violation. Publicly allowing a violation of the rules in order to prevent a violation of a rule would also be advocated by some impartial rational persons. However, no impartial rational persons would advocate publicly allowing the infliction of greater evil than would have been publicly allowed as the punishment for the violation of the rule unless significantly greater evil is being prevented. If these provisions are not met, then I do not see the possibility of any impartial rational persons still advocating that it be publicly allowed.

Any significant violation of these rules with regard to one person in order to obtain goods for other people, including oneself, is an unjustifiable violation. No impartial rational person would advocate that this kind of violation be publicly allowed. Although some impartial rational person might advocate that a minor violation of these rules be publicly allowed in order to promote a great deal of good for many people, others would not. Some impartial rational persons would never publicly allow inflicting even a minor evil on an unconsenting innocent person unless it was to prevent even greater evil being suffered. No impartial rational person would publicly allow killing and torturing for pleasure, profit or scientific information. It is clearly immoral. However, killing and torturing to prevent greater killing and torturing may sometimes be publicly allowed by some impartial rational persons.

We now see that impartial rational persons may disagree about whether some violations should be publicly allowed. Although all impartial rational persons agree on the moral rules and the appropriate moral attitude to be taken toward them, this does not eliminate genuine cases of moral disagreement. Genuine moral disagreements are those that occur within the larger framework of agreement where it is allowed by impartial rationality to advocate either alternative. In genuine moral controversies each individual has to decide for herself what violations she, considering the question as an impartial rational person, would advocate be publicly allowed.

Providing a justification of some violations of the moral rules does not provide a mechanical decision procedure for settling moral questions. Although some genuine moral disputes can be settled by simply applying the moral attitude to the moral rules and getting clear about the facts, many cannot. All that I have attempted to do is to provide a limit to genuine moral disputes, to show that outside this limit impartial rational persons can no longer disagree about what morally should be done. However, before this limit is reached, no application of what has been said will settle the issue. Impartial rational persons must decide on their own whether they would advocate that the violation be publicly allowed. Therefore, I have not provided anything that functions like an ideal observer, or Aristotle's practically wise person, to whom one can take any moral problem for his pronouncement of what ought to be done. The cases which can be answered clearly by what I have said are those cases in which most people have had no doubt about what is morally right. I have not only not provided a complete guide to life, I have not even provided a complete guide to the moral life.

Summary

I realize that my justification of the moral rules may be considerably weaker than what has been generally sought. I realize that many would have liked to be shown not only that impartial rationality requires taking the moral attitude toward the moral rules, but also that rationality requires acting in the way specified by that attitude. I should have liked to be able to show it. In Chapter 11, I shall try to explain further why the most that can be done is to show that rationality allows acting morally, but I shall provide the best reasons I know of for acting in this way. In the present chapter, I have been concerned only with showing that impartial rationality requires the moral attitude toward certain rules when considered as moral rules. It is important not to confuse these two distinct tasks. It is impossible to justify acting morally in as strong a sense as it is to justify taking the moral attitude toward the moral rules.

This chapter has shown that, given the constraints discussed earlier in this chapter, all impartial rational persons will take what I call the moral attitude toward each of a certain set of rules when considered as part of a public system that applies to all rational persons. This attitude presently goes as follows. "Everyone is to obey the rule with regard to everyone except when an impartial rational person can advocate that the violation of the rule be publicly allowed. Anyone who violates the rule when an impartial rational person could not advocate that such a violation be publicly allowed may be punished." Showing that impartial rationality requires the moral attitude toward a moral rule is what I call justifying that moral rule. Further, only those rules toward which impartial rationality requires the moral attitude count as moral rules, or justified moral rules. Our discussion of the justification of the moral rules has therefore served a dual function: it has justified our attitude toward some commonly accepted moral rules, and it has also furnished us with a criterion for determining if a rule is a justified moral rule. In the following chapter we shall not only see toward what other rules impartial rationality requires the moral attitude, we shall also examine the moral attitude in greater detail.

7

JUSTIFICATION
OF THE MORAL RULES—
THE SECOND FIVE

In the last chapter we saw that there were five rules toward which all impartial rational persons would advocate the moral attitude. These rules: "Don't kill," "Don't cause pain," "Don't disable," "Don't deprive of freedom," and "Don't deprive of pleasure," are five basic justified moral rules. However, they are not the only basic justified moral rules. In fact, these rules include only two of the original seven moral rules listed in Chapter 4 (p. 67). Three of the basic justified moral rules: "Don't disable," "Don't deprive of freedom," and "Don't deprive of pleasure," are thus, in a sense, new moral rules. However, this is not in any way disturbing, for these three rules share all the relevant characteristics of "Don't kill" and "Don't cause pain." Further, though they are not ordinarily listed as moral rules, anyone who unjustifiably disabled a person or deprived him of freedom or pleasure would be considered to be acting immorally. To talk of moral rules is just a convenient way of talking about kinds of actions that we consider to be immoral unless one has an adequate justification or excuse. So we can say that these three rules were always implicitly moral rules. Indeed we must say this, for moral rules are discovered, not invented, and they are unchanging.

I have still not discussed five of the seven original rules taken as paradigm cases of moral rules: "Don't lie," "Keep your promise," "Don't cheat," "Don't commit adultery," and "Don't steal." Are all of these rules justifiable moral rules? Would all impartial rational persons adopt the same attitude toward these five rules as they did toward the five rules discussed in the last chapter? Are there any other rules that should be added to this group of rules? Should any of these rules be reworded? What changes, if any, should be made in the formulation of

125

the moral attitude? Since being a rational person only requires avoiding suffering evils without an adequate reason, why should impartial rational persons be concerned with rules at all? These are the questions that will be answered in this chapter.

Don't Deceive

I shall start with the rule "Don't lie." What would be a rational person's attitude toward this rule? Being lied to does not necessarily involve suffering an evil in the way that violation of the first five rules does. No rational person wants to be killed, to be caused pain, to be disabled, or to be deprived of freedom or pleasure; but must rational persons have a particular aversion to being lied to? It may be true that most people dislike being lied to most of the time, but why should they? Is there anything in human nature or the human social situation that makes this aversion rationally required? Let us define lying as making a false statement in order to lead someone to have some related false belief. It then becomes clear that if it is rationally required to want others not to lie to one, this is not because a false statement is being made, but because one is being led to have a false belief. A rational person would want to avoid being led to have a false belief by silence, by gestures, even by a true statement made in a certain tone of voice; it is being led to have a false belief that is important, not that it is done by making a false statement. Thus the rule should be concerned with prohibiting acting so as to lead someone to have a false belief. I shall formulate this rule as "Don't deceive."

As with the first five rules, the rule concerning deception can be interpreted differently in different societies. With regard to deception as with the previous five rules, rights sometimes determine what counts as deception. If someone has a right to know then silence can be a violation of this rule, whereas if they have no such right, then anything short of a false statement may not be considered a violation of the rule. It is because lying, i.e., making a false statement in order to get someone to have some related false belief, is unambiguously a violation of the rule prohibiting deception, that many have preferred to state the moral rule in terms of lying rather than deceiving. However, whether some common social remark such as "You haven't changed at all" counts as a lie is also subject to differing interpretations.

The question that should therefore be considered is, "What is a rational person's attitude toward the rule 'Don't deceive'?" Does a rational person want himself and those for whom he cares to be protected from deception? Obviously so, for to be deceived generally increases one's chances of suffering an evil and lessens one's chances of obtaining those things which one is seeking. If we remember that a person can use only rationally required beliefs and then add the constraint that one is impartially concerned with all, or that he is considering the rule as a moral rule, he will want everyone to obey the rule prohibiting deception unless an impartial rational person could publicly allow the violation. Thus, by a process whose details need not be repeated here, it can be shown that an impartial rational person would adopt the same attitude toward the rule "Don't deceive" that he adopted toward the first five rules.

One must remember that an impartial rational person's attitude toward the moral rules does not require absolute obedience but, on the contrary, allows for justified exceptions. Some deception is strongly justified, i.e., there are some situations in which all impartial rational persons would publicly allow violation of this rule. No paradoxes arise even when we take deception absolutely literally, for all impartial rational persons will advocate that deception be publicly allowed when it is done with the consent of the deceived and for their benefit. Thus, magicians are not morally prohibited from performing their shows, for it is clear that their deception is with the consent of and for the pleasure of the deceived. Since justified exceptions are allowed by the moral attitude, it can easily be seen that an impartial rational person would adopt the same attitude toward the rule "Don't deceive" that she adopted toward the previous five rules.

Keep Your Promise

The next rule, "Keep your promise," is unique, so far, in that it is the first rule to be stated positively. However, the negative formulation "Don't break your promise" is exactly equivalent, so that there is no need to adjust any of our arguments. This equivalence of negative and positive formulations is not trivial. It is not repeatable with any of the previous rules. "Don't deprive of pleasure" does not even seem to have a plausible equivalent positive formulation. Both "Prevent the loss of pleasure" and "Promote pleasure" demand positive action in a way that the original negative rule does not. The rule against depriving of freedom can be obeyed by doing nothing. The same is not true of any positive formulation, e.g., "Prevent the loss of freedom" or "Promote freedom." The positive actions taken by countries as well as individuals in order to follow these positive guides should make it quite clear that they require far more than does obedience to the original rule. "Don't disable" obviously has the same relationship to "Prevent disabilities" as the previous rules had to their positive formulations. "Don't cause pain" and "Don't kill" obviously require less action than the positive formulations: "Prevent the causing of pain" or "Relieve pain"; and "Prevent killing" or "Preserve life."

I do not know what the positive formulation of "Don't deceive" would be, but if we take "Don't lie" as the rule, then "Tell the truth" seems a plausible positive formulation. However, this plausibility is short-lived. For "Tell the truth" demands positive action, whereas "Don't lie" allows one to refuse to answer. The moral rules prohibit certain kinds of actions; they do not require positive action, except in those cases where there is no difference between requiring action and prohibiting it. There is no difference, except in style, between saying "Keep your promise" and "Don't break your promise." Acting in accordance with or violating either one necessarily involves acting in accordance with or violating the other. (This will also be the case with some of the rules considered later.)

We have already seen that "Tell the truth" does not mean the same as "Don't lie." It might seem that one could make it equivalent by adding the phrase "If you talk." But it is clearly possible to talk without either telling the truth or lying, e.g., by asking questions. It should now be obvious that the point of the rule is to prohibit certain kinds of talk, viz., lies, not to require that one talk. Although "Keep your promise" is phrased positively, its point is also negative, to prohibit the breaking of promises. This rule can be phrased positively because, unlike all of the previous rules, this rule presupposes that some previous action has taken place, viz., that one has made a promise.

The previous six rules can be broken with regard to people we may not have come into contact with previously, either directly or indirectly. The rule concerning promises obviously can be broken only with regard to people to whom we have made promises. If we have not made any promises to anyone, then we cannot break this rule. The fact that the rule concerning promises presupposes some action on the part of the person who is subject to the rule has led some philosophers to consider this rule to be significantly different from all of the previous rules. However, I do not see any morally significant difference between this rule and the one against deception. The action that is presupposed before this rule can be broken is one which any moral agent who is part of a society would have performed many times.

The Nature of Promises

Some may object that there may not be promises in every society. They may claim that promising is similar to marriage in that it is not universal, that there are societies without promises. This claim seems to me to be mistaken. Any society composed of persons who are subject to the previous moral rules will have a practice of promising. Every society demands some degree of cooperation among its members, some division of labor, some postponements of rewards. This, in turn, requires some practice whereby society can arrange for this cooperation, division of labor, and postponements of rewards. This practice will necessarily involve what we now call promising, including mutual promises (what is more formally called making contracts) or some close equivalent. Any person who is part of a society will not only have the opportunity to make a promise, it is almost inevitable that he will make some. Thus this rule has the required universality.

Although I have talked of the practice of promising, I do not regard promising as involving any elaborate conventions. In any society where people have the ability to express their intentions, they have the ability to make promises. In our society we have evolved verbal (and legal) formulas which help us to distinguish promises from other statements of our intentions. By saying "I promise" we make it clear that the person to whom we are promising can count on our doing what we say. But even now we do not have to say "I promise" for our statement of intention to be a promise. Promising need only involve stating your intention to do something in certain kinds of circumstances. The clearest case is one in which the intention is expressed hypothetically; e.g., "I will do x, if you do y," and we both know that x is an action you want me to do and that y is an action I want you to do. This is merely the clearest example of a statement of intention becoming a promise.

John promises Jane to do x may be defined as (1) John states to Jane his intention to do x (2) both John and Jane believe (2a) that Jane wants John to do x and (2b) that the point of John's stating his intention to Jane is to lead her to count on John's doing x. A statement of intention in these circumstances will quickly come to have the features that many philosophers have listed as part of the practice of promising. It is not surprising that verbal formulas have arisen which make it explicit that John intends Jane to count on his doing what he says he intended to do. The close relationship between promising and stating your intention to do something for someone that both of you know she wants you to do can be seen by noting that in order to make sure it is not taken as a promise one often says, "But don't count on my doing it."

Promising and Deceiving

This account of promising shows how closely related the rule about promising is to the rule concerning deception. It may even seem plausible to say that the rule concerning deception tells one not to lie about the past or present; the rule concerning promises, not to lie about the future. What is wrong with saying this is that it ignores the fact that one can lie about the future when this involves no promise and that even when no lie is told when the promise is made, the promise still can be broken by some act in the future. Not only may one change his mind, he may also forget about his promises. Making a lying promise is already prohibited by the rule against deception, although when we fail to keep our promise we break this rule as well. The main point of this rule is to prohibit breaking promises that were made in good faith. Thus we should keep the rule concerning promises distinct from the rule concerning deception.

This account also makes clear that all impartial rational persons would adopt the moral attitude toward the rule "Keep your promise." The necessity of promises for any large scale cooperative enterprise and the harm that everyone would suffer if one could not generally depend on people keeping their promises make it clear why a rule requiring the keeping of promises is one of the paradigm moral rules. A rational person would certainly not want to have promises broken with regard to himself or those for whom he is concerned for, like deception, the breaking of a promise increases one's chances of suffering evil and lessens one's chances of obtaining those things he is seeking. Using only rationally required beliefs, an impartial rational person would adopt the same attitude toward the rule "Keep your promise" as he did toward the previous six moral rules, especially when he is considering it as a moral rule, which requires that it is understood and can be accepted by all rational persons.

Don't Cheat

The somewhat surprising neglect of the concept of cheating by philosophers leads to two objections against including "Don't cheat" in a list of basic moral rules. It is objected that it is unnecessary because cheating, like lying, is simply a subclass of deception. Or it is objected that cheating is a special case of breaking one's promise. Both of these objections are plausible. Most cheating, if not all, does seem to involve deception; the question is, "Is this necessarily so?" Also, cheating seems very similar to breaking a promise; it seems, in fact, to be the breaking of an implicit promise. In order to reply to these objections, an analysis of the concept of cheating is necessary.

Cheating, in its basic form, takes place only in voluntary activities with built-in goals and which are governed by a public system. The rules of this system can be drawn up explicitly, as in most games, or simply grow out of custom, as in generally agreed-upon practices in buying or selling. Cheating involves the violation of this system in order to gain these goals, but not merely this. It is a violation for which the activity includes no explicit penalty except perhaps expulsion from the activity. Cheating usually involves the violation of a rule of the public system that applies to all participants which it is expected that none of them would violate. It is, in this respect, like deception, the violation of trust or faith. This may be all that is meant by those who regard cheating as the breaking of an implicit promise, but this may involve a distortion of the concept of a promise. Further, since cheating is primarily done in order to obtain the built-in goals or benefits of participating in the activity, for it to be successful, one cannot normally let other participants in the activity know of one's cheating. We can see why cheating seems to involve deception. People who know about the violation are not generally going to allow themselves to be cheated.

Although cheating is closely connected to both the breaking of a promise and deception, it is distinct from both, and hence to rule out cheating we still need a separate rule concerning cheating. Promises are always made to a particular person or group of persons. Even with genuine implicit promises this is also the case, e.g., this kind of promise is sometimes characterized by saying, "Silence gives consent." Here, one is made an offer and by not refusing implicitly promises to carry out his part of the bargain. One can cheat, however, never having come into contact with anyone who can claim that a promise, implicit or explicit, was made to him. Cheating is a social rather than personal phenomenon; it is failing to live up to certain standards expected by all who participate in the activity. Entering a game may sometimes involve making a promise to the other players that one will abide by the rules of the game, but usually this is not the case. Claiming that there is always an implicit promise, even when there is no communication between the players, by simply claiming that cheating must always involve the breaking of a promise, is not very plausible. Such a claim will probably result in someone holding that when you cheat at solitaire you have broken a promise to yourself. On any clear account of promises, a rule prohibiting the breaking of a promise will not rule out all cases of cheating.

Although cheating generally involves deception, the account given above shows that deception is not essential. If one participates in an activity with others and fails to abide by the rules expected of all participants, he generally will try to conceal this from others, especially as he expects to gain some benefit thereby. But we can easily imagine special cases where all of the people participating in the activity are, in an important way, dependent on one person. Then we can imagine this person taking advantage of his position outside of the activity to cheat without even bothering to conceal this from the others. The boss who plays golf with his subordinates may sometimes cheat quite openly. He may not count missed strokes, or he may remove the ball from the rough without taking a penalty. Of course, if he cheats too much, one might say that he is not really participating in *that* activity, e.g., that game. But in a sense, cheating just is "not playing the game," and so this is not a serious objection. One need only notice the reactions of the people being cheated to realize that they do not consider themselves playing a different game. This analysis explains why we talk of cheating at solitaire, even though no one else is involved, and so it is not really a moral matter.

Cheating is not reducible to either the breaking of a promise or deceiving, though, as mentioned before, it is possible that all three of them might be considered the violating of a trust or faith. However, this would be to use "violation of faith" in a very vague sense. I think it preferable to have the rules as precise as possible consistent with reasonable scope. I should note that, as I have explained it, cheating, like deceiving and the breaking of a promise, is something one may be justified in doing. I mention this explicitly because justified cheating seems almost a contradiction. It may be hard to imagine a case of justified cheat-. ing, but, though they may be outlandish, such cases are certainly possible. If I play cards with someone who will kill my family if he wins, I am certainly justified in cheating. (If he will kill them if he loses, I am not cheating if I let him win.) Cheating, although it may seem different from the other kinds of actions prohibited by the rules, is like them in the relevant respects.

The rule against cheating does have one characteristic that none of the other rules have. One cannot break this rule unintentionally. There seems to be no such thing as unintentional cheating. With the first five rules, it is clear that violations can occur unintentionally. To act in a careless or thoughtless way with the result that someone suffers one of the evils that these rules prohibit causing, will generally count as a violation of the relevant moral rule. The same is true with the rule concerning promises; breaking of promises not only occurs intentionally, one can also break a promise unintentionally by simply forgetting about it. Both count as violations of the rule. The claim that only an intentional action counts as a violation of a moral rule can be seen to be completely mistaken.

Although it is not clear what, if anything, "unintentional deception" normally refers to, one can, without too much difficulty, find a natural referent. Impartial rational persons adopt the moral attitude toward the rule prohibiting deception because being deceived generally has bad effects. A rational person is as concerned with natural deception as with intentional deception. Were ice to give the appearance that it would support the weight of a person when it would not, then an impartial rational person would advocate a sign warning of this. A rational person wishes to avoid being deceived by nature as much as by a person, for it is the consequences of deception that she wishes to avoid. In adopting the moral attitude toward the rule prohibiting deception, some actions not intended to deceive would naturally count as unintentional deception, e.g., telling jokes to naive people who might be misled by them, passing on gossip which you have no good reason to believe true. Such actions would count as violations of the rule prohibiting deception.

It is much more difficult to find a clear referent for "unintentional cheating." However, since cheating is failure to abide by the rules of the public system of some voluntary activity in which one is engaging, we can easily describe something that might plausibly be called unintentional cheating. A most plausible case is where one breaks one of the rules unintentionally, discovers it later, but does nothing about it. I do not claim that this is now called unintentional cheating; I am not even sure that it would actually be called either cheating or unintentional. There is no intentional breaking of the rules, yet there is an intentional concealing of a past violation. Obviously, this kind of activity would be prohibited by the rule against cheating. Further, one would expect people to take reasonable care that they do not unintentionally violate the rules, for the violation of those rules which would clearly be cheating if intentional generally is against the interests of all the other participants in the activity. Thus the rule against cheating must be understood as requiring reasonable care that one does not violate the rules of any voluntary activity in which one is participating. This, of course, requires that one not enter any activity unless one knows the rules by which it is governed. Although its significance is probably so small as not to warrant calling it a moral matter, the attitude of people toward someone who enters a game not knowing the rules is close to moral condemnation. Expulsion is not unjustified.

Cheating as a Model for All Immoral Behavior

The concept of cheating is an extremely interesting and important concept which has unfortunately been almost completely neglected by philosophers. Investigation of it is very helpful in understanding the nature of morality, for cheating provides in miniature the nature of immoral action. We have already pointed out that cheating in its basic form involves violating the rules of the public system governing an activity that one is participating in voluntarily in order to gain some advantage over others participating in that activity. (This is why students do not normally regard cheating on exams in the same way that they regard cheating in a game. Taking exams, except at the more advanced levels, is not a voluntary activity. Nor do students realize, unless they are graded on the curve, that the cheating affects them in a disadvantageous way.) The close parallel between cheating and all immoral action can be seen if we simplify and redefine cheating, using the terminology that we have already introduced. Cheating is participating in a voluntary activity and violating the public rules applying to all persons participating in that activity when no impartial rational person would publicly allow such a violation. This redefinition of cheating shows how closely it parallels immoral action in general. We need only remove from the redefinition any reference to a voluntary activity and include all rational persons in the class of people to whom the public rules apply in order to have a general definition of an immoral action.

This extraordinary parallel between cheating and immoral action in general helps to explain why cheating seems the paradigm case of an immoral action. Indeed, many philosophers have considered all immoral action to be cases of cheating. Although they are not generally aware of it, all those who make fairness central to morality are using cheating as the model of immoral action. Similarly, cheating provides the model of immoral action for the social contract theorists. Their talk of promises, especially implicit promises, becomes more easily understood when we recall the close connection between cheating and breaking an implicit promise. Also, we can more easily understand their effort to view society as a voluntary association.

However, despite the close parallel between cheating and immoral action, using cheating as the model of immoral action has had some bad effects. It has resulted in overemphasis on the notion of consent. This has resulted in the view that one can perform an immoral action only with regard to someone who is participating in some voluntarily shared activity. Coupled with the view that only people in the same society participate in voluntarily shared activities, the conclusion follows that one can be immoral only with regard to someone in one's own society. This is an argument which leads some people to accept ethical relativism.

That this view has immoral consequences comes out with great vividness in Chapter 10, section 2 ("The Notion of Duty") of Stephen Toulmin's book *The Place of Reason in Ethics* (Cambridge, 1949). In considering an island composed of two communities, C 1 and C 2, he seems to hold that nothing the members of C 1 might do to the members of C 2, or vice versa, can be immoral. This same point has been taken up by Gilbert Harman in his book, *The Nature of Morality* (Oxford, 1974). He holds that only those who accept the same standards can regard one another as immoral.

Another serious fault with using cheating as the model of immorality is the trivialization of morality. Cheating generally results only in the lesser of the evils that the moral rules prohibit causing. Thus Toulmin holds that morality is designed to prevent "causing to other members of the community some inconvenience, annoyance, and suffering. . . ." There is no mention of death or disability. Although cheating should not be taken as the model for all immoral action, it is clear that it is generally immoral to cheat. All impartial rational persons will take the same attitude toward the rule prohibiting cheating as they do toward the previous seven rules. Thus "Don't cheat" becomes the eighth justified moral rule.

Adultery

In order to evaluate "Don't commit adultery," I must make explicit what is meant by adultery. For purposes of this discussion I will define adultery as having sexual intercourse with someone other than one's spouse when one is married. Some deny that this rule is a basic moral rule because they hold that a society might lack an institution of marriage. If no one in the society is married, then no one can commit adultery, and so the rule would not apply to all people in all societies and hence would not be a basic moral rule. This does not mean that adultery is not immoral, for the immorality of adultery may not depend upon there being a basic moral rule against adultery. It may be that in any society with an institution of marriage adultery violates some other basic moral rule. However, it might also be that it is only in societies with an institution of marriage like ours that adultery is immoral.

I am encouraged to take this latter view because I do not feel that adultery by the Eskimos, if sexual activity between married persons and those who are not their spouses is openly accepted, as reported by anthropologists, is immoral, whereas I do feel that adultery in our society generally is. It seems to me that adultery in our society is immoral because of the kind of institution of marriage that we have. Marriage, in our society, involves participating in a practice in order to gain the goal of exclusive possession of a sexual partner. Of course, marriage is supposed to be much more than this, and often is, but exclusive sexual activity is central to it. Adultery involves gaining the goal of marriage, an exclusive sexual partner, without abiding by the standards of that practice, i.e., being an exclusive sexual partner. Adultery is a form of cheating. This is, in fact, reflected in our ordinary talk about adultery, as when we talk of persons cheating on their spouses. If the institution of marriage is as I have described it, it follows that adultery is immoral, for adultery is cheating and cheating is immoral. But as mentioned earlier, cheating, like violations of all other moral rules, can in certain instances be justified.

Further arguments can be made against adultery. It generally involves deceit. It may also be said to involve the breaking of an implicit promise. Although this is true, it is the same kind of thing that can be said against most kinds of cheating. In fact, it supports the view that given the institution of marriage that we now have, adultery is cheating. Nothing in what has been said involves approval or disapproval of our present institution of marriage, but only that given that institution, adultery is generally immoral. It may be argued that this institution should be changed or, perhaps, should be adopted by all societies. This question, luckily, does not fall within the scope of our investigation. However, some points should be made about the relationship of morality to sexual activity.

Sex and Morality

Sexual relationships are important to all people in all societies. It seems to many to be an issue on which there ought to be a moral rule. However, philosophers, in contrast with the general public who often regard morality as concerned primarily with sexual matters, have almost completely ignored sexual matters. To say that adultery is immoral because it is cheating may seem to most people a thoroughly implausible answer. Adultery is wrong, they might say, because any sexual relationship between two people who are not married is wrong. They hold that premarital sexual intercourse is also wrong, and this is obviously not a case of cheating. Those who defend premarital sex are sometimes accused of holding a "new morality." Those who uphold the traditional standards of sexual behavior and those who uphold the new are often thought to be having a fundamental moral dispute. This is a mistake. Whatever side one takes on this issue should not affect, in the slightest, one's attitude toward any of the other moral rules we have discussed.

This is an extremely important point and one that cannot be overemphasized. Some defenders of tradition equate sexual freedom with moral anarchy. They agree with some defenders of the "new morality" who hold that showing that any moral rule prohibiting sexual freedom is unjustifiable proves that no moral rules are justifiable. Both think that there is a rule governing sexual behavior that shares all the features of the other basic moral rules. That they are mistaken can easily be seen by trying to formulate an independent moral rule concerning sexual behavior toward which all impartial rational persons would adopt the moral attitude. Of course, rape is immoral. But it is immoral not because it is concerned with sexual matters, but because it necessarily involves a violation of one or more of the first five moral rules. Rape involves the infliction of pain and the deprivation of freedom. Denying that there are any independent moral rules concerning sex does not involve denying that rape is universally immoral and that adultery is immoral in any society with an institution of marriage like ours.

Whether premarital or postmarital sex is immoral or not depends on the institutions and laws in the society concerning these matters. I am now talking about nonmarital sex between mutually consenting adults. Unless nonmarital sexual relations between consenting adults causes harm to someone, no impartial rational person would favor a public rule prohibiting such activity. On the contrary, given that sex can provide some of life's more enjoyable moments, it would seem that the deprivation of this pleasure is itself immoral unless one can show that such deprivation is necessary for avoiding greater evil. Whether this can be shown or not, I do not know, but certainly the burden of proof is on those who seek to deprive anyone of the pleasures of sex. However, given the importance of sexual activity to one's life, it would be imprudent not to think very carefully about the consequences before engaging in it.

Stealing

Eight basic moral rules have now been justified, and only one of the original seven rules listed in chapter four, "Don't steal," must still be considered. It does not require a new argument to show that all impartial rational persons would adopt the same attitude toward the rule "Don't steal" as they did toward the previous eight rules. A rational person usually does not want to have anything he owns or anything owned by those he cares for stolen. To steal something from someone generally deprives him of pleasure or freedom. Using the same arguments we have used before it seems clear that all impartial rational persons would adopt the moral attitude toward the rule against stealing.

However, insofar as stealing results in the deprivation of pleasure or freedom, no special public rule is needed against it. The point of including a rule in the list of basic moral rules is that it prohibits some action impartial rational persons want prohibited but is not already prohibited by some other rule. To show that an independent rule against stealing is needed, one must show that it prohibits some actions not prohibited by any of the other rules. Consider the following; we can steal from the estates of the rich who will not even miss their money, or from companies who will simply add a penny to everyone's bill.

These cases do not seem to be prohibited by the rules against depriving of freedom or pleasure so that the rule against stealing does seem needed.

Now a new problem arises. Just as adultery requires the practice of marriage, which it is not clear that all societies have, so stealing requires the practice of owning property, which it is not certain that all societies have. Since the immorality of stealing in our society would not be put in doubt by the discovery of a society with no practice of ownership, the immorality of stealing cannot depend on there being an independent rule against stealing. The immorality of adultery was accounted for by showing that, in our society, adultery is prohibited by the rule prohibiting cheating; however, none of the previous eight rules seems to cover all cases of stealing. We need another rule in order to account for the immorality of stealing.

Stealing involves taking that which is owned by another; the concept of ownership depends upon the concept of law. Whether you own something, and under what conditions, is determined by the law. Stealing is not merely taking that which is owned by another, it is taking it unlawfully. Thus every case of stealing will be a case of breaking the law. Including as a basic moral rule the rule "Obey the law" guarantees that stealing is immoral, without having an independent rule against it. Another reason for having the rule "Obey the law" as a basic moral rule is that we generally regard as acting immorally those who break the law when an impartial rational person could not advocate publicly allowing such a violation. Including "Obey the law" as a basic moral rule allows us to continue regarding these actions as immoral without making individual laws into moral rules.

An Account of Law

Since I regard "Obey the law" as a basic moral rule, I must give an account of law such that every society has laws, for I have required of a basic moral rule that it be applicable to all rational persons in all societies. I realize that it is impossible to give an adequate account of law in a few paragraphs. It may even be that the condition which I require to be satisfied, viz., that every society have laws, will make it impossible to give an account of law which even hints at the complexities that law has in sophisticated societies. However, all that I wish to provide is a set of characteristics which are sufficient for calling something a law. I realize that in sophisticated societies laws will have characteristics that I do not mention. It may even be that some will regard these unmentioned characteristics as necessary features of law, and will regard societies that do not have rules with these features as pre-legal societies. On my view there are no pre-legal societies, and all I require is that every society have laws in the sense I provide.

Laws are rules, and thus disobeying the law will be similar to cheating. The important difference between laws and those rules or standards, the violation of which is cheating, is that cheating is violating the rules of a voluntary activity, one which a member of the society can choose to participate in or refrain from. In a sense, one chooses to be subject to the rules or standards, the violation of which is cheating. One cannot always choose to be subject to the law; whether or not one is subject to a law is often determined by the law. This difference between laws and the rule concerning cheating is related to another difference: violating a law often has an explicit penalty; cheating usually has no explicit penalty.

I define a law as follows: *A law is a rule which is part of a system of rules which is known to (almost) all rational persons in the society and which, directly and indirectly, significantly influences their behavior. Some of these rules apply to members of that society whether they wish to be subject to them or not, and some of them have explicit penalties for violation.* A law directly influences one's behavior when one's behavior is affected primarily by one's knowledge that there is such a law. It indirectly influences one's behavior when one's behavior is affected primarily by the knowledge that others know that there is such a law.

This account says nothing of the origin of laws. Laws are not necessarily those rules which are instituted by authorized legislators. Although it is trivially true that laws guide the conduct of those subject to them, a law, in the sense I have given it, may arise from custom, so that it may serve no purpose. One would like to say that laws are for the benefit of society, but this would rule out as laws far too many laws. Even the weaker qualification that laws must be believed to be for the benefit of society rules out too many laws to be included as part of an account of what a law is. Although this account of a law is purely descriptive, laws generally have the result of producing order and stability in society, of allowing greater predictability of the actions of members of the society. Laws enable people to plan their lives with greater assurance.

With this minimal account of law, is it possible to provide a justification for the rule "Obey the law"? This rule, unlike the previous eight rules, presupposes the institution of a society with a system of rules that applies to all of its members. The first six rules apply even in what might be called desert island situations. Coming upon a stranger who is minding her own business, we should neither kill her, cause her pain, nor disable her. Nor should we deprive her of freedom or pleasure. Also, we should not deceive her. Obviously we cannot break a promise to a person to whom we have never made one, so that the seventh rule presupposes some prior contact and at least some ongoing social interaction. When the social situation has evolved so that promises can be made, once a promise has been made, then it ought to be kept. This does not depend on the keeping of promises being enforced by the society. The situation with cheating is the same; if appropriate activities evolve, one ought not cheat when participating in them. Thus the first six rules apply even when there has been no prior contact between individuals, and the next two rules presuppose only what I call an informal social situation, not the establishment of a system of rules governing all members of the society.

The violations of each of the first eight rules normally is with regard to particular persons, e.g., the person killed, deceived etc. The attitude of rational persons develops from their aversion to having the rule violated with regard to themselves or those they care for. Each of the first eight rules prohibits something which may be done to me or those I care for. When the condition of impartiality is imposed, or the rules are being considered as moral rules, rational persons will adopt the moral attitude toward the rule. The present formulation of this attitude is: "Everyone is to obey the rule with regard to everyone, except when an impartial rational person can advocate that the violation of the rule be publicly allowed. Anyone who violates the rule when no impartial rational person can advocate that such a violation be publicly allowed may be punished."

This formulation does not seem appropriate when applied to the rule "Obey the law" because normally one does not obey or disobey the law with regard to anyone, one merely obeys or breaks the law. Further, it is not possible to formulate the egocentric attitude toward this rule in the way it was formulated for the previous eight rules because one does not normally disobey the law with regard to particular persons, e.g., those for whom I am concerned, even though particular persons often suffer some evil because of one's breaking of the law. Thus one cannot build up an impartial rational person's attitude toward "Obey the law" by adding constraints to the egocentric attitude in the same fashion that was done for the previous eight rules.

A similar problem, though not as acute, arises with the rule "Don't cheat." Although when one cheats, one normally cheats someone, sometimes there may be no particular person, if anyone, who has been cheated. Cheating provides a kind of bridge between personal and social moral rules. For violations of the first seven moral rules, there is necessarily some one or more individuals with regard to whom one is breaking the rule. For the eighth rule, this will usually be true, but not necessarily so. Cheating has an impersonal aspect; it is the violation of the standards governing an activity. Violations can occur and yet, even when all the facts are known, it may be impossible to pick out any individual of whom we would want to say he had been cheated. Thus it seems that the present formulation of the moral attitude makes it sometimes inappropriate for the eighth and ninth rules.

However, the first part of the formulation "Everyone is to obey the rule with regard to everyone" can easily be replaced by "Everyone is always to obey the rule." Simply replacing "with regard to everyone" by "always" and changing the word order makes it quite appropriate to take the moral attitude toward the rule "Obey the law." The moral attitude is now formulated "Everyone is always to obey the rule unless an impartial rational person can advocate that violating it be publicly allowed. Anyone who violates the rule when no impartial rational person can advocate that such a violation be publicly allowed may be punished." When considering only one society, we can even substitute "law" for "rule" in the moral attitude and then put in particular laws where we had previously put in the individual moral rules. This parallelism between particular laws and the individual moral rules is not accidental. Adopting the moral attitude toward a rule is very like advocating that the rule be made a law. The law is often talked of as the embodiment of impartial reason, and particular laws often embody the moral rules. Unfortunately the law is not always the embodiment of impartial reason, and some particular laws may even require violating a moral rule when no impartial rational person would publicly allow such a violation.

Is "Obey the Law" a Justified Moral Rule?

Given what has just been said it may seem that impartial rational persons would not adopt the moral attitude toward the rule "Obey the law." However, we must remember that the moral attitude allows the possibility that disobeying the law can be justified. In adopting the moral attitude toward the rule "Obey the law," an impartial rational person is not advocating an end to all civil disobedience. Civil disobedience usually occurs when one believes that the law is causing significant evil. It is never justified unless one has an adequate reason to believe that a significant amount of evil is being suffered and that disobeying the law will do something toward lessening that evil. Adopting the moral attitude toward the rule "Obey the law" only commits one to holding that unless an impartial rational person can advocate that ignoring or breaking the law be publicly allowed, one should obey it.

I have admitted that it is not possible to develop an attitude that all impartial rational persons will adopt toward the rule "Obey the law" in precisely the same way that it was developed for the preceding rules. However, as we shall see in what follows, not much modification is needed. All rational persons know that they and those for whom they care may suffer some evil when the law is broken. Thus all rational persons would take the following egocentric attitude toward the rule "Obey the law," "I want all others to obey the law when not doing so increases the likelihood that anyone for whom I am concerned (including, of course, myself) will suffer an evil, unless I have (or would have if I knew the facts) a rational desire that they not obey the law in those circumstances."

In order to eliminate the egocentricity, we add the constraints of impartiality or that the rules be considered as moral rules, i.e., as public rules that apply to all rational persons. With these constraints it now seems that all impartial rational persons would adopt the moral attitude toward the rule "Obey the law." But do these constraints result in their adopting the moral attitude toward the rule "Obey the law" rather than toward the more complex rule "Obey the law whenever not doing so increases the likelihood of anyone suffering any evil?" Reflecting on this question makes it clear that the same question arises when we consider the rules concerning deceit, promises, and cheating, that is, any rule the successful violation of which does not necessarily result in someone suffering an evil. The problem we have uncovered here is not one that is peculiar to the rule "Obey the law," but affects all the rules considered in this chapter.

A Problem in Justifying Some Moral Rules

This problem did not seem to arise in discussing the rules concerning deceit, promises and cheating because it seemed as if every unjustifiable violation of any of these three rules must result in someone suffering some evil or being deprived of some good. Of course, this is not true. Unjustified deceit may result in my getting some undeserved good, while no one suffers in any way from that particular act. A promise may be unjustifiably broken even though no one suffers because of it. Unjustified cheating seems so obviously immoral that no one even considers that unjustified cheating can clearly occur without anyone suffering any evil because of that particular act. Just think of someone who cheats on an exam not graded on a curve, because it is easier, even though he could pass if he worked at it. The question thus arises if it has been shown that all impartial rational persons would adopt the moral attitude toward the rules under consideration in this chapter or only, as with the rule "Obey the law," toward some related but more complex rule.

This question arose in the discussion of the rule "Obey the law," not merely because it necessitated a change in the wording of the moral attitude. Far more important, I think, is that "Obey the law" seems to be a much less likely candidate for a basic moral rule than any of the rules discussed previously. We are suspicious of this rule, and thus I had to be more careful in examining its justification. And these suspicions seem to have been warranted. All that I seem to have shown is that impartial rational persons will adopt the moral attitude toward the rule "Obey the law whenever not doing so increases the likelihood of anyone suffering any evil," not to the simpler rule "Obey the law." Now it seems that the same inadequacy is present in the justification of the three previous rules. To justify these rules as originally formulated it must be shown that all impartial rational persons would adopt the moral attitude toward the original rules without any qualification about the particular violation resulting in increased chances of someone suffering some evil.

Although it seems as if all impartial rational persons would adopt the moral attitude toward the corresponding complex rule rather than toward the original simple rule, I do not think this is the case. I do not deny that impartial rational persons will sometimes advocate that violations of each of the last four rules in their original formulations be publicly allowed. Nor do I deny that sometimes this will happen when they have good reason to believe that no evil will be caused by that particular violation. What I do deny is that simply the fact that one has a rational belief that the particular violation will not cause anyone to suffer any evil is enough to lead an impartial rational person to advocate that such a violation be publicly allowed.

Consider an exam in which everyone's grade and whether they pass or fail is completely independent of what others do on the exam. A person may cheat on this exam without causing anyone to suffer any evil. Suppose an impartial rational person were to refuse to adopt the moral attitude toward the rule prohibiting cheating in its original simple formulation. This means that she holds that anyone who has a rational belief that no one will be hurt by his cheating may cheat without being liable to punishment. If such a person is discovered to be cheating, no penalties at all are to be administered, not even a scolding. Taking such an attitude involves accepting that such exams be eliminated, for the purpose of the exam is to distinguish between those who have the ability tested by the exam and those who do not. Thus, only if an impartial rational person is prepared to accept the elimination of these exams can she refuse to adopt the moral attitude toward the original simple rule prohibiting cheating. But sometimes, considering the matter as an impartial rational person, one would not be prepared to accept the elimination of these exams. In these cases, one must adopt the moral attitude toward the original rule prohibiting cheating.

The Same Kind of Violation

When an impartial rational person advocates that a violation of a moral rule be publicly allowed, that violation must be describable in a way that is understandable to all rational persons. The only considerations that an impartial rational person can use in deciding whether to advocate that a violation be publicly allowed are those that can be understood by all rational persons. Any particular facts that she uses count as considerations only insofar as they are instances of more general facts that would be understood by all rational persons. When an impartial rational person advocates that a violation be publicly allowed, he is not advocating that this particular violation in all of its individuality be publicly allowed, rather he is advocating that all violations of the same kind be publicly allowed. It therefore becomes extremely important to determine what counts as the same kind of violation.

Philosophers have usually qualified the claims that they make in moral arguments by adding a *ceteris paribus* clause. It has been noted that often it is this clause that is doing most of the work. Everyone recognizes that saying that this kind of violation is justified, *ceteris paribus,* is usually intolerably vague. I am attempting to specify what counts as the same kind of violation without using the *ceteris paribus* clause so that one can make a claim about a kind of violation being justified without using any phrase like "other things being equal." The only way in which one can specify what counts as the same kind of violation with sufficient precision is to provide a list of all of the morally relevant features of the violation. However, if this list is to be of any use it cannot be too long. This requires the morally relevant features to be formulated at a fairly high level of generality. It would be pointless to have headaches, stomach pains and extreme anxiety count as distinct basic categories of morally relevant features. When concerned only with their moral relevance, all of the above count as pains. It might be thought that pain should count as a distinct basic category, and the same with the rest of the evils prohibited by the moral rules. But once we realize that people may rank different kinds of pain differently, we see that there is no need to make each of the evils a separate category; rather, we can include all of the evils in a single category.

Morally Relevant Features

A morally relevant feature of a particular violation is a feature that if changed would affect whether or not some impartial rational person would advocate that this violation be publicly allowed. If all of these features are the same for two violations then they are the same kind of violation, and if an impartial rational person would advocate that one of them be publicly allowed then she must also advocate that the other be publicly allowed. It follows that if one advocates that a particular violation be publicly allowed, but does not advocate that another that seems similar be publicly allowed, then, as an impartial rational person one must show how the two violations differ with regard to, at least, one of these morally relevant features.

I shall now list what seem to me to be all of the morally relevant features of a violation of a moral rule. I regard only the answers to the following questions as providing features that would affect whether or not some impartial rational person would advocate that the violation be publicly allowed. I count only these features as morally relevant, i.e., only these features are relevant in deciding whether a particular violation of a moral rule is of the same kind as some other violation.

1. What moral rule is being violated?
2. A. What evils are being caused by the violation?
   B. What evils are being avoided by the violation?
   C. What evils are being prevented by the violation?

In addition to specifying the kinds of evils, one must include their severity, the length of time they will be suffered, and their probability of occurrence. If more than one person is involved, the distribution of these evils among these persons must also be specified. That there are different kinds of evils, e.g., death, pain, and loss of freedom, that impartial rational persons may rank differently accounts for most of the moral disagreement that occurs when there is genuine agreement on the facts. However, in real life situations most moral disagreement is the result of different beliefs about the facts, especially different beliefs about the probability of various evils occuring; it is not due to differences in the ranking of evils at all. Insofar as people agree on what evils will be caused, avoided or prevented by a particular act, including kind, severity, duration, probability, and distribution, they will agree on whether that act is of the same kind as some other act.

3. What are the relevant desires of the person toward whom the rule is being violated? There are several possibilities. (1) The person has rational desires that result in his wanting the rule to be violated, e.g., a patient desires to live and wants the pain of treatment because he believes it necessary. (2) The person has rational desires that result in his not wanting to have the rule violated, e.g., a defendant desires to be free so he does not want to be convicted and to spend the next year in prison. (3) The person has desires that are relevant to his wanting the moral rule violated, but these desires are not rational, e.g., a young woman desires to die because her fiance has been killed in a motorcycle accident so she does not want doctors to treat her. (4) The person has no desires at all that are relevant to the moral rule violation, e.g., he is so demented he does not have any desires that would be affected by the proposed violation of the moral rule.

The relevant rational desires of a person are morally relevant even if, because of the lack of relevant rational beliefs, he does not see the connection between his rational desires and the moral rule violation. For example, one person who has a rational desire to live even if this means enduring significant pain may not want a painful operation because he does not realize that it is necessary to save his life; another person has a rational desire to die rather than to endure significant pain and so does not want a painful operation even though he knows that it is necessary to save his life. At least some, if not all, impartial rational persons would advocate that treating these two persons differently be publicly allowed even though neither wants to have the operation.

4. What are the relevant beliefs of the person toward whom the rule is being violated? Again there are several possibilities. (1) The person understands all of the relevant consequences of the rule being violated and of its not being violated. All of his beliefs about how he will be affected by the violation are rational and based on the best available evidence. (2) The person understands some of the relevant consequences; some of his beliefs about how he will be affected by the violation are rational and based on the best available evidence, but others are either irrational or would be irrational if the person had a higher level of intelligence or knowledge. (3) The person understands none of the relevant consequences; he either has no beliefs about how he will be affected by the violation, or none of the beliefs he has would count as rational if he had a higher level of intelligence or knowledge. As the example in the previous paragraph shows, what a person knows about the consequences of his decisions may influence whether impartial rational persons would advocate that violating a moral rule with regard to him be publicly allowed. This consideration arises quite often in medicine when deciding whether or not to violate a moral rule with regard to a person for his own benefit, but without his consent, what is commonly known as paternalistic behavior.

5. Is there a relationship between the person violating the moral rule and the person toward whom it is being violated such that the former has a duty to violate some moral rules with regard to the latter independent of the latter's consent and is in a unique or almost unique position in this regard? This feature accounts for the fact that, in our society, parents' relationship with their children is morally relevant. That is, when we are considering the violation of a moral rule, it is morally relevant whether or not it is parents that are violating the rule with regard to their children. For example, parents' violation of the rule against depriving of freedom with regard to their children does not count as the same kind of act as a violation of the same rule by an adult toward a child with whom he has no special relationship even when the evils, caused, avoided, and prevented, and the relevant desires and beliefs of the child are the same.

This feature also accounts for the fact that the relationship between governments and their citizens is morally relevant. This means that a government depriving one or more of its citizens of some freedom is not the same kind of act as one citizen depriving another one of the same amount of freedom, even when the evils caused, avoided and prevented, and the rational desires and beliefs of the person being deprived of the freedom are the same. Of course, both acts of deprivation may be morally unjustified, but since they are not the same kind of act, it may be that one of them is justified and the other not. This feature makes it possible that a government may be justified in inflicting an evil on one of its citizens, or parents on one of their children when people without these special relationships are not justified in inflicting an evil in what may otherwise count as the same kind of situation.

6. What goods (including kind, severity, probability, duration, and distribution) are being promoted by the violation? My personal view is that, except for trivial violations of a moral rule, or outlandish philosophical examples, this feature is morally relevant only when the previous feature applies. Normally, only when we are dealing with a violation by someone who has a duty to violate the moral rules with regard to the person toward whom the rule is being violated, are the goods being promoted relevant. I call this kind of situation a political one. A consequentialist view which counts only evils as morally relevant, e.g., negative utilitarianism, seems to be much closer to our moral intuitions than a consequentialist view that treats both goods and evils as relevant, e.g., classical utilitarianism, when dealing with individuals. However, when dealing with governments, the reverse seems to be true. Although I do not hold either kind of consequentialist view, taking features five and six together allows me to incorporate the strong points of each version. It is worth explicitly noting that this feature concerns only the promotion of goods; depriving of a good is the same as causing an evil and so is included in feature two.

7. Is the rule being violated toward a person in order to prevent her (1) unjustified, or (2) weakly justified violation of a moral rule? These features are used to distinguish deception by those involved in undercover police work from deception by those seeking to gain scientific knowledge, even when the amount of evil caused, avoided and prevented is the same. These same features can be used to distinguish between spying and other activities by one government with regard to another in order to prevent the unjustified or weakly justified violation of moral rules, from spying which is not done to prevent such violations. Also one may be willing to publicly allow more serious violations to prevent unjustified violations of a moral rule than to prevent weakly justified violations.

8. Is the rule being violated toward a person because he has violated a moral rule (1) unjustifiably, or (2) with a weak justification? These are very important features when discussing punishment. Many will claim that the infliction of an evil does not count as punishment unless it is done because of an unjustified or weakly justified violation of a moral rule. I agree that it would be inappropriate to call the infliction of an evil "punishment" unless the person is being inflicted with the evil because of such kinds of violations. It is, of course, morally relevant whether the violation is weakly justified or completely unjustified, e.g., one may inflict greater penalties for the later kind of violation, even if all the other features are the same. But justifying punishment as part of a general moral theory means that what needs to be justified is the infliction of an evil, whether or not it is appropriately called "punishment." This feature is also relevant to the justification of war, and here there is no question of "punishment" in its standard sense.

I do not claim to have shown that these are the only morally relevant features; indeed, I think that one of the most important tasks for moral philosophers is to discover if there are additional features that are morally relevant. However,

I have not found any morally relevant features that do not fit into one of the basic categories listed above, and so I shall treat the list as complete. It is important to note that agreement on what counts as a morally relevant feature does not eliminate disagreement concerning whether any given violation does have that particular feature. However, if two persons agree that two violations have all the same morally relevant features then they agree that they are the same kind of act. My experience has been that most moral disagreements are disagreements about the facts of the case, that is, the people who disagree about whether or not to publicly allow a given violation do not regard it as the same kind of act.

The Morally Decisive Question

The answers to the previous eight questions provide a list of features that determine the kind of violation one is considering. Once one has used all of the previous listed morally relevant features that apply, then one proceeds to the next step, which is to decide whether or not as an impartial rational person one would advocate that this kind of violation be publicly allowed. If the answers to the first eight questions are the same for two violations, then they are the same kind of act and any impartial rational person who advocates that one be publicly allowed must also advocate that the other be publicly allowed. However, although this is not usually the case, different impartial rational persons can agree that two violations are of the same kind and yet one person advocate that both be publicly allowed and another person advocate that neither be publicly allowed. The decision that one makes on this point is determined by the answer that one would give to what I call *the morally decisive question.*

"What effects would this kind of violation have, if publicly allowed?" The answer to this question is the morally decisive feature. Unlike the morally relevant features listed above, this morally decisive feature does not determine what counts as the same kind of act; it determines whether or not one, as an impartial rational person, would advocate that that kind of violation of a moral rule be publicly allowed. Disagreement on whether or not to advocate that a violation that two impartial rational persons consider to be of the same kind be publicly allowed is based on two distinct factors. The first is a factual disagreement about what the effects of publicly allowing this kind of violation would be. The second is a disagreement in ranking of these effects; this disagreement can occur even when there is agreement on the effects of publicly allowing this kind of violation. However, it is often not clear which of these two factors is responsible for the disagreement.

For example, one person may believe that publicly allowing deception in order to avoid a certain degree of anxiety or displeasure for the deceived would result in a substantial decrease in the amount of anxiety and displeasure suffered, while another believes that publicly allowing this kind of violation would result in increased anxiety because of additional uncertainty due, in part, to increased violations. Although this disagreement may simply be a factual disagreement, since the facts are not available and are most likely not to become available, the dispute has become known as ideological. An ideological dispute is one in which the disagreement on whether to advocate that a certain kind of violation be publicly allowed does not depend on any factual disagreement which can be settled and also does not arise from any explicit disagreement on the rankings of the various evils involved. It is usually put forward as a dispute about human nature or the nature of human society, but I suspect it also involves a difference in the rankings of the different goods and evils. It usually has a significant political dimension and involves different views about the way the government should act, e.g., allowing more or less paternalistic deception by the government, or favoring more or less government restriction on the behavior of its citizens.

Kant's Categorical Imperative Versus Advocating That a Violation Be Publicly Allowed

Kant's Categorical Imperative, "Act only according to that maxim whereby you can at the same time will that it should become a universal law," can be plausibly interpreted as stating that you should act only on a rule that as a rational person you would put forward as a public rule that applies to all rational persons. I do not claim that this is what Kant intended by the Categorical Imperative; I do claim that it is only on this interpretation that we can explain why Kant's Categorical Imperative has had the influence that it has had among so many who know nothing about its metaphysical basis. The Categorical Imperative not only provides a formula for determining what counts as a moral rule, it also states that all of one's actions should be in accordance with such rules. If Kant's formula for determining what counts as a moral rule were correct, then in one fell swoop he would have not only determined what morality is, but also that one should be moral. This interpretation of the Categorical Imperative, by showing how it seems to solve the two main problems in ethics, explains why it has had so much influence.

The Categorical Imperative does not adequately determine what counts as a moral rule because Kant does not have an adequate account of rationality. When rationality is defined in the kind of formal way that Kant defines it, the Categorical Imperative is totally inadequate as a means of identifying moral rules. Identifying moral rules as any rules that any person can consistently put forward for governing everyone's behavior would permit far too many rules to count as moral rules. Since this has been generally recognized, the Categorical Imperative has been interpreted as ruling out as immoral any act done on a maxim that one could not will to be acted on by everyone. But this rules out as immoral many acts that clearly are not immoral, e.g., acting on the maxim "never be the first to arrive at (or the last to leave) a party."

Kant has other serious problems in deriving rules from his Categorical Imperative. He seems to have conflated the concept of universality, applying to all rational persons at all times and places, and the concept of absoluteness, not having any exceptions. Thus even if the Categorical Imperative did generate the moral rules, it would still be inadequate for Kant never provides any way of deciding when one can justifiably violate these rules. However, given some of

Kant's examples, one might consider the Categorical Imperative, not as determining what counts as a moral rule or for determining the morality of any act, but rather as a means of identifying justifiable exceptions to the moral rules. Kant would then simply be taking the common moral rules as genuine moral rules, which is quite dubious. On this (implausible) interpretation, a violation of the moral rules is justifiable only if one can will that it be acted on by everyone. That this is still inadequate can be seen from considering the following examples. It is certainly possible for everyone to will that one cause significant pain to one person when doing so provides pleasure for some large number of people, e.g., ten thousand, yet this is not a justifiable exception to the rule prohibiting the causing of pain. And while it may not be possible to will that everyone commit a certain kind of violation, e.g., non-violent civil disobedience when one will suffer the penalties imposed by the law, this might still be a justifiable violation because an impartial rational person can advocate that it be publicly allowed because she believes that not everyone will actually commit it.

Regardless of what Kant intended, the value of Kant's Categorical Imperative is in its incorporation as central to morality the features of both impartiality and publicity. But when considering the violation of a moral rule, neither impartiality nor publicity require that one determine the consequences of everyone committing the same kind of violation. Impartiality only requires that one not make a special exception for anyone, including oneself or one's friends. Satisfying this requirement does not involve preferring the state of affairs where everyone commits a given kind of violation, only that you prefer the situation where everyone is publicly allowed to commit that kind of violation. (Marcus George Singer, in Chapter 4 of *Generalization in Ethics* [New York, 1961], vainly tries to save Kant by inventing the notions of "invertibility" and "reiterability.") Determining what would happen if everyone were publicly allowed to commit that kind of violation only requires that it be known by everyone that everyone is allowed to commit that kind of violation. That a violation be one that an impartial rational person can advocate be publicly allowed determines what counts as a justifiable violation of a moral rule far better than determining it by considering the effects of everyone's actually committing that violation. Kant's Categorical Imperative, no matter what interpretation it is given, does not provide an adequate account of how to determine the morality of an action.

There is one way that one can provide an understanding of Kant that not only is in the spirit of Kant, but also provides a fairly adequate account of morality. One would have to provide Kant with the proper understanding of rationality, but once one had done this, the only change needed would be to replace the term "maxim" and "law" by the term "system of laws." Then Kant's Categorical Imperative becomes "Act only on that system of laws whereby you can at the same time will that it should become a universal system of laws." This is then interpreted as act only on that system which you can put forward as a public system that applies to all rational persons. If we take the Categorical Imperative as ruling out immoral acts, we can formulate it explicitly in a negative way, "Never act in any way that you cannot advocate be publicly allowed." This could be put in a positive formulation as well, "Act only in that way that you can advocate be publicly allowed." When all of this playing around with Kant is done, then one can see that among his other errors is one that he shares with almost all other philosophers who have sought to provide a justification or foundation for the moral rules: he treats each rule separately rather than seeing it as part of a system which includes not only rules, but also a procedure for determining justifiable violations of the rules.

Morality Must Be Public

A moral system must be public; that is, it must be known to all those to whom it applies, and it must be such that it could be accepted by all of them. Since a moral system applies to all rational persons, all rational persons must know all of the moral rules; that is, they must all know that certain kinds of behavior, e.g., killing and cheating, are immoral unless one can justify such actions. But a moral system must contain more than the moral rules; it must also contain a procedure for determining when it is justifiable to violate the rules. The moral attitude describes the procedure for determining justifiable violations. When one puts forward an exception to a rule, that is, when one advocates that certain kinds of violations be publicly allowed, this is part of the moral system. Since the total moral system must be public, all parts of the system must also be public, so that the procedure for determining justifiable violations must be known to and acceptable to all rational persons. Also, the exception itself, must be such that it could be part of a public system. This is why one must consider whether one could advocate that such a violation be publicly allowed, that is, whether the violation is one that can be understood and accepted by all rational persons.

A moral system must be public because it provides a guide to conduct for all rational persons. It cannot provide such a guide if it is not known to and cannot be accepted by all. This is why a moral system cannot depend on any beliefs that are not known to all rational persons, why the moral rules must be formulated in a way that is understandable to all rational persons, why the morally relevant features must be formulated in the same way. It also explains why the procedure for determining justified exceptions to the rules must be that an impartial rational person can advocate that they be publicly allowed. Since morality applies to all rational persons, it must be known to and acceptable to all rational persons.

The public character of morality is also closely related to the kind of impartiality that is recognized by all as an essential feature of the moral rules. Impartiality with respect to the moral rules requires that there be no special exceptions for anyone, that every rational person be required to obey the rules in the same way. Unless the moral rules, including the allowed violations, are public, everyone cannot be required to act in the same way. Requiring that the violations be publicly allowed is a way of guaranteeing that the moral system retains the proper kind of impartiality. If one only advocated that everyone be allowed to violate the rule, not that the violation be publicly allowed, one would have a moral system in which there would be a distinction between those who knew the violation was allowed and those who did not know, and this would be incompatible with the kind of impartiality required by the moral rules.

Why Be Concerned with Rules at All?

Even if it is granted that all impartial rational persons would adopt the moral attitude toward all of the rules under discussion if they considered them as moral rules, it may be asked why they need be concerned with rules at all. A rational person need not be concerned with rules, only with consequences. The only beliefs that count as basic reasons, that is, that can make otherwise irrational acts rational, are beliefs about the consequences of that act. Why should it make any difference if impartiality is added to rationality? Why should an impartial rational person be concerned with anything other than the consequences, direct or indirect, of a particular action? That an action is in accordance with a rule, obedience to which is generally beneficial, does provide a reason for performing that action, but only because it makes it more likely that one's action will have beneficial consequences. Why should a rational person be concerned at all with whether that action is a violation of a moral rule? This is not asking why a rational person should be impartial; everyone agrees that if we are concerned with the morality, impartiality is essential. But why be impartial with respect to rules; why not be impartial solely with respect to consequences?

This is the fundamental dispute between consequentialists, who hold that only consequences are important and deontologists, who believe that rules are an essential feature of morality. It is not that one group is in favor of impartiality and the other is not; it is not even that they are impartial with regard to a different group. Both consequentialists and deontologists may pick the same group as the appropriate group toward which one should be impartial. They differ in the respect with which one should be impartial with regard to this group. Many consequentialists claim that one should always act so as to bring about the greatest balance of good over evil, or in its more plausible negative form, should always act so as to bring about the least amount of evil. All consequentialists hold that it is irrelevant whether or not bringing about the least amount of evil requires the breaking of a moral rule, except insofar as doing this makes it more likely that there will be an increase in the amount of evil suffered in the future. Moral rules are simply considered useful maxims warning one of kinds of acts likely to bring about evil consequences, but they play no essential role in moral reasoning.

Not all impartial rational persons would pick that moral system which results in the least amount of evil being suffered; some may also be concerned with the distribution of the evil. Even if all rational persons would prefer one day of continuous pain to a thousand hours of pain, one hour a day, it does not follow that all impartial rational persons would advocate causing one day of continuous pain to one person in order to prevent a thousand persons from suffering one hour of pain. This is the case even if we eliminate any mention of violating a moral rule. Not all impartial rational persons would advocate relieving the pain of a thousand people suffering one hour of pain rather than relieving the pain of one person who is suffering continuously for a day. Both consequentialists and deontologists can take distribution considerations into account. An impartial rational consequentialist may hold that one person suffering one day of continuous pain is worse than one thousand persons suffering one hour of the same intensity of pain even though all rational persons may prefer twenty-four hours of continuous pain for themselves to one thousand hours of pain spread evenly over one thousand days.

I admit that consequentialism may include a concern for distribution, but for it to present a distinct point of view, one that is opposed to any kind of deontology, consequentialism must be limited to theories that consider the foreseeable consequences of a particular act as ultimately the only morally relevant considerations. A consequentialist can consider the foreseeable consequences of that act on whether other people will perform similar acts and thus give some weight to the following of beneficial rules, but he must really be considering the foreseeable consequences of that particular act. For example, if he is considering cheating, he must consider it morally relevant whether or not other people are likely to find out that he has cheated, for this changes the likelihood that they will be affected by that particular act of cheating. A consequentialist cannot take into consideration what would happen if, contrary to fact, everyone knew she was allowed to cheat in these circumstances. This does not involve a consideration of the foreseeable consequences of the act under consideration; it is at most a consideration of what the consequences would be if something that is not going to happen were to happen. This latter sort of view has been called "rule consequentialism," but it seems to me to be no more a consequentialist view than a false friend is a friend. (I call this fallacy the fallacy of ignoring the modifier.) Rather, this kind of "rule consequentialism" is a kind of deontological view, and with some significant modifications, it is the kind of view I am defending.

Given this account of consequentialism, consequentialists may claim that I have misrepresented their theories, that they do not really want people to act on a consequentialist system. Rather, they may claim that consequentialist theories are intended to provide a test for moral systems. One should adopt the moral system that, allowing for distribution considerations, results in the least amount of evil being suffered. However, the character of that system, given the facts of human nature and of a moral system, especially the limited knowledge of persons, and the public nature of a moral system, need not be consequentialist. It may be that taking the above factors into account, the moral system should be deontological. If the consequentialist says this, then I have no dispute with him. He is simply claiming that the point of morality is to lessen the amount of evil in the world, and I agree completely with this. My claim is about the character of a moral system; I have claimed that it should include impartiality with respect to rules, not merely with respect to consequences; this is what I mean by saying that the moral system should be deontological. This claim is based on two factors, (1) the public character of morality and (2) the limited knowledge of persons.

The public character of a moral system, has already been discussed, but it is worth mentioning here that the fact that it must be known to all who are governed by it means that it must be capable of being taught to those who are about to be governed by it, i.e., children. That all rational persons are judged by it makes it essential that a moral system should be taught to everyone, that adherence to it should be endorsed by all members of society whose endorsement is of significance, and that everyone be urged to follow it. The question that is under discussion is what moral system, given that a moral system must be public, and that people have only limited knowledge, is most likely to result in the least amount of suffering; is it a consequentialist moral system or a deontological one, one which requires impartiality only with respect to consequences or one that also requires impartiality with respect to rules?

Limited Knowledge

It is limited knowledge which makes it impossible for an impartial rational person to advocate that cheating be publicly allowed simply on the grounds that the violation will cause no harm. To advocate that such a violation be considered a justified exception is to advocate that anyone who has good reason to believe that his particular violation will cause no harm should be publicly allowed to cheat whenever he wants. This means that one should not be punished, or in any way condemned for cheating on an exam, in a situation where one has good reason to believe that no one will be harmed by her cheating and that some people, e.g., she and her parents, will be spared the evils that might come from her flunking the exam. We all know that persons are sometimes mistaken in their beliefs about the future, even when they have good reasons for such beliefs. This is especially true when the beliefs concern the consequences of their own actions.

The limited knowledge of persons, their inability to know all the consequences of their actions, is usually neglected in discussing moral rules. But limited knowledge is important not only for explaining why an impartial rational person would not advocate that cheating be publicly allowed simply on the grounds that no one will be hurt by it, but also for explaining why we need any moral rules at all. If all persons were omniscient, knew all of the consequences of their actions (if it is even possible that this be known), then they would have no need for rules. An impartial rational person would then advocate that everyone simply act so as never to increase the amount of evil in the world. He would be unconcerned whether or not these actions were violations of the moral rules. Consequentialism, of which Utilitarianism is a particular form, is the right kind of theory for a society of omniscient persons. But there are no omniscient persons; it is irrational to hold that any person, including oneself, can know all the consequences of her actions. Consequentialism remains so popular with philosophers because they usually present their examples in such a way that there is never any doubt about what the consequences of one's action will be.

Since persons are not omniscient, they need rules in order to provide a guide that can actually be followed. Given the limited knowledge of people, were they to act solely on what they believed would bring about the best consequences, independently of whether it involved violating a moral rule, they would act in ways that would result in more evil being suffered than if they followed the moral attitude toward the moral rules. The order and stability provided by people taking the moral rules as their guide explains why the moral attitude requires that an impartial rational person be able to advocate that the violation be publicly allowed before it can be considered justified. This requires her to consider the consequences of this kind of violation being publicly allowed, i.e., everyone knowing that everyone is allowed to break the rule in these circumstances. Recognizing the dangers posed by the limited knowledge of others serves as an important reminder that one's own limited knowledge also poses a danger. Holding that because of one's superior knowledge and intelligence, one can violate rules which, because others are inferior, one would not advocate being publicly allowed is a sign of arrogance. Arrogance is incompatible with impartiality. Violations of moral rules when no impartial rational person could advocate that those kinds of violations be publicly allowed is, in the long run, accompanied by a greater amount of evil being suffered.

Justifying the Moral Rules Again

I have shown that the fact that a particular act of cheating does not cause any harm is, by itself, not sufficient for an impartial rational person to advocate that everyone be publicly allowed to commit such a violation. I have not shown that an impartial rational person would adopt the moral attitude toward the original rule against cheating. The situation being considered is one in which an impartial rational person cannot advocate that cheating be publicly allowed whenever a person has a rational belief that no one will suffer because of her cheating, because that would be equivalent to accepting that a valuable activity be abolished. If all rational persons wish to protect this activity, they must discourage people from cheating even when their individual acts of cheating would cause no harm. Discouragement requires liability to punishment, and thus we have shown that all impartial rational persons would indeed adopt the moral attitude toward the original rule "Don't cheat" without the added qualification.

Does this same argument work with the rule "Obey the law"? It seems to me clear that it does. The two rules are perfectly parallel. If the law is a bad one, then the moral attitude may allow it to be broken. It will allow a violation when an impartial rational person can advocate that everyone be publicly allowed to commit such a violation. But if the law is a good one, then the fact that an individual violation would do no harm is not sufficient to allow an impartial rational person to advocate that it be publicly allowed to commit such a violation. Indeed, she must advocate that the rule not be violated in this situation, and this results in an impartial rational person adopting the moral attitude toward the rule "Obey the law." If all that one knows about a given action is that it is a violation of the law, then one ought not to do it. One needs to know enough about the consequences of violating it that one can advocate that such a violation be publicly allowed before that violation is justified. This is all that is needed to show that "Obey the law" is a moral rule. This argument also shows that it would be misleading to revise the rule so as to talk of "just laws," for there may be occasions on which an impartial rational person would advocate that a violation of a just law be publicly allowed and occasions on which no impartial rational person would advocate that a violation of a bad law be publicly allowed.

I do not think it is necessary to go through the argument again to show that impartial rationality requires adopting the moral attitude toward the rules "Don't deceive" and "Keep your promise" without qualification. The undesirable consequences of the erosion of trust that would result from publicly allowing violations of these two rules simply because one believes such a violation will cause no harm is evident to all. Breaking any of the four rules under discussion in this chapter, when an impartial rational person could not advocate that such a violation be publicly allowed, is acting immorally. Even if one's particular violation causes no harm, one is generally acting hypocritically. The effect on one's character provides an additional reason for an impartial rational person to advocate the moral attitude toward the four moral rules as originally formulated. I shall discuss this in more detail in Chapter 10, but even without this reason, we have shown that our rules as originally formulated are justified moral rules. Hence we can see that the earlier conclusions were correct even though adequate arguments had not yet been provided.

Independence of Each Moral Rule

I have now shown that an impartial rational person would adopt the same attitude toward the rule "Obey the law" as toward the previous eight rules. Since stealing always involves breaking the law, stealing is immoral even though there is no basic moral rule against stealing as such. For all practical purposes, one can treat "Don't steal" as a basic moral rule. I have not done so because "Don't steal" can be deduced from the rule "Obey the law." I have attempted to make all the moral rules logically independent of one another. Someone who breaks one of these rules does not necessarily break any of the others, though the breaking of one may always involve the breaking of some other. The rule "Obey the law" does not entail the rule "Don't kill" even though most, if not all, societies have laws against killing. Even if a society did not have a law against killing, it would be immoral to kill, or to break any of the previous moral rules, unless an impartial rational person could advocate that such a violation be publicly allowed. Thus it should not be thought that this rule in any way renders superfluous any of the previous rules. However, it sometimes helps determine what counts as a violation of some of these other rules.

All of the common moral rules listed in Chapter 4 (p.67) have now been considered. We have seen that all of them can be justified, though not in the same way. Some of them, "Don't kill," "Don't cause pain," "Keep your promise," and "Don't cheat," are basic moral rules. The rule "Don't lie" was changed to "Don't deceive" to broaden its scope. "Don't steal" was justified in that it could be deduced directly from the basic moral rule "Obey the law." "Don't commit adultery" was the only rule that did not have a universal justification, but it could be justified in any society with our institution of marriage. Given that institution, the rule against adultery could be deduced from the rule against cheating. In addition to these rules, three other rules were discovered which should be considered basic moral rules, "Don't disable," "Don't deprive of freedom," and "Don't deprive of pleasure." This gives us a list of nine basic moral rules. I may be influenced by tradition, but this list does not seem to me to be complete. I believe one more rule is necessary to complete the list. This rule I have formulated as "Do your duty."

Do Your Duty

This rule provides for those actions in society not covered by the rule "Obey the law," and yet not necessarily falling under any of the previous eight rules. All societies have a division of labor; many different jobs or offices need to be filled, each with specific duties. As I am using the term "duty," duties are primarily connected with jobs, offices, positions, etc. A teacher has certain duties, so does a night watchman; the recording secretary and the treasurer have specified duties that are spelled out by the rules of the organization in which they hold office; a father has duties, and so do children. Some of these duties are specified very precisely; some are extremely vague. Judges and umpires are required to make their decisions impartially; it is their duty to do so. Failure to do so, e.g., to favor one side, is to violate the rule "Do your duty." For it is not only one's duty to do certain things, e.g., a night watchman must make his rounds, but it is also often part of one's duty to do things in a certain way. A judge must not only show up for trial and make decisions; he must also make them impartially.

Although duties, in general, go with offices, jobs, roles, etc., there are some duties that seem more general. Some would say that it is the duty of every citizen to uphold the law. Although it may not be incorrect to say this, it is usually said only in very special circumstances. These circumstances are when an appeal is made to a very large number of citizens to obey the law, e.g., to white southerners when the civil rights laws were passed. Here, one does appeal to the duty of a citizen to uphold the law of the land. One who steals, however, is not normally thought of as failing to do his duty, but simply as violating the law. Even where the appeal is made to all citizens to do their duty by obeying the law, it is violating the law that is condemned; no further reference is usually made to failure to do one's duty as a citizen.

In these contexts, "it is your duty" means little more than "you ought." It is this use which philosophers have taken over when they maintain that we have a duty to obey the moral rules. I do not use the term "duty" in this extended sense. A person has a duty, in the basic sense in which I am using it, because of some special circumstances, e.g., his job or his relationships. I think that defining "duty" in the extended sense, but, without realizing it, making use of implications that only follow from the basic sense, has led some philosophers to accept ethical relativism. Toulmin's discussion of duty referred to earlier (see p. 133) is an excellent sample of this. Also, extending the term "duty" to cover everything that one morally ought to do leaves no term available for formulating a rule equivalent to "Do your duty."

Although duties are generally voluntarily incurred, they are not always so. A soldier who is drafted has no fewer duties than one who enlists. Children have duties to their parents, though in our society these are extremely vague. Duties can arise from circumstances also. In any civilized society, if a child collapses in your arms, you have a duty to seek help. You cannot simply lay him out on the ground and walk away. This duty cannot simply be called the duty to aid those in distress, for we do not have a duty to send money to those who are starving. It is, of course, morally good to do this, but we have no duty to be morally good.

In most civilized societies one has a duty to help when (1) one is in physical proximity to someone in need of help to avoid a serious evil, usually death or serious injury, (2) one is in a unique or close to unique position to provide that help and (3) it would be relatively cost free for one to provide that help. These are the features of the kind of example usually presented to show that there is a general duty to help those in distress, e.g., you are on the beach alone and see a small child drowning in shallow water whom you can rescue with no danger whatsoever to yourself. The duty to help does not have precise limits and it is sometimes impossible to say whether a person neglected a duty to help or simply failed to do what was morally good when he had a special opportunity to do so. I do not deny that you ought to prevent evil; I only deny that, except in special circumstances, you have a duty to do so. There is no general duty to prevent evil.

I am concerned with clarifying what I mean by "duty," for otherwise it may seem that the rule about duty makes some of the previous rules superfluous. We have already seen that it is possible to take the rule "Do your duty" as eliminating the need for the rule "Obey the law." It is also possible to maintain that this rule eliminates the need for the rule "Keep your promise." For it could be maintained that it is your duty to keep your promises. It could also be said that we have a duty to play fairly, and so the rule against cheating is superfluous. It has been maintained that we have a duty to tell the truth, so that the rule against deception might also be eliminated. Thus it might seem that the second five rules could all be reduced to the rule "Do your duty." But as I noted above, I do not wish to use "duty" in such a wide sense.

The question, "Why should I give the book to him?" depending on the circumstances, could be answered by citing several different rules. One obvious answer would be "You promised to give it to him," and the circumstance that makes this reply appropriate is simply the fact that you did promise. We can also imagine circumstances where the appropriate reply is "It is your duty as president of the organization to give the book to the winner of the contest." Sometimes the reply "Because the judge ruled that the book was legally his" is the appropriate one. We can even imagine circumstances in which the reply "Because it would be cheating not to" would be an appropriate reply.

Trying to reduce all of these replies to "It is your duty" is pointless, for this reply carries no more weight than the replies that it is supposed to replace. The rules against deceiving, breaking promises, cheating, and breaking the law are justified as directly as the rule demanding that you do your duty. If one does not see the point of these other rules, why should he see the point of the rule concerning duty? However, it is one of the standard practices of philosophers to try to reduce the moral rules to a single one, or failing that, at least to some smaller number than is generally accepted. One of the aims of social contract theorists was to reduce the rule "Obey the law" to "Keep your promise"—although had they thought of the rule against cheating, they would have tried to use it instead. I see no point in reducing the number of rules, especially when doing so makes one stretch the scope of the remaining rules beyond what is generally accepted. I regard "Do your duty" as a basic moral rule that is on a par with the other rules, not one that includes the others within it.

I have not yet shown that all impartial rational persons would adopt the moral attitude toward this rule. However, this is very easy to do. The reasoning is identical to that used to justify the rule "Obey the law." All rational persons know that they, or someone for whom they are concerned, may suffer some evil when someone fails to do his duty. Thus all rational persons want all other persons to do their duty when their not doing it increases the likelihood that anyone for whom they are concerned will suffer evil. When this attitude is put in a form that is acceptable to all impartial rational persons, it loses its egocentricity. We thus arrive at the moral attitude toward the rule "Do your duty whenever your not doing it increases the likelihood of someone suffering an evil."

Realizing that allowing everyone to neglect his duty whenever he has a rational belief that the particular act would result in no harm to anyone may destroy valuable activities that depend upon general obedience to the rule, all impartial rational persons would adopt the moral attitude toward the rule "Do your duty" without any qualifications. This argument also applies to the duty that some people have to punish violations of the moral rules. Refusing to carry out this duty when an impartial rational person could not advocate that this refusal be publicly allowed, is itself an immoral act. That one may refuse to do this duty because of compassion simply shows that compassion may lead one to act immorally.

I am aware, in these days of totalitarianism, that doing one's duty has been used to justify the grossest immorality. I am aware that business executives often try to justify acting in accordance with immoral company policy, claiming that their duty is to increase profits. The term "duty" is not synonomous with "what I am paid to do." One's job involves duties only to the extent that the job does not require one to unjustifiably violate a moral rule. It is not the duty of a professional killer to kill his innocent victim, though he may have been paid a sizable sum to do that. One cannot have a duty to unjustifiably violate a moral rule. The term "duty" in the rule "Do your duty" is unlike all of the terms in the previous moral rules in this important respect: it depends on knowledge of these other rules in order to be fully understood.

All of the terms in the other rules are understandable independently of our knowledge of any moral rule. Our understanding of what "kill," "deceive," or "cheat" mean does not depend upon our knowing about any moral rules. Understanding fully what counts as a violation of "Do not kill" may depend upon our knowing of the rules "Do not deceive" or "Keep your promise," what the term "kill" means does not. However, we do not understand what the term "duty" in the rule "Do your duty" means until we know that one can have no duty to do that which is an unjustifiable violation of a moral rule. To show that what a person claims to have a duty to do is an unjustifiable violation of a moral rule is to show that he does not really have a duty to do it. This does not mean that the rule "Do your duty" cannot conflict with other moral rules; it can. But the conflict must be one in which some impartial rational persons would advocate that doing your duty be publicly allowed, even though it involves violating another moral rule. If no impartial rational person would advocate that breaking the other rule in order to do what one claims it is one's duty to do be publicly allowed, then one does not have a duty to do it. Even with this understanding of duty, an impartial rational person is not advocating blind devotion to duty; indeed, he is not advocating blind obedience to any of the moral rules. All that is being maintained is what seems to me a completely uncontroversial view, that when an impartial rational person cannot advocate that disobeying this or any of the other moral rules be publicly allowed, one should obey them.

Summary

We now have ten rules:

1. Don't kill.	6. Don't deceive.
2. Don't cause pain.	7. Keep your promise.
3. Don't disable.	8. Don't cheat.
4. Don't deprive of freedom.	9. Obey the law.
5. Don't deprive of pleasure.	10. Do your duty.

It should be remembered that I regard the first rule as prohibiting causing the permanent loss of consciousness; the second rule as prohibiting various forms of mental suffering as well as physical pain; the third rule as prohibiting causing a loss of ability; the fourth rule as prohibiting interference with the exercise of any of one's abilities, so that it prohibits the deprivation of opportunity as well as the deprivation of freedom; and the fifth rule as prohibiting depriving of future as well as present pleasure.

Toward each of these rules considered as moral rules, i.e., as public rules that apply to all rational persons, the following attitude would be taken by all impartial rational persons: "Everyone is always to obey the rule except when an impartial rational person can advocate that violating it be publicly allowed. Anyone who violates the rule when an impartial rational person could not advocate that such a violation be publicly allowed may be punished." To adopt the moral attitude toward the moral rules is to recognize that the public system that we regard as morality includes not merely the moral rules but also the procedure for determining justified violations of the rules that is described by the moral attitude.

In Chapter 4 I listed the characteristics that all moral rules are believed to have. Any rule that has all of these characteristics is one toward which all impartial rational persons would adopt the moral attitude and any rule toward which all impartial rational persons would adopt the moral attitude has all of these characteristics. This shows that all of these characteristics fit together and are not merely an ad hoc collection of features which happen to have become associated with the moral rules. Showing that there are some rules toward which all impartial rational persons would adopt the moral attitude shows that some rules have all of the characteristics that genuine moral rules are believed to have and so shows that some rules are genuine moral rules. Showing which rules are those toward which all impartial rational persons would adopt the moral attitude not only shows which rules are genuine moral rules it also shows that these rules are justified moral rules. In an important sense, therefore, discovering what rules are genuine moral rules is justifying those rules.

I have tried to make clear when it is morally justifiable to violate the rules, viz., only when an impartial rational person can advocate that such a violation be publicly allowed. I have shown what morally relevant features determine the kind of violation and what feature of the kind of violation an impartial rational person must use in deciding whether or not to advocate that that kind of violation be publicly allowed. I showed how the public character of morality and the limited knowledge of persons were essential elements when impartial rational persons consider the effect of publicly allowing this kind of violation, i.e., that everyone knows that is is allowed to violate the rule in these circumstances. It must be kept in mind that an impartial rational person advocating that a violation be publicly allowed must be able to describe it in such a way that all rational persons can understand the reasons offered for the violation and could accept them as adequate.

I should also like to point out again that the "except" clause of the moral attitude does not mean that an impartial rational person never advocates punishment for a violation of a moral rule when an impartial rational person can advocate that such a violation be publicly allowed. Only if all impartial rational persons would advocate that such a violation be publicly allowed would no impartial rational person advocate punishment. When the violation is only allowed by impartial rationality, i.e., when impartial rational persons disagree on whether or not to advocate that the violation be publicly allowed, then rational persons also will disagree on whether or not the person should be punished. An impartial rational person need not exempt from liability to punishment another impartial rational person who has violated a rule because the latter would advocate that such a violation be publicly allowed. Evils are ranked in too many diverse ways for all impartial rational persons to be willing to permit any violation that some impartial rational person would advocate be publicly allowed. This is one explanation of why there is sometimes a divergence in moral judgment and legal judgment. We agree that the person has morally justified his violation; but since those in charge of enforcing the law, acting as impartial rational persons, would not have advocated publicly allowing such a violation, they are willing to advocate punishment. They may be morally justified in punishing him.

It should be clear from the preceding that in justifying the moral rules, I have not eliminated all moral disagreement. But I have set limits on such disagreement. I am able to set these limits because I have limited my discussion to impartial rational persons and to the concept of morality. My accounts of the concepts of rationality and of the kind of impartiality that the moral rules require, and of the public character of morality, are what allow me to provide a formal criterion of moral rules which has precisely the content that those opposed to formal criteria usually want. The debate between the formalists and those who demanded content can now be seen to be like most other debates in philosophy. Both parties are partly right, but because both lack an adequate account of some basic concepts they are unable to reconcile their differences.

The debate between the deontologist and the consequentialist is resolved in a similar manner. The deontologist is right about the need for rules; the consequentialist is right about morality having a point or purpose. The former fails to see that moral rules, like all other rules, must be interpreted, and that a rational person will always interpret them by reference to the point of the rules. The latter fails to see that an impartial rational person, in order to provide a public system that can be used by all rational persons and achieve the point of morality, must make use of rules. Once we have the concept of an impartial rational person and recognize that morality must be public and that people have only limited knowledge, we realize the need both for the moral rules and for the moral attitude which tells us how to obey these rules. I hope that the concepts of an impartial rational person and of the moral attitude are not only useful in resolving moral disputes, but equally helpful in resolving philosophical disputes about morality.

8

MORAL IDEALS

Although the moral rules are the most important part of morality, they are not all of it. Morality consists not only of rules, but also of ideals. This has been noted from the very first chapter, but emphasis on the moral rules has been so great that it may very well have been forgotten. In the first chapter I noted that moral judgments are judgments on actions, intentions, etc., using some moral rule or ideal. In the previous two chapters the role of the moral ideals in providing a justification for violating the moral rules was noted. But there has as yet been no detailed discussion of the moral ideals, no attempt to identify them or to distinguish them from other ideals. This shall be done in this chapter.

Just as the moral rules might be summarized as "Don't cause evil" or "Don't do that which causes or is likely to cause anyone to suffer evil," so the moral ideals can be summarized as "Prevent evil" or "Do those things that lessen or are likely to lessen the amount of evil suffered by anyone." Particular moral ideals can be paired with particular moral rules. Substituting "prevent" for "don't" and changing the wording slightly generates a moral ideal from each of the moral rules. "Prevent killing," "Prevent the causing of pain," "Prevent disabling," "Prevent the deprivation of freedom," "Prevent the deprivation of pleasure," "Prevent deceit," "Prevent the breaking of promises," "Prevent cheating," "Prevent the breaking of the law," and "Prevent the neglect of duty" are all moral ideals.

These moral ideals can be followed in a number of different ways. One way is by teaching people to adopt the moral attitude toward the moral rules. Someone who tries to persuade others to do this, e.g., the writer of this book, is following the moral ideals; but trying to persuade others to adopt the moral attitude toward the moral rules does not indicate anything about the moral character of the person doing the persuading. In normal circumstances all rational persons will openly support adopting the moral attitude toward the moral rules. Nothing I say in this chapter or in any other chapter of this book is a reliable indication of my moral character. This is as it should be, for what I say should be judged entirely on its own merits. If it is claimed that I am preaching rather than doing moral philosophy, my response is that I am preaching what one should expect any rational person to preach. That we expect all rational persons to preach that people act in accordance with the moral attitude toward the moral rules helps to explain the popularity of the maxim "Practice what you preach."

Following the moral ideals merely by preaching that everyone follow the moral attitude toward the moral rules when this preaching requires no sacrifice or risk, as in writing this book, does not count for much. However, there are occasions in which preaching morality does have significant moral worth. Someone who speaks out openly against the immoral action of some powerful person or group of persons is following a moral ideal in a significant way. Someone who urges his country to stop acting in immoral fashion often undergoes significant risk in so doing, and his action deserves moral praise. Even someone who does not undergo any risk but merely devotes a great deal of time to encouraging people to act morally may deserve moral praise. Of course, much depends on the motive for the action, but this needs no special comment here.

The moral ideals that encourage one to prevent those actions that count as violations of the moral rules are not the basic moral ideals. The most important moral ideals are directly concerned with lessening of such evils as death, pain, and disability. People who volunteer for the various relief agencies which aid the innocent victims of war, famine, floods, earthquakes and other man-made and natural disasters are clearly following the moral ideals. Those who work with the deprived peoples of the earth, trying to help them deal more effectively with the evils they suffer, are also clearly following the moral ideals. Since disease is also a cause of so much death, pain, and disability, helping to fight disease is also a way of following the moral ideals. When one is talking about disease it may sometimes be more appropriate to talk of the moral ideals of "Preserving life," "Relieving pain," and "Lessening disabilities." In former times it was thought that these moral ideals were the primary motives for those who went into the practice of medicine, and so doctors used to be regarded as among the morally best persons.

Although it may not be as obvious, there are also moral ideals directly connected with the evils that are the concern of the fourth and fifth moral rules. These ideals, "Prevent the loss of freedom," and "Prevent the loss of pleasure," need not be related to violations of the moral rules. Freedom and pleasure may be lost by the operation of natural causes, as well as by the acts of other persons. For example, those who work to save the homes and prized possessions that are threatened by fire are trying to prevent the loss of freedom and pleasure. Of course, it is also following a moral ideal to try to prevent the loss of freedom and pleasure when these are caused by other persons, e.g., burglars. An extraordinary amount of evil is neither the result of natural causes, nor of particular unjustified violations of moral rules, but stems from social causes. Those who work to eradicate slums and poverty are generally following the moral ideals. War, justified or not, causes immense amounts of all of the evils. Those who sincerely work to achieve and preserve peace are almost always acknowledged to be following moral ideals. "Blessed be the peacemakers" is a sentiment shared by all impartial rational persons. In fact, since war is one of the greatest single causes of the evils suffered by humankind, the prevention of war and the preservation of peace must be among the most important goals of those following moral ideals.

Negative Utilitarianism and the Point of Morality

Like the moral rules, the moral ideals are concerned with evil rather than good. However, whereas the moral rules require that you not cause anyone to suffer evil, the moral ideals encourage you to prevent or lessen the evil being suffered by anyone. Morality requires that everyone be careful always to obey the moral rules; it only encourages people to act on the moral ideals as much as they can. When what you are required to do by the moral rules conflicts with what you are encouraged to do by the moral ideals, you must decide whether your breaking of the rule is justified. I have already pointed out that these cases cannot be decided in the abstract, but that each case must be treated on its own merits. One could maintain that one ought to choose that alternative which, all things considered, results in the least amount of evil being suffered. If this principle, which might be called the principle of negative utilitarianism, does not require that an impartial rational person be able to advocate that violations of moral rules be publicly allowed, it not only conflicts with our clear moral intuitions in some cases; but, as shown in the previous chapter, it also does not take either the public character of morality or the limited knowledge of persons sufficiently into account. If it does require that an impartial rational person be able to advocate that violations of moral rules be publicly allowed, the principle is superfluous.

Further, the principle, although it pretends to provide a precise procedure for making decisions, is so vague as to be almost totally useless. It does not say what ought to be considered. Should it merely be the evils directly avoided, caused, and prevented? Should it include the effect on the moral character of those involved? Should it include the effect on respect for the rule by others? What is the weight of these various considerations? How does one weigh one kind of evil against another? None of these questions is answered by the general principle of negative utilitarianism. It seems to me best to regard the principle of negative utilitarianism as a device to remind oneself of the point of morality, the minimization of evil, rather than as a guide to be rigorously applied to individual cases of moral conflict. Misuse of this principle is what leads to the view that those who violate the second five moral rules but do not intend to cause evil to anyone are really not acting immorally.

Distinguishing Moral Ideals from Utilitarian Ideals

Because the goal of morality is the minimization of evil it is important to distinguish moral ideals from all other ideals, particularly utilitarian ones. A utilitarian ideal, i.e., an ideal which encourages us to promote some good, does not normally justify the breaking of a moral rule, although this is obscured by the fact that often when we talk about "doing good," e.g., doing volunteer work in a hospital, we are not talking about what I call promoting goods, but rather preventing evils. The evils of death, pain, and disability are obviously the proper subject of moral ideals. But when one considers the evils of loss of freedom and loss of pleasure the distinction between moral and utilitarian ideals may not seem so clear. I do not claim that there is an absolutely clear distinction between the moral ideals "Prevent the loss of freedom" and "Prevent the loss of pleasure" and the utilitarian ideals "Increase freedom" and "Increase pleasure." In fact, increasing the freedom and pleasure of those whom I call "deprived persons" is following moral rather than utilitarian ideals. I shall have more to say about this in Chapter 12, when discussing morality and society. Here I am merely noting that there is some distinction between preventing or lessening a loss of goods, which counts as minimizing evils, and simply promoting goods.

Normally, in morality one must start with the status quo. The moral rules prohibit changing the status quo by causing evil. Moral ideals encourage changing the status quo by lessening the amount of evil. This is the only change encouraged by morality. It does not discourage promoting good as long as this does not involve violating the moral rules, but it is not the goal of morality to promote the greatest good for the greatest number. Nor does morality demand that the goods of the earth be equally distributed among all its inhabitants. Moral ideals are not revolutionary, except in those societies where immoral action by those in power is taken for granted, or when there are great numbers of deprived persons. Unfortunately, in the world today there are many societies where moral ideals are revolutionary.

Moral Ideals and Impartiality

Moral ideals, like the moral rules, make no mention of person, place, group, or time. This may lead some to the view that in following moral ideals we must exclude all personal preferences as rigorously as when obeying the moral rules. This is a mistake. Personal preference does not justify violating a moral rule with regard to someone one does not care about in order to follow a moral ideal with regard to someone one does care about. For example, that you love someone cannot justify killing an innocent stranger in order to save her life. The moral rules require obedience with regard to all persons impartially, but the moral ideals do not require impartial action with regard to all persons. When no violation of the moral rules is involved, one may choose to follow a moral ideal with regard to some group of persons with whom one has some special relationship. The NAACP has no need to justify concentrating its efforts in following moral ideals toward aiding black Americans. The United Jewish Appeal need not justify concentrating its efforts toward aiding other Jews. Nor does the government of the United States need to justify being primarily concerned with aiding the deprived citizens of America. It is pointless to try to follow moral ideals with regard to all persons impartially. Everyone is more likely to act more effectively if she is allowed to choose the persons or groups toward whom she will concentrate her efforts. In fact, it seems most likely that it is impossible to follow the moral ideals impartially; hence no moral system would require that the moral ideals be followed in this way.

Even were it possible to follow moral ideals with regard to all persons impartially, one would not be morally required to do so. One is not required to follow moral ideals at all, much less to follow them with regard to all persons impartially. The view that one should follow moral ideals impartially usually amounts to no more than the view that one should follow moral ideals impartially with regard to all those with whom one comes into personal contact. I do not see how this is in any way morally preferable to following moral ideals with regard to some more traditionally specified group. What gives it an air of being morally preferable is that if one chooses to follow moral ideals impartially with regard to everyone with whom one comes into personal contact, one is less inclined to unjustifiably violate a moral rule in order to follow a moral ideal. But if one adopts the moral attitude toward the moral rules and is clear about the distinction between moral rules and moral ideals, I see no advantage in excluding personal preferences. The only exception to this might be if one decides to do that which will result in the greatest relief of evil regardless of any relationship to oneself.

Religious and Other Ideals

I have up to now limited my discussion of ideals to moral and utilitarian ideals. These are not the only ideals that all impartial rational persons would include in a public system that everyone is encouraged to follow, but they do seem to be the only ideals directly concerned with actions that would have universal support, e.g., all of the major religions of humankind urge their adherents to follow moral and utilitarian ideals. Religions have also put forward ideals, not directly related to actions, which would be supported by all impartial rational persons, e.g., that people develop certain personality traits. At its highest, religion has put forward the ideal of loving-kindness, which goes beyond what is encouraged by moral ideals. Although the highest ideals of religion actually urge following of moral ideals, this is generally obscured because these ideals often are not distinguished from the ideals that are peculiar to the particular religion. The harm done by this failure to distinguish moral ideals from ideals which depend essentially on belief in a particular religion cannot be overestimated. Failure to distinguish between moral ideals and those ideals which depend on some particular religious belief has contributed to the mistaken view that these latter ideals, which no impartial rational person could advocate as part of a public system, sometimes justify violating the moral rules.

Whenever the ideal that a religion supports rests essentially on a revelation, or scripture, viz., anything that is not known to all rational persons, impartial rational persons cannot advocate that a violation of a moral rule be publicly allowed in order to follow it. It is never morally justifiable to follow these ideals when this involves violating the moral rules. Failure to realize this has permitted the infliction of an extraordinary amount of evil. Nations, also, have put forward ideals for which no impartial rational person could advocate that a violation of a moral rule be publicly allowed. The evils caused by pursuing these ideals, even when this involves violating the moral rules, may now outweigh the evils caused by the unjustified violations of the moral rules for religious ideals. Persons of various races are putting forward ideals that no impartial rational person can advocate be publicly allowed to be followed when doing so involves violation of the moral rules. It may be that the evil caused by racist ideals will outweigh the evils of both religious and nationalistic ideals. I am not maintaining that following these ideals must lead to evil. If one recognizes that pursuit of these ideals does not justify violation of the moral rules, then many positive benefits may come from following these ideals. Indeed, persons need some ideals beyond those provided by morality.

Although morality does not and should not provide a complete guide to life for all persons, there is a sense in which it provides the supreme guide. Morality provides a guide to conduct that all impartial rational persons advocate that no one ever be publicly allowed to violate for the sake of any ideal which cannot be part of a public system that applies to all rational persons. Only ideals or ends which an impartial rational person can advocate as part of such a public system justify a violation of a moral rule. This means that only for moral ideals and, in special circumstances, for utilitarian ideals can one justifiably violate moral rules. In general, this view is largely accepted today. We would consider as a fanatic anyone who thought it justifiable to do what is morally wrong in order to promote some ideal or cause which an impartial rational person could not advocate as part of such a public system. In fact, this is an acceptable definition of a fanatic. A religious fanatic is one who thinks it permissible to do what is morally wrong in order to do what God commands or his religion demands. A nationalistic fanatic is one who thinks it permissible to do what is morally wrong in order to advance the interests of his country. A racist fanatic is one who thinks maintaining the purity of his race permits his doing what is morally wrong. A scientific fanatic is one who thinks that the gaining of scientific knowledge makes it permissible to do what is morally wrong.

The proper understanding of the oft misused saying "The end does not justify the means" is "No end justifies immoral means." Of course, what counts as "immoral means" depends to some degree on the end that is sought. Breaking a moral rule does not count as using immoral means if the ideal one is following is such that an impartial rational person could advocate that such a violation be publicly allowed. It should be clear from the above that morality does not have any positive goal at all; rather it sets the limit on what can be done in following any positive ideals, e.g., the positive ideals presented by the different religions. Morality seeks only to minimize evil, but as long as the positive ideal does not violate the demands of morality, it is compatible with the moral guide to conduct. Although morality does not provide a complete guide to life, it does provide a supreme one; for impartial rational persons, nothing else is permitted to overrule it.

Happiness

I have not yet discussed what I shall call the personal ideals. These involve the goals that a rational person seeks for herself. Some of these are goals that are shared by all rational persons, and some are not. Philosophers and others have historically concentrated on those ideals that are shared by all rational persons, and I also shall limit myself to these. Traditionally, happiness has been considered as a goal that is sought by all rational persons. However, there are so many diverse views of happiness that even were it accepted as the goal sought by all rational persons, this would not mean that all rational persons had the same personal ideal except in a purely verbal sense.

If we want happiness to be something which all rational persons seek above all other things for themselves and for all those for whom they are concerned, then there is almost certainly nothing that will count as an acceptable account of happiness. A happy life is not the same as a life of pleasure. Not all rational persons prefer pleasure to every other good so that happiness should not be confused with pleasure, though everyone agrees that there is a close connection between the two. Although a life of pleasure may be a happy life, it also may not be, for one may not look back upon it with pleasure. One way to relate happiness and pleasure is to regard a happy life as one that is remembered with pleasure, which a life of pleasure need not be, for one may come to regard it as a wasted life. Happiness would not be remembered pleasure, but that which a rational person remembers with pleasure.

On this account of happiness, to say "This is the happiest moment of my life" is to make a prediction, not merely in the literal sense that one is denying that she will ever have a happier moment. It is the prediction that one will remember that moment with great pleasure for the rest of one's life. Often the happiest times of one's life are those in which one is so absorbed in the activities of living and doing that at the time one often complained of having no time simply to enjoy life. This account of happiness is obviously incomplete, e.g., it does not specify the conditions under which one remembers the past, but it does have the virtue of partially explaining why happiness has been thought to consist of so many diverse elements. There are very many different kinds of things that rational persons can remember with pleasure. It is also plausible that a happy life, as that which is remembered with pleasure, might be preferred by all rational persons to anything else. It is interesting that the so-called Utilitarian paradox, that one best achieves pleasure by not aiming for it, seems not to be true for pleasure, but does seem to hold for happiness on this account of happiness. Thus it seems pointless to list happiness as a personal ideal, for it involves a goal that one is more likely to achieve by not seeking it directly.

In my discussion of the personal ideals, I shall discuss only those goals that a person is more likely to achieve when she sets out to attain them. Generally speaking, persons think of the ideal life in two quite different ways. For some an ideal life consists primarily in the attaining of as many personal goods as possible. For others, an ideal life consists primarily in being a certain kind of person. In older and somewhat more colorful language, for some the ideal is a life of pleasure, for others a life of virtue. However, this colorful way of putting it is quite misleading. There are other personal goods in addition to pleasure, and virtue is not a homogeneous whole. Moreover, all rational persons desire some goods, and all rational persons wish to have some virtues. Indeed one might claim that the personal ideal shared by all rational persons is to be a person of virtue and to have a high degree of all the personal goods, which is very close to Aristotle's definition of happiness. However, plausible as this seems, I think that it is false.

The *Summum Bonum* or Greatest Good

The lure of the *summum bonum* is almost irresistible. It is extraordinarily difficult to accept the view that there is no one thing, or some simple combination of things, that all rational persons are seeking. Even those who realize the impossibility of formulating any intelligible account of a *summum bonum* continue to use the term. Perhaps this is due to feeling that denying that there is a *summum bonum* would be denying that there is any objective goal to human life. But there can still be objective *goals*. Failing to see this may be partly due to a failure to realize the diversity of personal goods. I have already shown that not all rational persons seek all personal goods, that insofar as there is agreement on goals, it is an agreement to avoid suffering any evil. We must allow different people to have different personal ideals, even if that ideal is describable as wanting to have a personal good. Some persons may desire pleasure, in the ordinary sense of that term, others knowledge, and others certain kinds of physical and mental abilities. This latter ideal is often described as self-realization. Nothing is gained by trying to include all of these goals in a *summum bonum*.

It would probably be less misleading to describe preferences for these different personal ideals as primarily a difference in emphasis, but to do this would encourage the mistaken view that all persons really want the same thing, only in somewhat different proportions. Moreover, we must also guard against the similar error that each person has his own *summum bonum* or matter of ultimate concern, even though it may be different from some other person's. Most rational persons have a number of personal goods that they wish to attain, and though one may be more important than any of the rest, it is rarely more important than all the rest put together. It is generally as misleading to talk about the *summum bonum* with regard to an individual person as it is to talk about it with regard to all rational persons. Pursuit of these personal ideals clearly does not justify immoral behavior, but the failure to distinguish morality from other guides to conduct has obscured this, and so pursuit of quite worthy personal ideals has often led to immoral conduct.

Not all personal ideals involve attaining personal goods; some are concerned with becoming a certain type of person. Generally this involves certain traits of character or virtues. Virtues will be discussed in more detail in the following chapter, but something should be said here about their place in the personal ideals. Some virtues, which I shall call the "personal virtues," e.g., prudence, temperance, and courage, are desired by all rational persons. These virtues, however, generally form only a small part of one's personal ideals. The virtues that form the most significant part of some people's personal ideals are the moral virtues: honesty, trustworthiness, etc. For Plato and Aristotle, all of the moral virtues went together under a name that we have come to call justice. Biblical thought added another virtue, sometimes called charity, or kindness. These two virtues, justice and charity, or kindness, were thought to comprise all of moral virtue by Hobbes and almost all thinkers after him. As I shall show in the following chapter, they can be considered substantially correct. Even though attaining these moral virtues is a personal ideal for many rational persons, we must remember from our previous discussion of morality that not all rational persons wish to act morally.

Authenticity

Recently, as objective morality has fallen into disfavor, another trait of character has come to the fore as forming a significant part of the personal ideal of many people. The most popular name for this trait of character is authenticity. Authenticity is not to be understood merely as truthfulness, which would make it merely one of many specific moral virtues. Rather, authenticity seems as if it were designed to replace all of the moral virtues. On at least some accounts, authenticity requires only rationality and lack of hypocrisy. It is relatively easy to see how authenticity on this account seems to encompass all of the moral virtues. If we regard a rational person as necessarily making moral judgments, then he presents himself as accepting the moral system as the appropriate guide to behavior. Since authenticity excludes hypocrisy, the authentic person must act in the way that he presents himself, i.e., as acting on a public system that applies to all rational persons. Such a person will have all of the moral virtues. I doubt that such thoughts prompted those who advanced authenticity as a personal ideal for all, but it seems compatible with much that has been written on the matter.

In much talk about authenticity there is great emphasis put on the fact that we entered a world we did not make and will soon leave, willingly or not. This emphasis on our dependence on a world we did not make and on death fits in nicely with the view of authenticity presented above. Acknowledgement that one is dependent on others and mortal may lead one to view oneself as like other persons in the most important respects and hence to adopt the guide to conduct provided by morality. Recognizing that one will die and the world continue, just as it has for all the people who have gone before and will do for all of the people who come after, is a powerful antidote to arrogance. The same is true of acknowledging one's dependence on other people and on society in general.

Interpreted in this way, authenticity is a worthy personal ideal; it is identical to the personal ideal of being a morally good person.

However, authenticity is not always understood in this way. The failure to distinguish morality from other guides to conduct, and the desire for one encompassing guide, affected the concept of authenticity, as it did more traditional ethical concepts. Authenticity most closely resembles the ancient Greek doctrine of living according to one's nature. The Greeks, of course, regarded a person's essential nature as that of a rational being, and so living according to nature was interpreted very much like living rationally, but with no distinction made between living as rationality requires and as impartial rationality requires. However, today a person is no longer regarded as essentially a rational being. Thus authenticity requires a person to follow his nature without telling him what that nature is. Perversion of the concept was inevitable. Authenticity was taken as requiring only that one act naturally, interpreted as acting as one feels, free from the artificial constraints imposed by society. No distinction was made between the constraints imposed by the moral rules and those imposed by non-moral social conventions. On this account an authentic person believes that he should violate the moral rules whenever he feels like doing so. The "hero" of Gide's *The Immoralist* is someone who adopted the confused concept of authenticity as a personal ideal.

Tolerance

It should be noted that most of what I have said about the moral ideals does not apply to tolerance. Yet tolerance is regarded by some as one of the most important moral ideals. Tolerance is not a moral ideal. It is required by the moral rules. Tolerance, properly understood, does not involve doing anything; rather, it consists in not doing certain things. To be intolerant is to violate any of the moral rules, particularly the first five, with regard to someone because of some morally indifferent characteristic he possesses. A tolerant person will not kill, cause pain to, disable, deprive of freedom or pleasure, any person because of the color of his skin, his place of birth, or his religious beliefs. An intolerant person is necessarily an immoral person, for he violates a moral rule unjustifiably. Legislation enforcing tolerance is completely justified, for it is simply legislation enforcing the moral rules. This is quite different from legislation that seeks to enforce the following of some moral or utilitarian ideal, e.g., that one must strive to benefit some disadvantaged group. Impartial rational persons can disagree about this kind of legislation.

Those who say that you cannot make people moral by legislation usually fail to distinguish the moral rules from moral ideals. Every civilized society enforces the moral rules. The criminal law is designed for precisely this purpose. In civilized societies the violation of every moral rule is punishable by the criminal law; this is even true of the rule "Obey the law," for violation of it, even if the original law broken was not part of the criminal law, becomes a matter of the criminal law. You cannot make people follow a moral ideal by passing a law, for the passing of such legislation makes what would have been an action encouraged by a moral ideal into an action required by a moral rule. This seeming paradox is no argument against such legislation, but it may explain why some hold the silly view that moral action should not be enforced by legislation.

Neither morality nor tolerance requires one to give equal consideration to all views. Some views may not deserve serious consideration. But the expression of absurd views, even of immoral views, though not to be encouraged, should usually not be suppressed. Freedom of speech and related freedoms are not moral ideals; they are required by the moral rules. The only justifiable limitation of freedom of speech is provided by moral ideals. The only justification for violating a moral rule with regard to someone who expresses an immoral view is to prevent people from suffering sufficient evil that an impartial rational person would advocate that such a violation be publicly allowed. Dislike for, even disgust with, the views being expressed does not justify violating a moral rule with regard to the person expressing the view. Similarly, dislike for or disgust with the personal preferences or habits of others, by itself, does not provide a justification for violating a moral rule with regard to them. Cleanliness may be next to godliness, but unless it results in increasing the risk of others suffering some evil, it has little to do with morality.

It is important to distinguish the moral rules and ideals from those rules and ideals that are often confused with them. Failure to do so allows some to violate the moral rules with regard to those whom they dislike or with whom they disagree. This permits intolerance, which is immoral, to masquerade as morality. This masquerade is no better when the intolerant are sincere than when they are not. In fact, when one sincerely believes that morality supports his intolerant actions, he is likely to cause more evil than when he is aware of the masquerade. Witness the extraordinary evil caused by those who sincerely believed that it was morally right to persecute those who held different religious beliefs. Witness the evil still inflicted on those who refuse to conform to the non-moral social customs of a society.

Religious tolerance is fairly well established now in most democratic countries. Very few would hold it morally justified to violate the moral rules with regard to anyone because of his religious beliefs. I do not think that this is due primarily to an increase in moral understanding, but to a decrease in the importance of religious beliefs. The fundamentalist sects are notoriously less tolerant of people holding different religious beliefs than are the more liberal denominations. I do not believe this reflects a difference in moral character or moral understanding. It reflects what is admittedly the case, that religious belief is much more important to members of fundamentalist sects. Very few people are tolerant of different views on matters they consider important. Many people are quite prepared to violate the moral rules with regard to those who express sufficiently unpopular views on political matters. But tolerance only demands not violating the moral rules with regard to the person expressing the views; it does not demand politeness. The vigor of one's response to views one dislikes, particularly immoral views, is not restrained by tolerance. Tolerance simply demands that this vigor not express itself in the unjustified violation of a moral rule.

I do not want to be understood as maintaining that politeness is not important. Indeed, politeness taken as a character trait involving acting so as to avoid giving offense to others even counts as a moral virtue. But politeness is a moral virtue only when properly understood. Politeness can never require either unjustified violation of a moral rule or conflict with justifiably following a moral ideal. Since one moral ideal is to teach people to follow the moral rules and ideals, it is a misunderstanding of politeness to think it requires one never to challenge someone who has put forward immoral views. Most people would probably prefer to continue this misunderstanding, for it takes some considerable courage to challenge the views of others in the service of morality.

The close connection between tolerance and morality makes it seem unlikely that anyone would seek to undermine the latter in order to promote the former. Yet this seems to be what those anthropologists who espouse ethical relativity are doing. These persons wish to encourage tolerance of the customs and mores of the peoples they study. They hold, quite rightly, that it is morally unjustified for outsiders to come into a culture and try to force changes in the way these people live. Although they do not express it in this way, they hold that one should not violate a moral rule with regard to these people in order to get them to adopt a different way of life. However, they sometimes support this perfectly correct view by maintaining that there are no universal moral rules, that morality is completely a matter of one's own culture. But if my culture allows the violation of moral rules with regard to those who live differently, morality would provide no reason to be tolerant of the culture of different peoples.

The anthropologists' confusion is one that we have discussed repeatedly. They have failed to distinguish the moral rules from the non-moral customs of a society. They wish to maintain that we should not impose our non-moral customs and practices, particularly sexual ones, on other cultures because doing so would be immoral. However, having failed to distinguish morality from those aspects of a culture which are peculiar to it, they do not have the concepts to express their views correctly. They advocate tolerance without realizing that in so doing they are advocating obedience to the moral rules. It is ironic that these people, who are so morally sensitive and sophisticated, should argue for the correct moral view by attacking morality.

Centrality of the Moral Rules

Although this chapter is supposed to be devoted to moral ideals, discussion of the moral rules continually seems to take over. I do not apologize for this. The moral rules are central to morality, not only from a philosophical point of view, but also from a practical one. Emphasis on moral ideals results in a view of morality that is too idealistic. This is not only philosophically incorrect, it has bad practical consequences. An idealistic morality is too easy to dismiss as being all right in theory, but of no use in real life. To hold that morality requires everyone to follow moral ideals is a misguided attempt to encourage such action. It is misguided because no philosophical theory will have much force in persuading people to follow moral ideals. The result of this attempt is more likely to provide an excuse for those who wish to dismiss morality as impractical or too difficult for ordinary human beings like themselves. Distinguishing sharply between the moral rules and moral ideals, and emphasizing the former, does away with this excuse. Morality requires that one obey the moral rules; it only encourages one to follow moral ideals. The demands of morality are not too difficult for ordinary human beings.

Emphasis on the moral rules does not result in a purely negative morality. That moral ideals are not required does not mean they are not encouraged. Those who wish to go beyond what is required by morality do have moral ideals to provide them with a positive guide to life. I do not think that moral philosophy will persuade many people to follow moral ideals. Those who are inclined to follow them generally will do so without the aid of moral philosophy. Those who are not so inclined generally will not do so, regardless of their agreement with a particular moral philosophy. Moral philosophy has as its primary practical function that of preventing people from doing what is morally wrong because of a misunderstanding of morality. Lack of the proper understanding of morality can lead to morally wrong actions. I believe that this book may result in some people avoiding an immoral action that they might otherwise have done. But I do not believe that this book will result in anyone doing a morally good action, i.e., following a moral ideal, which they would not have done without reading this book.

Compassion

One may follow moral ideals because she has compassion for other persons. However, misguided compassion for one person may lead one to follow a moral ideal when this is the morally wrong thing to do. There is a possibility that an understanding of morality may prevent this. But a perfect understanding of morality, without compassion, generally will not lead one to follow moral ideals. To have compassion for others is to suffer because of their suffering. Thus compassion may lead one both to avoid causing anyone to suffer and to relieve the suffering of others. There are degrees of compassion, and most people have more compassion for those they love than they do for others. But it is not unusual for everyone to have some compassion for all humankind, even if it is only a very small amount. To see others seriously hurt, especially children, even though we do not know them, is distressing to almost all people.

I do not use the term "compassion" as a term of praise. It is understandable how it comes to be so used, for we expect a compassionate person to be a kind person. But compassion need not lead to kindness. It depends, in part, on the depth of one's compassion, but more depends upon the breadth of one's compassion. One who has compassion only for a limited group, such as his family, may be ruthless in dealing with other people. What is most important however, are the actions that result from one's compassion. Even one who has a great depth of compassion for all humankind will not necessarily be a kind man. He may seek to relieve his suffering by trying to forget about others. This can be done in many ways: drink, drugs, searching for excitement and adventure, even complete dedication to sor . intellectual pursuit. He may even be overcome by his compassion and completely avoid those whose suffering causes him to suffer. If one's goal is merely to relieve oneself of the suffering of compassion, following moral ideals may not be the most satisfactory way of proceeding; one always has the sufferings of others clearly in mind. Nonetheless, there is some personal benefit to the compassionate person in following moral ideals. He does get some pleasure in seeing some suffering being relieved or prevented.

Being morally good is not primarily a matter of feelings. It is a matter of action. The feelings are morally important only insofar as they lead to morally good actions. It is a confusion to hold that a morally good person is really no better than one who always acts selfishly, as each is simply trying to minimize his own pain and to increase his own pleasure. Apart from the fact that this is not even true, it is beside the point. As long as one's motive for following the moral ideals is not one that depends on others' being aware of what one is doing, then it is morally insignificant what that motive is. Further, as we have already pointed out, a compassionate person has ways of relieving his compassion other than following moral ideals. We do not praise a man morally because he is compassionate, but because his compassion leads him to follow moral ideals.

Love

Compassion should be distinguished from love. One may have compassion for someone without loving her. *To love someone is to take pleasure in her pleasure.* This is what is common to all forms of love: of parents for their children, of men and woman for their spouses, or of a saint for all humankind. Each kind of love includes something more than love, and we do not usually talk of one person loving some other individual unless they get more pleasure from seeing that person pleased than they do from seeing others pleased. One job for psychologists is to determine statistically meaningful relations between love and various other feelings, desires, and actions. I am trying to provide some clear concepts so that they can begin to do this job. It is easy to see that love is intimately related to compassion. Generally, we do not even talk of someone as genuinely loving another unless she also feels compassion for him, even though it is common to feel compassion for someone without loving him. Love without compassion is shallow, superficial, etc., but I do not think that we should deny it is love. However, since it is so rare to love someone without feeling compassion for him, I shall consider love as always being accompanied by compassion. Again it should be clear that I am not using the term "love" as a term of praise. However, unlike compassion, the feeling of love is, in itself, a pleasant feeling.

The expressions of love, I call the acts of love. In the acts of love, I include sexual acts, for the acts of sex are among those in which people can express their love most directly. But there are many other ways in which they can express their love. Parents express their love for their children when they bring them toys in order to watch the look of delight on their faces. The spontaneous attempt to give someone pleasure is the surest sign of love. People often treasure this far beyond the particular pleasure they have received. To be loved is to have someone take pleasure in your pleasure. To love someone who loves you is one of the most glorious things that can happen, for pleasure builds on pleasure as is possible in no other way. This is not merely true of love between a man and a woman, but also of love between parents and children or indeed between any two people. This is why it is truly a loss to be unable to love. To be unable to love is to be unable to enjoy the pleasures of others. This means the loss of a significant amount of pleasure.

The proposed definition of love explains much of what we normally say about love. It explains why we say that some babies are lovable; it is almost impossible not to take pleasure in their pleasure. It also explains why a behavioristic analysis of love is unsatisfactory. Love is not behavior; it is a feeling, a feeling of pleasure at the pleasure of another. But we can also see why behavior is so important in determining if one truly loves another: if one loves another, one generally will act in certain ways toward him. If Jane gets pleasure from pleasing John, one would expect acts on her part in order to please him. It is now also clear how Jane can suddenly discover that she is in love with John. What she discovers is the feeling of pleasure she gets in seeing him pleased. She may find herself going to considerable efforts to please him, and not considering them a sacrifice at all. Falling out of love is discovered in the same way. She discovers that she no longer gets pleasure in pleasing him, that efforts to please him really are efforts.

Jealousy and Envy

Unselfish love, i.e., delight in the pleasure of another regardless of who causes it, is the most satisfactory kind. Unlike selfish love, which delights only in the pleasure that one causes oneself, it cannot give rise to jealousy. Jealousy is displeasure caused by the thought that the person one loves is being pleased by someone other than oneself. One who loves another selfishly may actually seek to deprive him of pleasure that is caused by someone else. But it is not only love between men and women that can be selfish. A parent may have a selfish love for his children. It is even possible for a person to love God selfishly, though this would probably manifest itself in annoyance at others who seek to please God, rather than toward God himself. Given this understanding of jealousy, it is natural that it can also be taken as displeasure at the thought of losing the love of someone, but although this is often taken as the essential feature of jealousy, I do not think it is. One can be jealous of a woman whom one knows does not love one, as long as one loves her. Jealousy also has a wider sense in which it involves feeling displeasure at the thought one might lose anything one values to another, not merely the love of a person, but also a position of power, etc.

If I love a woman selfishly and some other person pleases her, I am said to be jealous of him. But the phrase "jealous of him" is misleading. It should be "jealous because of him." He causes my jealousy by pleasing the woman I selfishly love. Exactly the same is true when brothers and sisters are said to be jealous of each other; rather, all love their mother selfishly, and each is displeased when she is pleased by the other. Because one often envies the person who causes him to be jealous, jealousy and envy are often confused. I can only be jealous of one whom I selfishly love, though my jealousy may be caused by another because he pleases her. He is important only because of his relationship to the woman I selfishly love. It is the fact that she is pleased by another that causes my jealousy.

Envy is different. To envy someone is to be displeased because of his having something which you desire but do not have. I can envy a man because he pleases some beautiful woman, but unless I love her, I am not jealous because of that. Similarly, a child of one family can envy a child in another because that child's mother is pleased by her child, but he cannot be jealous because of that child. He can only be jealous if his own mother is pleased by that child. Envy is not primarily related to displeasure that is caused by another's having a love one wants for oneself; envy can be caused by another's money, fame, or musical talent. Jealousy, in its primary sense, does not seem as bad as envy because in order to be jealous, one must at least love someone. Both jealousy and envy can lead to hate. To hate someone is to be displeased because of his having some good, whether or not one desires that good oneself. Even worse, hate may come to include pleasure because of that person suffering some evil. Hate may thus not only be opposed to love, but also to compassion.

Love, Liking, and Pleasure

Although love is fundamentally a matter of taking pleasure in the pleasure of another, it so naturally becomes a matter of taking pleasure in any good obtained by another that often no distinction is made. We are said to love someone whenever we are pleased by her obtaining some good. Love in the basic sense is always love for individuals, for only an individual can feel pleasure. But in the natural extension, we can be said to love a country, and perhaps any other group or organization, when we are pleased by its achieving some good. When the country we love is our own, then love of country becomes pride in country. This pride, if it is felt only when the successes of the country are not obtained by immoral actions, is most properly called a feeling of patriotism. When pride is felt for successes even when obtained by immoral actions, then it is properly called a feeling of nationalism. Love of country, like all other love, needs to be restrained by morality. Without such restraint it can lead to serious immoral actions.

That loving someone involves getting pleasure from her accounts for another extension of the term "love," viz., as when someone says "I love fishing" or "I love New Hampshire in the fall." But when we are talking about a person from whom we get pleasure, but one whom we do not love in the strict sense, then we should use the word "like." Liking someone involves getting pleasure from being in their company, usually because of the way that they behave. Of course, liking someone is almost always accompanied by some love, and loving someone, almost always accompanied by some liking. In the ideal case we like and love the same person, but sometimes one is clearly predominant. Romantic love and romantic infatuation both involve sexual attraction and the pleasure one gets from the look and touch of the other, but the former also includes love in the strict sense, pleasure in the pleasure of the other, and the latter does not. Perversely, it is often romantic infatuation that people are referring to when they talk of romantic love.

It is important to distinguish between liking and loving, for though liking is almost always accompanied by some love, love may be accompanied by little or no liking. This may not be possible with romantic love, for that always includes sexual attraction, even though we do not normally talk of this in terms of liking. But even here someone may always feel more pain than pleasure when in the company of a loved one, thus making it appropriate to talk of love without liking. This rather sad state of affairs is also common but less often remarked upon in the relationship between parents and their grown-up children, especially when they hold opposing religious or political views. That the parents and children do not like each other is clear to anyone who sees them together; that they, nevertheless, still love each other is clear to anyone who knows them.

Self-love can also be understood as a natural extension of love. A person who enjoys her successes, who is pleased when she achieves her goals, would be one who should be described as having self-love. Such a person need not be selfish; indeed, she may be one of the most altruistic of persons. For to love oneself is not incompatible with loving others. On the contrary, it is very doubtful that someone who does not love herself will love others. Just as self-love may increase the chances of love for another, so love of one may make it more likely that one will love others. One of the most delightful features of love is that the pleasure we get from loving one person may increase rather than decrease when we love someone else besides. A husband and wife's love for each other often increases after they have a child whom they have come to love.

Concern or Caring

This short digression on love and related emotions is not entirely beside the point. I admit that it is primarily due to my dissatisfaction with other accounts of love, but it is important in discussing morality to distinguish clearly between love and compassion. It is also important to distinguish both of them from being concerned with or caring for a person. When I talk of being concerned with or caring for a person, I do not mean that one either loves him or has compassion for him. I mean only that *the belief that doing something will help him to avoid suffering some evil is a motive for doing that thing.* Compassion for people naturally leads one to care for them. But the degree of compassion is not necessarily linked to the degree of concern. The strength of one's concern is the strength of the motive, and that strength can be affected by many things besides one's compassion. It will certainly be affected by the way one has been brought up. It may be affected by one's religious beliefs. A similar relationship is present between love and what I call taking an interest in a person. *To take an interest in a person means that the belief that doing something will help him to gain some good is a motive for one's doing it.* I shall talk about taking an interest in a person as involving caring for her in the same way that I talk about love as involving compassion.

It is often said that morality requires one to "Love thy neighbor as thyself." It should now be clear that this is not correct. There are several different mistakes involved. First, morality does not require you to have any feelings toward anyone; it only requires you to act in certain ways. Second, morality does not even require that you act as if you loved your neighbor as yourself. Morality does not require that you act as if you regarded your own good and evil and that of another impartially. Morality requires only that you avoid breaking the moral rules with regard to your neighbor unless an impartial rational person can advocate that such a violation be publicly allowed. The moral ideals do not encourage you to take as much interest in the good of your neighbor as you take in your own good. They can be taken as encouraging being as concerned with the evil suffered by your neighbor as with the evil suffered by yourself. It is because of this that the question "Who is my neighbor?" need not indicate any lack of the proper moral feeling, but only a realistic sense of one's power to act according to moral ideals. If "Love thy neighbor as thyself" is taken to be what morality requires, "love" must be changed to "compassion." Then "compassion" must be taken as "concern." Further, even understood in this way, it is not a statement of what morality requires, but only a way of encouraging action according to moral ideals. This "only" does not mean that encouraging people to follow moral ideals is unimportant; it is extremely important. But I refuse to confuse the demands of morality with what is encouraged by it. This confusion only encourages some people to dismiss the demands of morality as utopian.

People generally seem to prefer the loftiest kinds of statements when talking about morality. They can repeat these to each other, feel some sort of warm glow, and then forget all about them when they go about their daily lives. If someone presents some statement which does not demand very much, they often dismiss it as cynical. They dismiss it because it presents demands that can actually be followed by all persons. "Love thy neighbor as thyself" is one of the favorite sayings. No one feels compelled to live by it; obviously only the very saintly can even approach it. "Live and let live," on the other hand, is often regarded as merely advocating the easy way out. But "Live and let live" is probably the best statement of what the moral rules demand. Do not interfere with others; do not cause them any evil. If one wishes to go beyond the moral rules to moral ideals, one can change it to "Live and help live." These maxims do not have the emotional appeal of the more lofty statements, but they are maxims that all persons can actually live by.

Morality should not be regarded as providing a guide by which all rational persons should try to live, though with no hope of ever actually doing so. Morality should be regarded primarily as being the public system of rules which every rational person must obey no matter what his personal aim in life is. Only after this is clearly understood should morality be regarded as something which also provides a positive guide to life. Nonetheless, the moral ideals seem to embody the point of morality, the lessening of evil, even more clearly than the moral rules. As long as an impartial rational person can publicly allow it, any action that seeks to lessen the amount of evil in the world is encouraged by the moral ideals. But neither the moral ideals nor morality itself has a final goal. The elimination of evil can never be reached as long as human beings continue to live. The task of morality is never-ending, but the guide provided by morality can be followed by any person.

9

VIRTUE AND VICE

Although morality provides a guide for all rational persons, it is more likely to be followed by those who have a good moral character. Indeed, this is little more than a tautology, as we assess the moral character of persons by the degree to which they follow the guide provided by morality. To bring up children so that they will act morally and to bring them up to have a good moral character are, generally speaking, simply two ways of saying the same thing. In a discussion of moral character, even more than in the discussion of other aspects of morality, a moral philosopher must keep in mind the raising of children. All impartial rational persons will advocate that children be brought up to have a good moral character. This needs no argument, as it follows directly from the view that all impartial rational persons advocate that all persons act morally.

Training Children to Act Morally

Everyone not only agrees that children be trained to act morally, all impartial rational persons also want this training to involve as little infliction of evil as possible and to be as effective as possible. The best way to train children is to set a good example, to refrain from immoral action and to act in morally good ways, for this not only involves no infliction of evil, but actually results in less evil being suffered overall. Combined with this, it is useful to teach children what counts as moral and immoral, to discuss moral matters with them, explaining the point of morality and why it requires certain kinds of behavior. All impartial rational persons want the most effective training because this offers the most protection for everyone from violations of the moral rules, but they also want the training to inflict as little evil as possible. In this respect an impartial rational person's attitude toward the training of children will exactly parallel her attitude toward punishment. As with punishment, some rational persons will place more emphasis on the one goal; others, on the other.

Even with this disagreement in emphasis, some points will be agreed to by all impartial rational persons. If a lesser punishment is as effective in training as a greater, all impartial rational persons will advocate using the lesser. (It seems, oddly enough, that lesser punishments may be even more effective than greater ones in training children. If so, then all impartial rational persons would advocate using lesser punishments.) If it is as effective to train children by rewarding them for making morally right decisions in tempting or difficult situations as it is to punish them for making morally wrong choices, then all impartial rational persons would advocate training by reward. However, it is extremely unlikely that children can be trained to act morally if they are never punished for unjustifiable violations of the moral rules. Although an impartial rational person does not want evil inflicted when it is not the most effective way of training children to act morally, she may allow it when it is most effective. As an impartial person she is not merely concerned with the children being trained, she is as concerned with the people who will be affected by the immoral behavior of the children when they grow up.

No impartial rational person wants children to be trained to follow the moral rules blindly. He wants them to obey them in the manner specified by the moral attitude, for he knows that there are occasions in which all impartial rational persons would advocate that a violation of a moral rule be publicly allowed. He would also like to encourage children to follow the moral ideals. Further, he wants children to be trained so that they act in these ways even when they believe that no one knows of their actions. He wants this because he knows that life provides many occasions where one has opportunities both to act immorally and to do something morally good when there is little chance that anyone will discover it. A rational person's primary concern with motives is with their effectiveness in leading to the desired actions. However, she has one other concern: she does not want the motives to be such that they are more likely to result in more evil or less good to the person having them, or to others, than some other motives that are equally effective, i.e., she would prefer people to act out of love rather than guilt.

Motives and the Morality of an Action

Some may claim that motives are more important than I acknowledge because sometimes it is the motive which determines if one is acting morally or not. They grant that some actions are immoral no matter what the motive, viz., killing an innocent person knowing that this will not result in anyone avoiding a serious evil, but they hold that there are some cases where the motive determines the morality of the action. If I deceive in order to ingratiate myself or those I represent, then my action is immoral even if no harm is done; but if I deceive in order to save someone from suffering severe anxiety, when the truth would have no future benefit, then my action may not be immoral. Similarly, stopping treatment for an incurable cancer patient who had made a valid refusal of treatment, would be immoral if I did it in order to benefit myself or someone I cared for, but not if I did it in order to prevent the victim's suffering.

Persuasive as this reasoning sounds, the conclusion is false. It is not the motive which determines the morality of the action; it is whether an impartial rational person can advocate that such a violation be publicly allowed. If so, then the violation is not morally wrong no matter what the motive; if not, then it is immoral, regardless of the motive. Two factors serve to obscure this point: (1) We do not distinguish carefully enough between the moral judgment that is appropriately made of the act and the moral judgment we should make of a person who acts from certain kinds of motives. (2) We believe that certain kinds of motives lead people to violate moral rules even when no impartial rational person can advocate that such violations be publicly allowed, while other kinds of motives naturally lead only to violations that impartial rational persons can advocate be publicly allowed. It is primarily this second belief, which is probably true, that accounts for the false view that the motive determines the morality of an act. What determines the morality of a violation of the moral rules is whether an impartial rational person can advocate that such a violation be publicly allowed. The motive, at most, determines the moral worth of the action, i.e., how much it indicates anything about the moral character of the agent.

Personality Traits

Personality traits primarily concern a person's feelings, not her actions. This is often overlooked because a person's feelings have an important effect on the way she acts, and we often judge what a person is feeling by the way she acts. Since the normal pattern is for a person to act according to her feelings, words which refer to personality traits are often mistakenly thought to apply primarily to dispositions to act. Describing someone as shy is often taken as saying something about her disposition to avoid meeting new people, but shyness, as a personality trait, is the disposition to suffer anxiety at meeting new people, rather than the disposition to avoid them. This can be seen from the fact that we can say of someone who acts like a politician at election time that she is really shy, but that she has overcome her shyness. It is not the feelings themselves, but the disposition to have those feelings in certain kinds of circumstances that are the personality traits.

We normally talk of personality traits only when having the disposition to have a kind of feeling occurs in circumstances that are described in a way that all rational persons are likely to confront them. Shyness is a personality trait because the anxiety occurs when meeting new people, a circumstance that is clearly one that everyone is likely to confront. Dispositions to feel anxiety when seeing snakes or being in small enclosed spaces, are not personality traits because they are not circumstances that every rational person is likely to confront, but timidity, the disposition to feel anxiety in any, even slightly, dangerous situation, is a personality trait because described in this way the circumstances are so general that it is likely that every rational person will confront them.

The disposition to feel anger whenever the computer goes down is not a personality trait, but if one is disposed to feel angry whenever one's plans are disrupted in any way, then one is irascible. Irascibility is a personality trait, for any rational person in any society is likely to have his plans disrupted at some time. Affability, feeling pleasure when interacting with others, is obviously also a personality trait. Being compassionate, the disposition to feel sad whenever one is confronted with the suffering of others, is a very significant personality trait. The listing and analysis of personality traits is a fascinating undertaking, but in this book I am primarily interested in personality traits because of their connection with character traits.

Character Traits

A person's character is continually being shaped by the actions she performs. A person's character consists of a number of traits, each trait concerning a range of actions. Character traits, like habits of action, are strengthened and weakened by the actions we perform. A misunderstanding of psychoanalysis has led philosophers and others to the view that character is relatively unchangeable after the age of five. This misunderstanding is due to a failure to distinguish between character and personality. It may be true that personality does not change after an early age; it is not true of character. A child of five does not yet even have a character. It is primarily character, not personality, that we are concerned with in this chapter.

Character traits, like habits, are dispositions to behave, but they differ from habits in several ways, one of the most salient being that they involve a much wider range of actions. Whereas habits are dispositions to behave in a specific physical or mental fashion, traits of character are dispositions to respond to a situation in a characteristic way. For example, I may habitually put on my right shoe before my left, or always add a column of numbers starting from the bottom, but neither of these would be a trait of character. A trait of character, e.g., imprudence, the disposition to respond to a situation which may have significant future consequences without considering these consequences adequately, has no specific physical or mental behavior that necessarily accompanies it.

Not all ways of responding to situations are character traits; the situations must be general enough that they are likely to be encountered by everyone. Ways of responding to danger, fear, temptations to act immorally, the suffering of others, opportunities to excel, are all character traits. In almost all cases, character traits are ways of responding which have been formed, to some important degree, by free, intentional, voluntary acts so that normally each person is to some degree responsible for her character. Personality is quite different. Although a person may change her personality by free, intentional, voluntary acts, e.g., engaging in some form of psycho-therapy, most persons do not. A person's personality is not something she is usually considered responsible for. This can be seen from the fact that we talk of the personality of children before they reach an age at which they are held responsible for anything.

Personality traits are sometimes used to explain character traits, e.g., someone is cruel because she is sadistic. Character traits are not generally used in explanations. One can, of course, explain a particular action by citing a character trait, but this is simply to fit it into a general pattern of behavior, e.g. she tortured him because she is a cruel person. Although personality traits and character traits are quite distinct, they are often confused with one another. This is especially true when the personality trait is one that could be used to explain the character trait. For example, to say that a person is sadistic is to cite a personality trait, viz., that she enjoys seeing others suffering pain . This personality trait may explain why a person is cruel, viz., she acts so as to inflict pain on others unjustifiably. Distinguishing between being sadistic, a personality trait, and being cruel, a character trait, enables one to recognize that a sadistic person need not be a cruel one, nor need a cruel person be sadistic. The failure to distinguish clearly between personality and character, and to recognize that only the latter is the concern of morality, can result in people being unfairly condemned for undesirable personality traits.

I recognize the extraordinary impact of personality on character and am aware of the importance of developing in children a personality that is most conducive to their achieving a moral character. All impartial rational persons would advocate that children be raised so as to develop a personality such that they come to enjoy acting morally. This is a significant matter, for it not only affects the way the children will feel when acting morally, it also affects the likelihood of their acting in this way. Although personality traits are often used to explain why we act as we do, persons do not act merely on the basis of their feelings; they are also capable of guiding their actions by reasons. Reasons can lead a person to act in a way opposed to her feelings. A sadistic person need not be cruel or malicious even though she enjoys seeing people suffer. Many factors are important in forming a person's character: personality, though important, is only one; another is the actual actions of the person, for dispositions to respond are usually strengthened by acting on them. Character traits are dispositions to respond in a standard way to situations that all rational persons are likely to confront. Virtues and vices are those character traits that all rational persons, or all impartial rational persons, judge in the same way.

Moral Vices and Virtues

My primary concern in this chapter is not with character formation, but with the nature of the specific character traits that are called virtues and vices. When a character trait is such that all rational persons, or all impartial rational persons, would judge it in the same way, then that character trait is a virtue or a vice. Associated with each of the second five moral rules are specific character traits. Some of these are moral vices. To have a moral vice is to have a disposition to unjustifiably violate a moral rule, i.e., to have a disposition to respond to conflicts between what a moral rule requires and one's interests or inclinations, in a way that involves unjustifiable violation of that rule. Associated with the rule concerning deception is deceitfulness; with promises, untrustworthiness; with cheating, unfairness; with obeying the law, dishonesty; and with doing one's duty, undependability. I realize that this is a somewhat arbitrary pairing of moral vices with moral rules; e.g., dishonesty might also be linked with the rule against deception, and failure to perform some duties involves callousness rather than undependability. These pairings are primarily for ease of exposition; a more careful examination of the moral virtues would reveal a more complex relationship.

All the moral vices connected with the second five rules have corresponding virtues. In fact, except for deceitfulness, to which the corresponding virtue is truthfulness, the names of all of these other vices can be changed into those of the corresponding virtues simply by removing the prefix. These moral virtues are dispositions to avoid unjustified violations of the moral rules. It follows that all impartial rational persons advocate that everyone have these moral virtues. It would be inconsistent to adopt the moral attitude toward the second five moral rules and not hold that others acquire the associated moral virtues and avoid the associated moral vices. The moral virtues connected with the second five rules, truthfulness, trustworthiness, fairness, honesty, and dependability, are not very exciting. They are not those traits of character that all rational people necessarily seek for themselves, but rather those that they want others to have. It is obvious why this is so. Rational persons advocate obedience to the moral rules to avoid having evil done to themselves. However, except in unusual circumstances, rational persons must, at least, pretend to cultivate these virtues in themselves, and thus we have the truth of the saying "Hypocrisy is the homage that vice pays to virtue."

The moral virtues and vices that we have been discussing, those connected with the second five moral rules, seem to lie on a single scale. As one becomes less truthful, she becomes more deceitful, less trustworthy, more untrustworthy, etc. We can rank people on this scale, and it makes little difference when we switch from the virtue to the vice. A person may be completely dependable, generally dependable, fairly dependable, somewhat undependable, usually undependable, or completely undependable. The virtue and the vice are such that as one moves away from the one end, she necessarily moves toward the other. The degree to which one has a particular moral virtue or vice is determined by the frequency and circumstances in which one unjustifiably breaks the corresponding moral rule. We can, in fact, restate the second five moral rules in terms of either the virtues or the vices. The rules might be either "Be truthful, trustworthy, fair, honest, and dependable" or "Don't be deceitful, untrustworthy, unfair, dishonest, or undependable." In Chapter 11, we shall see the significance of this close association between the second five rules and the moral virtues and vices.

Although most of what are normally regarded as the moral virtues and vices are connected with the second five moral rules, some moral virtues and vices are not. Cruelty, or maliciousness, is a moral vice which is not connected to any of the second five moral rules. In fact, although most obviously related to the rule prohibiting the causing of pain, it does not seem restricted to this rule; rather it seems related to all of the first five moral rules. Cruelty can manifest itself in unjustifiable violations of any of the first five rules, i.e., any unjustifiable infliction of evil on someone. Of course, some people are more cruel than others; whereas some people are willing to kill and torture, others may only be willing to deprive of pleasure. There are no distinct vices for each of the first five moral rules, only, perhaps, degrees and kinds of cruelty.

Unlike the moral vices connected to the second five moral rules, as cruelty decreases, we do not necessarily get an increase in what might be taken as the corresponding moral virtue, kindness. Between kindness and cruelty sits indifference. Unlike the moral virtues connected to the second five rules, honesty, fairness, etc., kindness does not consist in obeying the moral rules. Rather, kindness is a disposition to follow the basic moral ideals when this does not involve unjustifiably violating a moral rule; it is a disposition to act so as to relieve the suffering of others. This explains the presence of indifference. Kindness is not simply lack of cruelty as honesty is lack of dishonesty. Nor is cruelty simply lack of kindness as dishonesty is lack of honesty. Lack of kindness is indifference; when regarded as a moral vice, it is known as callousness, and is closely related to cruelty.

I have listed only six moral virtues and seven moral vices, but I do not think that these are the only ones. On the contrary, any character trait that necessarily involves failing to follow the moral ideals when this can be done justifiably or to unjustifiably violate the moral rules is a moral vice; any character trait that involves avoiding unjustifiable violations of the moral rules or justifiable following of the moral ideals is a moral virtue. If we wish, we can characterize moral virtues and vices without mentioning the moral rules or ideals. We can define them in terms of the attitudes of all impartial rational persons. A moral virtue is any trait of character that all impartial rational persons would advocate that all persons possess. A moral vice is any trait of character that all impartial rational persons would advocate that no person possess. It is not my task here to list all of the moral virtues and vices. They will all be involved in a very intimate way with the moral rules and ideals.

Many character traits that have been considered by some to be moral virtues and vices actually are not. Of the so-called cardinal virtues: justice, prudence, temperance, and courage, only justice should be classified as a moral virtue. Justice is unlike the moral virtues discussed previously: it is not related to any particular moral rule; rather, a just person does not unjustifiably violate any of the moral rules. In this sense, of course, justice is not merely one moral virtue among many; it is the combination of all the moral virtues connected with the moral rules; a just person is one who has all of the moral virtues related to the moral rules. Justice is not related to the moral ideals, so that although justice is necessary to moral goodness, and lack of justice makes one immoral, being just only makes one not immoral and is not sufficient for moral goodness. Moral goodness requires not only justice, but also kindness.

Personal Vices and Virtues

Prudence, temperance, and courage are not moral virtues at all, nor are their opposites moral vices; rather, they are what I call personal virtues and vices. On the account of moral virtues as dispositions to avoid unjustified violations of the moral rules or to justifiably follow moral ideals, these three virtues do not even seem to be moral. On the account of moral vices as dispositions to unjustifiably violate moral rules imprudence, intemperance, and cowardice are clearly not moral vices. However, it may seem that all impartial rational persons would advocate that all persons possess the character traits of prudence, temperance, and courage and advocate that no one possess the character traits of imprudence, intemperance, and cowardice. But this is not the case. No impartial rational person would advocate that those who were cruel or malicious acquire the personal virtues. This would increase the chances of people suffering more evil consequences from unjustified violations of the moral rules.

Unlike the moral virtues, all rational persons personally want to have these three cardinal virtues, and to avoid the corresponding vices. This is why I call prudence, temperance, and courage personal rather than moral virtues and their opposites, imprudence, intemperance, and cowardice, personal vices. One can, in fact, define the category of personal virtues as those character traits that all rational persons want personally and personal vices as those that no rational person wants personally. All rational persons want to have these cardinal virtues personally, but they need not advocate that all other persons have them. If one were a rational egoist, she might very well prefer that all her enemies have the personal vices rather than the virtues although, insofar as it was possible, probably she still would want them to have the moral virtues.

Personal Virtues and Reasonable Expectations

It is not necessarily the case that everyone either has a personal virtue or else has the corresponding vice and that no one has neither. Many people are neither courageous nor cowardly, neither prudent nor imprudent. In order to explain this fact, the analysis of virtue and vice must take into account what it would be reasonable to expect a person to do. If a person is in a situation in which it would be reasonable to expect anyone to be so affected by danger or fear that she would act irrationally, then if she does so act, we do not count the action as showing her to be cowardly, but we do count it as showing that she is not courageous. Being courageous involves acting rationally even in those situations in which it would be reasonable to expect anyone to act irrationally. One counts as having courage to the extent that one acts rationally in situations where it would be reasonable to expect a person to act irrationally; the greater the expectation that a person will act irrationally, the more courage is shown when one acts rationally. Of course, this analysis also allows for persons to be courageous when faced with some kinds of dangers or fears but not with others. Physical courage might be distinguished from other kinds of courage if it turned out that some people regularly acted rationally when faced with physical dangers that made it reasonable to expect a person would act irrationally, but did not act rationally when faced with public disapproval or economic loss.

Cowardice is shown when one acts irrationally when it is reasonable to expect a person to act rationally in that situation. If one does act rationally in this kind of situation, then this does not show courage, but is necessary for courage. Although courage is shown by acting rationally when this is not what it is reasonable to expect, it also requires acting rationally when it is reasonable to expect this kind of behavior. Courage necessarily excludes cowardice even though it is not merely lack of cowardice. Extreme cowardice, that is, acting irrationally when faced with a very low risk of evil, or a risk of a very small evil, may cease to be a vice and become a pathological condition, such as a phobia. There is no sharp line between having a pathological condition and having a personal vice. This is true not only of cowardice, but also of intemperance and imprudence, indeed of all personal vices. We are often not sure whether we are dealing with a genuine volitional disability or only a weakness of will, even though intemperance is sometimes simply described as weakness of will. This close connection between the personal vices and pathological states may explain our attitude toward those who exhibit the personal vices; we are not sure whether to condemn or to pity.

Rationality and Virtue

It is one of the premises of this discussion that all rational persons want to have all of the personal virtues, e.g. courage, prudence, and temperance, themselves. No account of these virtues or of rationality can conflict with this premise. If it does, I take that to be conclusive evidence of its inadequacy. This means that having one of these virtues cannot require having some other personal vice, for if it did then rational persons could not seek to have all of the personal virtues. This provides us with some clue as to the proper interpretation of the personal virtues and vices. No virtue can require some other vice, e.g., prudence must be given an interpretation that does not result in its requiring cowardice, and courage cannot require imprudence. Given this relationship between the virtues and the vices, it becomes clear that the virtues and vices cannot be regarded primarily as involving distinctive ways of responding to the same situation, at least not if one of the virtuous ways of responding requires acting in what is correctly described as exemplifying a personal vice. If this were the case then it would be impossible for a rational person to seek all the personal virtues and, as noted above, this is not an allowable conclusion.

A clear understanding of this point shows the inadequacy of some possible interpretations of courage and prudence. Suppose that one took courage to be the trait of acting so as to overcome the present danger regardless of the possible harmful consequences to oneself and that one took prudence to be the trait of acting so as to minimize the possible harmful consequences to oneself. Both of these accounts have some plausibility, but given what we have said in the previous paragraph we can see that they cannot both be correct. If they were, when faced with danger, one sometimes would be forced to choose between being either courageous and imprudent or prudent and cowardly; one could not be both courageous and prudent. Many accounts of the personal virtues and vices lead to this same difficulty; one can discover a situation that requires one to exemplify one vice when exercising another virtue. This difficulty is partly a result of not distinguishing clearly enough between the virtues and vices and the personality traits that are related to them.

Following Aristotle, we all realize that courage can be considered a mean between the extremes of rashness and cowardice. (I am not putting forward Aristotle's more general account of virtue as the correct one.) However, all too often we simply contrast courage with cowardice and forget about rashness altogether. This results in our tending to equate courage with fearlessness and cowardice with fearfulness even though fearlessness can lead to rash action as easily as, if not more easily than, it leads to courageous action. It is a serious mistake to equate courage with fearlessness, for courage is a virtue, a trait of character all rational persons want for themselves, but fearlessness is a personality trait that some children are born with, and is not necessarily a trait that all rational persons want. It may be that very early childhood training, rather than heredity, is responsible for a child's fearlessness or fearfulness, but it is quite clear that children can be fearful and fearless at ages far below those at which it is appropriate to ascribe any character traits especially virtues or vices, to them at all.

If we are to guarantee that courage be a trait of character that all rational persons want for themselves, then it is necessary that courageous action must always be rational. If courageous action were ever irrational then it would not be the case that all rational persons would want to be courageous. How can one guarantee that courageous action will always be rational? The simplest and most direct way to do this is simply to include as part of the definition of courage that it involve acting rationally. Obviously, this is not a sufficient account of courage, for what we have said of courage also applies to prudence and temperance; both of these virtues must also include in their definition that they involve acting rationally.

If courage, prudence, and temperance all involve acting rationally, what is it that distinguishes them from each other? This seems fairly straightforward; what distinguishes the virtues from one another is the situation or circumstances in which their exercise is called for. Courage is the trait of character that involves not allowing danger or fear to make one act irrationally. Prudence is the trait of character that involves not allowing present concerns to make one act irrationally by neglecting significant future consequences with regard to oneself or those for whom one is concerned. Temperance is the trait of character that involves not allowing strong emotions or desires to make one act irrationally.

Interestingly, this account of the personal virtues naturally achieves the unity of the virtues that Plato and others have sought. The personal virtues are distinguished from one another by the situation that calls for the virtue, e.g., danger or fear call for courage; strong emotions and desires call for temperance. The virtues are consistent with a very wide range of personality traits, desires, emotions, etc.; they require only that one act rationally when faced with certain kinds of situations. It does not make any difference how many separate personal virtues one invents or discovers; all of them will be consistent with each of the others, for they will differ from one another only in the situation that calls for them. Fortitude will be the character trait of not allowing continuing hardships to make one act irrationally. Perhaps patience can be defined as the character trait of not allowing long delays to make one act irrationally. This account of the personal virtues shows quite clearly that the vices are more fundamental than the virtues, for each of the vices can be defined by simply leaving out the "not" in the definition of the corresponding virtue, e.g., intemperance is allowing strong emotions or desires to make one act irrationally.

I am sure that others far more skilled in depicting situations will be able to give a more adequate account of each of the particular personal virtues and vices. If they apply the schema that I have outlined, then it will be quite clear that it will be possible for someone to have all of the personal virtues or to have all of the personal vices or to have some of one and some of the other. The account I have given of the personal virtues and vices allows both for their complete coexistence and also for their existing independently of each other.

If prudence, temperance, and courage are to be personal virtues, i.e., character traits that all rational persons want personally, then they must be understood in the proper way. Prudence cannot simply be timidity or a dislike of risks; a rational person may enjoy some risk-taking. Temperance cannot simply mean abstaining from smoking and drinking, for a rational person may desire to smoke and drink. Courage cannot simply be adventuresomeness or the enjoyment of risks, for a rational person need not enjoy all risks. Indeed on these accounts courage and prudence would seem to be incompatible. If they are personal virtues, this cannot be, for a personal virtue is one that all rational persons wish to have personally. Knowing they are incompatible, all rational persons cannot want both of them. I shall try to provide a brief account of prudence, temperance, and courage, such that they are all compatible and that all rational persons would like to possess all of them.

Prudence

If prudence is to be a personal virtue, it must be a trait of character that all rational persons, regardless of the personalities they have, would like to have. Prudence cannot be a trait of character that appeals only to persons who primarily enjoy safe activities, e.g., stamp collecting; it must also appeal to those persons who enjoy more dangerous activities, e.g., mountain climbing. Prudence should not be confused with timidity, which is a personality trait, not a trait of character. A prudent person is one who carefully considers the consequences of her actions when these are likely to be serious, and who does not take unnecessary risks in seeking to reach her goal or satisfy her desires. This does not mean that the prudent person takes no risks, but that she does not take them unless they seem to be the best way to obtain what she is seeking. A person who enjoys action and adventure is not excluded from being a prudent person. For her, risks are enjoyable. As long as she takes care to prepare herself and has considered the evil risked in the light of the good to be gained, she may be a prudent person even if she is a lion tamer.

The prudent person is generally opposed to the rash or impulsive person, the person who undertakes a course of action that is likely to have important consequences without considering these consequences. This does not mean that the prudent person never acts on impulse, but that she does not do so in cases where the consequences are likely to be momentous. The prudent person is one who has a concern for the future, who does not sacrifice a greater future good to a lesser present one through lack of concern for the former. We can define a prudent person as one who standardly responds rationally to situations where the consequences of her action for herself and those for whom she is concerned may result in significant evil or failure to achieve significant goods. Defined in this way, it is quite clear that prudence is a personal virtue. All rational persons certainly want to avoid significant evil or failure to achieve some significant good for themselves and those they care for.

Temperance

Temperance seems to be a part of prudence, but there is a difference in emphasis. Whereas prudence primarily involves having appropriate concern for the future, temperance primarily involves avoiding losing control in the present. A temperate person is one who standardly responds rationally when in the grip of some strong emotion or desire. This does not mean that temperance always demands the overcoming of this emotion or the refusal to satisfy the desire. If it did, temperance would not be a trait of character that would be desired by all rational persons. Rather, considered as a virtue, temperance simply requires that one not allow a strong emotion or desire to make her behave irrationally. This permits circumstances in which it is not intemperate to satisfy a strong desire or express a strong emotion. Intemperance is a vice only if the indulgence of one's present desires or emotions leads one to act irrationally.

I am not attempting to describe temperance as it is ordinarily thought of; I am attempting to describe what temperance must be like if it is to be a personal virtue. Temperance is frequently regarded as merely abstention from, or great moderation in, the use of alcohol and tobacco. This is unfortunate. There is some need for the concept of temperance as a genuine personal virtue, one desired by all rational persons, not merely by a genteel middle class. This is the concept of temperance with which philosophers have traditionally been concerned. A temperate person need not have weak desires or emotions, as the degraded concept suggests. If one does not have any strong desires or emotions, one has little need of temperance, for temperance consists in having that strength of character that allows one to resist acting on a strong desire or emotion when to satisfy it would be irrational.

The "cool moment" aspect of rationality (Chapter 2) provides the clearest background for understanding the concept of temperance. On the "cool moment" account of rationality, it is irrational for a person to act on a desire which in a cool moment she would decide was significantly less important than the desire or set of desires she would frustrate by so acting. (The "cool moment" theory is incorporated into my account of rationality as an account of the ranking of the goods and evils.) A person who is quick to anger may decide in a cool moment that giving vent to her anger results in the sacrifice of that which she considers significantly more important. Nonetheless, when she is angry, she may not be able to control her anger. She is unable to act rationally when in the grip of her anger. I call such a person intemperate. Although the more important desires a person sacrifices by failing to control her present emotions or desires often concern her own self-interest, they also often concern those she cares about. It can also happen that the more significant desire that is sacrificed is the desire to act morally. When this is the case, philosophers have often talked of "weakness of will." That lack of temperance is sometimes the cause of immoral action explains why some have regarded temperance as a moral rather than a personal virtue. Defining a temperate person, as I have done, as one who does not let her present desires or emotions make her act irrationally makes clear that temperance is indeed a personal virtue, one that all rational persons desire for themselves and those they care about.

Courage

A courageous person is one who standardly responds rationally to danger or when she is suffering from fear. Since fear is an emotion, this may produce an overlap between temperance and courage, and there are circumstances in which we would call some reactions to fear intemperate, even though we generally call them cowardly. It should be no surprise that there is an overlap between the various personal virtues and vices. What distinguishes one personal virtue from another is the circumstance that in which one acts rationally. This explains Plato's attempt to equate virtue and wisdom, for Plato treated all virtue as personal virtue. What distinguishes one vice from another are the circumstances that lead one to act irrationally. Circumstances cannot always be clearly distinguished, so it should not be surprising that there are occasions in which it is equally appropriate to praise a person as either temperate or prudent, and others where we may condemn her for either intemperance or cowardice.

When one is faced with some significant present danger it is usually courage, not temperance or prudence, that is called for. Courage does not require always facing the danger and attempting to overcome it. Some dangers are severe enough to make a rational person modify her plans, or even to give them up entirely. If being courageous required always trying to overcome every danger, it would not be a personal virtue. Most, if not all, rational persons would prefer not to have such a character trait. If courage is to be a personal virtue, it must consist in not allowing fear or danger to make one act irrationally. Courage should not be confused with adventuresomeness, which is a personality trait, not one of character. A courageous person must be one who after consideration of the danger involved acts in a rational fashion. She attempts to overcome it, if this seems most likely to benefit herself or those she cares about, and abandons her plans if this seems most beneficial. Only when understood in this way can courage be considered a personal virtue.

Courage seems to have a more intimate connection with the moral ideals than either temperance or prudence. It is more natural to associate temperance with the moral rules, for, as noted previously, lack of temperance often results in violation of a moral rule. Although prudence is required if one is to act according to the moral ideals most effectively, it does not seem intimately connected with either the moral rules or the moral ideals. Courage, though sometimes required to obey the moral rules, is most often required in order to follow the moral ideals. It takes courage to prevent a mob from killing or torturing an individual. It takes courage to try to stop people from depriving others of their freedom and opportunity, especially when they have been doing it for a long time. It is no wonder that courage has often been considered a moral virtue, for it is so often required by those who would like to follow moral ideals. It is no wonder that it is often valued so highly, for it is a rare commodity, and that which is rare is generally highly prized. Courage is not isolated from the values we have. The courage generally shown by parents when their children are in danger shows quite clearly that courage can be had when we value something enough. It is not, I think, a lack of courage that is primarily responsible for the few people who show it in the pursuit of moral ideals. Rather, it is that so few people care enough about following moral ideals.

Personal Virtues as the Mean Between Two Extremes

It is interesting, though I am not sure how important, that the three personal virtues seem to fit Aristotle's account of a virtue as the mean between two extremes. Prudence is the mean between rashness, i.e., too little concern for the future, and overcaution, i.e., too much concern for the future. The prudent person does not allow concern for the consequences of her actions to inhibit her, but neither does she ignore these consequences. It is quite appropriate to advise someone to care not too much, yet not too little for the future. As a bit of practical advice, it might even be worthwhile to tell her to aim at erring in the direction of that extreme toward which she is not naturally inclined. All of this suggests what Aristotle says.

Temperance also is plausibly described as a mean between two extremes. On the one side, we have the extreme of intemperance or overindulgence, in general, a failure to control one's present desires and emotions. On the other side, we have asceticism or puritanism in which one refuses to satisfy any strong desire or display any strong emotion. This kind of generalized masochism is probably more common than one thinks; however, since it generally does not result in overt harm to others, it is not so commonly remarked upon. Intemperance is sometimes taken as the opposite of temperance, as if it were impossible to err by controlling one's present desires and emotions too much. A rational person would advise one for whom she was concerned to steer the middle course between indulging all of her present emotions and desires and indulging none of them. Again, it would be practical to tell her to err in the direction of that extreme toward which she is not naturally inclined.

The extremes between which courage lies are cowardice on the one side, and foolhardiness or rashness on the other. The former consists in letting fear or danger dissuade one from carrying out one's plans even though, all things considered, it would be rational to attempt to overcome the danger and proceed as planned. Foolhardiness or rashness consists in trying to overcome some danger when, all things considered, it is irrational to try to do so. However, when a person refuses to do something rash, we usually say she acted prudently rather than courageously. Conversely, even when it is prudent to try to overcome some danger, we generally praise a person for courage when she acts rationally. This, together with the fact that prudence is confused with timidity, and courage with adventuresomeness, explains why prudence and courage are sometimes thought to be incompatible.

Although courage is sometimes shown by the overcoming of fear, it is not necessary to fear in order to be courageous. Someone who recognizes the danger that she faces, but does not fear it, is no less courageous when she rationally decides to face it than the person who does so even though she fears it. We might praise more highly the action of the person who fears, as it is a more difficult act, but we would praise more the person who does not fear, as she is the kind of person we would prefer to be. The courageous person is one who has the proper respect for the dangers she faces; she does not let them overawe her, nor does she ignore them. To do the former would be to give up unnecessarily an opportunity to obtain some goods; to do the latter would be to increase unnecessarily one's chances of suffering evil. The rational person does not desire either of these, but always seeks to minimize the chances of either herself or those she cares about losing some good or suffering some evil. As in the case of prudence and temperance, the rational person would advise the timid person to err on the side of foolhardiness, the adventuresome person not to fear erring on the side of cowardice. For this is more likely to result in their achieving the mean of courage.

Relationship Between the Personal Virtues and Morality

In saying that prudence, temperance, and courage are personal rather than moral virtues, I do not mean to suggest that all rational persons want these virtues only for their own self-interest. Although a rational egoist may desire these traits simply in order to benefit herself, a rational person who desires to act morally may want them in order to enable her to act morally. Prudence, temperance, and courage are not only an aid to the person pursuing her own self-interest, they are an equal aid to the person who seeks to act morally. I am not suggesting that because prudence, temperance, and courage are personal rather than moral virtues they conflict in any way with moral action. On the contrary, the personal virtues are necessary for reliable moral behavior.

The point of distinguishing between the personal virtues and the moral ones is to stress that the former have no necessary connection with being moral. It is possible for a person to be prudent, temperate, and courageous and yet to be thoroughly immoral. We might not call such a person prudent, temperate, or courageous, because to assign a personal virtue to a person is to praise him, and we hesitate to praise immoral persons. Yet there is no doubt that a person can have all the personal virtues without having any moral ones. It is extremely unlikely that a person could have the moral virtues without having the personal ones. This latter fact accounts, perhaps, for the inclination to consider these virtues as moral ones. I think this inclination should be resisted.

Can Virtues Conflict?

Truthfulness clearly involves not unjustifiably violating the moral rule prohibiting deception. Just as clearly, truthfulness as a moral virtue involves not following this rule when this would be unjustifiable. Truthfulness involves avoiding deception except when an impartial rational person can advocate that it be publicly allowed. Kindness involves not causing suffering except when an impartial rational person can advocate that it be publicly allowed. I shall try to show how this understanding of the virtues enables one to deal adequately with the situation where these two moral virtues seem to come into conflict with one another.

It sometimes arises, especially in the practice of medicine, that one has a duty to tell painful news. On these occasions not telling this news, a grim diagnosis or prognosis, counts as deception as clearly as making a false statement. However, telling the news will clearly cause suffering. Here it seems as if being truthful requires that one be unkind, whereas kindness requires that one be deceitful. If truthfulness demands telling and kindness demands not telling, there does seem to be a conflict between the virtues. It may be that one can tell, but tell in such a way that minimizes the suffering of the patient, thus seeming to satisfy the demands of both truthfulness and kindness, but this is too easy a way out. Although one can and should minimize the suffering of the patient by telling in certain ways, it will still often be the case that significantly more suffering will occur if you tell, no matter how, than if you deceive either by not telling or by making a false statement.

This situation requires more precision in the account of the virtues than I have provided so far. Up till now I have characterized the personal virtues as if they were character traits that involved responding rationally to different situations, and I have characterized the moral virtues as character traits that involved responding to different situations in a way that impartial rational persons would advocate. I have claimed that what distinguishes one personal virtue from another is the situation in which the exercise of the virtue is called for, and have made a similar claim with regard to the moral virtues.

This claim strongly suggests that the virtues cannot conflict with one another because they are called for in different situations. This suggestion neglects the possibility that the same situation can call for the exercise of two personal or moral virtues such that if one of these virtues is exercised, it seems to rule out the exercise of some other virtue. This seems to be the situation we have been discussing where both truthfulness and kindness are called for, yet it does not seem possible to exercise both. A similar situation can occur with the personal virtues where one may be in a dangerous situation that calls for both courage and prudence and yet if one acts in one way it will be appropriately described as courageous, but not as prudent, and if one acts in the other it will be appropriately described as prudent, but not as courageous.

Does this show that courage and prudence must sometime come into conflict so that courage sometimes requires imprudence and prudence, cowardice? Is the same true for truthfulness and kindness? If so then it cannot be correct that all rational persons seek all of the personal virtues and seek to avoid all of the personal vices or that all impartial rational persons seek all of the moral virtues and seek to avoid the moral vices. Since I think that these claims are correct I must reconcile them with the situations described above. To seek the virtue is not necessarily to seek to *exemplify* it in every situation. One may feel that in some situations it would be preferable to exemplify a different virtue. A situation may allow different choices to be made, among them one that exemplifies courage and another one that exemplifies prudence. In choosing to act in the way that exemplifies courage one is not thereby committed to the view that acting in this way is imprudent, only that prudence is not the virtue that one's action is intended to exemplify. Similarly, acting in the way that would be called prudent does not require that one regard the action as cowardly, only that courage was not exemplified by the action.

Situations which seem to call for prudence or courage to the exclusion of the other should not be seen as showing the incompatibility of the virtues, but only the difficulty of performing an action which exemplifies both of them. The same point can be made about the seeming conflict between truthfulness and kindness. On the account I have provided, one can exercise a virtue without exemplifying it, for *exemplifying* a virtue requires acting in a way that one takes as paradigmatic, whereas *exercising* the virtue only requires acting in a way that is compatible with having the virtue. The view that virtues can conflict is partly the result of confusing exercising a virtue with exemplifying it. The realization that exercising courage, i.e., acting rationally in the face of danger, does not always require trying to overcome that danger, which is what is required for exemplifying the virtue, provides a much better understanding of the virtues.

The view that exemplifying one moral virtue must sometimes require exemplifying another moral vice may arise from the fact that impartial rational persons can disagree about what morally ought to be done. If two people do disagree, one holding that a given choice would count as kind, e.g., not telling the patient the truth, and another person holding that it would be deceitful not to tell, then it seems as if there is a real conflict between the virtues. This is a mistake; to the persons involved there is no conflict, the one who thinks it kind not to tell does not regard it as deceitful, and the one who thinks it deceitful not to tell does not think it kind. Rather, one thinks it is justified to deceive and the other does not; thus they have different views about what is the morally acceptable way to act. They disagree about whether not telling counts as an act of kindness or not and this disagreement is a disagreement about whether or not this avoidance of causing suffering counts as a morally adequate reason for not telling this patient the truth.

This account does not have any place for misplaced kindness. One is not showing kindness when it is morally unjustifiable for one to prevent suffering. Misplaced kindness is not kindness anymore than a false friend is a friend or a rubber duck is a duck; thinking that it is, is to commit the fallacy of *ignoring the modifier*. If one knows that it would be wrong not to tell the patient, and yet one cannot bring oneself to tell him this is not kindness, at least not kindness if it is to be regarded as a moral virtue. Rather, it is a manifestation of the personality trait of compassion or pity. It is, of course, true that someone with compassion is more likely to be kind than someone without compassion, but confusing kindness with compassion is as much a mistake as confusing courage with fearlessness. It is very important to distinguish between the virtues and the personality traits that are related to them in such an intimate way. Recognizing that all impartial rational persons favor all of the moral virtues makes clear that misplaced kindness is not really kindness at all.

Similarly, someone who claims that one is not being truthful if one refuses to tell, even when all impartial rational persons would advocate not telling, is confusing the virtue of truthfulness with compulsive truth telling. A truthful person never deceives when it is morally unjustifiable to deceive, but when it would be morally wrong not to deceive, a truthful person deceives. Although this sounds paradoxical, it is clear that if truthfulness is to be a moral virtue it must never require doing what is morally wrong. Someone who tells the truth regardless of consequences is not truthful but tactless. The names of the virtues are sometimes misleading. The view of the virtues as necessarily desirable is essential for coming up with an adequate analysis of them.

Virtues and the Nature of Persons

The attitude that a rational person takes toward the moral virtues, and hence toward the moral rules and ideals, as well as the attitude she takes toward the personal virtues, depends upon the nature of persons. If persons could not suffer the evils which the first five rules prohibit causing, then not only would these rules be pointless, but also the second five rules would lose their point and so there would also be no point in acquiring the moral virtues. Nor, as we shall see, would there be any point in acquiring the personal virtues. That persons can suffer the evils that the first five moral rules prohibit causing is a fundamental fact that plays an essential role in any adequate account of morality, as well as in any adequate general account of virtue and vice. This can be seen most clearly if we imagine a world in which impartial rational beings would not advocate obedience to any of the first five moral rules.

These beings must be such that they cannot be killed. If they die, and we can imagine it either way, they die from internal causes which cannot be affected by others. These beings would certainly have no need for a rule against killing, if they could even understand such a rule. Let us further suppose that these beings can suffer no physical pain. This is relatively easy to imagine, there now being some human beings who, due to a defect in their nervous system, feel no pain. These beings would have limited use for the second rule, "Don't cause pain," and would understand it in a limited way. The third and fourth rules, "Don't disable" and "Don't deprive of freedom," belong together. Why a rational person does not want to be disabled or deprived of freedom is that she thereby lessens her chances of escaping death and pain and of obtaining those things that she might desire or get pleasure from. We shall imagine that our beings desire nothing but to contemplate the mysteries of the universe. Further, their ability and freedom to do so cannot be affected by anyone. The third and fourth rules now become pointless, and perhaps unintelligible. To complete the picture, let us say that they get pleasure from nothing but this contemplation, and that no one can deprive them of it. The fifth rule, "Don't deprive of pleasure," now goes the way of the first four. This also makes the second rule pointless because there is no possibility of causing mental suffering.

It is not clear that the beings described in the previous paragraph are rational. According to our description, they do nothing except, perhaps, for contemplating aloud. Nothing allows us to distinguish this verbal behavior from a recording. These beings have no desires, goals, or aversions that can be affected by anyone. They show no purposive activity; in fact, they show no activity at all, except, perhaps, verbal activity. Even this is limited. They cannot interfere with one another at all. They cannot deprive one another of pleasure by talking too loudly and destroying the pleasures of contemplation. We are imagining beings who are completely independent of anyone else. They can neither be helped nor harmed in any way by anyone. Even if they are aware of others, they are completely indifferent to them. Such beings, which seem to be regarded as ideals by some religions and even some philosophers, are certainly quite different from human beings. We can, I think, regard them as rational beings only if we provide them with a history. So that we must first picture a group of beings like those which Shaw presents in *Back to Methusala,* and then allow for changes until the beings have the characteristics I have described above.

I am not sure that even with such a history we would regard such beings as rational. Even if we do, it is quite clear that the first five moral rules would have no application in a world populated solely by such beings. These rules have application only to people who can suffer the evils which the first five moral rules prohibit causing. It is pointless to have a rule "Don't kill" when no one can be killed. Similarly it is pointless to say "Don't cause pain" when no one can suffer pain, or "Don't deprive of pleasure" when it is impossible to do so. And if, in addition, no one has desires that can be thwarted by anyone else, then there is no point in having the rules "Don't disable" and "Don't deprive of freedom." The beings we have described are such that none of the first five rules have any point with regard to them. The questions that now arise are "Do any of the second five rules have any point?" and "Is there any point in acquiring the virtues, moral or personal?"

The second five moral rules are justified; i.e., all impartial rational persons adopt the moral attitude toward them, because violation of them generally results in someone suffering one of the evils prohibited by the first five rules. In the world we are now imagining no one can suffer any of the evils prohibited by the first five moral rules. Hence this justification of the second five moral rules no longer holds. Is there any other justification for these rules? Not only can I see no justification for the second five moral rules, but given this world of completely independent beings, I can see no justification for having any rules governing one's behavior toward others at all. It is pointless to have such rules if no one benefits from them. In the world we are now imagining no one would benefit from anyone following either moral rules or moral ideals. It follows immediately that there is no justification for the moral virtues, for all of the moral virtues are connected with the moral rules or ideals, and these are pointless in a world without evil.

The pointlessness of the second five rules, and consequently of the moral virtues associated with them, can be seen most clearly if we slightly modify our world without evil. Imagine the beings we have described at some earlier stage. Here they remember what it was like when they could be seriously harmed by others. Now in their joy at being free from the necessity to follow any rules, moral or otherwise, they take pleasure in deceiving, breaking promises, cheating, disobeying the law, and neglecting their duties. These beings therefore differ from the beings described in the previous example. They take pleasure in something other than mere contemplation of the world. Apart from this change, and any further changes that are required by this change, they are the same as the beings described in the previous example. No one ever suffers any evil as a consequence of deception, a broken promise, being cheated, a law being broken, or a neglected duty.

In this situation would an impartial rational being adopt the moral attitude toward the second five rules, or the acquiring of the associated virtues? I do not see why she would. No one has anything to gain from universal obedience to the second five rules or having the associated moral virtues. Of course, having read Kant, she may know that it is impossible for everyone to deceive all of the time, never to keep a promise, etc. Being aware that universal deception, breaking promises, etc., is impossible, self-frustrating, or unintelligible, an impartial rational being would advocate sufficient obedience to the rules so that it is possible to break them. But since the whole point of establishing the rules is simply to provide the opportunity to violate them, no impartial rational being would advocate that everyone always obey them.

The Inadequacy of Kant's Categorical Imperative

Consideration of this imaginary world shows the inadequacy of using the lack of formal universalizability as conceived by many philosophers, especially Kant, as the criterion of an immoral action. In this imaginary world, it is as impossible to completely universalize deception, promise-breaking, etc., as in our actual world. Whereas in our actual world it is immoral ever to do these things simply because one feels like doing so, in our imaginary world, it is not. No impartial rational being in this world would advocate that an evil be inflicted on someone because she violated one of the second five moral rules simply because she felt like doing so. However, all impartial rational beings might advocate punishment for a course of action reminiscent of an ordinary violation of the moral rules. These beings would advocate that one not violate the moral rules all of the time; they might even advocate punishing those who did.

Punishment would consist in depriving the violator of the pleasure of violating any of the rules. No one would pay any attention to anything she says or does, thus eliminating the possibility of deception; all promises would be forgiven; she would not be allowed to participate in any voluntary activities; she would be declared exempt from all laws and be excused from all duties. For the only evil that can be inflicted on these beings is to deprive them of the pleasure of breaking the moral rules. The strangeness of this punishment makes it clear that there would be another kind of activity for which these beings might advocate punishment. This would be any unauthorized activity designed to keep others from violating the moral rules. Any being who prevented others from violating the moral rules would, in this strange world, herself be acting immorally. She would be unjustifiably violating the one moral rule that retained its point in this world, the rule "Don't deprive of pleasure."

In the course of a moral argument one sometimes says, "What would happen if everyone acted like that?" but this question has more rhetorical than logical force. For one thing, it is not even clear what the question means. In the world we have been imagining, it is possible to ask someone who lies, "What would happen if everyone acted like that?" Part of the ambiguity in the question becomes clear if she should reply, "Do you mean 'What would happen if I and everyone else lied every time we spoke?' or 'What would happen if everyone lied whenever she felt like it?' It is only if you mean the first that lying becomes impossible, self-frustrating, etc. If you mean the second, then nothing much may happen at all."

Violations of the second five moral rules are not always immoral. When they are immoral it is not because they are not universalizable, but because no impartial rational person would advocate that such a violation be publicly allowed. In considering whether or not to advocate that such a violation be publicly allowed, an impartial rational person is not concerned with what would happen if everyone actually were to commit such a violation or even if it is possible for everyone to actually commit this kind of violation. It is only the consequences of everyone being publicly allowed to commit such a violation that are important; these are compared with the consequences of no one being publicly allowed to commit it. If no impartial rational person would advocate that the violation be publicly allowed, it is unjustifiable; if all impartial rational persons would advocate that the violation be publicly allowed, it is strongly justifiable; if some impartial rational persons would advocate that the violation be publicly allowed, it is weakly justifiable, but punishment for the violation may also be justifiable. Unjustifiable violations generally result in an increase in the amount of evil consequences being suffered overall.

The same points hold when considering violations of the first five rules. It is impartiality that is important, and universalizability is not necessary for impartiality; what is necessary is that the violation be publicly allowed. Every violation of these rules has evil consequences; thus a rational person, if she is impartial, wants everyone to be protected from these evils. She cannot allow anyone, including herself, to violate these rules in circumstances in which an impartial rational person can not publicly allow everyone else to do so. It is because impartiality is required toward the moral rules that one must consider the evil consequences that would result from publicly allowing this kind of violation of the moral rules. That a rational person can publicly allow all others to commit the same kind of violation is sufficient to guarantee the impartiality of her violation of the rule. Impartiality does not require that she consider what would happen if everyone committed the violation, unless she believes that this is what would happen if everyone were publicly allowed to do so.

Why should impartial rational persons care if the maxim of their action satisfies Kant's Categorical Imperative: "Act only according to that maxim whereby you can at the same time will that it should become a universal law"? It is extremely unlikely that it will become a universal law. In addition, there are extraordinary difficulties in applying the Categorical Imperative because almost any action can be claimed to be based on a maxim that one would universalize. If I steal from a person richer than I, even though I am not poor, I can claim that the maxim for my action is "Increase your income." It may be objected that I have left out the important aspect of my action, viz., that it involved stealing, but that is just the difficulty with the Categorical Imperative: it provides no guide in deciding which aspect of the action is important. It provides no guide for determining how to formulate the maxim that one must be willing to universalize. By universalizing a maxim or making it a universal law, I understand Kant to mean advocating that everyone act on it.

The difficulties in applying the Categorical Imperative are not the main thing wrong with it. It is simply false that a rational person is acting immorally whenever she acts on a maxim which she would not advocate that everyone act on. Even if all impartial rational persons would advocate that no one act in some way, acting in this way need not be immoral; it may only be imprudent or cowardly. Only when your action can be correctly described as a violation of a moral rule must an impartial rational person be able to advocate that everyone be publicly allowed to act in this way. Unless a person has violated a moral rule, there is usually no need for her to justify her action morally. It is absurd to demand that a moral person always will that the maxim she acts on be adopted by everyone else.

I do not want all persons to become professional philosophers. I do not even want all qualified persons to do so. There are quite enough professional philosophers. Those who are qualified to become professional philosophers are usually also qualified to enter some other profession. I think it preferable for many of them to do so. Yet, I do not think that anyone would consider me immoral for becoming a professional philosopher. Confusion results if we talk of willingness to universalize one's maxims of action as a necessary condition for acting morally. Lack of universalizability does not make an action immoral. Moreover, even if an action is a violation of a moral rule, that it cannot be universalized is not what makes it immoral, but that it would not be publicly allowed by any impartial rational person.

Kant's Categorical Imperative is worthless for discovering or testing moral rules. It is not even adequate for testing what counts as a justifiable violation of a moral rule, although it is closer to the mark for this task. But even when one is considering violations of a moral rule, it is a misleading test of impartiality. Impartiality is, in fact, achieved by considering what would happen if everyone were publicly allowed to commit the violation, not by considering what would happen if everyone were actually to commit it. The kind of violation that no impartial rational person would publicly allow is the kind of action that makes it more likely that there will be an increase in the suffering of evil. This is why all impartial rational persons advocate liability to punishment for those who commit such actions.

Evil Is Necessary for Most Virtues to Have a Point

Evil, or the possibility of avoiding it, is also what makes prudence, temperance, and courage worthwhile. Although a virtue such as patience may have a point in a world without evil, since it can facilitate the gaining of goods that might not be gained if one lacked patience, most personal virtues become pointless in a world without the possibility of evil. If one does not need to be concerned with the future, nor to control one's desires, nor to face any danger, then one does not need prudence, temperance, or courage. It is the possibility of suffering evil that gives a point to the acquiring of the moral and personal virtues. This may explain why some religious thinkers "solve" the problem of evil by claiming that evil is necessary for the cultivation of those character traits, including both the moral and personal virtues, that we now value so highly. Of course, we now value these character traits so highly precisely because there is so much evil in the world, so that I am not clear how much force this "solution" has.

Let us now change the original imaginary world so as to allow the beings to deprive each other of the pleasure of contemplation by talking very loudly. Most if not all of the virtues become possible. For example, these beings might carelessly talk too loudly when particularly excited by something they were contemplating. This might invite reprisals by others. The virtue of temperance would now be desirable. Since reprisals might provoke counterreprisals, prudence would also be called for. It may be inappropriate to talk of courage, but fortitude would be possible. We can even imagine the point of some organization in which certain beings were designated as officials whose duty is to warn those who begin talking too loudly and to punish those who do not heed their warnings. I do not know if we could generate the possibility of all the moral virtues with this simple world, but it is clear that some of them could be. The point of this example is to show that very little evil is required before some of the moral and personal virtues become possible again.

Let us now add the possibility of pain to this world; e.g., certain kinds of talk not only deprive of pleasure, but actually inflict pain. It may now be that all of the moral and personal virtues become justified again. Perhaps this accounts, in part, for the view of the Classical Utilitarians that morality is concerned only with pleasure and pain. In the imaginary world we are considering, the utilitarians would not be so far wrong, but in the real world, their view is vastly oversimple. Not only is there the matter of life and death, but the ways in which one person depends on and can interfere with another are vastly more complex. Morality must be understood with reference to the real world, not with reference to some more simple imaginary world.

10

MORAL JUDGMENTS

Having presented the background necessary for making moral judgments, a moral system which includes moral rules and a procedure for determining justified violations of these rules, moral ideals, moral virtues and vices, I shall now give an account of moral judgments. In the first chapter I showed that all previous accounts of moral judgments were inadequate because they provided no clear distinction between moral and nonmoral judgments. Some of these theories were unable to provide a clear distinction because they were primarily theories about the function or purpose of making moral judgments, not about the nature of these judgments. It is not that the various linguistic theories of moral judgments are mistaken, rather they are not theories about the nature of moral judgments at all; what they say applies equally well to many kinds of nonmoral judgments. Even though none of these theories provides an account of the nature of moral judgments, they all have something of value to say about the purpose of making moral judgments.

Linguistic Theories of Moral Judgments

The imperative theory, which regards moral judgments as a special kind of command, points to the fact that moral judgments are primarily used to tell people what to do or, more frequently, what not to do. This theory is most persuasive for moral judgments concerning actions that have not yet been performed. These judgments, e.g., "You ought to do it" or "You shouldn't do that," do resemble commands in many ways.

The commending theory is most persuasive for moral judgments about people. These judgments, e.g., "She is a good person," do resemble the kinds of evaluations we make of plays, paintings, tools, etc. This theory acknowledges that moral judgments are made upon the basis of standards, but it says nothing about these standards. Like all of the linguistic theories, this theory is compatible with the universalist account of morality I have provided as well as with theories that regard moral systems as dependent solely upon the customs of each particular society.

The emotive theory regards moral judgments as expressions of our emotions or feelings. This theory is most persuasive when we consider those moral judgments, e.g., "But cheating is wrong!" which are made when we wish to register our feelings about what is being done. Suppose we see a good friend of ours cheating or about to cheat. Telling her that cheating is wrong would serve more as an expression of our feelings than it would inform her of something she did not know.

The view that moral judgments are statements of fact is most persuasive when characterizing moral judgments that are made in the context of a philosophical or historical discussion. After providing an account of the morally relevant features of a situation, to conclude that a proposed course of action is morally right is very like stating a fact.

The examples of moral judgments given in the preceding paragraphs contain the words "ought," "shouldn't," "good," and "wrong." However, it is not because they contain these words that they are moral judgments. In fact, most judgments containing these words are not moral judgments, but prudential or aesthetic, etc., and most moral judgments do not even contain these words. Rather than simply tell someone that he ought to do something, we usually say something more specific; e.g., "You promised to do it," or "It is your duty to do it." Similarly, in making moral judgments about people we do not generally say that they are good or bad, but something more specific, e.g., that they are kind and trustworthy, or cruel and deceitful. Moral judgments about actions also generally contain more specific terms than "right" or "wrong," such as "That would be cheating." Insofar as general terms are used in moral judgments, they are more likely to be the kinds of terms that do not usually appear in books on moral philosophy or in print at all.

Distinguishing Between Moral and Nonmoral Judgments

The various linguistic theories of moral judgments are not serious attempts to distinguish moral judgments from nonmoral judgments, but are primarily accounts of the many different functions of making moral judgments. Most of the theories which attempt to distinguish moral judgments from nonmoral judgments do so by bringing in the attitude of the person making the judgment. I have already mentioned the view that a judgment counts as a moral judgment only if the person making it not only is prepared to act on it, but also is willing to universalize such action. Sometimes this view is combined with the view that the person also has to consider a moral judgment as one that cannot be overridden, i.e., that she is always prepared to act on this judgment regardless of any

conflicting nonmoral judgment. This is supposed to distinguish it from prudential, aesthetic, legal etc., judgments which can sometimes be overridden because
of moral considerations. A moral judgment, on the other hand, can never be
overridden by nonmoral considerations, though it might be modified by other
moral considerations.

This set of related views concerning moral judgments, unlike the linguistic
theories, is an attempt to distinguish between moral and nonmoral judgments.
By making the distinction on the basis of some distinctive attitudes of the person
making the judgment it allows one to distinguish between genuine moral judgments and those that merely seem to be such judgments. If one is prepared not
only to act on the judgment but also to universalize the judgment and accept the
resulting actions, it is a genuine moral judgment; if not, except for unusual cases,
it is not a genuine moral judgment. This view also allows one to distinguish
between correct and mistaken moral judgments; mistaken moral judgments are
those judgments that the person believes that she takes the appropriate attitude
toward, but were she placed in the relevant kind of situation she would realize
that she does not.

One obvious objection to this view is that it allows any action to be the subject
of a moral judgment. Not only do the judgments of fanatic Nazis favoring the
extermination of non Aryans become moral judgments, but the judgments of
fanatic devotees of Esperanto or English as the universal language, favoring the
use of that language, become moral judgments. Any judgment toward which
anyone takes the appropriate attitude becomes a moral judgment. Modifying
this view so that the individual has to be rational, in the sense described in
Chapter 2, does eliminate some of these objections, but not all of them. In particular, unless we limit the judgments to those based on beliefs that are shared
by all rational persons, there is no way to distinguish between moral and religious views. For it makes people's religious judgments, if they want all people
to act on them and consider them their supreme guide to conduct, into moral
judgments. This makes it impossible for anyone to claim that religion should be
considered a more important guide to conduct than morality or vice versa.

This view, though it seems quite sophisticated, has a touching innocence. It
assumes that everyone takes morality as his supreme guide to conduct. It is as
if all one needs to do in order to get someone to act morally is to convince him
that he would want everyone in similar circumstances to act in that way. This
view denies that those people who do not care whether or not their behavior is
universalizable, or even if it is moral in some more normal sense, ever make
genuine moral judgments. On this theory, fanatics can make moral judgments
on any kind of action they want, but hypocrites can never make any genuine
moral judgments at all. But hypocrites not only make genuine moral judgments,
they often make correct ones. That is why we do not want them to be hypocritical, but to act on their judgments. It is possible to make genuine and correct
moral judgments even though one does not intend to act on such a judgment
were it to apply to oneself. A genuine and correct moral judgment only requires
that the judgment one makes is made on the basis of a moral system that one
could put forward as a public system that applies to all rational persons. Such a

judgment need not be a mere "inverted commas" moral judgment, perhaps stating what my society regards as moral, but a judgment that I personally regard as morally correct even though I am not prepared to act on it. On my account of moral judgments, it is not whether the person is prepared to act on the judgment that determines whether or not it is a moral judgment, it is whether that judgment is based on a moral system that has a specific subject matter.

The Subject Matter of Moral Judgments

We make moral judgments not only of particular actions, intentions, motives, persons, policies, and organizations, but also of kinds of actions, intentions, etc. The subject matter of moral judgments is limited to those actions etc., which are governed by a moral system, primarily those that are covered by some moral rule or moral ideal. I call these "moral matters." I count a judgment as a moral judgment only if it is about a moral matter. This allows for disputes about whether a judgment is or is not really a moral judgment, for one may be mistaken about whether or not it is really about a moral matter. The current debate about various sexual practices, e.g., homosexual behavior, is best understood as a disagreement about whether or not homosexual behavior is a moral matter. This debate is complicated because one may claim not that homosexual behavior is immoral per se, but is so only because it is contingently related to some other matter which is a moral matter. My claim about moral judgments is that they must be judgments about something that is a moral matter, either directly or indirectly.

Next, the judgment must be believed to be one that could be made by an impartial rational person on the basis of a public system that applies to all rational persons. It either must be a judgment that itself is understood and could be accepted by all impartial rational persons, what I call a "basic moral judgment;" or it must be related to a basic moral judgment in the appropriate ways. One way is for the judgment to be restated as a basic moral judgment by replacing more specialized terms with more general terms, e.g., "trigeminal neuralgia" by "severe facial pain." Another way is for the judgment to be deducible from a basic moral judgment together with what one believes to be true factual judgments. Moral judgments are mistaken if either the factual beliefs are false or the belief that the judgment could be made on the basis of a public system by any impartial rational person is false. As I use the phrase "moral judgment," it does not mean the same as a judgment made on a moral matter, for one can make judgments on these matters without caring whether or not any impartial rational person using a public system could make that judgment. In fact, one can make judgments on these matters that one knows to be inconsistent with the judgment that would be made by any impartial person using a public system that applies to all rational persons.

I have already made clear that moral judgments need not contain certain words. Whether a judgment is a moral judgment does not depend upon the words contained in it. A moral judgment can be made without actually saying anything at all; in some situations one can simply shrug one's shoulders. In fact, "good," "bad," "right," "wrong," "ought," and "should" are far more often used in making nonmoral judgments than in making moral judgments. Nonetheless examination of these words will be of some value in getting clear about moral judgments, for each of them does occur in moral judgments that can be used to represent a wide range of similar moral judgments. By comparing their use in moral judgments to their use in nonmoral judgments, we may be able to clear up some problems that have arisen about the nature of moral judgments.

"Morally Good" and "Morally Bad"

In Chapter 3 I provided an account of the use of "good" and "bad" in nonmoral judgments, so that I shall now consider their use in moral judgments. We say of an action that it is morally good, generally, when it is not in violation of any moral rule and is following some moral ideal. In most cases, giving to various charitable organizations, e.g., UNICEF, is morally good. Giving to museums, however, is generally following utilitarian rather than moral ideals. Working for organizations like the American Civil Liberties Union is usually morally good, for these organizations seek to prevent the deprivation of freedom without themselves violating moral rules. When the prevention of evil involves the violation of a moral rule, the situation is more complex and shall be investigated when discussing what it is to say that an action is morally right or wrong. An unjustified violation of a moral rule is always morally bad. Sometimes an act which does not involve breaking a moral rule, but which is an indication of a bad moral character, e.g., refusing to act according to a moral ideal when this does not involve any significant personal sacrifice, is regarded as morally bad.

A morally good person is one who seldom or never does morally bad actions, and often or generally does morally good ones. In judging a person we do not simply consider her actions, but also her intentions and motives. A morally good person must intend to do morally good actions and intend to avoid morally bad ones. We do not call a person morally good who accidentally acts in accordance with the moral ideals, and does not do morally bad actions simply because things don't turn out as she intends. This is a situation that generally occurs only in slapstick movies. It is worth mentioning to avoid the impression that it is only the consequences of a person's action that count toward her being judged morally good or bad. Consequences are important. A person who always tries to prevent evil but never does is not generally thought of as morally good. Of such a person, we may say that she means well, but, contrary to Kant, some results are necessary before we call her morally good.

Good results, even if intentional, are not sufficient to make a person morally good; motives are also important. A person who follows the moral ideals and obeys the moral rules, but does so solely or primarily from fear of punishment or desire of praise, is not usually considered a morally good person. A morally good person must do morally good actions and avoid doing morally bad ones for certain kinds of motives. These motives are not limited to acting out of respect for the moral law, but include actions based on some emotions as well. I will discuss these motives in greater detail when considering why one should be moral. Generally we call a person morally good if she intentionally does morally good actions and avoids morally bad ones, and her motive for doing this is one that can be depended on to operate even when she believes that no one will know about her action.

A brief reminder of the analysis of "good," "bad," "better," and "worse," used in judgments describing particular kinds of things shows how the use of these terms in moral judgments fits the general analysis. A good x is an x that all qualified rational persons would choose when they wanted an x for its normal function unless they had a reason not to. A bad x is an x that no rational person would choose unless etc. A morally good person is one that all rational persons would choose when they were selecting persons to live with, unless they had a reason not to. A morally bad person is one no rational person would choose to live with, unless he had a reason. Unless they had a reason, all rational persons would pick the morally better persons when choosing persons to live with so that all rational persons would select the morally good person over the morally bad one. We can now see that moral judgments of persons using the words "good" and "bad" are very similar to judgments made of tools, and even more similar to judgments made of athletes. This does not require that persons be regarded as tools, or even as athletes, performing a function of any sort. It simply makes explicit the fact that rational persons are interested in the moral character of others because of the consequences for themselves and those for whom they are concerned.

"Right" and "Wrong"

Before I can show that the use of the words "right" and "wrong" in moral judgments is very similar to their use in nonmoral judgments, I must provide some account of their use in nonmoral judgments. "Correct" and "incorrect" can often be substituted for "right" and "wrong." In theoretical problems, an answer is right (correct) if all the people qualified to deal with this problem would agree on the answer. An answer is wrong (incorrect) if all qualified people agree that it is not the answer. It is important, but often ignored, that lack of agreement on what is the right answer is completely compatible with complete agreement that almost all of the proposed answers are wrong. If there is a disagreement among qualified people, or if there is disagreement about who counts as a qualified person, then there may be no right or wrong answer to the problem.

That we do not now know enough to determine what the right answer is does not show that there is none; we may lack either knowledge of all the relevant facts or appropriate techniques. The latter, in pure form, is primarily found in mathematics and logic. Here all that one needs to determine if a theorem is correct is to provide a proof acceptable to all qualified mathematicians. In some cases, lack of knowledge of facts is simply due to failure on the part of people to look for them. If, in the absence of the agreement of all qualified people, we continue to maintain that a certain answer is right or wrong, we must be holding that some new technique or information can be found which will result in the agreement of all qualified people. If we do not believe this, then we should abandon calling our answer right or wrong, for we are doing no more than expressing our feelings. This is what those who adopted the verifiability principle were, in a misleading fashion, trying to say.

It is not only answers to theoretical problems that are called right and wrong; we also talk of practical decisions or courses of action as being right or wrong. In these cases, what is right or wrong is often determined after the fact. We often call a decision right or wrong only after seeing whether or not it leads to the desired result. Where equally qualified persons would make different decisions, the one that leads to the desired result is usually called the right one. That a person makes the right decision does not mean that she is to be praised for it, for she may have been simply lucky. However, if a person generally makes right decisions, we tend to give her credit for them, even if we cannot see why her decisions generally turn out right. Talk of intuition or insight is common here, and a person who gets such a reputation often acquires a number of followers, e.g., stock market analysts.

Sometimes all qualified persons would make the same decision. In this kind of case, we can talk about the right decision independent of its outcome. It is because of this kind of case that "right decision" does not mean simply "decision that leads to the desired result." We can imagine a case in which all qualified persons would agree that a person who decides to stay in a burning building rather than to climb down the fire escape has made the wrong decision, the person herself included. Yet it may be that the desired result, saving her life, was in fact achieved by her staying put, and would not have been achieved had she climbed down the fire escape. For it may be that a meteor brushed the side of the building, tearing down the fire escape while she would have been on it, and the wind from the meteor was strong enough to blow the fire out. Although she achieved the desired result by staying put, and would not have achieved it by climbing down the fire escape, this does not alter the fact that the decision to do the latter was the right decision, and the decision to do the former, the wrong one. Right decisions can have tragic results. Decisions or courses of action, like answers to theoretical problems, are right when all properly qualified persons would advocate them; they are wrong when no properly qualified person would advocate them. When there is disagreement, then we often call the decision that leads to the desired result the right decision.

"Morally Wrong" and "Morally Right"

A morally wrong action is usually an unjustified violation of the moral rules. Any action that can be called "morally wrong" can also be called "morally bad," but not vice versa. "Morally bad" has a much wider application than "morally wrong;" this should be clear from the fact that we often use "morally bad" to describe people, motives, and intentions, as well as actions, whereas "morally wrong" is usually restricted to actions. Although "morally wrong" is related to the nonmoral use of "wrong," it differs from it in that what is morally wrong is always determined by what all qualified persons would decide at the time of acting or deciding and is never determined by an outcome that no qualified person would have foreseen. The same relationship holds between "right" and "morally right." We use "morally wrong" when we wish to emphasize the objective character of our judgment. A morally wrong action is one that *all* impartial rational persons would advocate not doing. Since "morally bad" is related to the nonmoral use of "bad," it is generally used when we wish to emphasize that the action is to be avoided or not to be done. A morally bad action is one that all impartial rational persons advocate *not* doing.

A morally right action is not merely one that is in accordance with the moral rules, for since all the moral rules are, or can be, stated as prohibitions, any action that is not a violation of a moral rule is in accordance with it. Counting all such actions as morally right would mean that an action like putting on my right shoe before my left is a morally right action, but in the first chapter, I had already noted that this kind of action is not subject to moral judgment. We generally talk of a morally right action only in those circumstances where we think the action reflects on the moral character of the person. These circumstances are primarily those in which a morally wrong action seems a genuine alternative. There are two kinds: (1) those circumstances in which a person has, or might be expected to have, a strong desire or motive to violate a moral rule unjustifiably, and (2) those circumstances in which a person has, or might be expected to have, difficulty in determining whether or not all impartial rational persons would advocate that violating a moral rule be publicly allowed. We can, therefore, talk of two kinds of morally right actions. The first is where one ignores or overcomes some significant temptation. It is this kind of action that seems most straightforwardly related to one's character. The second kind of morally right action is done in circumstances where we think it difficult to determine what all impartial rational persons would advocate. Here we often talk of moral insight. The former may involve only the moral rules; the latter almost always involves both the moral rules and the moral ideals.

The clearest case of a morally right action of the first kind is when we credit a persons's personal virtues for her doing the morally right action, e.g., when it takes courage to tell the truth. In these cases if the morally wrong action had been done, we would have said that it resulted from a lack of the appropriate personal virtue, e.g., she lied because she didn't have the courage to tell the truth. It is this kind of immoral action that is appropriately described as proceeding from weakness of will. Not all morally right actions of the first kind are due to strength of will. Sometimes we are tempted to unjustifiably violate a moral rule because of self-interest or the interests of others, and it is not the personal virtues but the moral virtues that are put to the test. These cases are similar because there is no doubt about what the morally right action is; what makes it worth calling the action or (non-action) morally right is that there is a significant temptation not to do it. Philosophers have mistakenly stressed the overcoming of self-interest as most important for the first kind of morally right action, but often one must overcome the motives provided by one's family, one's religion, or one's country.

When family, religion, or country provide the motives for immoral action, then the overcoming of temptation is complicated by the difficulty in coming to see whether all impartial rational persons would or could advocate that the violation be publicly allowed. It is often no easy matter to see what could be advocated by impartial rational persons in the same situation. Morally irrelevant considerations are extraordinarily difficult to eliminate. That *my* family or country will benefit and those I do not care for will suffer are considerations that almost invariably affect my judgment. Distortion of the facts is almost inevitable. It is the recognition of the difficulty of being impartial in a case in which one is involved with any of the parties that accounts for the rule that judges disqualify themselves in such cases. Nonmoral considerations, e.g., that it is *my* family that is involved, usually lead to following a moral ideal when this involves unjustifiably breaking a moral rule. Explicitly describing the situation using only those general terms that can be understood by all rational persons provides some help in eliminating egocentric biases.

Sometimes uncritical following of the moral rules, especially obeying the law, leads to doing the morally wrong action. One may mistakenly think that one has a duty to do something even though no impartial rational person would advocate one's acting in that way. Although one should never violate a moral rule unless an impartial rational person could advocate that such a violation be publicly allowed, whenever obeying the rule causes someone to suffer, one should always consider whether impartial rational persons would advocate that violating the rule be publicly allowed. Doing the morally right action when it involves overcoming one's habit of automatically obeying the moral rule is among the most difficult of all morally right actions.

When, given all the facts known by the agent (or which she should have known), all impartial rational persons would advocate that violating the rule in order to follow the ideal be publicly allowed, then doing so is morally right. When no impartial rational person would advocate that violating the rule in order to follow the moral ideal be publicly allowed, then breaking the rule is morally wrong. When fully informed impartial rational persons disagree about whether to publicly allow breaking the rule or not, then we cannot say that breaking the rule is either morally right or wrong. If we believe that some further information is now available which would lead all impartial rational persons to agree, then we can continue to maintain that the action is either morally right or morally wrong. If we believe no information is now available which would result in the agreement of all impartial rational persons, then to maintain that the action is either morally wrong or morally right is primarily to express one's attitude, which is better expressed by saying that the action either ought or ought not be done. Most moral disputes are disputes over the facts of the case, as is acknowledged even by those who hold that moral judgments are simply expressions of feelings.

The account of "morally right" given above allows a more precise account of "morally wrong" than that given earlier. On that earlier account I said that a morally wrong action is usually an unjustified violation of the moral rules. We can now include as a morally wrong action one that is in accordance with a moral rule when all impartial rational persons would advocate that violating the rule in order to follow a moral ideal be publicly allowed. This class of morally wrong actions differs from the unjustified violations of the moral rules in that only for the latter do all impartial rational persons advocate liability to punishment. To complicate the matter still further, it will sometimes be one's duty to violate a moral rule in order to follow a moral ideal. A doctor may have a duty to inflict pain on a person or to restrict her freedom in order to prevent much greater evil, and so may a judge or a policeman. Where we have not only a conflict of moral rules with moral ideals, but of moral rules with one another, impartial rational persons may advocate liability to punishment for doing the morally wrong action. In all of these cases there is not only the failure to follow a moral ideal, there is also a violation of a moral rule.

"Morally Indifferent"

Those actions that I call justified exceptions to the moral rules are not the same as what are sometimes called morally indifferent actions. Those justified exceptions which all impartial rational persons advocate be publicly allowed are not morally indifferent; they are morally right, and impartial rational persons will advocate doing them. Those justified exceptions which some impartial rational persons advocate publicly allowing, while others do not, are not properly described as morally indifferent either, for this suggests that all impartial rational persons are indifferent about such actions. Although some impartial rational persons may be indifferent about these actions, some impartial rational persons would advocate that they be prohibited while others would advocate doing them. A morally indifferent action should be one that all impartial rational persons agree that, morally speaking, it makes no difference whether or not the action is done. Some of these actions may be those in which the forseeable consequences of two actions are the same, except that different people will be suffering those consequences. However, the largest class of actions that are normally described as morally indifferent belong in the class of actions that fall outside the scope of morality. Although all of these actions are ones toward which all impartial rational persons would be morally indifferent, we normally use the phrase "morally indifferent" in describing an action only when one is denying, perhaps in anticipation, that the action is a moral matter, e.g., various kinds of sexual activity between consenting adults.

Moral Judgments of Persons

A person involved in moral matters, who never or almost never does what is morally wrong or bad and always or almost always does what is morally right, I call a just person. Note that such a person must sometimes follow the moral ideals. Of course, such a person must also have the appropriate intentions and motives, as we noted in the discussion of the morally good person. It is not necessary that a just person be continually tempted to do what is morally wrong. In fact, it is doubtful if a person who was continually tempted would be a just person. Although a just person may be tempted to do what is morally wrong from time to time, one would expect that situations that would tempt most persons will most often not tempt her. Of two persons facing the same temptation, we may praise the morally right action of the person who is tempted more than we praise the morally right action of the person who is not, but we admire the character of the latter more. This is similar to two persons facing the same danger, where we praise the courageous action of the person suffering from fear more than we praise the courageous action of the person who is not, but admire the character of the latter more. What I call a just person is sometimes called a conscientious person, a person of integrity, or sometimes simply a moral person. When justice is combined with charity, or the just person is also kind, she is what I call a morally good person. She is also called a kind person, a charitable person, a humane person, or sometimes simply a good person.

Moral Standards

To call someone a morally good person or even to call her a moral person is to praise her. We normally reserve these praises for persons we consider to be much better than we believe persons usually are. I use the phrase "moral standards" to mean the standards used in determining how much moral praise or condemnation a person deserves. The higher the moral standard, the more morally right and good actions we require for a person to be praised as moral or morally good. The lower the moral standard, the more morally bad or wrong actions we require for a person to be condemned as immoral or morally bad. Some rational persons have higher expectations of how persons usually act; they will demand more of a moral person than someone who has lower expectations.

Since it is our expectation of how persons do act that determines how high or low our moral standards are, any narrowing of the range of acceptable moral standards must be accomplished by narrowing the range of acceptable expectations about how persons do act. This latter narrowing can be done, in part, by examining the way that persons actually act. If no person has ever lived a full life without committing some immoral actions, it is pointless to demand no immoral actions before we call a person moral. In fact, we do not usually apply the term "immoral" to an act unless we think it serious enough to count against the person being called a moral person. If the morally best person one has ever heard of spent only one fourth of her time in following the moral ideals, it is absurd to demand that a morally good person devote half of her time to following the moral ideals. It is in discovering how persons actually behave that psychology, sociology, and anthropology have relevance to morality. Our moral standards should be determined, in part, by the findings of the sciences I have mentioned, but since behavior can be changed by education and training, it might be worthwhile to also have some higher standard in mind, e.g., what impartial rational persons would expect of people. If, as seems plausible, all impartial rational persons would expect that people give up at least some luxuries to provide others with necessities, then our moral standards will be much higher than they presently seem to be. And a change in our moral standards will result in a change in our moral judgments.

Moral Worth of Actions

Moral standards not only determine our moral judgments of people, but also those of particular actions. A judgment of the moral worth of an action is a judgment concerning how much the action indicates about the moral character of the person. Telling the truth when this has serious consequences for oneself is an action that has significant moral worth. Rescuing a child at great risk to oneself also has significant moral worth. Both of these actions are a strong indication of good moral character. A donation to charity involving no sacrifice has little moral worth, for it does not indicate much about the moral character of the person. Normally we talk of the moral worth of an action only when it is an indication of a good moral character. We do sometimes talk of an action that is not morally wrong as being morally bad when we mean that it is a strong indication of bad moral character. A morally bad action need not involve either an unjustified violatiɔn (or the unjustified keeping) of a moral rule; it can simply be a callous action, failing to act on a moral ideal when the normal expectation is that a person would do so.

I do not suggest that language is used with such precision, nor do I advocate, or even believe it possible, that it be used in this way in the future. However, I think the following may be of some value for being clear about the use of the phrases "morally good," "morally bad," "morally right," and "morally wrong." *Morally good* actions are those that all impartial rational persons advocate doing, but do not advocate liability to punishment for not doing. *Morally bad* actions are those that all impartial rational persons advocate not doing, without considering the question of punishment. *Morally right* actions are those that all impartial rational persons not only advocate doing, but also generally advocate liability to punishment for not doing. *Morally wrong* actions are those that all impartial rational persons not only advocate not doing, but also generally advocate liability to punishment for doing. The notions of morally right and morally wrong are closely connected with the notion of punishment, while the notions of morally good and morally bad are not usually connected with it. Despite this, it can be seen that "morally bad" and "morally wrong" can often be applied to the same actions, whereas "morally good" and "morally right" usually apply to quite different actions.

Responsibility Standards

Judgments about whether, or to what degree, a person is responsible for some action which falls under the scope of the moral system are judgments of blame and credit. In contrast with judgments of moral worth, which are usually made of morally good actions, judgments of responsibility are usually made of morally wrong actions. If a person is totally excused from responsibility for an action, then she gets no moral blame or credit for it; if she has a partial excuse, then she has to take some responsibility for the action, though not as much as someone who has no excuse. It is in situations where there is some question about whether or how much to hold a person responsible that we usually talk of credit and blame.

I call the standards one uses to determine how much credit or blame a person should get for a particular action "responsibility standards." These standards do not usually result in what I call moral judgments, but in those judgments which determine to what degree, if at all, a person should be subject to moral judgment. The standard punishment for a certain kind of violation of a moral rule, e.g., killing a person, is designed for the person who is fully responsible. To judge that she is not completely to blame is to decide that her punishment should be somewhat less than the standard punishment. This is why it is important what responsibility standards are adopted, for judging how much one is to be blamed affects how much she is to be punished.

Blame and Credit Versus Praise and Condemnation

The usual ways of talking about praise and blame have obscured the distinction between moral standards and responsibility standards. Praise is not the opposite of blame, but of condemnation, and is related to our moral standards. Blame and its opposite, credit, are related to responsibility standards. It is easy to see how the confusion arose. To call a person morally good is to praise her. We only praise a person as morally good if she does morally good actions. But the amount of positive moral worth that her actions have depends upon her being responsible for them. If an action that normally has a certain amount of positive moral worth is one for which we do not give complete credit, this will lessen the amount of moral worth. It will do so because by taking away some credit the action is no longer as strong an indication of the moral character of the person. Since the assignment of credit affects the assignment of moral worth, the two have not always been clearly distinguished. In similar fashion, how much we condemn a person for an immoral action will depend upon how much we hold her responsible for it. Thus blame and condemnation are often not distinguished.

Praise and blame are mistakenly regarded as opposites because each is the dominant member of its pair. Judgments about moral worth are primarily made of morally right and morally good actions. We are interested in encouraging moral and morally good actions, and ranking positive moral worth provides some extra incentive. Rewards are not usually available for such actions. Degrees of punishment do provide a scale for ranking most immoral actions; hence there is little need for judging negative moral worth. Further, we are interested in discouraging all immoral behavior; thus there is little point in ranking negative moral worth. Judgments of responsibility are primarily concerned with morally wrong or morally bad actions, for there is little need to be concerned about assigning full responsibility for morally good actions; no one usually suffers if more credit is given than is deserved. Normally it is important to be concerned about assigning responsibility for morally wrong actions, for someone suffers unjustifiably when she is blamed more than she deserves.

How much credit or blame a person deserves will depend upon the responsibility standards that are adopted. The stricter the standards, the greater the excuse needed to reduce the amount of blame. Stricter responsibility standards will probably result in people taking more care not to act immorally, but they will probably also result in more punishment being inflicted on people. Whether or not these statements are true cannot be determined *a priori,* but only by a study of how people actually behave. Just as the proper amount of punishment is determined by seeing what comes closest to maximum deterrence with minimum infliction of evil, so the proper responsibility standards are those that most closely approach this ideal. Psychology, sociology, and anthropology are all relevant in determining the proper responsibility standards, but no science can decide between two different standards that result in the same amount of evil being suffered.

Some prefer stricter standards with fewer violations, though there is then an increase in the amount of punishment. Others prefer the more lenient standards, though the decrease in punishment is offset by an increase in violations. But of two standards both equally effective in discouraging violations, the more lenient is the better. This is exactly parallel to determining the amount of punishment. It is most unlikely that there is a unique determination of either how much a given violation should be punished and how much a given person should be held responsible. This is why the question of what a person deserves has never been answered to everyone's satisfaction.

In applying the responsibility and moral standards, considerations of person, group, place or time are as irrelevant as when applying the moral rules. What may make it seem as if these things are relevant is that we know that people in certain societies or in earlier times lacked some characteristics that are relevant in applying these standards. We do not blame people in a primitive society for an immoral action as much as we would people in our society, not because they live in a different society, but because we feel that people in that society lack some relevant characteristic, usually knowledge. We would assign the same amount of blame to someone in our own society who lacked these same characteristics. The standards used both in determining the moral worth of an action and in determining how responsible a person is for her actions are universal standards. They can be applied to all persons in all societies.

"Ought" and "Should"

"Ought" and "should" have often been considered peculiarly moral words. In fact, many have considered them to be the most important words to understand if one wanted to understand moral judgments. Although the two words cannot always be substituted for each other (in fact, it seems as if only "ought to" rather than simply "ought" can be substituted for "should"), it makes no difference to my points which word is used. Thus I shall use the one that sounds to me most natural in the context, and shall not be concerned about establishing conclusions about "ought" from premises about "should." Before I try to give an account of these words as they occur in moral judgments, I shall, as I did with the words "good," "bad," "right," and "wrong," try to provide an account of their use in nonmoral judgments. For, as the slightest consideration of these words shows, "ought" and "should" are most often used in nonmoral judgments, not in moral ones.

The following examples not only show some of the many nonmoral judgments in which "should" and "ought" occur, they also show that "ought to" and "should" are often interchangeable. "You should (ought to) see that movie." "You should (ought to) get some sleep." "I ought to (should) leave now." "You should (ought to) use a lighter shade of lipstick." "You should (ought to) have thought of that sooner." "She ought to (should) have an operation immediately." "She ought to (should) be up by now." "She should (ought to) have three teeth by now." "This bridge should (ought to) have four lanes each way." "All of us ought to (should) quit smoking." "I should (ought to) be studying for the exam now." "I know I should (ought to) have tried harder, but I didn't feel like doing it." "I know I should (ought to) be studying, but I don't feel like it." "There ought to (should) be more blue in that corner." "The lighting should (ought to) suggest a foggy night." "What should (ought) I (to) do now, wash the dishes, or make the bed?" "I don't know what I should (ought to) do."

It is, or should be, clear after looking at the sentences in the preceding paragraph that no simple account of "should" or "ought" will be adequate. To regard statements containing "should" or "ought" as commands is plausible for some of the examples given above but obviously implausible for others. It is, in general, most plausible for those sentences starting with "you" and in the present tense. It has less plausibility for sentences starting with "I," and has almost no plausibility for those sentences starting with "she" or in the past tense. In addition, some of the sentences do not seem to be imperatives in even the widest sense of that term, e.g., "She ought to be up by now," and "She should have three teeth by now."

"Ought" and "Should" in Practical Judgments

Our discussion of "right" and "wrong" showed that they were used to describe answers either to theoretical questions or to practical questions. It should not be surprising that "ought" and "should" are also used in two somewhat different contexts; although, as with "right" and "wrong," we should expect that the description of their use in one context will be very similar to the description of their use in the other. In contrast with "right" and "wrong" which are more commonly used in theoretical judgments, "ought" and "should" are most often used in practical judgments.

I shall start by attempting to describe their use in nonmoral practical judgments. As used in these judgments, the terms "ought" and "should" are used to advocate a course of conduct. When they are addressed to a particular person, they must advocate a course of conduct that a rational person concerned with that person would advocate. To say to a person that she ought to do something is to imply that you, as a rational person concerned with her, advocate that course of action, and usually suggests that you take an interest in her. To say to a person that she ought to do something, when you do not think that any rational person concerned with her would advocate that course of action to her, is close enough to lying to be a violation of the rule "Don't deceive." In fact, if you said "I think you ought to do it," and thought that the action was one that you as a rational person would not advocate to anyone for whom you were concerned, then you could properly be accused of lying. For to tell a person that she ought to do something is to imply that you are concerned with her.

Nothing said above should be taken as implying that in every situation there is only one course of action that ought to be followed. As was pointed out in Chapter 2, two persons can act in incompatible ways and both be acting rationally. One person may maintain that I ought to do x, and another maintain that I ought to do y, where x and y are incompatible courses of action, yet both may be using "ought" correctly. Disagreements about what ought to be done can have several different causes. Even though two people take an interest in me, they may disagree about what is really in my best interest. These disagreements often involve different rankings of the goods and evils and can usually not be resolved even when there is complete agreement on the facts. Even if two persons agree about what is in my best interest, they may disagree about the best way in which to obtain the desired goal. These kinds of disagreements can sometimes be settled, e.g., it may be that one person knows me or my situation better than the other, and upon acquainting the other with this additional information, both would agree upon the course of action they would advocate.

Agreement on all the relevant facts does not guarantee that rational persons will agree upon the course of action they maintain that I ought to follow. When the disagreement cannot be resolved, there is no right course of action, and the course of action that we say ought to be followed will generally reflect our own individual attitudes and desires. An economist and a banker, advising a young person with the ability to be either, may very well advise her to follow different careers, even though they do not disagree on any facts, and both are interested solely in the welfare of the person they are advising. In these cases, it might be better to say "My advice is to . . . " rather than "You ought," but one cannot say the latter phrase is being misused in this sort of situation.

In some situations every rational person knowing the same relevant facts and concerned with the individual or individuals involved will advocate the same course of action, e.g., all qualified doctors will agree that in my condition, I ought to have an operation immediately. It is incorrect to say that I ought to do x, if, given all the facts, no rational person concerned with me would advocate my doing x. Thus, unlike commands, statements containing "ought" or "should" can be incorrect. Of course, someone can make a mistake in *giving* a certain command; one may not mean to say what she did, or obeying the order may produce results other than those intended, but you can give a command to an individual for whom you have no concern. However, when you tell a person that she ought to do something, what you tell her to do must be something that a rational person concerned for her might advocate her doing. If it is not, you were either mistaken in telling her she ought to do it, or you were deceiving her.

It should not be thought, however, that every practical judgment containing "should" advocates a course of action intended to benefit the person to whom it is addressed. Although saying "you ought to do x" implies that I am a rational person concerned with you, it does not imply that doing x will benefit you personally. It is not incorrect to tell you that you ought to do something that will benefit someone else, especially, but not solely, if you care for that other person. We often tell people what they ought to do in order to benefit someone for whom they are concerned. This is a perfectly acceptable use of "ought." If Jane cares for someone, it is acceptable to tell her that she ought to do something that will benefit him, even if her doing so will not benefit her personally.

This creates the possibility of even greater disagreement among rational persons about what I ought to do. For one course of action might benefit me personally; another might benefit someone for whom I am concerned. Given all the facts, it may therefore be that rational persons will disagree about the course of action they advocate for me to take. One may advocate a course of action designed to benefit me personally; another may advocate a course of action designed to benefit someone for whom I am concerned. But in either case, it is correct to tell me that I ought to do x, only if x is an action or course of action that a rational person concerned with me could advocate, and if it is one which you, in fact, being concerned with me, do advocate.

This analysis of "ought" is easily adapted to statements in the first, second, or third person, and in either present or past tense. When I say that I (you, she) ought to do x, I mean that I, as a rational person concerned with myself (you, her), advocate that I (you, she) do x. When I say that she ought to have done x, I mean that I, as a rational person, concerned with her, would have advocated that she do x. In some cases, we may be making an even stronger claim, namely that all rational persons would advocate her doing x, or would have advocated her doing it.

I realize that it may sound somewhat strange to talk of my advocating a course of action to myself, but on reflection I hope that this strangeness will disappear. It is not at all unusual for someone to tell herself that such and such is the rational thing to do. Nor is it always the case that one does what she considers the rational thing to do. The proposed analysis accounts as well for statements such as "I know I should have done it, but I didn't feel like it," as it does for the more straightforward statements like "You ought to have an operation."

Adapting the analysis to statements such as "This bridge ought to have four lanes each way," and "The lighting ought to suggest a foggy night," also presents no difficulties. Insofar as these statements are addressed to someone who is going to build the bridge or to control the lighting, they are to be understood in the same way as second person, present tense statements containing "should." If we do not wish to rewrite the statements, they can be understood in the following way: "I, as a rational person concerned with the people affected by the bridge (lighting), advocate that the bridge have four lanes each way (that the lighting suggest a foggy night)." Here, again, one may or may not be claiming that all rational persons would agree. Whether one is claiming that or not will become clear from what one does if someone disagrees with what one says.

"Ought" in Theoretical Judgments

So far I have been concerned solely with the use of "ought" in nonmoral practical judgments. I shall now turn to the use of "ought" in nonmoral theoretical judgments; judgments such as "She ought to be up by now" and "She ought to have three teeth by now." "Ought" is used much less often in judgments of this sort, and most accounts of "ought" have completely ignored its use in this kind of judgment. In these judgments, nothing is being advocated, much less commanded; rather something is claimed or asserted. Depending on the context, "She ought to have three teeth by now," can be taken as a prediction that she now has three teeth or as a claim that she deviates from the normal, generally, though not always, with the suggestion that this is a bad thing. If we do not know how many teeth she has, then our statement is most likely a prediction. If we know that she only has one tooth, it is a claim that she has fewer teeth than is normally expected of a child her age.

The prediction and the claim are much more closely connected than they seem at first glance. For the prediction is generally made on the basis of one's belief about how many teeth children of her age generally have. Of course, both the prediction and the claim can be made on somewhat narrower grounds than what is normal for children of her age. If, for example, everyone in her family has been an early teether, then "She ought to have three teeth by now," can be based on one's beliefs about the age that her brothers and sisters got their teeth. But one must have some reasons for one's prediction or claim, for the use of "ought," even in theoretical judgments, implies that one has reasons for one's judgment. If one says "She ought to have three teeth by now," and upon being asked why, does not have any reason, then one has misused the language. We should use "ought" in nonmoral theoretical judgments only when we have beliefs that would lead some rational person to accept the judgment. Of course, sometimes a belief that leads one rational person to accept a judgment will not lead another one to accept it; but this is a consequence that we should now expect.

Disagreement about whether to accept a particular "ought" judgment of this kind sometimes rests on disagreement about the beliefs that are used to support it. These disagreements can sometimes be settled by finding out the facts, but not always. Rational persons may differ in the weight they give to the support provided by certain facts. Sometimes, however, the facts are such that any rational person acquainted with them would accept certain "ought" judgments. Suppose we know that a child has always napped for one hour and then played quietly in her bed for another hour. Then, in the absence of any reason to believe anything is unusual today, her mother's remark made one hour and forty-five minutes after she went to sleep that she ought to be up by now would be acceptable to all rational persons.

Nonmoral practical judgments like nonmoral theoretical judgments containing "ought" sometimes make a stronger claim, sometimes a weaker one. If we say "She ought to be up," then we must, at least, be claiming that we have some beliefs which would lead some rational persons to accept our judgment. The

presence of new information can drastically change our assessment of a judgment. For example, in the case of the mother's remark about her child being up
from a nap, information that the child had been given a sleeping pill just before
she went to bed today would make us less likely to accept the mother's judgment. Since "ought" judgments are generally made on the basis of many beliefs,
a change in one or more need not affect our assessment of an "ought" judgment,
but sometimes, as in the example sketched above, it will.

Nonmoral theoretical judgments can be analyzed into a kind of nonmoral
practical judgment, viz., I, as a rational person, advocate believing this prediction or claim. A rational person would advocate believing a prediction or claim
only if it was supported by some belief which she accepted and which she
thought provided adequate support for the prediction or claim. Although nothing is lost by analyzing nonmoral theoretical judgments into practical ones, a
nonmoral theoretical judgment containing "ought" should always be distinguished from a nonmoral practical judgment containing the same words. It is a
testimony to the power of language that there are occasions when a theoretical
judgment is made with the tone of a practical one and sometimes it is not clear
which of the two is meant. "She ought to be up by now," said of a teenager rather
than a baby, could be either a practical or theoretical judgment. There may be
times when even the person who made it is not clear which she meant. So that
if you asked her, "Do you mean that you think she's up, or that you think she
ought to get up?" she may be unable to answer, or will reply "Both. I think she
is up, but if she isn't I think she ought to get up."

This may be the time to emphasize again that I am not primarily concerned
with providing an account of ordinary language. I am, at most, providing an
account of an "idealized" ordinary language. By "idealized," I do not mean a
better one, i.e., one that all rational persons would prefer, but only one that has
less flexibility and more precision than ordinary language. As will be most
apparent in the account of "ought" and "should" as they occur in moral judgments, the distinction between making a moral judgment and making a nonmoral one is not precise. Nonetheless I believe that the distinction is helpful and
that understanding the analyses that I provide should enable one to be clearer
about the actual use of moral judgments and of nonmoral ones.

"Ought" and "Should" in Moral Judgments

Moral judgments containing "ought" or "should" are practical judgments that
one believes are based on a public system that applies to all rational persons.
They are judgments, involving a moral rule or a moral ideal, that any impartial
rational person could make. They include judgments in which a person advocates doing morally right and morally good actions and advocates avoiding
doing morally wrong and morally bad actions. They also include judgments on
which impartial rational persons disagree. Not all practical judgments that are
made on the basis of a public system applying to all rational persons, or that one
makes as an impartial rational person, are moral judgments. Such judgments
may be prudential, aesthetic, or utilitarian judgments. A moral judgment must

also be about a moral matter, an action etc., that is related to a moral rule or moral ideal.

A significant amount of objectivity of any moral judgment containing "ought" is guaranteed by the fact that such a judgment must be one that any impartial rational person could make. In making the moral judgment "You ought to do x," I am implying that I, as an impartial rational person concerned with you, advocate your doing x. However, I am not implying that I would advocate that everyone in morally similar circumstances do x. When I make a moral judgment containing "ought," if it is not concerned with the violation of a moral rule, I do not have to be willing to universalize it in the strict sense suggested by Kant or Hare. Only when the judgment concerns the violation of a moral rule does the impartiality required by the moral rules demand that one be willing to make the same judgment in all situations which are the same in all morally relevant features. Otherwise one need only allow that any impartial rational person could make the same judgment.

Whenever I claim to be making a moral judgment when I say "You ought to do x," then I must be willing to acknowledge the appropriateness of that judgment of anyone to whom the same morally relevant considerations apply. When the judgment concerns the violation of a moral rule, even though I must always make the same judgment, I do not have to maintain that anyone who makes an incompatible judgment is mistaken. The acceptability of my judgment to all morally similar cases is all that is needed to give moral judgments their universal quality, a characteristic that all moral philosophers agree that they have. It is not even necessary that I be prepared to make the same judgment about all people to whom the same morally relevant considerations apply. When no violations of moral rules are involved, there is nothing wrong with telling two people to whom all the same morally relevant considerations apply that they ought to do different things, e.g., telling one that she ought to help those in her home town, and telling the other that she ought to join the peace corps and help those in the poorer countries.

I pointed out previously that rational persons sometimes disagree about what ought to be done; sometimes even impartial rational persons will make incompatible moral judgments about what ought to be done. In this situation, an impartial rational person who makes a moral judgment saying what ought to be done is expressing her personal attitude. Of course, she is not doing just this. For even if there are several different courses of action that could be advocated by impartial rational persons, there are many more that no impartial rational person would advocate. Even when impartial rational persons disagree about what action ought to be done, if they are making moral judgments, there is a limit to what they can say. When making a moral judgment a rational person must believe that all impartial rational persons could make the same judgment.

Two people who make different moral judgments about what ought to be done can sometimes be led to agree, not by producing new information, but by getting one person to see that no one who was impartial and rational, not even she, would make this same judgment if, e.g., it were not her child that was involved. But even in those cases where impartial rational persons cannot agree about what morally ought to be done, there is agreement about what the morally relevant considerations are, and about what considerations are not morally relevant. Although they may disagree about this case, they can agree that if the facts were somewhat different, they would agree. In most actual cases all impartial rational persons agree on what morally ought to be done.

All impartial rational persons agree that one ought to do what is morally right, and that one ought not to do what is morally wrong. This is a mere tautology. But, given the analysis of morally right and morally wrong, it shows that moral judgments about what one ought to do are capable of being mistaken. Someone making the moral judgment that x ought to be done can be shown that she is mistaken by showing that doing x is morally wrong. Further, moral judgments about what one ought to do, even if they cannot be lies, can be deceitful. For we can know that an action is morally wrong and claim to be making the moral judgment that one ought to do it. Acceptable moral judgments containing "ought" or "should" cannot be made simply according to the whim, or even the reflective attitude, of the person making them. In some cases, only one moral judgment is correct. In others, although there may be several acceptable moral judgments, this number will generally be quite small in proportion to the moral judgments that are not acceptable.

"Ought" occurs in moral judgments in which one advocates obeying a moral rule, or when one advocates following a moral ideal. In either of these cases, one may find complete agreement, or partial disagreement. I have already pointed out that there are occasions in which not all impartial rational persons agree that one ought to obey a moral rule. It is even clearer that impartial rational persons can disagree about whether to advocate following a moral ideal. The latter case allows room for much more disagreement since though all impartial rational persons advocate following the moral ideals, they do not, as with the moral rules, advocate that everyone always follow them.

When "ought" is used in those moral judgments advocating obedience to a moral rule, and no impartial rational person would advocate that violating the rule be publicly allowed, then "ought" has a greater force than when advocating following the moral ideals. In these cases all impartial rational persons not only agree in advocating obedience to the rule, they also advocate liability to punishment for disobedience. We can describe this sense of "ought" by saying that it is used when all impartial rational persons *require* that a certain course of action be followed. It is this sense of "ought" that philosophers seem to have in mind when they use the words "oblige" and "obligation." I prefer not to use these words for it seems to me that they have their normal use primarily in connection with the three positively stated moral rules: "Keep your promise," "Obey the law," "Do your duty." To stretch the use is to invite misunderstanding. I have not been concerned with these words because it is not philosophically important to distinguish the positively stated rules from the negatively stated ones. It is not that there is nothing philosophically interesting to say about obligation; it is only that what one says about obligation does not have any important bearing on moral philosophy.

Although a judgment that Jane ought to do x is not correct unless a rational person concerned with her could make that judgment, one need not be concerned with a person in order to make a moral judgment that she ought to do *x*. However, when actually making a moral judgment to some person about what she ought to do, one is generally expected to have some concern with her. If I tell a person for whom I obviously have no concern "You ought to do *x*," even if I intend this to be a moral judgment, she may legitimately reply, "You can't tell me what I ought to do; you don't care about me." The legitimacy of this reply stems in part from the fact that moral and nonmoral judgments are not totally distinct. Although we can tell anyone that a certain action is morally right or morally wrong, when we say to someone that she ought to do something, even when making a moral judgment, we suggest that we are concerned with her. Most moral judgments telling people what they ought to do also must have a characteristic of a nonmoral judgment, namely that one be concerned with the person to whom one is making the judgment. This brings us to the question we shall discuss in the next chapter, "Why should one be moral?"

11

WHY SHOULD ONE
BE MORAL?

Many philosophers have held that the question "Why should one be moral?" is a senseless or pointless question. I believe that this is due to their misunderstanding of the question. They interpret the question as "Why would an impartial rational person advocate that one be moral?" Taken in this way, the question is pointless, for the answer is obvious. All impartial rational persons must advocate that everyone act morally. But the question is not asking what an impartial rational person would advocate; rather, it is asking what a rational person, not necessarily impartial, but concerned for me, would advocate. Understood in this way the question becomes "Why would a rational person concerned for me advocate that I be moral?" This is not a senseless question. It may very well be that some rational persons concerned for me will advocate that I not be moral. However, some rational persons concerned for me will advocate that I be moral. Why they would advocate this provides the answer to the question "Why should one be moral?"

Talking to Children

This question must be asked by someone who thinks you are concerned for him. To really appreciate its force, consider that you have been asked it by one of your children or a younger sister or brother. What would you answer? There are many things you could say. You could point out that it was generally in one's self-interest to be moral, that people who were moral were generally happier than those who were not. When talking to those whose character is not yet formed, this point takes on even more significance. If you were religious, you could add that God wants one to be moral, and that He will reward those who are. But you could say more than this. You could talk of your ideal of a person, one with all the virtues, moral and personal, and say that you wanted him to be such a person. To want him to become your ideal of a person certainly shows your concern for him. You could talk of integrity and dignity, pointing out that since he will most likely be making moral judgments on the behavior of others, it would be hypocritical not to act morally himself.

Finally, you could point out to him that though you were concerned for him, you were also concerned for others, and that in large measure, you advocate his being moral, not so much out of your concern for him as out of your concern for everyone. There is nothing wrong, morally or otherwise, with advocating a course of action to someone for whom you are concerned, which is not advocated out of concern for him. As long as you would advocate this course of action to anyone for whom you are concerned, you need not advocate it out of your concern for him. If he has had instilled in him a concern for others, then this final answer will have the most force. If he has not, then there is a good chance that none of your answers will seem persuasive.

Many attempts to answer the question seem to take it as asking for reasons of self-interest for being moral. Although it is usually in one's self-interest to be moral, it will sometimes not be so. It is not even always in one's self-interest to seem moral, though in any morally acceptable society it almost always will be. No answer in terms of self-interest is completely satisfactory. What is desired by those who ask the question, "Why should one be moral?" is an answer that will apply always, and not just generally. What is desired is an answer in terms of the intrinsic nature of morality. This was partially realized by Plato, who tried to offer reasons of self-interest for being moral, but at the same time to make these reasons intrinsic to morality. The result of this was to make morality intrinsically self-interested, though with a strange kind of self-interest, viz., harmony of the soul. As we have seen, acting morally is not necessarily in one's self-interest. There is a connection between self-interest and morality, but any attempt to make this direct results in a distortion of the concept of morality or of the concept of self-interest, or both.

Not all reasons are reasons of self-interest; rationality is a wider concept than self-interest, and allows a concern for the welfare of others. In asking, "Why should I be moral?" one need not be asking, and, I think, generally is not asking, "What's in it for me?" but rather, "What is the point of my being moral?" Since being moral is often regarded as simply obeying a certain set of rules, it is not self-evident that there is anything to be gained by anyone by acting morally. This is especially true if there is no distinction made between those moral rules which can be justified, either with or without reference to the customs or institutions of one's society, and those which do not have a justification at all. In many societies the genuine or justifiable moral rules are not distinguished from those rules or traditions which the society, by some accident or design, has grouped together with them.

I imagine that the question, "Why should I be moral?" or its practical equivalent in many circumstances, "Why shouldn't I do it if I want to?" is most often asked in connection with rules concerning sexual activity. "Why should I refrain from having sexual intercourse before marriage?" Simply to say it is immoral to have sexual relations outside of marriage is not a sufficient answer. If no one is hurt, what is wrong with my breaking what some in my society consider a moral rule? I am only concerned with the question, "Why should I be moral?" when restricted to justified moral rules. To the question, "Why should I obey the rules that my society regards as moral?" I can provide no answer, because there is often not an adequate reason to obey these rules. Others have not made the distinction between justified moral rules and unjustified ones. They have simply used morality to mean justified morality. They would say that there was no answer to the question "Why should I obey the justified moral rules?" This is not what I am saying at all. I am simply pointing out the obvious truism that there is no intrinsic reason to obey unjustified moral rules.

It could, of course, be claimed that there is an intrinsic reason to obey even unjustified moral rules: namely, you will be punished if you are caught violating the rules. Though this answer is correct, its very correctness shows us that it is not the answer we were looking for, for this answer gives us no better reason for obeying the justified moral rules than for obeying the unjustified ones. Even though the analysis of morality provided in the previous chapters makes clear why punishment is not just accidentally connected to unjustified violations of the moral rules, punishment does not provide the kind of answer that is wanted. "You will be punished" does not really answer the question "Why should I be moral?" but only the question "Why should I seem moral?" One might, of course, claim that it is impossible to seem moral without being moral. But this claim, though it may hold generally, certainly does not hold universally. We are interested in finding a reason that holds universally.

Religious Answers

One way of making this answer hold universally is to bring in God. God always knows if you are really moral or only seem to be, and He will punish you if you are not really moral. This is why some claim that belief in God is a necessary support of morality. In this context, this claim seems to be based on the view that only self-interest, in this case avoidance of the wrath of God, can provide the reason for acting morally. The answer in terms of religious self-interest avoids one of the difficulties that all answers in terms of natural self-interest have. It is simply false that it is always in our natural self-interest to act morally. However, the religious self-interest answer is not primarily an answer to the question "Why should I be moral?" but rather to the question "Why should I do as God commands?" Of course, if God commands us to be moral, then we do have an answer to our original question also.

The religious self-interest answer to the question "Why should I be moral?" is not the only religious answer. There is also what I prefer to call the genuine religious answer, viz., the love of God. The genuine religious answer to the question "Why should I be moral?" is that God will be pleased if you are. And since God knows when one only seems to be moral, it provides a reason for actually being moral. But this reason, like that of religious self-interest, does not distinguish moral from non-moral rules. In both cases we obey the moral rules because God happens to command us to. However, it does make sense for God not to command us to obey the moral rules; and in fact, to command us to break one of the rules unjustifiably, e.g., God commanded Abraham to sacrifice his son Isaac.

On a practical level, the most serious defect with both religious answers is that they depend upon belief in a God, and a God of a very special sort, viz., one who commands obedience to the moral rules. A rational person need not believe in such a God. So these answers provide no reason at all for him to be moral. What is needed is an answer that all rational persons must acknowledge as an adequate reason, so that it would not be irrational for any person to act morally. I say only that it would be acknowledged as an adequate reason by any rational person, not that it would be considered to be irrational not to act on that reason. On the contrary, I emphatically deny the possibility of such an answer, as it would have as a result that all immoral action was due to ignorance or irrationality.

Immoral Action and Irrational Action

I am not only not claiming to be able to provide an answer to the question "Why should one be moral?" such that every rational person, if aware of this answer, would act morally, I am not even claiming that they would all even be slightly inclined to act morally. I am not claiming that the reason for being moral must provide a motive for all rational persons. All that I am claiming is that an adequate answer to the question "Why should one be moral?" must provide an answer such that it would always be rational to act on the reason provided by that answer. It must always be rational to act morally, but it cannot always be irrational to act immorally.

Some would maintain that all immoral action is either based on a mistaken belief or irrational. Plato tried to show, at least on some interpretations, that no one ever knowingly did evil. However, Plato did not clearly distinguish between immoral action and irrational action. Unless one has an adequate reason, it is true that acting so as to bring evil on oneself or those one cares about is acting either unknowingly or irrationally. It is not true that all immoral action is either unknowing or irrational. Immoral action usually involves causing evils to those we do not care about (or care about enough) in order to please or benefit ourselves or those we do care about. There is nothing irrational in this, unless we accept the very dubious Platonic account of the harmony of the soul. There is a great temptation to accept such an account. Freud has often been twisted in such a way as to yield the conclusion that an immoral person is always sick. Although most murders may be due to mental illness, it is completely implausible to account for all immoral action in this way.

It is equally implausible to hold that all immoral action is followed by painful feelings of guilt. The wicked suffer torments of the soul only if they have a certain kind of superego, which all of them do not have. Even if all of the wicked do suffer some pangs of conscience (a very doubtful view), it is very likely that their ill-gotten gains very often more than compensate for such pangs. To hold that the wicked never profit from their wickedness is a view that I, as much as anyone, would prefer to be true. Unfortunately, all of the evidence appears to show that it is false. But there is another view, which I think my account of morality supports, namely, that a moral person stands a better chance of being happy than an immoral one. I think the evidence appears to show that this view is true. I am only denying that there is any plausible account of human nature such that it is never in one's self-interest to unjustifiably violate a moral rule.

The Moral Reason for Being Moral

The question "Why should one be moral?" is most likely to be asked by those concerned with morality, such as Glaucon and Adimantus; thus we should be wary of dismissing the question as a request for proving the self-interest of morality. Providing an answer to this question is one good way of distinguishing bogus from genuine or justifiable morality. If we cannot give an answer to it, then we should begin to question the justification of that morality. Since we do have a justification of some moral rules we should be able to give a satisfactory answer, though, of course, not one in terms of self-interest.

The moral rules prohibit acting in those ways that cause or increase the likelihood of someone suffering an evil. This provides us with a ready-made answer to our question. One should be moral because he will cause or increase the likelihood of someone suffering evil if he is not. Note that this is a moral reason or answer to the question "Why should one be moral?" As such, it should apply in all cases rather than merely generally. We can now distinguish between being moral and the reasons for being moral. Included among these reasons is what I shall call *the moral reason*, to avoid causing or increasing the likelihood of someone suffering an evil. Note that this is a perfectly acceptable answer to the question. It is one that might serve to convince someone who had actually asked the question. Pointing out to him that others will suffer because of his immoral action may be sufficient to make him give up that course of action, for he may not have thought of this, or have given it sufficient weight.

It is because one usually knows the moral rules before one knows their justification that it is possible to fail to distinguish justifiable moral rules from unjustifiable ones. And it is primarily the presence of unjustifiable moral rules that leads some to ask "Why should one be moral?" It is important and interesting that "Because you will cause or increase the likelihood of someone suffering an evil if you are not" is an appropriate answer only when asked about the justifiable moral rules. It also is a reason for actually being moral rather than only seeming to be so. It thereby differs from all answers in terms of self-interest. Unlike the religious answers, it is also an answer that derives from the point of morality itself, not one that has only an accidental relation to morality.

Although this answer, indeed an even stronger one, "You will cause someone to suffer an evil if you are not" can always be given to anyone contemplating a violation of the first five rules, it is not always an appropriate reply to someone contemplating a violation of one of the second five rules. And it is with regard to the second five rules that the question is more likely to be asked. Although violations of any of the second five rules generally result in at least an increase in the probability of someone suffering an evil, some unjustifiable violations of each of the second five rules do not seem to increase this probability. When no one will suffer an evil because of this particular violation, one may wonder why one should not, e.g., deceive when doing so would be in one's best interest. Why should one be moral in this case? The straightforward answer "Because you will cause or increase the likelihood of someone suffering evil" is not adequate here. Although this would be an appropriate answer for not lying most of the time, it does not seem appropriate in the particular case we are considering.

I am not concerned now with the question "Why in general shouldn't I deceive, break my promise, cheat, disobey the law, or neglect my duty?" The answer to these questions is the same as for the first five rules: "You will cause someone to suffer evil consequences." Thus it might seem as if the answer to the question "Why in this particular case shouldn't I deceive, cheat, etc.?" is our original answer, "You will cause or increase the likelihood of someone suffering evil consequences." But in some cases this is not true; your act will not cause or increase the likelihood of someone suffering evil consequences. From the fact that disobeying these rules generally results in someone suffering evil consequences, it follows that many individual acts of this sort are likely to have these consequences. But it does not follow that some particular act is likely to have them. It is the offering of this reason in the cases where it does not fit that renders it suspect. It is a good reason not to violate a moral rule on a particular occasion that it causes or increases the likelihood of someone suffering evil consequences. But it is not a good reason when this is not the case.

I now wish to provide an answer to "Why should one be moral?" when this question is asked about an unjustifiable violation of a justifiable moral rule and cannot be answered by "Your act will cause or increase the likelihood of someone suffering evil consequences." If I cannot do this, I must admit that there is an unbridgeable gap between the justification of the moral rules and the possibility of always answering the question "Why should one be moral?" But even admitting this gap in some cases should not make us overlook that there is no gap in the most important and most clear-cut cases. Thus the justification of the moral rules provides an answer to the question "Why should one be moral?" in very many cases. The answer is not a religious one or one of self-interest, but a moral one, one which is intrinsic to morality.

The Role of the Virtues

I am now discussing a very limited class of actions, those actions which are an unjustifiable violation of a moral rule, and yet one cannot say that someone will suffer or is more likely to suffer evil consequences because of that particular act. These are those violations of the second five rules, particularly the last three, when a single violation causes no harm; but an impartial rational person cannot advocate that such a violation be publicly allowed because publicly allowing such a violation would have serious evil consequences. Here the moral virtues come into play very importantly. I noted that no moral virtues are specifically connected to each of the first five moral rules. We do not need them, for our moral reason is sufficient to offer an answer to the question "Why should one be moral?" But each of the second five moral rules is connected quite tightly to a moral virtue: to the rule concerning deceit we have truthfulness; to promises, trustworthiness; to cheating, fairness; to obeying the law, honesty; and to duty, dependability. (One may prefer different names for these virtues, this will make no difference to anything that follows.)

The answer to the question "Why should one be moral?" when it is not likely that the violation will have evil consequences for anyone is connected to the moral answer by means of the virtues. As noted in Chapter 9, virtues and vices are built on habit and by precedent. Following the moral rule generally builds the virtue, and contrary action generally builds the vice. The reason for following the moral rule in the peculiar situation when no one would be harmed by an unjustified violation sounds like a prudential one; i.e., it builds your character. This may sound more like a Platonic reason of self-interest than a moral reason. But it is not, for a virtuous person is much less likely to cause evil consequences to others. Building one's virtue makes one less likely to unjustifiably break moral rules when this will increase the likelihood of someone suffering evil consequences.

It should not be surprising that the moral answer to the question "Why should one be moral?" is direct and universally connected with the first five moral rules, and only generally and indirectly connected to the second five. For we saw in the justification of the moral rules that the first five rules were directly connected to the evils that all rational persons desire to avoid, but that the second five were only indirectly connected to these evils. Hence it is not surprising that the moral answer to the question "Why should one be moral?" is indirect when applied to these second five rules. Although indirect and involving the moral virtues, the second five rules are by no means loosely connected with the moral reason. The moral virtues, when properly understood, necessarily lead to causing less evil than the vices; however, blind following of the moral rules, especially the second five, could have disastrous consequences.

The Virtuous Answer

I have admitted that the moral answer to the question "Why should one be moral?" sometimes requires one to make use of the virtues. The virtues need not figure solely as an aid to the moral answer to the question. There is what could be called the virtuous answer to the question "Why should one be moral?" This answer makes use of the fact that some persons aspire to a good character. The most plausible view of a good character is that it contains all of the virtues, both moral and personal. If one aspires to a character of this sort, then he must act morally, for clearly one cannot have the moral virtues unless he acts morally. One who acts morally because he aspires to a good character need not even be concerned with others. Rather, he need only be concerned with attaining a goal that he has set himself. It is certainly a worthy goal, one that all impartial ratio-nal persons would advocate that all persons aim toward. I do not think, how-ever, that the virtuous answer will have much appeal to anyone for whom the moral answer has no force. Although one needs no reason for aspiring to a char-acter which includes the moral virtues, it is very unlikely that one will aspire to it unless he does have a reason. The most persuasive reason for wanting such a character is the moral reason, but the virtuous answer, like the moral answer, has an intrinsic connection to morality. Further, it always provides a direct answer to the question, "Why be moral?"

The Rational Answer

There is a third answer that has an intrinsic connection to morality. This answer makes use of the fact that all rational persons, insofar as they are adopting an attitude toward the moral rules that could be accepted by all other rational per-sons, must adopt the attitude that all impartial rational persons could advocate, viz., the moral attitude. One may be persuaded to act morally because impartial rationality requires acting in this way. I call this answer the rational answer to the question "Why should one be moral?" If one aspires to act in the way that impartial rationality requires, then he must act morally. The rational answer is quite similar to the virtuous one; neither one requires concern for anyone else. Yet both can always provide a direct answer to the question, "Why be moral?" However, neither of them by itself seems to me to be very persuasive. Of course, one needs no reason for wanting to act as impartial rationality requires, but unless one accepts the moral reason as persuasive, I do not see why anyone would want to act in this way.

There is one illegitimate motive for wanting to act this way. It is illegitimate because it is based on a confusion. The confusion involves the relationship between what impartial rationality requires and what rationality requires. "Impartial rationality requires acting morally" simply means that all impartial rational persons advocate acting morally. "Rationality requires acting morally" means that it is irrational to act immorally. As I have continually pointed out, and shall discuss again later in this chapter, rationality does not require acting morally; it only allows acting in this way. Rationality does not require acting in the way impartial rationality requires. If one does not clearly distinguish between what rationality requires and what impartial rationality requires, then he may conclude that it is irrational to act immorally. It seems likely that Kant was involved in this confusion.

Although I believe that neither the rational answer nor the virtuous answer is as important as the moral answer, I believe that they are important. It may be that some persons have been brought up so as to desire to have a character including all the moral virtues, and that other persons have been brought up to desire to act in the way that impartial rationality requires. If they have, I have no desire to discourage them. More important, these answers strengthen the moral answer. It may be that the moral answer, making no reference to oneself, is, by itself, not enough to persuade most people to act morally. These latter two answers, though grounded in the moral answer, go beyond it and carry some significant force of their own. Indeed, this is evidenced by the fact that some common emotions, with obvious power to move people, are related to these answers as well as to the moral one.

Moral Emotions: Compassion, Remorse, Pride, Shame, and Guilt

Compassion is intimately connected with the moral answer. Combined with a proper understanding of morality, compassion may lead one to genuinely accept the moral answer. I believe that those who sincerely ask "Why should one be moral?" do not lack the necessary compassion. They do have compassion for others, but they do not see how morality, which they regard as simply a traditional set of rules, has any relationship to it. The moral answer is the answer they want, if only they can be made to see it. Even some who do not generally feel compassion often suffer remorse when they see someone suffering because of something they have done, even if unintentionally. To suffer remorse is to feel sad because of some harm you have caused. Unlike compassion, remorse is felt only under special circumstances. The special circumstances are those in which you consider yourself responsible for someone suffering some evil. A compassionate person will often feel remorse when someone suffers because of his immoral actions. Violations of the first five rules are most likely to cause remorse.

The emotions most closely connected with the virtuous answer are pride and shame. Of course, pride is appropriate to more than one's virtues. One can take pride in one's abilities, work, family, or country. One can take pride in anything that one believes related to oneself and that lives up to a standard that one accepts or that makes one superior to other persons. To feel pride in something is to feel pleasure because one believes that thing which is related to oneself lives up to some standard one has accepted or that it makes one superior to other persons. Since most rational persons consider a character containing the moral virtues to live up to an accepted standard and to be superior to one not containing them, it is obviously appropriate to take pride in one's moral virtues. One who does take pride in his moral character will suffer shame when he acts immorally. To feel shame is to feel sad due to loss of pride or because of something related to one that fails to live up to an accepted standard or that one believes makes one inferior to other persons. The desire to maintain one's pride and to avoid feeling shame provide strong motives to some for being moral. Pride and shame are also closely related to the moral ideals. One often feels pride when acting on the moral ideals, and shame is commonly caused by failure to act.

The feeling of guilt seems most closely connected with the rational answer. One is found guilty of having unjustifiably broken some rule. Although guilt is often most closely associated with legal rules or laws, one can also be guilty of having unjustifiably broken some moral rule. The feeling of guilt is anxiety due to one's belief that one is guilty. Children often feel guilt when they violate the rules laid down by their parents or teachers. Adults may not feel guilt unless the rules they violate are ones that they consider justified. The rational answer emphasizes that the moral rules are rules toward which all impartial rational persons, including oneself, advocate obedience. For one who accepts the rational answer, it is very common to feel guilt for unjustifiably violating any of the moral rules, even when no one is hurt, as in some unjustified violations of the second five moral rules. The desire to avoid feeling guilt may provide a strong motive for acting morally.

Conscience

The rational answer can also be used to explain and justify some of our talk about conscience. This should not be surprising, as pangs of conscience are often considered identical to guilt feelings. By regarding what your conscience tells you as the attitude you would take as an impartial rational person, we can come to understand how this identification was made. Letting your conscience be your guide is equivalent to guiding your actions by what you would advocate as an impartial rational person. Going against your conscience is doing what you know you, as an impartial rational person, would advocate not doing. Regarding conscience as one's attitude as an impartial rational person, rather than as the superego, takes conscience out of psychology and brings it back to morality where it belongs. However, it is easy to understand how conscience came to be identified with the superego. Most of our attitude as an impartial rational person was learned from our parents. Concerned primarily with the explanation of behavior and not its justification, Freud and his followers made no attempt to distinguish between that internalized parental teaching which was justifiable and that which was not. Thus conscience was swallowed up by the superego and lost its moral significance. By identifying conscience with one's attitude as an impartial rational person, we give conscience back its traditional moral authority.

The rational answer is also connected with the concept of authenticity. Authenticity excludes hypocrisy. Hypocrisy is not exactly deceit, but is closely related to it. It consists in making judgments of other persons' behavior, thereby suggesting that one acts in accordance with those judgments, when, in fact, one does not. Some people have maintained that authenticity is all that is required for acting morally. That is correct only if one makes moral judgments. Since most people do make moral judgments it is plausible to maintain that an authentic person must be a moral person. If one makes judgments according to one's conscience, and acts accordingly, one would be acting authentically. In somewhat older terminology, which I prefer, such a person would be called a person of integrity.

If one takes cheating as the model of immoral action, one may look upon the moral rules as the rules which govern the game of life. Looking at them in this way, one may regard it as beneath her dignity to be immoral. She may think that if she cannot win the game of life without violating the moral rules, she does not deserve to win. One who views morality in this way may also find the rational answer most persuasive. The difference between dignity and integrity is very small. I think, however, that dignity has a closer relationship to pride. To act beneath one's dignity is to suffer shame; to violate one's integrity is to suffer guilt. A person of dignity is one who truly believes "It matters not whether you win or lose, but how you play the game." Unless one accepts the moral answer, however, I do not see why one should accept the moral rules as the rules for the game of life.

Summary of Reasons for Acting Morally

Although I believe that desires for authenticity, integrity, or dignity may lead one to act morally, I doubt that they will do so unless one also has compassion. However, if one has dignity and integrity, in addition to compassion, then she has additional reasons for being moral. Being moral is required to avoid not only remorse, but also shame and guilt. But all of these reasons have an air of self-interest about them. I do not think self-interest, no matter how far it is extended, provides the fundamental reason for being moral. The fundamental reason for being moral is to avoid causing evil for others. The fundamental reason for being morally good is to prevent or relieve the suffering of evil by others. All of the other reasons seem to me to have little force unless these reasons have force, although I grant that the force of the moral reason is increased significantly by the addition of these other reasons.

I have provided a number of answers to the question "Why should one be moral?" Some, like the answers in terms of self-interest and those which involve religious belief, I have found wanting, for these answers do not really address themselves directly to the question. I admit that acting morally is generally in one's self-interest; indeed I have tried to show why this is so, but I cannot admit that it is always so. Further, I think that those who ask the question are really not looking for an answer in terms of self-interest but for one which explains the point of morality. The religious answer may satisfy some, but I, personally, do not find it self-evident that I should do what it is claimed that God commands. The answer that I find most satisfactory is the moral answer. This answer is truly an answer to the question. It stems from the very nature of morality. Once one accepts this reason, I think it can be supported by other reasons: those involving integrity and dignity, but the fundamental reason for being moral is to avoid causing evil for others.

I think that these are the best reasons one can provide for acting morally, unless one is prepared to make some highly dubious hypotheses about human nature, or the nature of the world. I am not prepared to make these hypotheses. First, any that would even be plausible would provide no better reasons than these reasons. Second, these reasons are good enough. They are good enough reasons to make it completely rational for any person to act morally at any time. However, I do not claim, in fact, I deny, that they are good enough reasons to make it irrational for one ever to act immorally. Although the moral reason, even with its supporting reasons, will not lead all rational persons to act morally, it will lead some. Further, even those who do not accept the moral reason for acting morally would be rational if they did so.

Impossibility of Giving Conclusive Reasons for Acting Morally

Some might take the previous paragraph to be an admission of ultimate failure to answer the question "Why should one be moral?" I have stated, or at least implied, that it is perfectly sensible to ask "Why should one avoid causing evil for others?" They might conclude that giving the answer "You will avoid causing evil for others" does not really answer the question. This conclusion is not warranted. Simply because it is sensible to ask "Why should I avoid causing evil for others?" it does not follow that avoiding causing evil for others does not provide an adequate reason for being moral. The objection claims that if I can sensibly ask "Why should I do X?" when X is the reason for doing Y then X can't be an adequate reason for doing Y. When stated in this general way, we can see the mistake involved. It is due to a concept of a reason which I have shown to be false that an adequate reason for doing a particular action is one that provides a motive for all rational persons.

What some people desire when they ask the question "Why should I be moral?" is an answer that will show that it is always rationally required to act morally, not merely that it is always rationally allowed to so act. I have already shown that rationality rarely requires acting in one way rather than another. I think that the reluctance to accept this answer is due to the belief that rationality does always require one kind of action, action in one's own self-interest. The equation of rational action with action in one's self-interest is so strong that the question "Why should I do X?" is often taken to mean no more than "How will doing X benefit me?" The question "Why should one be moral?" is considered not really answered by "Because you will avoid causing evil for others." Although this gives me a reason of sorts for being moral, it is not really the right kind of reason. It does not provide a motive for all rational persons, and so not all rational persons will act in accord with it. The only answer that provides a motive for all rational persons is a reason of self-interest, so supposedly the only answer that all rational persons will act on is "Because it is in your self-interest." I have admitted that this answer cannot always be truthfully given.

Self-Interest Does Not Provide Conclusive Reasons

Even though I agree that only reasons of self-interest provide motives to all rational persons, I should now like to show that the answer "Because it is in your self-interest" does not provide conclusive reasons, i.e., reasons that all rational persons must act on. However, first I should like to discuss a slightly different question so as to provide as close a parallel to the moral case as possible. Let us consider the question "Why should I be prudent?" This is a question that is asked, though perhaps not in exactly these terms, by many people, especially by teenagers. Just as "Why shouldn't I do it if I want to?" is sometimes equivalent to "Why should I be moral?" so it is also sometimes equivalent to "Why should I be prudent?" In the former case, the answer is "You will cause someone to suffer an evil;" in the latter, "You will suffer an evil yourself." We are inclined to think it perfectly rational to go on and ask "Why shouldn't I cause others to suffer evils?" but to be irrational to reply "Why shouldn't I cause myself to suffer evils?" This inclination is not merely due to a prejudice in favor of oneself over others. The two questions are not usually asked in the same circumstances. When we ask "Why shouldn't I cause others to suffer an evil?" a further clause is generally understood, viz., "if it benefits me." The question is really "Why should I be concerned for others rather than myself?" I have already stated that rationality does not require being concerned for others, especially when it is at some cost to oneself.

The question "Why shouldn't I cause myself to suffer an evil?" is not understood in the same way, i.e., with the unstated clause "if it benefits me." With the question "Why shouldn't I cause myself to suffer evil?" the unstated clause is generally something like "if I want to." When asking why we should not harm others, we implicitly oppose concern for others to self-interest. When asking why we should not harm ourselves, we oppose self-interest to irrational desires. Someone who smokes, or drinks, or takes drugs when told that his excessive use will harm him, may reply, "So what, I want to." Here, if we think the harm is significant, we consider the action irrational. Thus it seems as if asking "Why shouldn't I cause myself to suffer evil?" is, if it is a serious evil, an irrational question, one that no rational person would ask. Hence it seems that the answer "You will harm yourself if you do that" is one that all rational persons would accept as conclusive for not doing something, whereas "You will harm someone else if you do that" is not conclusive to all rational persons.

We are not yet clear enough. When asking why I should not cause evil for others, I opposed this to benefitting myself. However, when I asked why I should not cause evil for myself, I did not oppose it to the prevention of evil to others, but to an irrational desire. It is not that, considered by themselves, "Why shouldn't I harm others?" is a perfectly sensible question and "Why shouldn't I harm myself?" is a senseless one. The sense of the question depends upon the unstated clause that goes with the question. It is not senseless to ask "Why shouldn't I harm myself?" if the unstated clause is "if I can thereby prevent harm to others." This question with this unstated clause is one that is asked, though perhaps not in these words, by many people, particularly young men and women. It is not unusual to hear a father try to persuade his daughter not to join the Peace Corps or not to join the fight for civil rights, by pointing out that she may suffer harm. And it is not unusual to hear the daughter reply that this is not a good enough reason, that avoidance of harm to herself does not take precedence over trying to help others. Thus it can be seen that "Why shouldn't I harm myself?" is not always a senseless question. Avoidance of harm to oneself does not always provide a conclusive reason for all rational persons, one that they will always act on in preference to avoiding harm to others.

It is, of course, possible to call irrational all those who are willing to sacrifice their own interests for the interests of others. But one who did this could only do so by arbitrarily defining rational action as action done for one's own self-interest. We do not ordinarily limit rational action in this way, as I showed in

Chapter 2. Since it is rational to sacrifice your interests for the interests of others, the reply "You will harm yourself if you do that" is not a conclusive reason for all rational persons. It does provide a good reason for not doing something, but in doing this it does no more than the reply "You will harm others if you do that." Although avoidance of harm to oneself provides a motive for all rational persons, whereas avoidance of harm to others does not, this does not mean that when they conflict the former motive is always stronger than the latter. Both as motives and reasons, beliefs about avoiding harm to oneself and beliefs about avoiding harm to others are such that it is rationally allowed to guide one's action by either one. Of course, one who always regards the avoidance of causing harm to others as the more important reason will be very likely to act morally, while one who always considers his own self-interest as most important will probably not. Neither person will be irrational. While I have shown that reason always allows acting morally, I have also shown that it allows acting immorally.

Rationality, Self-Interest, and Morality

It now seems as if rationality is of no use as a guide to action. This, of course, is not so; rationality is incompatible with many kinds of action, as pointed out in Chapter 2. It is true that in the important decisions about whether or not to act morally, rationality does not provide the guide. When morality and self-interest conflict, even when morality and the interests of friends or family conflict, rationality takes no sides. Disappointing as this conclusion seems at first, we should see that any other conclusion would be worse. Were rationality ever to prohibit acting morally, we would be forced, in the case of conflict, to advocate either irrational or immoral behavior. If rationality were always to require acting morally, we would be forced to regard all immoral action as irrational, including that which was clearly in the self-interest of the agent. Contrasted with either of these alternatives, the conclusion seems far less disappointing than before.

I have shown that rationality does not always require acting morally, and I have also shown that rationality does not always require acting in one's self-interest. However, since I have shown that rationality always allows one to act morally or to act in one's self-interest, there is a danger that one will come to think that rationality prohibits acting in any way that is both immoral and contrary to one's self-interest. This has not been shown. Indeed, it is false. Rationality allows action that is both immoral and contrary to one's self-interest. This has generally been overlooked by those philosophers who have considered all rational actions to be either moral actions or those of self-interest. Further, some have held that these two kinds of actions not only exhaust the category of rational actions, but that they are mutually exclusive. They seem to hold that not only can self-interest never provide additional reasons for acting morally, but that self-interest always leads one to act immorally and that morality always requires one to act contrary to one's self-interest.

It should be immediately clear that self-interest cannot always require one to act immorally. So many actions that are in our self-interest fall outside the sphere of morality that this view is not even plausible. Further, even when our actions are covered by a moral rule or ideal, our self-interest may provide additional reasons for acting morally. This becomes clear when we remember the common emotions that are so intimately connected with the different answers that were given to the question "Why should one be moral?" It is in our self-interest to avoid shame, guilt, and remorse, and often we must act morally if we wish to avoid them. Further, the risk of punishment and the enmity of those affected by the immoral action may also lead one to act morally. It now should be clear that self-interest and morality are not mutually exclusive. In a country with a good government, self-interest and morality often provide reasons for doing the same action.

Reasons for Acting Immorally

The desire for revenge may lead one to act irrationally, and hate may have the same result. Since these are examples of acting immorally and against one's self-interest, some philosophers have thought that were they to show that self-interest always requires acting morally, they would have shown that immoral action is irrational. They thought this because they held that when self-interest and morality both require acting in a certain way, rationality prohibits acting in any other way. We have already seen that self-interest does not always require acting morally, but even if it did, this would not have made it irrational to act immorally. There are other reasons for acting immorally besides reasons of self-interest. These reasons are beliefs that our action will benefit some person or group in whom we take an interest. Such a belief may lead us to act even though we know the action is both immoral and contrary to our own self-interest. Parents sometimes act both immorally and contrary to their own self-interest for the sake of their children. Their interest in their children is greater than their concern for themselves and for morality. Lovers not only sacrifice themselves, but others, for the sake of the loved one. Rationality need not prohibit such actions.

Failure to realize that a rational action can be both immoral and contrary to one's self-interest, together with the view that all rational actions are either self-interested or moral, leads to the view that whenever a rational person sacrifices himself for others he is acting morally. Unjustified violations of the moral rules which are contrary to one's self-interest, perhaps even requiring risking one's life, are not just a logical possibility. On the contrary, without underestimating the amount of evil caused by immoral actions done from motives of self-interest, I think that considerably more evil has been caused by immoral actions that were contrary to the self-interest of the agent. Religions have provided motives for people to act in ways that were both immoral and contrary to their self-interest. Some of these actions may have been irrational, i.e., no one was believed to have benefited from them, but some were thought to benefit some people, either in this life or the next. The amount of evil caused by self-sacrificing immoral actions for religious reasons is incredible. So many persons have not only slaughtered others but risked their own lives in advancing the interests of their religion that it is impossible to hold that self-interest is the sole cause of immoral action.

Religion is only one of many sources of reasons for acting immorally. People often act immorally in order to advance the interests of their social or economic class. And sometimes these immoral actions require some sacrifice of self-interest. Persons often act both immorally and contrary to their self-interest, in order to advance the interests of their race or ethnic group. But today probably the greatest and most serious source of reasons for acting immorally come from one's country. Many persons are not only willing, but anxious, to sacrifice their lives for their country even when their country is engaged in an immoral war. The evil caused by immoral actions due to nationalism probably outweighs the evil caused by the immoral actions due to all other reasons put together. Taking an interest in one's country need not lead to immoral actions. To be willing to do whatever is in the best interests of one's country, except act immorally, is the mark of a patriot. A nationalist is one who is willing to advance the interests of his country even when this requires him to act immorally. To keep patriotism from degenerating into nationalism is impossible without a clear understanding of morality.

Reasons for Acting Morally

Pointing out that self-interest does not always provide the motive for immoral action is important for avoiding confusion. We have seen that self-interest often is not even an opponent of morality, but often sides with morality against the demands of country, race, or religion. To avoid misunderstanding, it should also be pointed out that religion, country, and race sometimes provide reasons for morally good actions when self-interest would lead to immoral action. In other words, self-interest, religion, race, and country all provide reasons which sometimes support morality and sometimes support immoral action. Why then has self-interest received so much attention as the opponent of morality? Mostly, I think, because of a misunderstanding of morality, and probably also because of an over simple account of rational action, but there is another explanation that deserves some consideration.

Concern for others is often centrally involved in acting in accordance with the moral rules. The same is true when acting to advance the interests of one's religion, race, or country. However, unlike religion, race, and country, the moral rules require impartial concern for all. Moral ideals, on the other hand, encourage one to minimize the evil suffered by any group of persons for whom one is concerned. If self-interest provides the only motive for one's actions, then one will never be a morally good person. Acting for patriotic, racial, or religious motives may lead one to follow the moral ideals. However, though race, religion, and country, unlike self-interest, may provide motives for morally good actions, they also provide more powerful motives for immoral action. Indeed, except for those motives provided by the moral answer and related answers, the motives which have the most power for moral good also have the most power for moral evil. But when religious conviction, racial pride, and patriotism come together in a person who has great compassion for all humankind, as they did in Dr. Martin Luther King, Jr., moral goodness achieves such power that even death seems to be overcome.

I realize that the question "Why should one be moral?" will be answered differently by different rational persons. I would expect most readers of this book to advocate that one be moral and to give some or all of the answers to the question that I have provided in this chapter. However, I am fully aware that some people, lacking that concern for all humankind that is essential for dependable moral action, may not advocate that someone for whom they are concerned always act morally. A rational mother, perhaps with bitter experience with persons outside of her family, may advocate to her daughter not to be moral, but only to seem to be. Such a person might provide her daughter with reasons why she should not be moral. She may argue that she will generally get the best of others if she is immoral and that she will be able to satisfy her own desires and the desires of those whom she loves much more completely and easily. In some situations this may be extremely persuasive, but in others it will not.

Equally common will be the father who advocates to his son to put his country above all else. He can also provide some powerful reasons for his son to adopt this course of action. His life will have a largeness of purpose and ideals which are lacking to the person who is concerned only with himself and some few loved ones. Indeed, such a person may have all the rewards that are normally associated with a moral life, including great honor and esteem. Putting one's race or religion above all else may be supported by similar reasons. It is not a service to morality to minimize the persuasiveness of these answers; they do not lose their persuasiveness if we ignore them. However, I think we may now have arrived at that stage in human history where the moral answer may prove to be more persuasive to many to whom it is clearly presented. Many persons now do have a concern for all humankind, and many religions now support this concern. Many nations have come to realize how small the earth is. And the evils that result from dividing the races have become apparent to all.

The difficulties of providing persuasive answers to the question "Why should one be moral?" is no greater than the difficulties of providing persuasive answers to the question "Why should one be immoral?" Unfortunately, in some societies, and in some parts of all societies, the answers to "Why should one be immoral?" may be more persuasive than the answers to "Why should one be moral?" It is, I think, the most important measure of a society, which answers are most persuasive to most of its citizens.

12

MORALITY AND SOCIETY

The society in which one lives not only influences the persuasiveness of the answers to the question, "Why should one be moral?" but also, by means of rights, the interpretation of the moral rules. That part of society which is most important in determining rights, as well as being extremely important in determining general attitudes toward morality, is the government of the society. Government is also that part of society that is generally responsible for the laws of the society. The moral system that has been described in the preceding chapters was developed primarily for individuals; however, I believe that the same moral system applies to governments as well. Indeed, there can only be one moral system, for if there were different moral systems for governments and for individuals, and they sometimes required different actions, any individual who was acting for a government could not avoid acting immorally.

In this chapter I shall show how the same moral system does apply to governments; I shall point out some of the morally significant similarities and differences between governmental action and actions by individuals. I shall, in part, be defending and explaining why what I listed (in Chapter 7) as morally relevant feature 5, concerning the relationship between the person breaking the rule and the person toward whom it is broken, is in fact a morally relevant feature. There I claimed that it is morally relevant if there is a relationship between the person violating the moral rule and the person toward whom it is being violated such that the former has a duty to violate some moral rules with regard to the latter independent of the latter's consent and is in a unique or almost unique position in this regard.

This feature accounts for the fact that the relationship between governments and their citizens is morally relevant. This allows for the possibility that a government is morally justified in depriving one or more of its citizens of some freedom when it is not morally justified for one citizen to deprive another one of the same amount of freedom, even when the evil caused, avoided and prevented, and the rational desires of the person being deprived of the freedom are the same. By showing how the actions of a government and of an individual, even if similar in all other respects, are not the same kind of act, I can explain why impartial rational persons may advocate that one kind of violation of a moral rule be publicly allowed and not the other. This allows me to apply the same moral test to governments that I apply to individuals, i.e., counting an action as morally justifiable only if an impartial rational person can advocate that this kind of violation of a moral rule be publicly allowed.

Minimal Duties of Government

One function of governments, some would say its primary function, is to keep the peace, to protect its citizens from one another. In order to do this governments deprive the members of the society of their freedom to violate the moral rules, at least with regard to other members of the society, by enacting laws enforcing the moral rules. In order to enforce obedience to the moral rules, governments must sometimes set up a legal system, with police, judges, jails, etc. This requires money, and so citizens have to pay taxes, or provide support in some other way, in order to provide the government with the money to protect them from the immoral behavior of each other. Even those who support a minimal state admit that governments have a duty to protect the citizens from the harms caused by immoral behavior. This duty requires them to violate the moral rules with regard to their citizens even without the latters' consent. Further, it is only governments that have this duty with regard to all citizens, so that they are in a unique position in this regard.

The same considerations allow governments to restrict freedom in order to prevent serious internal disorder. Civil war usually brings with it even more evil to the citizens of a state than individual acts of immoral behavior. Riots and general lawlessness threaten many with serious evil. Governments are allowed to limit the freedom of people in order to prevent civil disorder. As long as governments have a moral justification for limiting freedom, then they are not being immoral in doing so. Of course, people will sometimes disagree whether the risk of evil that the limitation of freedom is aimed at preventing is sufficient to justify that violation of a moral rule. Most of these disagreements are due to a disagreement about the facts. How serious is the risk of evil? How much freedom needs to be deprived in order to prevent it? Even complete agreement on the moral theory will not help in settling these questions for it is disagreement on the facts that is at issue.

It is, and ought to be, allowed to governments to deprive people of freedom and pleasure in order to prevent not only civil war, but also war with other countries, for all war not only results in loss of freedom and pleasure, but also brings the great evils of death, pain, and disability. Although phrases like "Give me

liberty or give me death" have a powerful rhetorical force, taken literally, most
rational persons would never use them as a guide to behavior. The death penalty
is almost universally considered more serious than life imprisonment. It is hard
to conceive of someone outside of prison being deprived of freedom any more
completely than he is by life imprisonment. Thus governments are generally
allowed to deprive their citizens of a substantial amount of freedom in order to
prevent the greater evils that generally accompany war, either civil war or war
with other countries.

Governments May Violate Moral Rules for Moral Ideals

Governments are often not only morally allowed to tax, but also allowed to
deprive people of their freedom and pleasure in other ways, if necessary to prevent significant evil. Since individuals are sometimes morally allowed to violate
moral rules to follow moral ideals, this does not distinguish governments from
individuals, although governments may be allowed to violate moral rules in situations that would be unjustifiable for individuals. One situation in which governments are morally allowed to violate moral rules when individuals are not is
in supporting medical research; governments may tax and otherwise limit freedom in order to support medical research, for medical research is an indispensable aid in following the three positive moral ideals of preserving life, relieving
pain, and lessening disability. The same considerations allow governments to
provide support for the training of doctors and nurses, the building of hospitals,
and in general, to do all those things which will help prevent people suffering
the evils of death, pain, and disability.

That a government may violate the moral rules in order to follow the moral
ideals is not what distinguishes the government from an individual, for an individual may also sometimes violate a moral rule in order to follow a moral ideal.
That one of the duties of government is to prevent the suffering of evil by its
citizens also does not distinguish the government from some private citizens,
for it may be the duty of some private citizens, e.g., doctors, to prevent others
from suffering evil. Insofar as the government is allowed to violate a moral rule
only in order to follow a moral ideal, even if it may do so in situations when
individuals may not, governmental action poses no serious problem for what
has already been said. The serious problem arises when the government violates
a moral rule in order to follow some utilitarian ideal, for I have claimed that
following a utilitarian ideal almost never justifies an individual, except a parent,
violating a moral rule.

Governments May Violate Moral Rules for Utilitarian Ideals

It seems to follow from this claim that governments usually act immorally. For
governments often violate one or more of the moral rules in order to act on
utilitarian ideals. Not only this, but given that I list both promoting pleasure
and increasing ability, which includes knowledge, as a utilitarian ideal, it seems
that I am forced to condemn as immoral government taxation in order to pro-

mote the arts, parks, or better schools for all. This seems to follow because in these cases taxation deprives people of freedom or pleasure, not in order to prevent death, pain, or disability, or even the deprivation of freedom or pleasure, but in order to increase ability and pleasure. Some philosophers, those supporting a minimal state, accept the conclusion that it is immoral to tax in order to support a superior school system, for they hold that whatever is immoral for an individual to do is also immoral for a government to do.

I do not accept the conclusion that it is immoral to tax in order to support a superior school system. I am not sure that it is positively immoral not to tax in order to support a better school system; I am certain that it is generally not immoral to do so. I shall try to show why the conclusion that it is immoral to tax in order to support a better school system does not follow from what I have said. In order to do this I must show why it can be morally acceptable for a government to violate the moral rules for utilitarian ideals when it would not be morally acceptable for an individual to perform what otherwise would be the same kind of act.

Social Contract Theory

Social contract theorists provide one answer to this problem. According to one interpretation of social contract theory, citizens agree to obey the laws if the government agrees not only to prevent evil but also to promote the general welfare. Since, on this account, the government has promised to promote the general welfare, in doing so, it is not merely following a utilitarian ideal, it is also obeying the moral rule "Keep your promise." It is generally acknowledged that a better school system promotes the general welfare; therefore, the government would be violating a moral rule if it did not support a better school system. In carrying out its promise, it is permitted to deprive people of some freedom or pleasure, e.g., by taxation, for were it not permitted to do this, it would be unable to fulfill its promise. Although this argument can also be applied to support of the arts and parks, it is not quite so persuasive here. There is not so close a connection between support of the arts and parks and the general welfare as there is between a better school system and the general welfare.

This argument depends upon there being some agreement between the citizens and the government concerning promotion of the general welfare, and this is extremely implausible. Although some politicians make promises to do various things if elected, governments, in general, do not enter into agreements with their citizens. To the claim that there is an implicit agreement, I offer the same objection I made when discussing cheating: there is often no one who even claims that a promise was made to him. Some modern versions of social contract theory regard the government as unfair if it does not promote the general welfare, but unless unfairness is taken as a synonym for immoral, this claim also does not have much plausibility. Governments do not usually enter into voluntary activities with their citizens such that failure to abide by them counts as cheating. The most plausible version of the social contract theory is that put forward by Hobbes in which he claims that it would show ingratitude for the government not to promote the general welfare, but even this version has serious difficulties, for it is not clear one is allowed to violate moral rules in order to show gratitude.

Another answer is that we do allow individuals to violate the moral rules with regard to someone else if they have good specific reasons for thinking that the person has a rational desire to have the rule disobeyed with regard to himself. Similarly, governments are allowed to violate the moral rules with regard to their citizens if they have good specific reasons for thinking that the citizens have a rational desire to have the rule disobeyed with regard to themselves. The justification of government violation of the moral rules in order to follow utilitarian ideals is like the justified violation of a rule by an individual toward people whom he knows have, or would have if they knew the facts, a rational desire to have the rule disobeyed with regard to them. The problem with this answer is that it justifies only violations of the moral rules by the government toward citizens whom it has good reason to believe want the rule violated with regard to themselves. This answer would not justify universal taxation in order to support a better school system, for not everyone wants to be taxed for this reason.

The Justification for Government Promoting the General Welfare

Since I hold that there is only one moral system that applies to both individuals and governments, I regard it as essential to account for why the government may violate a moral rule to promote the general welfare which is related to the moral system I have provided. With regard to the second five moral rules, all impartial rational persons would advocate that some violations be publicly allowed in order to follow the moral ideals. Of course, there will be disagreements on how much evil must be prevented before such a violation is justified, but this is a familiar problem. Both breaking promises and deceiving weaken the trust that is so important for citizens to have in their government, so that before an impartial rational person could advocate that the government be publicly allowed to violate these rules, he would have to be convinced that the evil to be prevented or avoided by the violation was significant. No impartial rational person could advocate that a violation be publicly allowed unless he believed that the evils prevented by publicly allowing such a violation would be greater than the evils caused by publicly allowing that kind of violation.

Allowing governments to violate the second five moral rules in order to follow moral ideals does not, by itself, require any change in the moral system, for individuals can also violate the second five moral rules in order to follow moral ideals. Whether impartial rational persons would advocate that violations be publicly allowed for governments that they would not allow for individuals depends upon examination of the consequences of publicly allowing violations by each. Another difficult question is whether governments can justifiably violate the second five moral rules to promote utilitarian ideals without the consent of those toward whom they are breaking these rules. Individuals are usually not allowed to violate any moral rules for utilitarian ideals without the consent of those toward whom the rule is being violated. No impartial rational person would advocate publicly allowing any significant violations by individuals when no evil is being prevented, and even deprived persons are not being benefitted, but only ability or pleasure is being promoted. It is also unlikely that any impartial rational person would publicly allow similar violations by a government, but examination of particular cases may be required. Few if any impartial rational persons would advocate that violations of any of the second five moral rules without consent of the person toward whom the rule is being violated, by individuals or governments, be publicly allowed except for the prevention of serious evils.

No impartial rational person would advocate publicly allowing any significant violation of any of the first three rules in order to follow some utilitarian ideal, either by individuals or governments. Although there may be particular cases in which a rational person would be willing to suffer death, pain, or disability in order to achieve some good, he would not be willing to let someone else decide when he should suffer these evils and for what goods. No impartial rational person would advocate that the government have the authority to kill or cause significant pain or disability in order to follow any utilitarian ideal. Throwing the Christians to the lions is not justifiable, no matter how many people enjoy it, and no matter how much they enjoy it; nor does gaining added knowledge about lions or Christians or their interaction justify it.

The fourth and fifth rules, "Don't deprive of freedom" and "Don't deprive of pleasure," remain to be considered. They are the only ones which can be plausibly described as being more concerned with goods than with evils. The first three rules demand that one avoid causing evil, the next two that one avoid causing loss of goods. This being the case it is quite plausible that impartial rational persons would advocate that governments be publicly allowed to violate these rules in order to follow utilitarian ideals. To allow governments to do this would simply be to allow the government to take away some goods in order to promote others. Of course, the good that is promoted must be significantly greater than the good that is taken away. If this limitation is heeded, then there are some situations in which all impartial rational persons would advocate that the government be publicly allowed to violate the fourth and fifth moral rules in order to follow utilitarian ideals.

This explanation of why some government violations of the fourth and fifth moral rules for utilitarian ideals are morally justified raises another question. If all impartial rational persons would sometimes advocate the deprivation of freedom and pleasure for utilitarian ideals by a government be publicly allowed, why would they not also advocate that what would otherwise be the same kind of violation by individuals be publicly allowed? The answer is that in every society there is only one government but many individuals. If individuals were publicly allowed to violate these moral rules in order to promote utilitarian ideals, the resulting disorder would lead to significant evils that all rational persons wish to avoid. Allowing the government to violate these moral rules in order to follow utilitarian ideals does not lead to disorder. This is why it is morally relevant that the government is in a unique position with regard to its citizens. This also explains why parents are sometimes morally allowed to violate these two rules with regard to their children in order to increase their ability or pleasure.

That there are many individuals but only one government is not the only important difference. Governments are not only uniquely related to their citizens; this uniqueness is morally significant. Individuals may never need to violate a moral rule without consent; governments must often do so. Simply enforcing those laws that are necessary in order to prevent violations of the moral rules, requires depriving people of freedom and pleasure. Since the government must violate the moral rules, it is faced with a decision about the way in which it will do so. The government needs money and must get it from its citizens, but the manner in which it gets it, e.g., income tax or sales tax, is a matter for decision. Whatever decision it makes will result in different people being deprived of different amounts of money. Since the government violates, though justifiably, the moral rules with regard to all of its citizens, it is in a different relationship to them than any individual is with regard to his fellow citizens. Morally relevant feature Five explains why governments are morally allowed to violate some rules when individuals would not be justified in doing so.

This special relationship blurs the distinction between the utilitarian ideals and some moral ideals. The distinction between preventing the depriving of freedom and pleasure and increasing freedom and pleasure becomes somewhat arbitrary. Promoting what I call the utilitarian ideals can often be plausibly described as following the moral ideals, for the government may claim that it is simply trying to lessen the amount of freedom and pleasure that it takes away from its citizens. Governments differ from individuals in that for governments, the distinction between some moral ideals and utilitarian ideals becomes more blurred. This is because a government has a duty to violate the moral rules with regard to it citizens, even without their consent. Further, governments are in a unique position to their citizens in this regard. Thus an action by a government with regard to its citizens is a different kind of act than an action by an individual which is otherwise identical in all of its morally relevant features. However, this does not put governments outside of the moral sphere, for governments cannot justifiably violate any moral rule unless an impartial rational person can advocate that the violation of that rule be publicly allowed. The difference between governments and individuals lies in this, that in some cases impartial rational persons can advocate that the government be publicly allowed to violate some moral rules for utilitarian ideals when they could not advocate that individuals be publicly allowed to do so.

Political Judgments

All impartial rational persons would advocate that the government be publicly allowed to violate the moral rules in some situations, and no impartial rational person would advocate that violations of them be publicly allowed in others. However, the bulk of the cases, at least of those that are seriously discussed, will be those in which impartial rational persons disagree about whether the government should violate the moral rules or not. Of course not all disagreements will concern whether the government should violate the moral rules; some will concern how they should do it. Political judgments, i.e., moral judgments of governments, involve more than is usually relevant in moral judgments of individuals, viz., a consideration of the goods that will result. Political judgments differ from other moral judgments in that promoting good as well as causing, avoiding, and preventing evil is normally a relevant consideration. This makes the distinction between the moral and utilitarian ideals less significant for governments. It was undoubtedly the Classical Utilitarians' preoccupation with governmental action that led them to neglect the importance of the distinction between promoting good and avoiding or preventing evil.

Although distinguishing between moral and utilitarian ideals is less important when talking of governments, this does not make political judgments about governments significantly different from moral judgments about individuals. A just government is one that seldom or never does what is morally wrong and always or usually does what is morally right. A just government almost never unjustifiably violates any of the moral rules with regard to any of its citizens, nor does it do so with regard to other governments or individuals. Almost all violations of a moral rule by a just government are those that at least some impartial rational persons would advocate. Of course, since impartial rational persons sometimes disagree, there may be disagreement about whether a government is just or not.

As with other moral disagreements, one would expect that if agreement is reached on all the facts, a particularly difficult task when considering governmental action, there will be a large measure of agreement. Disagreements should continue only in a very limited sphere. Like individuals, governments are judged not only by their actions, but also by their intentions and motives. If the government in power does what, to the best of its knowledge, will result in the least amount of evil being suffered, then it does not become unjust simply because its action actually resulted in more evil being suffered. Like individuals, however, good intentions are not enough to make a government just. The results must generally be the intended ones. An inefficient government may not be an unjust one, but neither will it be a just one.

Just Governments and Laws Versus Good Governments and Laws

The necessity of government to constantly violate the moral rules makes the distinction between a just government and a good one more difficult to make than the parallel distinction between a just person and a morally good one. Nonetheless, there is some point in the distinction. A just government is one that by positive action, as distinguished from not acting, neither intends to nor does unjustifiably violate any of the moral rules. A just government does not unjustifiably increase the evil suffered by anyone, but a just government may not be a good government. A morally good government, or simply a good government, is not only just, but intends to and does follow the moral and appropriate utilitarian ideals. A good government is one that by its positive action decreases the amount of evil suffered and increases the amount of good enjoyed. A government can be just without being good, if it does not follow the moral or utilitarian ideals, but simply refrains from unjustifiably violating the moral rules. A good government must also be a just government. A government that is unjust cannot be a good one no matter how much it attempts to decrease evil and increase good, for if it is unjust, this means that it unjustifiably violates the moral rules, and all impartial rational persons would advocate that this never be done.

Although it is generally difficult to judge individual laws, it is sometimes possible to do so. A just law neither intentionally nor unintentionally unjustifiably violates a moral rule. If a law intentionally violates a moral rule unjustifiably, it is an unjust law; if it does so unintentionally, it is simply a bad law. All just laws are good ones. This last statement needs to be defended, for it seems that there could be a just law that was not good. That is, the law neither decreases evil nor increases good, but neither does it intentionally or unintentionally unjustifiably violate a moral rule. But there cannot be a law meeting this description. If a law is not a good one, i.e., neither lessens evil nor promotes good, then it is bad, for it limits freedom unjustifiably. An unnecessary law is a bad one. By an unnecessary law I mean a law not needed either to lessen evil or to promote good.

I have been talking about governments and laws in such a way as to leave the impression that I am overlooking the obvious fact that governments are composed of persons and that laws are made by these persons. Although I am aware of these obvious facts, I do not think there is any simple way, if there is any way at all, to replace talk about governments and laws with talk about the persons who compose the former and make the latter. Although it is extremely unlikely, a good government may be composed primarily of bad persons, and a good law may be passed by persons whose motives were morally bad. It is far more likely that a bad government be composed primarily of good persons, and that a bad law be passed by persons whose motives were morally good. Of course, most often, good governments will be composed of good persons, and bad governments, of bad persons; good laws will be passed with good motives, and bad laws with bad motives. The goodness and badness of laws and governments are not, however, to be judged by the goodness or badness of the motives responsible for the former or the moral character of the persons who compose the latter.

Persons in Government Not Morally Required to Be Morally Good

The persons who compose the government and who make the laws are subject to the moral rules in exactly the same way that all other persons are. This means that they are required to obey the moral rules except when an impartial rational person can advocate that violating them be publicy allowed, and that they are encouraged to follow the moral ideals. It may seem that unlike others they are required to follow some of the moral ideals, for it is acknowledged by all that one duty of governments is to protect their citizens from the evils resulting from violations of the moral rules. Those in government are not merely encouraged to follow those moral ideals which urge one to prevent the violation of moral rules, they also have a duty to follow these ideals. I agree that some persons, in their role as members of the government, do have such a duty, but since it is their duty, I do not think this changes their relationship to the moral rules and ideals. People outside of government often have duties which require them to do things that would otherwise only be encouraged by the moral ideals. If one is required by one's duty, or by one of the other moral rules, to prevent others from suffering an evil, acting in this way does not count as following the moral ideals.

In these days, when everyone is aware of the vast number of deprived persons in almost every country, it may seem that more is required of persons, especially persons in government, than simply to obey the moral rules. To say that following the moral ideals is only encouraged, not required, seems to provide an easy way out for those who selfishly seek to preserve the status quo. Much as I would like to show that morality prohibits doing nothing to minimize the evils suffered by others, I cannot see how I can do so. Of course, such persons are not morally good, but one cannot be forced to be morally good. Indeed, the point of distinguishing between the moral rules and the moral ideals is to limit the behavior that others can force one to do. As we saw in the previous chapter, those who are motivated to act morally because they accept the moral reason will not care whether they are acting in accordance with moral rules or following moral ideals, for their goal is to minimize the amount of evil suffered. No practical purpose is served by distorting the concept of morality to make it require everyone to be morally good. If persons do not wish to be morally good, even a correct account of morality will not persuade them to be.

Even though it will probably have little practical effect, I should like to point out that the account of morality presented so far should not result in governments doing nothing to aid their deprived citizens in the way that it seems to. If no person in government were morally good, then it would, but one need not be naively optimistic to believe that in every country, and in every government, there are some morally good persons. If these persons introduce good laws, those that aid those citizens who are deprived, then the moral rules require that one not oppose such legislation unless an impartial rational person could advocate such opposition. To do so is to unjustifiably violate either the fourth or fifth moral rule. So although the moral rules do not require legislators to introduce good laws, they do require them to do nothing to prevent such legislation being enacted. Holding that morality only encourages, but does not require, following the moral ideals should not result in the preservation of a society with all of its social evils. If there is at least one morally good person, then morality requires that no one stand in her way as she seeks to eliminate the evils of her society. If there is not even one morally good person, no understanding of morality will be of any use.

Clearly much more needs to be said to clarify the relationship between morality and government. To be completely clear about this relationship one would have to develop a complete political theory, i.e., a theory about a rational person's public and personal attitude toward government. I hope to do this some day, but in this chapter I am concerned only with showing that what I have said about morality applies to governments as well as to individuals. Governments are just like individuals in that they are not justified in violating a moral rule unless an impartial rational person can advocate that such a violation be publicly allowed. It is only because governments have a duty to violate moral rules with regard to their citizens and are in a unique position in this regard that they are sometimes morally justified in violating moral rules when individuals would not be justified. I believe that this morally relevant feature is sufficient to account for the differences between governments and individuals and thus show that the moral system I have provided applies not only to the actions, intentions, etc., of individuals, but also to those of governments.

Who Counts as a Deprived Person?

I conceded that when talking about governments the distinction between some moral and utilitarian ideals becomes blurred. This blurring may also occur because rational persons may disagree about whether to say that we are lessening the deprivation of freedom and pleasure or that we are simply increasing freedom and pleasure. This disagreement will stem in part from disagreement about the minimal amount of freedom and pleasure that citizens in the society should have. This "citizens in the society should have" is probably best interpreted as "an impartial rational person knowing the resources and problems of the society would advocate every citizen having." I think that it could also be interpreted as "an impartial rational person knowing the resources and problems of the society would expect every citizen to have." All impartial rational persons, knowing the resources and problems of a society, would regard members of that society with less than some minimal amount of freedom and pleasure as deprived. When one got above this amount, impartial rational persons might disagree, some claiming that those who did not have some higher amount were being deprived, others claiming that they were not.

Liberal Versus Conservative (American Usage)

Generally speaking, those who advocate governmental action to aid the less fortunate members of the society seem to prefer talking of following the moral ideals rather than the utilitarian ones. They seem to claim that in a society with these resources and problems, no person should have less freedom and pleasure than will be provided by the governmental action they advocate. Indeed, they generally claim that even this governmental action will still leave too many people with less freedom and pleasure than the minimum they should have. Those who oppose such governmental action seem to claim that everyone or almost everyone has at least the minimum amount of freedom and pleasure they should have. They regard most governmental action of this kind as designed not to lessen the deprivation of freedom and pleasure, but simply to increase the amount of these goods. They oppose this kind of action because they feel that such governmental action necessarily results in depriving people of freedom and pleasure, and they do not think that it is justifiable for governments to violate a moral rule for utilitarian ideals.

Nowadays those who advocate more governmental action of this kind are called, in America, Liberals; their opponents, Conservatives. (In Europe and other countries, the terminology is different, and those who advocate more such governmental action are called Socialists or Social Democrats and those who are opposed sometimes are called Liberals. In my discussion I shall follow American usage.) There are, of course, differences in belief about the practical effects of governmental action, but generally even when the effects are agreed upon, there is often disagreement between Liberals and Conservatives. Conservatives generally place more emphasis on the moral rules; Liberals tend to emphasize the moral ideals. They also differ in the degree to which they view the government as an individual and the degree to which they think the distinction between utilitarian and moral ideals breaks down when dealing with governments.

Extreme Liberals hold that the distinction breaks down completely; extreme Conservatives, that it does not break down at all. Extreme Conservatives hold that the only duty of governments is to prevent violations of the moral rules. They are against most governmental actions to relieve or prevent evils not due to violations of moral rules, and they regard as immoral any governmental action that seeks to increase good, for they consider this as violating a moral rule for utilitarian rather than moral ideals. Extreme Liberals hold that with regard to government the status quo is of no importance, and thus there is no distinction between lessening evil and promoting good. In keeping with the present trend to deplore extremism of any sort, I do not accept either of these views.

Extreme Liberals do not recognize the importance of the status quo in moral matters. For them, the appropriate governmental action is one which more evenly distributes the freedom and pleasure enjoyed by members of the society. They see nothing wrong in depriving certain people of pleasure in order to give the same amount of pleasure to others who now have less. Of course, taking a thousand dollars from a very rich person and giving it to a very poor one probably gives significantly more pleasure to the poor person than it takes away from the rich person. I do not regard the negative income tax as an extreme Liberal measure. Further, attempts to help those people who are deprived, even though this involves depriving others of some good, are usually justifiable. If the people to be aided are not deprived, impartial rationality will require a significant difference between what is given and what is taken away. Morality does not allow a government to deprive some people of goods unless a significantly greater amount of good will result. Here there will be disagreements among impartial rational persons.

I regard the dispute between Liberals and Conservatives as limited to violations of the fourth and fifth moral rules. So I do not regard the Extreme Liberal as a Classical Utilitarian, simply advocating the greatest happiness for the greatest number. I think Utilitarianism not only an incorrect position, but an extremely dangerous one. Significant violations of the first three moral rules are never justifiable in order to promote goods, only to prevent or relieve significant evils. One who holds that it is justifiable to do so, as a Classical Utilitarian might, opens the door to the most extreme forms of totalitarianism. Communism, if practiced as preached, would be Classical Utilitarianism in action. It is devoted to the greatest happiness for the greatest number regardless of the consequences for some. Strange as it may seem, the path from John Stuart Mill, who defended liberty on Utilitarian grounds, to Communism, which denies it on the same grounds, is both short and easy to travel. Although the originators of the greatest happiness principle certainly did not intend it, their principle can be used to justify governmental actions which everyone would consider immoral. I have more than an academic interest in distinguishing my position from Utilitarianism.

I have already shown that Extreme Conservatism cannot be accepted because governments cannot be considered exactly like individuals, for they have a duty to violate moral rules and are in a unique position in this regard. It is simply a fact that governmental action has the effect of increasing freedom and pleasure for some, and decreasing them for others. In the real world, the distinction between some moral and utilitarian ideals does indeed become extremely blurred when applied to governments, especially governments of any size. Insofar as both Liberals and Conservatives accept what I have said about the moral rules and ideals, and their application to government, they will not be extreme, for both will acknowledge that a government is justified in breaking a moral rule only if an impartial rational person can advocate that the rule be publicly allowed to be broken in this case. If they agree on this, then both of their positions on whether the government should undertake a certain course of action count as morally acceptable. Even though some political disagreement cannot be settled by the moral system, employing the concept of what an impartial rational person can advocate be publicly allowed may be far more helpful in deciding political issues than is initially apparent.

Democratic Implications of Moral Disagreement

It may seem that a moral system that provides unique answers to every moral and political question is preferable to one that allows for some questions to have more than one morally acceptable answer. After all, a moral system is supposed to provide a way of settling disputes, so that a moral system that settles all disputes seems to be clearly preferable to one that does not. If there were a moral system that provided unique answers to every moral and political question and if these answers were accepted by all impartial rational persons, then I certainly would not discard it. As a practical matter, it would not make much difference if one did have such a system, for there would still be disagreements about the facts, i.e., about the nature and probability of the consequences of the various proposed alternative courses of action. And as I have pointed out before, most moral and political disagreements are disagreements about the facts.

The fact is that impartial rational persons do not always agree. Acceptance of the claim that a moral system always provides unique answers results in those taking different sides in a dispute regarding their opponents as either uninformed, partial, or irrational. A theory which claims to provide unique answers has a tendency to set up as the ideal form of government a kind of Platonic Republic, where philosopher kings, who are supposed to most closely approximate impartial rational persons, make all of the decisions. Such a theory has a tendency to regard democracies, where significant decisions are made by the votes of the mass of the population, as employing a defective decision procedure. If there is only one right answer then why not have those who are most qualified determine what it is? There is no need to involve all the people in these decisions, any more than the captain of a ship needs to consult his passengers about the way to run his ship.

A captain does not need to consult his passengers concerning the technical details of running the ship, but if it has not already been established where the ship is to go, then it is appropriate for him to consult them. He should tell them the capabilities of the ship, the risks they would encounter if they chose one destination rather than another, and also the benefits of each, but if he is running the ship on their behalf, then he should consult them on the destination. It is extremely doubtful that there is one destination that is intrinsically preferable to all of the others. It is the rational desires and preferences of the passengers that should determine where they go.

Not all members of a society rank the goods and evils in the same way. Some prefer a higher material standard of living ahead of more personal freedom, at least until the standard of living has become as high as Scandinavia or Switzerland. Others prefer more personal and political freedom to greater material prosperity even though the standard of living is lower than that of Ireland or Israel. Impartial rational persons need not always agree when there is a conflict between raising the material standard of living and having more personal and political freedom. Similarly, impartial rational persons may disagree on how much material prosperity they are willing to give up in order to alleviate pollution, thereby improving the health of the population.

All of the fundamental issues on which there is political debate between Moderate Liberals and Moderate Conservatives involve issues on which impartial rational persons can decide either way. Since both ways are morally acceptable and there is no morally right way, it is quite appropriate that the issue be decided by vote. This is not a second best way of deciding, it is the best way, for voting allows not only for all persons to express their own preference, it also allows for intensity of preference. Those who care more will work harder to win more votes. Of course, if one prefers democracy to oligarchy, care will have to be taken to avoid undue influence by those with extreme wealth or power. Force and fraud are already ruled out by the moral system, so that lack of a unique answer to every moral question does not mean that anything goes. That there is no single morally right action does not mean that there are not many ways of acting that are ruled out as morally wrong. Morality must be prior to politics, for one task of politics is to decide those questions to which there is more than one morally acceptable answer.

Moral System Allows for Moral Disagreement

Not only does morality not solve the issues between Conservatives and Liberals, as long as they are not extreme, it does not solve any of the moral issues on which fully informed impartial rational persons would advocate different positions. Morality sometimes leaves an individual with that dreadful freedom of choice about which some existentialist thinkers have written so fully and brilliantly. Because there is sometimes no morally right course of action, even a moral person is forced to choose between alternative courses of action. The anxiety caused by these choices is easily understood. One knows that she must either violate a moral rule or fail to prevent some evil, but she knows that neither choice is required by impartial reason. This kind of situation cannot but be distressing to any moral person.

Morality often fails to provide a unique answer to the genuine moral perplexities that confront us. This explains, in part, why such morally sensitive people as the existentialists have claimed that objective morality is a fraud or useless or both. This reaction, though understandable, is not justifiable. Just because morality does not always provide a unique answer, it does not follow that it never or even generally does not. Of course, those cases where morality provides a unique answer are not morally perplexing, so they have not attracted the attention of those concerned with moral perplexity. To desire morality always to present us with one clear answer may be a rational desire, but it is irrational to discard morality simply because it does not satisfy this desire.

It is not surprising that the existentialist rejection of morality has had a strong appeal even to those who have a more traditional view of God. We now have many works by theologians which decide the most perplexing moral issues in the most simple fashion. These works claim to be presenting a new kind of ethic or morality, sometimes called situational or contextual ethics. They claim to do away with the need for moral rules. Of course, this claim is false. The situations that these persons consider present moral dilemmas precisely because they seem to demand, or at least to allow, the violation of a moral rule. Like the existentialists, these theologians have become overly impressed with the obvious fact that there are occasions when it is justifiable to violate a moral rule, even occasions when it is the morally right thing to do. They have falsely concluded that there are no moral rules.

These persons are not presenting a new morality; they are not even denying the old morality. At most they are attacking a kind of moral fanaticism, which holds that it is never justifiable to violate any moral rule. However, having confused a fanatical attitude toward the moral rules with the appropriately moral attitude, they claim to have discarded moral rules entirely. If one is to find any positive value in these works, one must consider them as helping to solve a very limited, though important, problem that often arises in morality, viz., deciding what to do in those situations when impartial rational persons advocate different courses of action. If we take them to be dealing with this limited problem, then their answer, "Consider what God would tell you to do," is seen to be a legitimate one. In fact, one of the tasks of religion seems to be to offer a guide to moral action in those cases where morality provides more than one morally acceptable answer.

Morality and Religion

Religion also has another task connected with morality, namely that of providing persons with motives for being morally good persons. On the lowest level, this is done by claiming that God rewards persons who are morally good and punishes those who are morally bad. On a higher level, there is an attempt to inculcate a love of God, so that one is morally good because it pleases God. Religion can also try to get persons to care for their fellow persons, and so promote what I call the moral reason for being morally good. It can promote human concern in several ways: first, by trying to get a person to see herself and all others persons as children of one God; second, by providing as a role model some person who did have a concern for all humankind. So religion can provide some real support to morality.

When morality is supported by religion, there is always a risk that there will be a blurring of the boundaries of morality. Since religion may provide the motive to some people for being moral, they may fail to realize that it is not religion which determines what is moral, but that this is determined by the public system applying to all rational persons that would be advocated by all impartial rational persons. These people may fail to distinguish between a religion's support for morality and a religion's support for its own particular religious rules or ideals. This is extraordinarily dangerous. It leads some people to brand others as immoral when they are not immoral at all but simply fail to conform to the rules or ideals of some particular religion.

This problem becomes especially acute in those cases discussed earlier, viz., those cases in which there is no morally right course of action. It is a proper function of religion to offer guidance in these cases. Since these cases are truly in the sphere of morality, it is very easy for one to conclude that the answer given by his religion is the morally right answer. But it is not. This is not to say that it is a morally wrong answer, but simply to repeat that in this kind of situation there is no morally right answer. The occurrence of this kind of situation makes possible talk of Christian Ethics, Jewish Ethics, Moslem Ethics, etc. Christian Ethics differ from Moslem Ethics where there is no morally right course of action. An impartial rational Christian will advocate that one thing be done, while an impartial rational Moslem will advocate that something else be done. One must be very careful here, for it is very easy for the Christian to claim falsely that the Moslem is immoral, and vice versa. In truth, neither will be, but both must be extremely clear about the nature of morality, and distinguish it sharply from what their religion tells them to do. Otherwise, it will be almost impossible for them to keep from falling into this dangerous error.

Humility and Arrogance

The words of the prophet Micah, "What doth the Lord require of thee, but to do justly, to love mercy, and to walk humbly with thy God," are a stirring testimony to the support that religion can give to morality—and to the dangers that attend such support. For Micah, the Lord commands us to do what is morally right and to love what is morally good, and thus He provides a powerful support for morality. The Lord also requires one to walk humbly with Him, and Micah does not distinguish this requirement from the requirements of morality. One may be led to think that a person who does not fulfill this last requirement is to be condemned in the same way as one who does not fulfill the first two, leading atheism to be condemned as immoral. Hobbes, however, clearly pointed out that there is no ground for calling the atheist unjust. Believing in God and acting morally do not necessarily go together, one can do either one without doing the other.

Micah's remark about walking humbly with God can be be taken as extolling the virtue of humility. I have not discussed humility previously, because I did not feel confident about providing an analysis of it; however, I now have an analysis of humility that fits the context of Micah's remark and explains how humility is linked with justice and mercy. In this context, humility must be taken as very significant, for justice and mercy, which I take to mean kindness, together comprise all the moral virtues. Humility, in this setting, is the opposite of arrogance. Arrogance consists in viewing oneself as not subject to the constraints that morality imposes on all rational persons. Humility consists in recognizing that, no matter who one is or what one has accomplished, for humility is not inconsistent with pride, one is, like everyone else, still subject to the constraints of morality.

Humility and arrogance can be taken as involving more than an attitude toward the constraints of morality; they can be taken as involving a general attitude toward one's place in the world. Someone with humility genuinely recognizes that he is never a sufficient condition for his own successes. He realizes that an overwhelming number of events could have happened, which he had no part whatsoever in preventing, which would have made his success impossible. He is keenly aware not only of his dependence on the physical world, but also on the social world. He knows that he cannot even take complete credit for being the kind of person he is, that his family and school and society were indispensable factors in his being who he is and doing what he does. He recognizes himself to be in the most fundamental respects like everyone else and hence is willing to abide by the constraints that morality imposes on everyone.

The arrogant person does not appreciate his dependence on others; he regards himself as a self-made person. Of course, no rational person can deny his dependence on the physical world, or even on the social world, but the arrogant person does not regard himself as dependent on them in the same way as others. He may hold that he has been singled out by God as worthy of special consideration, or he may simply ignore how much he owes to others. He arrogates to himself the credit that belongs to others. He does not recognize that in the most fundamental respects he is like everyone else; rather he regards himself as different from others, as not bound by the same rules that they are bound by. He is therefore unwilling to abide by the constraints that morality imposes on everyone. Understanding humility and arrogance in this way helps one to appreciate why Micah appropriately links humility with justice and mercy.

Taking humility as recognizing that one is subject to the same constraints of morality as every other rational person and arrogance as believing that one is not subject to the same public system that applies to all other rational persons accounts for our ordinary views about arrogance as well as some otherwise very paradoxical relationships. On this account of arrogance it is quite clear why arrogance leads to immoral behavior. It is also quite clear why great wealth or power leads to arrogance. The arrogance of those with superior intelligence, great beauty or talent, or high social status is also easily understood. Less obvious, but made clear by this account, is why sincere and devout religious belief can lead to arrogance, as can any belief in the importance and righteousness of one's cause, political or scientific. Even the paradoxical arrogance born of despair is explained; one may believe that one has suffered so much that one is no longer subject to the constraints of morality.

A proper understanding of morality and of arrogance makes clear that the terrorist acts of the oppressed and the imposing of their wills on other smaller countries by the superpowers are both immoral acts brought about by arrogance. The behavior of Russia in Hungary and Afghanistan seems depressingly similar to that of the United States in Vietnam and Nicaragua. Power corrupts, absolute power absolutely, because the more power, the more likely one is to be arrogant. Failure to recognize this is the one major flaw in Hobbes's political views, although fortunately it is a flaw that can be removed with no important effect on his moral and political theory.

Ethical Relativity

The problem posed by religious support of morality is part of a larger problem which often goes by the name of ethical relativity. I have claimed that morality is universal, that the justified moral rules and ideals and the procedure for determining justified exceptions to the rules are the same everywhere and for everyone. There is a sense in which this is obviously not true. It is not true that everyone, everywhere, accepts the moral system as I have formulated it. Although the problem of ethical relativity is usually put forward as if it arises because different societies have different moral systems, the problem arises as much within a given society as it does between different societies. As we have already noted, followers of a certain religion may not distinguish between the moral rules and other rules put forward by their religion. Even the Ten Commandments combine moral and purely religious rules. I do not maintain that there is no difference of opinion about what rules are moral rules; there may even be a difference of opinion about what rules are justified moral rules. I think this latter difference of opinion can be settled. If it is settled, then I think that the former difference of opinion should be settled also. There is no point in continuing to call something a moral rule if it is acknowledged that it is not a justified moral rule.

Differing ethical beliefs are no more a problem for morality than are differing beliefs about the correct explanation of a given phenomenon are a problem for science. If people have not thought enough about a problem, or do not have the necessary information or techniques, then it is not surprising that they do not arrive at the correct solution. Most people have not thought enough about the nature and justification of the moral rules. Hence it is not surprising that they do not distinguish between genuine or justified moral rules and rules which only seem to be moral rules. Clearly distinguishing the moral rules from all other rules shows that the sphere of morality does not cover all of life. Showing the limits of morality and that morality allows for some personal and societal variations allows me to present a moral system that all impartial rational persons would accept. It is a consequence of accepting this account of morality that it is morally unjustified to deprive anyone of freedom or pleasure, let alone to disable him, cause him pain, or kill him, because he will not conform to a way of life not demanded by the moral rules.

It may be objected that since I include among the moral rules, the rules "Obey the law" and "Do your duty," my supposed universality is a universality in name only, for what is according to the law in one society may be contrary to it in another. What one society considers a duty, another society may not. I have also granted that there is some variation among societies in what counts as a violation of a moral rule, that the presence or absence of certain rights affects the interpretation of even the first fives rules, so when we come to specific cases, what is moral in one society may be immoral in another. This must be admitted, yet the consequences are not as damaging as they may seem.

First, I have shown that this variation in interpretation is relatively minor, that all intentional causing of evil counts as a violation of the rules. Second, the same kinds of acts are prohibited by the moral rules in all societies. Third, eight of the moral rules do not even differ much in content from society to society. Fourth, in any society, the specific act is considered to be moral or immoral by application of the same criterion. Would an impartial rational person advocate that this violation of the rule be publicly allowed? It is not considered an argument against the universality of morality that people promise to do different things; therefore, in specific cases, failure to do quite different things can be immoral. Such an argument would rightly be considered absurd. It is not immoral of me not to meet someone at the airport if I have not promised to do so; it is if I have. What makes the latter act immoral is that the moral rule concerning promises applies to it.

What is different about the rules "Obey the law" and "Do your duty"? As far as I can see, nothing. In one society it is immoral to have more than one wife; in another society it is not. There is no problem here: in one society there is a law against having more than one wife; in the other there is not. What makes the specific act immoral or not is that the moral rule about obeying the law applies to this case in one society and not in the other. In one society it is immoral for grandchildren not to take care of their grandparents; in another society it is not, but in one society grandchildren have a duty to provide for their grandparents, and in the other they do not. Again what makes the specific act moral or immoral is that a moral rule either applies or it does not.

It may be objected that some laws require the violation of a moral rule, and for no good reason. We may have a job that requires us to violate a moral rule, and for no good reason. But we may also have made a promise which if fulfilled would require violation of a moral rule for no good reason. The case of promising need be no different from the two others. In these cases, we have a conflict of moral rules, and hence the moral ideals come into play, as do considerations about the amount of evil to be caused, prevented, or avoided. I do not see how the inclusion of the rules "Obey the law" and "Do your duty" affects the universality of morality any more than the inclusion of the rule "Keep your promise." The moral system includes not only the universal moral rules, it also includes a procedure that allows for justified exceptions to the rules. The confusion between a rule being universal, i.e., applying to all rational persons without consideration of person, time, place, or group, and its being absolute, i.e., admitting no exceptions, has been one of the main sources of ethical relativity.

Moral Judgments Versus Judgments on Moral Matters

Since a moral judgment must be a judgment that one at least believes an impartial rational person could advocate, it is not possible to equate a moral judgment with a judgment made on a moral matter, i.e., that which is subject to moral judgment. Unfortunately this has not generally been recognized. Most of the so-called analyses of moral judgments have not in fact been analyses of moral judgments, but merely analyses of judgments made on moral matters. Considered in this way, they can be seen to be extremely plausible. Most people's judgments on moral matters are simply expressions of their feelings that are aroused by consideration of the act they are judging. Most people do not even consider whether their judgment is one that an impartial rational person could advocate, or rather they do not consider this unless their judgments are challenged. It is impossible to overestimate the amount of stupidity in the world. If emotivism is considered as an analysis of the unreflective judgments on moral matters made by most persons, I think it probably correct.

The feelings that are aroused by consideration of an act of which a moral judgment is appropriate usually reflect the views of one's society. Ethical relativism is also largely correct if taken as an analysis of the way in which most people make judgments on moral matters, especially if we consider unreflective judgments, those made simply on the basis of one's feelings. Not all judgments of moral matters are unreflective. After reflection some people make judgments of moral matters which conflict with the views which are dominant in their society. Indeed, some people, though undoubtedly a very small number, make judgments of moral matters which conflict with the way they presently feel toward the act in question. There is often a considerable time lag between coming to see what the correct moral judgment of an act is and coming to feel toward that act the way one thinks one ought to feel.

If one knows that no impartial rational person would agree with his judgment, then he is not making a moral judgment. But usually one does not know this. Usually one does not consider whether any impartial rational person could agree with his judgment. Sometimes one may even believe that some impartial rational person would agree with his judgment, but further reflection convinces him that this is not the case. It is this latter case that is most appropriately called making a mistaken moral judgment. It is not surprising that people often make mistaken moral judgments. It is not always an easy matter to determine what an impartial rational person could advocate. One must consider what one could advocate if one did not know who the parties involved were, but knew only the morally relevant facts. Sometimes considering the act with the two parties reversed is helpful. But not always. A judge should not consider what he would advocate if he were the criminal. What he must consider is what he would advocate as an impartial rational person.

The distinction between moral judgments and judgments made of moral matters allows one to make a simple statement about moral progress. Moral progress occurs as judgments of moral matters become moral judgments. This assumes, of course, that these judgments are not hypocritical. It is generally not realized how many judgments of moral matters are not even intended to be moral judgments. Many people realize that no impartial rational person would agree with their judgments, but do not care about this. They are not even concerned with the possibility of agreement among all rational persons, only with the agreement among a very limited subset of them. In primitive societies, this often includes only the other members of the society. In civilized societies, it may not even include this much. Some people make judgments that could only be agreed to by people with a similar social status. Some people make judgments that could be accepted only by people of the same race or religion. Indeed, in large societies a person is usually considered a highly moral person if his judgments of moral matters could be agreed to by all members of his society. Since most of the moral matters that one makes judgments of are matters concerning only those people in one's society, it is easy to overestimate the extent of moral progress. A person whose judgments of domestic matters make him seem a most moral person often is seen not to be so when he makes judgments of foreign policy.

One of the lesser, but nonetheless significant, evils of war is the reversing of moral progress. People whose judgments of moral matters had been genuine moral judgments no longer make the same judgments. Especially when the moral rules are unjustifiably violated by their country, they make judgments that could not possibly be agreed to by any impartial rational person. They no longer care whether there could be agreement among all rational persons; they are concerned only with agreement among their fellow citizens. They even condemn as unpatriotic those who continue to make genuine moral judgments of such matters. Thus nationalism overwhelms morality, not only as the basis for action, but also as the basis for judgment. Confusion about morality often allows nationalistic judgments to pass for moral ones, a confusion often not only supported by the leaders of the country but often shared by them. Sometimes, however, nationalism is explicitly put forward as superior to morality. "My country, right or wrong" is a slogan that war makes respectable even in the most civilized societies. War often causes people to lose that decent respect for the opinion of humankind that morality demands.

13

VERSIONS OF
MORALITY AS IMPARTIAL
RATIONALITY

In order to clarify the theory that I have put forward I shall contrast it with two other versions of the same kind of theory, i.e., that a moral system is a public system that applies to all rational persons and that a justified moral system is one that would be advocated by all impartial rational persons. I call this kind of theory, *morality as impartial rationality,* and the two versions that I have chosen to examine are those put forward by Kurt Baier in *The Moral Point of View*[1] and John Rawls in *A Theory of Justice.*[2] That these two philosophers provide two of the most well-known and well worked-out versions of this moral theory is sufficient reason to examine their books, but I have more personal motives; my own views were strongly influenced by both of them.

I was a graduate student at Cornell University in the late 1950's when Rawls taught there, and I took his seminar on Social Contract Theory. Although the first published edition of *The Moral Rules* came out in 1970, one year before *A Theory of Justice,* all of the influence goes the other way. Insofar as there are similarities between the two views, and there are many, we either arrived at these points independently or I borrowed, consciously or otherwise, from what I had learned from Rawls. My debt to Baier was initially less personal; I was strongly influenced by *The Moral Point of View.* How strongly has become clearer to me as I have continued to use this book in my classes. He also read a prepublication version of the first edition of *The Moral Rules* and made the suggestion, which unfortunately I have only now acted on, that I explicitly discuss the views of other philosophers showing how my view differs from theirs. The vigor of my attacks on these two books should be viewed as representing the effort needed to break away from their views: as an indication of the strength of their views, not of their weakness.

Morality

Both Baier and Rawls agree that morality must be a public system, that it must consist of rules or principles that are known and could be accepted by all those whose behavior is supposed to be governed by that system, and that for a moral system this includes all rational persons. They both agree that the content of that system should be determined by the agreement of impartial rational persons. These features are what make a theory a version of *morality as impartial rationality*. The publicity of morality is a crucial feature for both Baier and Rawls; they are concerned with the content of a moral system that would be openly used by everyone to determine the moral acceptability of an action. They both rule out as being inconsistent with the very nature of morality any system that could not be openly taught and defended. If a Utilitarian maintains that he has a system that will result in the greatest happiness of the greatest number, but only if no one knows that anyone else is using that system to guide his behavior, both Rawls and Baier would claim that the Utilitarian is not putting forward a moral system. They are interested in a system to which everyone can openly appeal, either as grounds for acting themselves or for judging the actions of others. My only criticism of them on this point is that they do not seem to fully appreciate the force of the claim that morality must be public.

That morality is a public system that applies to all rational persons places considerable constraints not only on the content of a moral system, but also on the foundations of that system, the moral theory that generates it. If a moral system must be such that it is understood and can be accepted by any rational person, it must be based solely on beliefs that are held by all rational persons, what I call rationally required beliefs. This not only rules out religious views as the basis of morality, it also rules out scientific views insofar as such findings are not known to all rational persons. Rawls, who allows those behind his veil of ignorance to have all general knowledge, including the findings of all the sciences, does not seem to fully appreciate that this is inconsistent with the public character of a moral system. A moral system that is based on the findings of the sciences could not be appealed to and accepted by all those to whom it applies, that is, to all rational persons. In fact, Rawls makes no use of the findings of any science in developing his moral system, but the fact that he thinks that it is allowable to use such findings indicates that he does not fully appreciate the constraints imposed by morality being a public system that applies to all rational persons.

Rationality

One of the most important features of the theory of morality as impartial rationality is that the question "Why should one be rational?" is not a sensible question. Rationality is regarded as the basic normative concept, one that can provide support for acting in other ways, e.g., morally, but for which it is inappropriate to attempt to provide support. No one we are prepared to take seriously will ever advocate doing an irrational action to anyone for whom they are concerned. There is complete agreement with Plato, Hobbes, and Kant that reason always ought to be in command. This agreement with the major non-sceptical philosophers concerning reason is not on its intrinsic character, for Plato, Hobbes, and Kant certainly provide stikingly different accounts of reason, but on the fact that reason should always be followed. It is accepted as given that everyone always ought to act rationally; no one ever ought to act irrationally.

Acceptance of the view that no one ever ought to act irrationally, that everyone always ought to act rationally, has led all proponents of morality as impartial rationality to attempt to provide an account of rationality that would appeal to every reader. Rationality must have an immediate and powerful appeal for the reader in order to gain acceptance for the moral system that depends upon it. One result of this is that self-interest plays a leading role in the concept of rationality. But rationality is not defined in terms of self-interest, for all want to allow it to be rational to act morally even when this is in conflict with one's self-interest. Examination of the details of the different accounts of rationality and of the views about the exact relationship between rationality, self-interest and morality shows that both Baier and Rawls have difficulty in providing an account of rationality that satisfies all these requirements.

Baier and Rawls on Rationality

Baier explicitly holds that it makes no sense to question whether one should be rational. (See Chapter 7.) He states, "Our very purpose in 'playing the reasoning game' is to maximize satisfactions and minimize frustrations" (p. 141). He thus seems to adopt the standard social science account of rationality that consists in identifying acting rationally with acting so as to maximize the satisfaction of one's desires, with no limitation on the content of one's desires. Later, however, he rules out certain desires as irrational, "It may be irrational as when, for no reason at all, we set our hand on fire or cut off our toes one by one" (p. 158), which suggests that he did not intend his previous formal account of rationality to be taken as his fundamental account.

For Baier, as for most contemporary philosophers who have attempted to put forward an account of rationality, there is a very close connection between acting rationally and acting on reasons. According to Baier, acting rationally simply consists in acting on the best reasons. Baier gives content to this formal account by providing a list of various kinds of reasons and ranking them according to their weight. He regards self-regarding reasons as having more weight than other-regarding reasons, though less than reasons of law, religion or morality. Baier wants an account of rationality such that for any course of action everyone will always agree whether the reasons supporting that way of acting are better, worse, or equal to the reasons supporting some alternative course of action.

Baier's particular ranking of reasons creates serious and unresolved problems when one's self-interest conflicts with the much greater interests of others. His strong distinction between moral reasons and altruistic reasons, the former being stronger than self-regarding reasons and the latter being weaker, prevents Baier from saying that it would be *morally* good to sacrifice one's own interests for the much greater interests of others, for this would erase the distinction between altruistic reasons and moral ones. When he discusses an actual case of this sort he uses the term "decent" to characterize acting for the interests of others and the epithet "selfish" to characterize acting in one's own interest and thereby, e.g., ruining a competing business firm (see p. 66). But on his own theory, he cannot consider these judgments of the alternative ways of acting to be moral judgments. It is clear that something has gone wrong.

Unlike Baier, Rawls does not define rationality in terms of reasons which have a content independent of the desires of the agent. Rather, Rawls defines rationality in terms of maximizing the satisfaction of one's desires with, except for what he takes to be a minor exception, no limitation on content. Except for this minor exception, Rawls intends that no desire be ruled out by its intrinsic character; a desire is irrational only if it conflicts with the satisfaction of other more important desires. Acting irrationally is acting in a way that is inconsistent with the maximum satisfaction of one's desires. Both a complete egoist and a complete altruist can be perfectly rational; rationality is determined for each person solely by his own plan of life, as long as he takes account of the formal aspects of rationality: efficiency, inclusiveness and greater likelihood (see Section 63). Rawls explicitly states, "It is clearly left to the agent himself to decide what it is he most wants and to judge the comparative importance of his several ends" (p. 416). On his account, rational persons need not be concerned exclusively, or even primarily, with their own self-interest. Following Hobbes and Hume, Rawls regards most rational persons as being motivated by limited altruism. (See Section 25 and Chapter VII.)

Rawls, much more than Baier, attempts to provide the kind of purely formal account of rationality favored by economists and other social scientists. When he begins to develop his moral theory, however, he does impose a slight limitation on the content of rationality. He says, "The concept of rationality invoked here, with the exception of one essential feature, is the standard one familiar in social theory" (p. 143). The exception is a special assumption "that a rational individual does not suffer from envy" (Ibid.). Rawls then continues, "He is not ready to accept a loss for himself if only others have less as well." Rawls seems to take this latter statement to mean the same as not suffering from envy. (Since Rawls simply goes from one to the other with no argument, this is another example of the ubiquitous fallacy of assumed equivalence.) But the two do not mean the same, the latter statement, which is the one Rawls needs for his theory, does not rule out all of envy and rules out much more than envy. Examination of this seemingly small exception shows that limitations on content play a much larger role in Rawls's account of rationality than he realizes.

That one is not willing to accept a loss in order that others have less as well does not rule out those envious actions in which one can make others have less with no loss for oneself. More important for the point I am concerned with, it rules out not only some actions motivated by envy, it also rules out some actions of the individual who has more than others but who is willing to have less if others are going to have even less, that is, if he increases the distance between himself and others. (See Rawls's account of grudgingness and spite, pp. 532 ff.) This ruling out of envy and grudgingness is not insignificant in political theory, for there is a very plausible hypothesis that once a minimum level of material well-being has been achieved, people regard status, which depends on comparing oneself with others, as more important than material goods.

This unwillingness to accept a loss in order to harm others also rules out certain kinds of revenge, viz., those acts of revenge in which the perpetrator of the revenge also suffers a loss. It also rules out some malicious desires, at least if these desires are deemed important enough that one is willing to suffer some personal loss in order to have them satisfied. What Rawls describes as the exclusion of envy thus involves a much more significant limitation of the content of rationality than initially acknowledged. It now turns out that it is irrational to act against one's self-interest merely in order to hurt others. I agree that such actions are irrational, but this conclusion could not come from a purely formal account of rationality of a non-envious person.

Rawls does not rule out as irrational pity or sympathy such that a person is ready to accept a loss for himself if only others have more, but he does not allow this to motivate the parties in the original position. It is interesting that in the original position accepting a loss for oneself if only others have less is ruled out as irrational, but accepting a loss for oneself if only others have more is only ruled out as a motivating force. Rawls allows that benefitting others may make it rational to act against self-interest, but does not allow that hurting others may do so. This is not only a very plausible position; it is a correct one, but it is important to see that it really is not compatible with Rawls's stated basic definition of rationality as the maximization of the satisfaction of desires.

If one is going to claim that going against self-interest is irrational when it is done to hurt others, but rational when it is done in order to help others, then quite clearly helping others and hurting others are related to rational actions independently of the formal definition of rationality as the maximization of satisfaction of desires. Further, one will also have to give some objective sense, that is, specified content, to self-interest or it will make vacuous the ruling out of accepting a loss for oneself if only others have less as well. Rawls does, in fact, provide such an objective content to self-interest, at least in the original position; it consists in maximizing one's primary goods.

In the original position, Rawls uses a definition of rationality that makes it irrational to sacrifice any primary goods in order to hurt others. Rather than the primary goods being deduced from the theory, as those goods that a person wants no matter what else he wants, they are actually used to limit the kinds of things that rational persons can want. A rational person is not only prohibited from acting out of envy or spite, but also from seeking revenge or from acting maliciously if acting in any of these ways causes him to suffer a loss of primary goods. Although, except for the exclusion of envy, Rawls claims to use a formal account of rationality, we have seen that his concept of rationality has a much more significant limitation on content.

I have mentioned so far only those limitations which arise from his ruling out a willingness to accept less if only others have less as well. However, it should be clear that Rawls also needs to rule out as irrational desires to have less for no reason at all. Also rationally prohibited are most suicidal desires as well as desires to mutilate or disable oneself and desires to be a slave. Only those who have mental disorders would have such desires, but an adequate account of rationality cannot ignore the desires of those suffering from mental disorders, it must account for their being irrational.[3] The fact that these desires are nowhere explicitly mentioned indicates that Rawls does not fully appreciate what his account of rationality actually involves. He does not realize that the formal account of rationality as the maximization of satisfaction of desires is not the operative concept in his theory. Rather, he has substantial content built into his account of rationality, even though the only hint of this content is given by his ruling out of envy.

The Relationship Between Rationality and Morality

Another important feature of the theory of morality as impartial rationality is that the question "Why should one be moral?" is a sensible question. As indicated before, morality is viewed as a public system that applies to all rational persons, but being rational does not require that one act on such a public system, even if as a rational person one would put forward that system as a public one. Kant, on the standard interpretations, would not agree with this view, for he took acting on the maxim you put forward as a universal law as a necessary feature of rationality.[4] The theory of morality as impartial rationality holds that a justifiable moral system is one which all impartial rational persons would not only advocate as a public system, but also one that they would use to guide their behavior. Different versions of morality as impartial rationality disagree concerning whether or not rational persons who are not impartial would always act morally.

Only because he is so confident that he has provided a concept of rationality such "that no one wants to become mad" (p. 143) does Baier make the ill-fated attempt to show that it is contrary to reason to act immorally.[5] Even before examining the details of his arguments, it should be clear that no argument could possibly have the result Baier wants, viz., that reason requires acting morally, and still retain the concept of reason that Baier started with and never explicitly gives up, viz., that everyone wants to follow reason. If it is shown that being rational requires me to tell the truth when I can make three million dollars with no risk to myself or anyone I care about by lying, then there will be quite a few people who will no longer want to be rational. Similarly, if it is irrational to contradict myself, but by doing so I can gain three million dollars with no risk to myself or anyone I care about, then there will be quite a few people who will not mind being irrational. This is why Alan Gewirth's view, in *Reason and Morality* (Chicago, 1978), that reason requires acting morally does not belong in that group of theories that I call morality as impartial rationality.

Baier's problem arises from an ambiguity in his account of the phrase "better reason." One sense of that phrase, "A is a better reason than B," entails that it is contrary to reason (irrational) to act on B rather than A when they conflict; no person acting rationally would do so. However, the other sense of that phrase, "A is a better reason than B" means that all rational persons, if they were choosing between a world in which everyone acted according to A and another world in which everyone acted according to B would always choose world A. Baier gives no argument for holding that what counts as a better reason in the latter sense also counts as a better reason in the former sense. Why should a rational person even care whether or not the reason he acts on is one that he would choose for everyone to act on if he were choosing between worlds? Baier's mistake is that at a crucial point in the argument, he incorporates impartiality, choosing between two worlds when all members of that world will be affected equally, into the concept of rationality.

If the concept of rationality is to provide a significant foundation for morality then the concept of rationality must be such that no one, at least no one we are interested in talking to, wants to act irrationally (contrary to reason). Since not everyone wants to be impartial, incorporating impartiality into the concept of rationality results in a concept of rationality such that not everyone wants to avoid acting irrationally. Any view that holds that no one wants to act irrationally, as morality as impartial rationality does, requires that the concepts of rationality and impartiality be kept distinct. Baier, unfortunately, in his attempt to prove that it is always contrary to reason to act immorally, mistakenly incorporates impartiality into the concept of rationality.

Rawls does keep the concepts of rationality and impartiality distinct. However, at least on his stated view of rationality, as the maximization of satisfaction of one's desires, he has come up with an equally counter-intuitive conclusion. This conclusion is that for certain people, in real life this may be the vast majority of people, it is often irrational to act morally. Whenever someone whose desires are limited to himself and those he cares about is confronted with a situation in which he and those he cares about will suffer if he acts morally and those he does not care about will benefit, then it becomes irrational for him to act morally. In such a case, maximizing the satisfaction of his desires, which are limited to himself and those he cares about, requires his acting immorally.

Although Rawls does not explicitly draw this conclusion, it is clearly implied by his definitions, and David Richards, in *A Theory of Reasons for Action,* a book which consciously builds upon Rawls's theory, does explicitly state this conclusion. When talking about a person who can successfully further his own interests by acting immorally, Richards states, "For such a person, it will be irrational to be moral, assuming most other persons are moral, since he can successfully profit from their morality without himself undergoing all the costs of being consistently moral in all cases."[6]

Richards explicitly distinguishes between rationality and reasonableness[7] and Rawls in his Dewey Lectures[8] seems to use a similar distinction. Richards puts the distinction in the following way. "Roughly, in terms of their application to acts, the distinction may be put thus: questions of rationality involve the agent's aims and the best way to realize them, whereas questions of reasonableness involve the assessment of the pursuit of one's own aims in the light of the morally justified claims of others."[9] This terminology has the odd consequence that it is sometimes irrational to be reasonable and sometimes unreasonable to be rational.

Moreover, morality as impartial rationality seeks to develop a moral theory by combining the concept of impartiality with rationality rather than reasonableness.[10] It is the principles that rational agents would adopt behind the veil of ignorance that count as moral principles. Given that we are concerned with rational agents because it is assumed that everyone wants to act rationally, we have the troubling result that some rational agents, behind the veil of ignorance, will adopt as moral principles, principles that it would be irrational for them to follow when they are no longer behind this veil. This strongly suggests that the account of rationality developed by Rawls in *A Theory of Justice* is inadequate and that Rawls and Richards were led to introduce the distinction between the rational and the reasonable because of this inadequacy.

Benefits of an Adequate Account of Rationality

The problems that arise in the accounts of rationality presented by Baier and Rawls are avoided by the account of rationality that was presented in Chapter 2. We have seen that Baier holds that it is always contrary to reason (irrational) to act immorally and that Rawls is committed to the view that it is sometimes irrational not to act immorally. Both of these conclusions are unacceptable, and the account of rationality presented in Chapter 2 avoids them both. Taking irrational action as basic allows "rational action" to be defined as "not irrational." This makes it possible for there to be conflicting rational alternatives in many situations. More particularly, in a conflict between self-interest and morality, it makes it *rationally allowed* to act either according to self-interest or to act morally. Baier and Rawls, like almost all other philosophers, take "rational" as the basic term to be defined and then regard as irrational or contrary to reason everything that does not meet that definition. This has restricted the use of rational to rationally required, and has been a factor in their problems.

Using irrational action as the basic concept and defining "rational" as "not irrational," yields an account of rationality which, together with impartiality, can serve as the foundation of morality. This account preserves an essential feature of morality as impartial rationality: no one ever wants to act irrationally; everyone always wants to act rationally. On this account, acting rationally has the following relationship to acting morally and to acting out of self-interest: (1) It is never irrational to act in your own self-interest; it is always rational (rationally allowed) to act in your own self-interest. (2) It is never irrational to act as morality requires; it is always rational (rationally allowed) to act as morality requires. When self-interest and morality conflict it cannot be irrational, but must always be rationally allowed, to act in either way. This means that rationality does not provide the strong support for acting morally that many philosophers have wanted, but we have already seen that this was a vain desire. Baier's account of rationality denies feature (1); Rawls's account denies feature (2).

We have already seen how Baier goes wrong in trying to show that reasons of self-interest are better reasons than altruistic reasons though not as good as moral reasons. On the present account of reasons, there is no ranking of self-regarding, other-regarding reasons, and moral reasons. All reasons for acting are beliefs about the consequences, direct or indirect, of one's actions for oneself or others; there are no independent moral reasons. It can be rational to sacrifice oneself for others or to refuse to do so. The adequacy of a reason depends upon the amount of harm avoided or benefit gained and does not depend upon who avoids the harm or gains the good. Denying Baier's claim that there is an objective ranking of reasons, with moral reasons counting as better than reasons of self-interest, avoids the unwanted conclusion that it is irrational to act immorally. This allows rationality to remain such that everyone always wants to act rationally. It is a vain desire to provide the strongest kind of motivation for acting morally that leads Baier to go from feature (2), It is never irrational to act morally; it is always rational (rationally allowed) to act morally, to (2a), It is always rational (rationally required) to act morally; it is always contrary to reason (irrational) to act immorally.

Ranking moral reasons higher than reasons of self-interest, and equating acting rationally with acting on the best reasons, forces Baier to hold that it is sometimes contrary to reason to act in one's self-interest, and thus he no longer has a concept of reason such that no one ever wants to act contrary to reason. The recognition that as long as one does not harm oneself one needs no reasons in order to be acting rationally allows acting rationally to be distinguished from acting on reasons, or acting on the best reasons. It is also important to distinguish between an adequate reason for doing x, a reason that makes it rationally allowed to do x, and a conclusive reason for doing x, a reason that makes it rationally required to do x. Morality always provides an adequate reason for acting against one's self-interest; it never provides a conclusive reason. Baier's failure to distinguish adequate from conclusive reasons (see p. vii) partly explains why he thinks he can go from (2), it is always rational to act morally, to (2a), it is always irrational to act immorally. Making the distinction allows us to hold that there are always adequate reasons for acting morally while denying that it is always irrational to act immorally.

Rawls realizes that there is no objective ranking of kinds of reasons, but he goes further, he holds that there are no objective reasons at all, that all reasons are related to one's desires. Each individual not only ranks reasons according to his own life plan, he determines whether or not something even counts as a reason. If a person's life plan only concerns himself and perhaps some friends and family, then he can have no reason to act contrary to these interests even if it is morally required that he do so. Even if a person knows that his actions will cause significant evil for others, if he does not care about those who will suffer that evil, if avoiding evil for them is not part of his life plan, he has no reason for not causing that evil. It is a consequence of this view that it is sometimes irrational to act as morality requires.

Suppose that such a person is in a situation where lying will promote his interests and those of his friends. Since refusing to lie goes contrary to his life plan, it must be irrational for him to refuse to lie. It is true that unless something else is added to the person's motivation, he will lie; it will be unintelligible on the account given so far if he refuses to lie. But rationality and intelligibility are not the same: the former is a normative term; the latter is not. It does not follow from his refusing to lie being unintelligible that it would be irrational for him to refuse to lie. Given that no one ever ought to act irrationally, the latter amounts to a recommendation that a person act immorally when morality requires any action against his life plan.

There is quite a difference between saying of a selfish immoral person that it would be inexplicable if he acts morally when it has significant cost and saying that it would be irrational for him to act morally if it has significant cost. The failure to appreciate this difference is a result of failing to distinguish between reasons and motives, of requiring all reasons to be motives. Failure to make this distinction makes it impossible to acknowledge the objectivity of reasons, for although a reason of self-interest must provide a motive for every rational person, a reason involving the interests of others need not. On the account of reasons that I have provided, beliefs that one will avoid death, pain, disability, loss of freedom or pleasure, or will gain greater ability, freedom or pleasure, are reasons that serve as motives to all rational persons; beliefs that others will avoid the evils or gain the goods are reasons that do not serve as motives to all, but they are reasons for a person whether or not they serve as her motives.

Baier does make the distinction between reasons and motives. (See p. 40ff.) He recognizes that morality provides an objective reason, if not a motive, for acting even if acting morally is not part of one's life plan. Unfortunately, Baier regards moral reasons as better than reasons of self-interest and thus makes it contrary to reason to follow an immoral life plan. Rawls realizes that it is never irrational to act according to one's life plan. Unfortunately, he does not acknowledge that morality provides objective reasons for acting independently of one's life plan, and thus he makes it irrational for some persons to act morally.

Impartiality

Morality as impartial rationality does not claim that all impartial rational persons advocate that the same violations be publicly allowed, e.g., resolve conflicts between the rules in the same way. This moral theory requires only that everyone agree on what counts as a morally relevant consideration; it does not require that everyone agree on the ranking of morally relevant considerations. Impartiality does not guarantee complete agreement; the view that it does probably stems from the vain desire to have a moral system which always provides unique answers to every moral question.

Morality as impartial rationality requires that any violation of a moral rule be one that an impartial rational person can publicly allow, but it is only when considering breaking a moral rule that impartiality is required. Morality as impartial rationality does not require everyone to always act impartially; when no violation of a moral rule is involved, impartiality is usually not even a consideration. Even when acting on the moral ideals, impartiality usually has no place; there is nothing morally wrong with making one's charitable contributions primarily to some group to which one has some special relationship or in which one has a special interest. Impartiality is required in formulating the moral system, guaranteeing that neither the rules nor the procedure for determining justified exceptions give special consideration to some moral agents e.g., oneself or those for whom one cares.

Impartiality simply is the absence of any bias in favor of or against any member of the group toward which one is supposed to be impartial. Everyone agrees that the impartiality required by morality involves a group that includes, at least, all moral agents. Baier tries to achieve this kind of impartiality by using "the condition of 'reversibility,' that is, the behavior in question must be acceptable to a person whether he is at the 'giving' or 'receiving' end of it" (p. 108). Rawls tries to achieve impartiality by removing from the rational persons who are to formulate the rules all information that would allow for any differences between them. Given the proper account of rationality, and the formal features of moral rules, neither of these procedures is adequate, each of them suffers from a serious flaw, which was discussed in the chapter on Impartiality.

As characterized above, impartiality is neither rationally required nor rationally prohibited; it is rationally allowed. A rational person can either be impartial or not; this is especially true of the impartiality required by morality. By defining acting rationally as acting on the best reasons and making impartial reasons the best reasons, Baier incorporated impartiality into his account of rationality and thus made it irrational not to be impartial. By defining acting rationally as maximizing the satisfaction of one's desires, Rawls made it irrational for a person with desires limited to the interests of himself and his friends to be impartial. Thus both Baier and Rawls distorted the relationship between the concepts of rationality and impartiality. Morality as impartial rationality requires that it be rational either to act impartially or to act with partiality. This must be true for all persons, regardless of their particular life plans.

The absence of any bias in favor of or against any member of the group does not require all impartial persons to agree completely in their moral judgments. Both Baier and Rawls formulate their accounts of impartiality in order to emulate the utilitarians and provide a decision procedure for every moral problem. Neither wants to allow for any moral disagreement among impartial rational persons who have the same factual information. Of course, they are not alone in making this attempt; almost every major moral philosopher who has provided a normative ethical theory has either assumed or argued for the view that all equally informed impartial rational persons will always agree. It is this claim that morality always provides unique answers which has made moral skepticism seem a plausible position.

Baier does not discuss impartiality in any detail, but he characterizes the "moral point of view" as the "God's eye point of view," (p. 107) and we all know that there is only one God. Perhaps Baier was afraid that if he allowed for any genuine moral disagreement among impartial rational persons, there would be no non-arbitrary place to draw the line and he would therefore end up in a position resembling that taken by R. M. Hare in *Freedom and Reason* (Oxford,

1963), where even the view of a fanatic Nazi cannot be objectively ruled out as morally unacceptable. Baier does not explicitly rule out moral disagreement, and given that, unlike Hare and Rawls, his account of rationality is not purely formal, he can allow for some disagreement without being forced to the conclusion that there are no correct answers. In fact, given that his test of impartiality seems to be reversibility, Baier may already have the mechanism for allowing limited disagreement; some rational persons would be willing to be on the receiving end of some behavior that other rational persons would not.

Rawls has no way of allowing for limited disagreement, indeed he definitely wants his moral system to provide a complete decision procedure. Had he tried to deal with some genuinely controversial issues of individual morality, he may have come to realize the error of explicating impartiality in such a way that it requires complete unanimity in answering every moral question. He admits that the questions, "how are these duties to be balanced when they come into conflict, either with each other or with obligations, and with the good that can be achieved by supererogatory actions?" (p. 339) have no obvious answer. He even says, "I do not know how this problem is to be settled, or even whether a systematic solution formulating useful and practical rules is possible" (pp. 339–40). None of this seems to give him any doubt that there are such priority rules, for he says on the very next page, "Here I imagine that the priority rules are sufficient to resolve conflicts of principles, or at least guide the way to a correct assignment of weights" (p. 341).

The only argument Rawls gives in favor of there being such priority rules has no weight at all. He says, "Obviously, we are not yet in a position to state these rules for more than a few cases; but since we manage to make these judgments, useful rules exist (unless the intuitionist is correct and these are only descriptions)" (p. 341). Note the phrase "we manage to make these judgments." Who are "we?" Certainly we all make moral judgments in situations when moral principles conflict, but do we all make the same judgments? For Rawls's point to have any weight, we would all have to make the same judgments. But clearly this is not the case.

People make different judgments in many cases of moral conflict. Even equally informed people whom we take to be rational and impartial sometimes disagree on the judgments they make in cases of moral conflict. It is the fact of genuine moral disagreement that gives an existentialist view or one like that presented by Hare in *Freedom and Reason* its plausibility. It is the denial of any genuine moral disagreement not based on a disagreement about the facts that makes normative ethical theories seem so clearly wrong that scepticism or indifference seems an appropriate attitude towards them.

A moral theory, and especially the view of morality as impartial rationality, is not committed to the view that there must be complete agreement on every moral question, i.e., that all equally informed impartial rational persons must always agree. Rawls is committed to unanimity because for him impartiality is determined by a veil of ignorance so complete that not only does one not "know his fortune in the distribution of natural assets and abilities, intelligence and strength, and the like," he does not even "know his conception of the good, the

particulars of his rational plan of life, or even the special features of his psychology, such as his aversion to risk or liability to optimism or pessimism" (p.
137). This complete ignorance is what allows Rawls to conclude "each is convinced by the same arguments. Therefore, we can view the choice in the original
position from the standpoint of one person selected at random" (p. 139).

Why does Rawls want the ignorance to be so complete? He wants those in the
original position to approximate, as closely as possible, Kantian noumenal
selves. He says "My suggestion is that we think of the original position as the
point of view from which noumenal selves see the world" (p. 255). This assumes
that all noumenal selves see the world in exactly the same way. Even granting,
for the sake of the argument, that all noumenal selves "desire certain primary
goods" (p. 253), why should we grant the much more dubious point, which
Rawls never discusses, that they rank these goods in exactly the same way? And
if they do not, then it is doubtful that they will make the same judgments when
there is a conflict.

Even if one does not know "the special features of his psychology such as his
aversion to risk or liability to optimism or pessimism" (p. 137), he still has those
features, and they may lead him to make different judgments in particular cases.
We should not adopt an account of impartiality which makes it impossible for
anyone to be impartial. Rawls simply assumes there is some privileged ranking
of the goods or psychological features such that all noumenal selves or impartial
rational persons will agree on the answers to questions such as how much material well-being is enough so that no more is worth any sacrifice of liberty. Rawls
cannot tell us what this level is, because it is impossible to come up with a precise statement of this level such that all impartial rational persons will agree with
it. More generally, there can be no confrontation of specific real controversial
cases in which one has to choose between evils, for then it would become
obvious how implausible it is to assume that one can come up with a unani-
mously agreed upon ranking of the goods and evils.

If there is no agreement on the rankings of the goods and evils then there is
no chance whatsoever of there being priority rules that will decide in every case
what should be done when moral principles conflict. Were Rawls to have made
a serious attempt to account for the exceptions to his duties and obligations,
which is the real problem for any moral theory—as Mill pointed out, there is no
real disagreement on the rules themselves—he might have given up his assumption that all impartial rational persons would rank all of the primary goods in
exactly the same way. It is not incompatible with impartiality for impartial rational persons to rank the goods and evils in different ways. Once this is realized
we can modify the account of impartiality provided by the veil of ignorance in
order to allow for some genuine moral disagreement. This does not result in
intuitionism, but rather allows us to say what the intuitionists should have said,
but did not, namely, that there are sometimes incompatible acceptable answers
to specific moral questions.

Realization that the amount of harm that can result from failure to obey any
of Rawls's duties or obligations can vary from very trivial to extremely great
should make clear that it is very unlikely that conflicts between the rules can be

settled by priority rules that depend primarily on the ranking of the various duties and obligations. The further realization that the harms or evils are not all of a piece, that death, pain, disability, loss of freedom and pleasure are distinct evils, and that impartial rational persons may differ in their rankings of them, some even preferring death to suffering a sufficiently high degree of the others, makes it completely implausible to think that there would be any agreed upon priority rules at all. It is interesting that Rawls never talks about pain and disability, and his only discussion of death comes when he admits that it would be an improvement to make prisoners of war slaves rather than killing them (see p. 248). In the development of his theory, Rawls seems to use liberty as the Utilitarians used happiness, in order to make it plausible that there are unique answers to every moral question.

Trying to deal with conflicts between rules, or more generally with determining justified exceptions to the rules, by means of priority rules leads one to neglect the individual differences present even among impartial rational persons. Accepting the fact that impartial rational persons can differ in their judgments permits a very simple and persuasive way of dealing with exceptions. Limit beliefs to those that are rationally required, thus eliminating the partiality that Rawls wants to eliminate by using his veil of ignorance, but allow all rational desires that do not depend upon any belief that is not rationally required, thus doing away with the unanimity imposed by Rawls's veil of ignorance. Those exceptions that any impartial rational person, using this appropriately modified veil of ignorance, *could* advocate count as morally acceptable, but it does not follow that all such persons *would* advocate the same course of action. This means that there will be some unresolved conflicts, but a moral system should not attempt to do the impossible, not all moral conflicts can be resolved. The system outlined above would allow some of the individuality that gives Hare's theory, in *Freedom and Reason*, its plausibility without allowing it to go as far as Hare, thus losing its plausibility.

Formulation of a Moral System

An ethical theory can have as its primary goal providing a system that can help one decide what one morally ought to do in an actual situation in which one now is; or it can have as its primary goal providing a guide for evaluating which state of affairs counts as the morally best state of affairs, without much concern about determining whether or how one can get there from where one now is. I shall call a theory with the former goal as primary a practical theory, a theory with the latter goal an evaluative one. Prior to the emergence of applied ethics, contemporary philosophers were more interested in evaluative ethical theories than with practical ones. For example, interest in G. E. Moore's *Principia Ethica* centers almost entirely on his claims about the good, and what counts as the best states of affairs, and there is almost complete neglect of his practical moral system. This is contained in the chapter with the unusual title "Ethics In Relation to Conduct," in which Moore admits that when deciding how one should act it is almost irrelevant to know what counts as good. According to the interpretation of Thomas Gray, John Stuart Mill regarded the principle of utility as an evaluative principle, not as a practical one. According to Gray, the fundamental practical principle for Mill is the principle of liberty.[11]

Baier and Rawls both present morality as impartial rationality primarily as an evaluative theory. Neither spends much time or effort in developing his theory in such a way as to provide a moral system that would be useful to people who want a moral guide to action. The most important part of such a moral system is the formulation of specific moral rules together with a method for determining justified exceptions. In failing to provide a useful moral system, the theories of most philosophers, including the versions of morality as impartial rationality presented by Baier and Rawls, have been seriously inadequate. Most time, of course, is spent developing the basic theory from which the moral rules will be derived. The formulation of the moral rules themselves is usually done quite quickly, and generally very carelessly. This may be due to the acceptance of Mill's view that the various schools of ethics "recognize . . . to a great extent the same moral laws; but differ as to their evidence, and the source from which they derive their authority."[12]

Although Baier never explicitly formulates the concept of a public system, he is clear that the moral rules must be public and formulates a number of features that guarantee that the moral rules will be public rules that apply to all rational persons: universal teachability, not self-frustrating, self-defeating, or morally impossible, and for the good of everyone alike (pp. 100–106). Rawls acknowledges his indebtedness to Baier's account (see footnote 5, page 130) even though he formulates the features of his principles (Rawls uses the term "principle" rather than "rule") in different terms (see section 23, pp. 130–136). However, neither Baier nor Rawls has a careful and detailed discussion of why they formulate a particular rule or principle in the way that they do.

For example, Baier spends less than three pages in the formulation of what he calls the moral rules. He specifically lists "Thou shalt not kill," "Thou shalt not be cruel," and "Thou shalt not lie" as moral rules. He then claims that "Don't do evil" is the most readily acceptable moral rule of all (p. 107). On the next page he lists "Killing, cruelty, inflicting pain, maiming, torturing, deceiving, cheating, rape, adultery," as instances of behavior violating "the condition of reversibility," thus leading one to believe that there are moral rules prohibiting all of these behaviors. Note the lack of precision. It is not clear why there is a rule against cruelty if there already are rules against inflicting pain, maiming, and torturing; indeed, it is not clear why one needs to mention torturing as a separate category.

This lack of attention to the actual formulation of specific moral precepts is probably in part responsible for Baier's failure to distinguish between moral rules, which should be enforced, and moral ideals, which it is inappropriate to force one to follow. Baier claims that "The principle of reversibility does not merely impose certain prohibitions on a moral agent but also positive injunctions. It is, for instance, wrong - an omission - not to help another person when he is in need and when we are in a position to help him" (p. 108). Supposedly it is a moral rule that "Thou shalt help those in need when in a position to do so." Baier claims that there is no significant distinction between this positive injunction and the prohibitions against killing and lying.

The failure to make such a distinction leads Baier into an internal inconsistency. He argues that it is absurd to regard "do the optimific act" as a moral duty because it "would have the absurd result that we are doing wrong whenever we are relaxing since on these occasions there will always be opportunities to produce greater good than we can by relaxing" (p. 109). However, given the state of the world during all of its history, almost everyone reading Baier's book is in a position to help someone who is in need instead of relaxing, and thus Baier's positive injunction to help those in need has the same absurd consequence as "do the optimific act."

Rawls agrees with Baier that there is no important distinction between what he calls the positive duty to help another in need and the negative duties not to harm. He says, "The distinction between positive and negative duties is intuitively clear in many cases, but often gives way. I shall not put any stress on it. The distinction is only important with regard to the priority problem, since it seems plausible to hold that when the distinction is clear, negative duties have more weight than positive ones" (p.114). This completely confuses the matter. It is not the priority problem at all that makes it important to distinguish Rawls's positive duties from his negative ones. It is true that we are not usually allowed to cause harm to one to prevent a similar amount of harm from being suffered by another, but when there is a great disparity in the harm being caused and the harm being prevented, even when the distinction between negative and positive duties is clear, it does not follow that it is always right to put more weight on the negative duty.

The real importance of the distinction between Rawls's positive duties and his negative ones rests upon the appropriateness of punishing failure to follow them. His positive duties are really moral ideals; they cannot be obeyed all of the time and hence one should not be forced, only encouraged, to follow them. On the other hand, his negative duties, together with the obligations, are moral rules; they can be obeyed at all times and should be enforced, unjustified violations of them making one liable to punishment. Rawls seems to partially recognize this distinction when he provides a fuller statement of his positive duties, but he does not appreciate its significance.

Rawls says, "The following are examples of natural duties: the duty to help another when he is in need or jeopardy, provided that one can do so without excessive risk or loss to oneself; the duty not to harm or injure another; and the duty not to inflict unnecessary suffering" (p. 114). Note the qualification "provided that one can do so without excessive risk or loss to oneself" which is included in the statement of the positive duty, but not included in the statements of the negative duties. This is not an idiosyncratic passage.

That Rawls does not appreciate the significance of this qualification comes out most clearly in his discussion of the supposedly positive duty of justice. "This duty requires us to support and to comply with just institutions that exist and apply to us. It also constrains us to further just arrangements not yet established, at least when this can be done without too much cost to ourselves" (p. 115; see also p. 334). Here Rawls seems to include within the duty of justice both the requirement to obey just laws, which is stated without qualification, and the moral ideal to further just arrangements, which does have the qualification, "when this can be done without too much cost to ourselves."

Rawls's failure to realize that only his positive duties have the qualification "without too much cost" (actually he phrases the qualification differently in each statement of it, but the intent is clearly the same) leads him to a very misleading account of supererogatory acts. He says, "Supererogatory acts are not required, though normally they would be were it not for the loss or risk involved for the agent himself. The person who does a supererogatory act does not invoke the exemption which the natural duties allow. For while we have a natural duty to bring about a great good, say, if we can do so relatively easily, we are released from this duty when the cost to ourselves is considerable" (p. 117).

Since Rawls has stated that there is no important difference between positive and negative duties, it seems to follow that we are also allowed to violate his negative duties when there is considerable cost or risk to ourselves. Although this is sometimes true, it is extremely misleading. We are not allowed to kill an innocent person in order to avoid our own death, but we are allowed not to act so as to prevent an innocent person from dying if we would thereby risk our life. There is an important distinction between what Rawls calls negative duties and what he calls positive duties, but it rests upon the enforceability of the former. Since Rawls rules out enforceablity as a feature of basic moral theory, he is unable to use it to make the distinction.

Rawls's description of supererogatory acts is designed to free him from the problem of making it morally wrong ever to relax. Baier noted that the utilitarians had this problem and then fell into it himself. Rawl's effort is not completely successful, but even more significant, Rawls's failure to distinguish his negative duties and obligations (moral rules) from his positive duties (moral ideals) plus his claim that "exemptions are included in the formulation of natural duties" (p. 117) creates a more serious problem. Violations of the moral rules are allowed which are completely at variance with our considered moral judgments about what should be allowed, as discussed in the previous paragraph.

Of the several factors that may be responsible for Rawls's failure to appreciate the significance of the distinction between his positive and negative duties, one of the most important is his adoption of "strict compliance" (p. 147) as part of the original position. Rawls holds that the parties in the original position assume that in real life all will obey the principles adopted behind the veil of ignorance. His position is that basic moral theory must assume strict compliance, rather than partial compliance, and that the question of punishment or enforcement does not enter into basic moral theory. This allows him to misuse the term "duty" in the typical philosophical fashion, where it does not entail that it is a feature of duties that they can be justifiably enforced.

Surprisingly, it is John Stuart Mill, in the last chapter of *Utilitarianism,* who correctly notes, "It is part of the notion of Duty in every one of its forms, that a person may rightfully be compelled to fulfill it. Duty is a thing which may be *exacted* from a person, as one exacts a debt. Unless we think it may be exacted from him, we do not call it his duty."[13] Rawls's complete neglect of the problem of enforcement makes it almost inevitable that he will not appreciate the real distinction between his positive duties and his negative ones, since that distinction rests upon which precepts impartial rational persons are prepared to enforce and which precepts they would not enforce.

Given that it is impossible to be following Rawls's completely general positive duties more than a small proportion of the time, it is not even clear how one could enforce them. Would one take a certain span of time, say a month, or a year, and if one had not done anything to further just arrangements, then he would be subject to punishment? Nor is it clear that anyone would want them enforced. Would anyone want Mozart forced to take time off from composing in order to further just arrangements? Merely asking the question shows the absurdity of regarding this positive duty as a duty in the ordinary sense that Mill describes.

Rawls's arguments for the adoption of his positive duties do not work if duty is taken in the ordinary sense as something to be enforced. Consider his argument for adopting the duty of mutual respect. "Now the reason why this duty would be acknowledged is that although the parties take no interest in each other's interests, they know that in society they need to be assured by the esteem of their associates" (p. 338). However, they can be assured of this esteem only if the duty of mutual respect is not a genuine duty, that is, if it is not a duty that is enforced. Only the unenforced acceptance of mutual respect can assure people of the esteem of their associates. His next argument, "Their self-respect and their confidence in the value of their own system of ends cannot withstand the indifference much less the contempt of others" has weight only if "others" is interpreted as "all others." Self-respect and confidence in the value of one's own system of ends can withstand the indifference and contempt of many others, as long as some show respect. Unenforced respect by some is more important for self-respect than enforced respect by everyone.

That Rawls's discussion of his positive duties involves the false dichotomy between accepting them as duties and no one acting on them at all comes out quite clearly in the following passage. "Thus while the natural duties are not special cases of a single principle . . . similar reasons no doubt support many of them when one considers the underlying attitudes they represent. Once we try to picture the life of a society in which no one had the slightest desire to act on these duties, we see that it would express an indifference if not disdain for human beings that would make a sense of our own worth impossible" (p. 339). The alternative to rejecting Rawls's positive duties as duties, however, is not to have no one have "the slightest desire" to act in the way that these "duties" prescribe. On the contrary, putting forward these ways of acting as moral ideals rather than duties that should be enforced would serve far more to develop self-respect, even if only a minority acted in these ways.

Rawls fails to include enforcement as part of his basic theory because he is primarily interested not in basic moral theory, but rather in basic political theory. It is not the duties for individuals that determines how he sets up the original position and its various features; rather, it is the two principles of justice. If one is primarily concerned with these principles, it is out of place to be concerned with enforcement. These principles are not ones that individuals can either obey or disobey; rather, they are principles by which one evaluates the institutions of the society in which one lives.

The priority that Rawls gives basic political theory over basic moral theory is clear from his claim that "in most cases the principles for obligations and duties should be settled upon after those for the basic structure" (p. 110) He offers no argument for this and indeed says that "it would be possible to choose many of the natural duties before those for the basic structure" (Ibid.). Indeed, all of his negative duties could be so chosen, and only his positive duty to support just institutions seems in any straightforward way to depend upon the two principles of justice. Rawls, like the classical utilitarians he is seeking to supplant, is more interested in basic political theory than individual moral theory.

This interest may explain why Rawls makes no distinction at all between "the duty to help another when he is in need or jeopardy" (p. 114) and "the duty to do something good for another" (Ibid.) or the "natural duty to bring about a great good" (p. 117). That is, he makes no distinction between following what I call the moral ideals, relieving or preventing evils, and what I call utilitarian ideals, promoting goods. This distinction is of lesser importance when considering governments, but it is quite important when talking about the actions of individuals, for in normal circumstances, only moral ideals, not utilitarian ones, can justify one individual violating a moral rule with regard to another.

Given that his positive duties are not really duties at all, and that Rawls designs his account of what is supererogatory primarily on the basis of his positive duties, it becomes quite clear that his account of the supererogatory is fundamentally flawed as well. One is left with very little of value in the details of his account of a moral system for individuals. None of this is due to a flaw in the theory of morality as impartial rationality; rather, the flaws are brought about by the failure to consider with sufficient care the moral system that is derived from the moral theory.

Conclusion

In summary, the faults commonly found in the theory of morality as impartial rationality are not faults intrinsic to the theory; rather, they are faults that stem from an inadequate statement of the theory. Baier and Rawls both provide inadequate accounts of rationality, neither fully recognizing that rationality should be analyzed in terms of content rather than form and that irrationality rather than rationality should be taken as basic. Both regard impartiality as requiring unanimity, and thus do not realize that equally informed impartial rational persons may, in many circumstances, advocate different ways of acting. Neither regards the question of enforcement as essential to basic moral theory, thus making it unlikely that they will provide an adequate moral system, one that distinguishes between moral rules, which may be enforced, and moral ideals, which should not be. Neither gives serious consideration to either the formulation of particular moral rules or to the procedure for determining exceptions to these rules.

Baier and Rawls never attempt to apply their accounts to particular ethical problems; they emphasize the evaluative rather than the practical aspects of morality as impartial rationality. This may explain, in part, why their moral systems are inadequate when one attempts to use them as practical guides to conduct. My criticism of their presentations of morality as impartial rationality is designed to show that one need not reject this theory if one does not accept their versions of it. If an ethical theory is going to be of any use as a moral guide, it must be as a practical theory. Morality as impartial rationality is, or can be presented as, a practical ethical theory. As such it can provide useful guidance to those who are looking for help in solving real moral problems. In the following chapter I shall provide some practical applications of the moral system that I have provided.[14]

14

APPLICATIONS OF
THE MORAL SYSTEM

In the preceding chapters I provide both a moral theory and a moral system. The moral theory involves analyses of the concepts of morality, rationality, good and evil, moral rules and ideals, and impartiality and demonstrations of how these concepts are related to each other. Using the analyses of these concepts together with their relationship to each other I generate the moral system that not only accounts for all the considered moral judgments on which people agree but also explains why they sometimes disagree. It is also a system that people can actually use in dealing with real moral problems. This system consists of moral rules and ideals and a procedure for determining when it is morally acceptable to violate a moral rule. In this chapter, I shall provide a very brief summary of the analyses of the concepts mentioned above, a somewhat fuller summary of the moral system, and a more detailed account of how the moral system can be applied to real cases.

Morality

This whole book should be taken as providing an adequate answer to the question posed by its first three words, "What is morality?" A summary definition of morality can be given by making use of the other concepts mentioned in the previous paragraph. Morality is a public system that applies to all rational persons insofar as their behavior affects others, its goal is the minimization of evil suffered, and the moral rules form a central part of it. A justified moral system is one that all impartial rational persons, using only those beliefs that are shared by all rational persons, would advocate adopting as a public system that applies to all rational persons. I believe that any system that satisfies the definition of morality will be a justified moral system. I also believe that there is only one such system, viz., the one described in this book.

A public system is a system that is understood and could be accepted by all those who are subject to it. Since morality is a public system that applies to all rational persons, this means that it is understood and could be accepted by all rational persons as a guide to their conduct and as a basis for making judgments on the conduct of others. Examination of the moral rules, which are the central part of morality, confirms both that morality is concerned with the behavior of rational persons that affects others and that an essential function of morality is to minimize the amount of evil suffered by rational persons. The main elements of the moral system are the moral rules which prohibit doing the kinds of actions which cause evil to be suffered, the moral ideals which encourage doing the kinds of actions which prevent or relieve the suffering of evil, and the procedure or attitude that is used to determine when it is justifiable to violate the rules.

Rationality and Good and Evil

Death, pain, disability, loss of freedom, and loss of pleasure make up the list which helps define both what counts as an irrational action and what counts as an evil. An irrational action is an action which increases the agent's chances of suffering an evil without an adequate reason. Another list—ability, freedom, and pleasure—defines what counts as a good and together with the previous list determines what counts as a reason for acting. A reason is a conscious belief, not obviously inconsistent with what one knows, that one's action will, directly or indirectly, help someone, oneself or someone else, avoid an evil or gain a good. The adequacy of a reason is determined by comparing the goods and evils caused, avoided, and prevented. A person can act rationally without having any reasons for her actions, she needs reasons for acting only if her action is likely to result in harm to herself or those she cares for. Although reasons and motives are both beliefs, not all reasons are motives for all rational persons, e.g., a belief that one's action will benefit someone else is not a motive for a rational egoist, nor are all motives reasons, e.g., a belief that someone I hate will be injured by my suicide, though it may be a motive, is not a reason. In conflicts between morality and the interests of oneself or those for whom one cares, it is rationally allowed to act in either way.

Impartiality

Impartiality is a more complex concept than generally acknowledged; it involves specifying not only who is impartial, but also toward what group one is impartial and in what respect. A person is impartial with regard to members of a group in a certain respect when his actions involving this respect are not influenced at all by which members of the group benefit or are harmed by those actions. Morality requires impartiality of all rational persons with regard to a group that includes, at least, all rational persons, with respect to obeying or violating a moral rule. Impartiality is not required with respect to following the moral ideals, for it would be impossible to satisfy this requirement. Impartial rational persons need not always agree on the answer they would give to every moral question, even if they are all fully informed and even if they have the same beliefs about the relevant risks and benefits, for they may rank the goods and evils differently. When all impartial rational persons agree on the answer to a particular moral question that is the morally right answer; when they do not agree, the limits of moral acceptability are determined by what impartial rational persons can accept.

The Moral System

THE MORAL RULES

1. Don't kill.
2. Don't cause pain.
3. Don't disable.
4. Don't deprive of freedom.
5. Don't deprive of pleasure.

6. Don't deceive.
7. Keep your promise.
8. Don't cheat.
9. Obey the law.
10. Do your duty.

The first rule prohibits causing permanent loss of consciousness, whether or not the organism dies; the second rule prohibits causing mental suffering as well as physical pain; the third rule also prohibits causing the loss of ability; the fourth rule prohibits causing the loss of opportunity, or any interference with the exercise of one's abilities; and the fifth rule prohibits causing loss of future as well as present pleasure.

THE MORAL ATTITUDE

The moral attitude, which in the moral theory is used to determine what rules are justified moral rules, in the moral system is the procedure used to determine what counts as a justifiable violation of a moral rule. It goes as follows: "Everyone is always to obey the rule except when an impartial rational person can advocate that violating it be publicly allowed. Anyone who violates the rule when an impartial rational person could not advocate that such a violation be publicly allowed may be punished."

The "except" clause of the moral attitude does not mean that all impartial rational persons agree that one is not to obey the rule when an impartial rational person can advocate publicly allowing such a violation, only that they need not agree that one should obey the rule in this situation.

MORAL IDEALS

The moral ideals, such as "Help the needy," "Relieve pain," etc. must be distinguished from the moral rules. The rules can be obeyed impartially with regard to all rational persons all of the time, twenty-four hours a day, seven days a week, fifty-two weeks a year. The ideals cannot be obeyed in this way. It is impossible to follow them impartially with regard to all rational persons all of the time. This point should become clear to the persons now reading this book when they realize that at this moment they are not violating any of the moral rules, but that they are also not following any moral ideals, though perhaps they are preparing themselves to do so. The distinction between the moral rules and the moral ideals is important, not because there is, or should be, a stronger internal motivation to obey the rules than to follow the ideals, nor because in any conflict between the rules and the ideals the rules should prevail over the ideals, but because it is not morally acceptable to use force to get people to follow the ideals. Punishment is morally acceptable only for some violations of the moral rules, it is never morally acceptable for simply failing to follow a moral ideal.

MORALLY RELEVANT FEATURES

When considering a violation of a moral rule only the answers to the following questions provide morally relevant features for determining the kind of violation. If all the answers to all of these questions are the same with regard to two distinct acts, then these two acts are the same kind of violation.

1. What moral rules are being violated?
2. What evils are being (a) avoided? (b) prevented? (c) caused?
3. What are the relevant desires of the people affected by the violation?
4. What are the relevant rational beliefs of the people affected by the violation?
5. Does one have a duty to violate moral rules with regard to the person, and is one in a unique position in this regard?
6. What goods are being promoted?
7. Is an unjustified or weakly justified violation of a moral rule being prevented?
8. Is an unjustified or weakly justified violation of a moral rule being punished?

When considering what evil is being avoided, prevented, and caused, and what good is being promoted, one must consider not only the kind of evil or good, and its seriousness, which includes its duration, but also its probability of occurring. One also must consider not only how many people will suffer the evil or gain the good, but also the distribution of the harm and the benefit.

Once the kind of violation has been determined then whether impartial rational persons would advocate that such a violation be publicly allowed depends upon what they believe to be the correct answer to the morally decisive question: "What effect would this kind of violation of the rules have if publicly allowed?"

For almost all violations by individuals, if it is clear that publicly allowing this kind of violation would result in more evil being suffered than not publicly allowing it, then no impartial rational person would advocate that it be publicly allowed. If it is clear that less evil would be suffered, then all impartial rational persons would advocate that it be publicly allowed. When it is not clear whether or not more or less evil would be suffered, either because the facts are not clear, or because rational persons rank the evils in different ways, then impartial rational persons will differ on whether to advocate that the violation be publicly allowed. For violations by governments one must usually also take into account the amount of good promoted: a worse balance of good and evil would result in no impartial person advocating that it be publicly allowed; a better balance, in all impartial persons advocating that it be publicly allowed; and disagreement among impartial rational persons when it is not clear whether the balance will be better or worse.

Applications of the Moral System

I shall be primarily concerned with problems in medical ethics because this is an area in which I have actually applied the moral system to real cases. Most of the cases on which I have been consulted do not provide any philosophical problems. Once everyone has become aware of all the relevant facts, there has almost always been complete agreement on what should be done. Further, this agreement is not the result of explicitly applying any particular moral system, but is almost spontaneous, even though application of the moral system has sometimes been helpful in making people feel more comfortable with their decision. This has reinforced my view that most moral disagreements are disagreements about the facts, not disagreements about values. However, there are two kinds of cases that do require some philosophical discussion, paternalistic behavior and euthanasia.

Paternalism

Informed or valid consent is such a morally significant part of medical practice because medical treatment almost always involves the violation of a moral rule, often the causing of pain, or a significant risk of suffering some other evil. Since medical treatment normally involves violating moral rules with regard to a patient, it requires justification. Usually the balance of evil prevented over evil produced by the treatment is not, by itself, sufficient to strongly justify the violation; often the balance is not, by itself, sufficiently great to even weakly justify the violation. Informing a patient of the possible harms and benefits of the proposed treatment and of medically acceptable alternative treatments, including no treatment at all, provides the patient with relevant rational beliefs about the treatment. The process also informs the physician of the patient's relevant desires concerning the treatment. If a competent patient with adequate relevant rational beliefs concerning the treatment has a rational desire that the physician violate whatever rules are necessary to carry out the treatment, then since the evil prevented or good promoted clearly compensates for the evil caused, the violations required by the treatment are strongly justified; all impartial rational persons would advocate that the violation be publicly allowed.

Paternalism in medicine involves acting without a competent patient's consent, on the belief that the balance of evil prevented over evil caused for that patient, by itself, justifies the violation of a moral rule with regard to him. Sometimes this belief is correct, but often it is not. Before one can determine when paternalism is justified, one needs a clear statement of what counts as a paternalistic action.

One is acting paternalistically toward a person if and only if (one's behavior correctly indicates that one believes that):

1. one's action benefits that person,
2. one's action involves violating a moral rule with regard to that person,
3. one's action does not have that person's past, present, or immediately forth-coming consent, and
4. that person is competent to give consent (simple or valid) to the violation.

Feature 1 explains why one considers oneself justified in violating the moral rule. Whether or not one is actually justified depends in part on the kind and degree of the benefit. There are two kinds of benefits: the first is to procure some good for that person, i.e., to increase his ability, freedom, or pleasure; the second is to prevent or ameliorate some evil he might suffer, such as pain or disability. Paternalistic acts can involve benefitting of either kind although, except for the government, parents, and others similarly situated, it is almost always only the paternalistic prevention of evils that is sometimes justified.

Feature 2 explains why paternalistic behavior needs justification, without restricting it to depriving a person of freedom for his own good. Paternalism can also involve violating the moral rules against killing, causing pain, disabling, depriving of pleasure, deceiving, breaking a promise or cheating. Although paternalistic behavior always involves the belief (or knowledge) that one is performing one of these kinds of actions, it does not require one to think of these actions as violations of moral rules. It is customary to talk about killing, deceiving, and breaking a promise as violations of moral rules, but there is no such linguistic tradition with regard to causing someone mental or physical pain or disabling him, although to do so without justification is clearly immoral.

Since paternalistic behavior always requires justification, refusal to follow moral ideals does not count as paternalistic, e.g., refusing to give money to a beggar because one believes he will only buy whisky with it which will be harmful to him. Such behavior may reveal a paternalistic attitude, that is, a willingness to act paternalistically toward the beggar if the situation arises, but it is not itself a paternalistic act. Only when one's action requires moral justification is it appropriate to call it paternalistic, as contrasted with paternal.

Feature 3 makes it clear that one morally relevant feature that could make it justifiable to violate a moral rule with regard to someone, viz., his consent, does not apply to paternalistic behavior. If one has the person's consent, or if she expects it to be immediately forthcoming, then an action which might otherwise be paternalistic is not so. For example, suppose one pulls someone from the path of an oncoming car which she believes he does not see. If she acts because she thinks that he will approve of the action immediately, the action is not paternalistic even though it may satisfy all the other conditions of paternalistic behavior. If she thinks that he is trying to commit suicide because of a temporary depression and that he will be thankful later when he recovers, then the act is paternalistic. Even when the expectation of future consent is a virtual certainty, the action is still paternalistic. For example, when a psychiatrist hospitalizes a depressed suicidal patient against his wishes, even though she knows almost for certain that the patient will be effusively thankful within two or three days, she is still acting paternalistically.

Feature 4 is presupposed in many accounts of paternalism but rarely is made explicit. We can act paternalistically only toward those whom we regard as competent to give either simple or valid consent. We cannot act paternalistically toward infants and comatose persons because they are not competent to give even simple consent. To be competent to give simple consent is to have at least some relevant rational beliefs about the violation of the moral rule with regard to oneself; to be competent to give valid consent is to have enough relevant rational beliefs about the moral rule violation that one can understand and appreciate all the information that an impartial rational person would consider adequate for deciding whether or not one wanted that rule violated with regard to oneself.

Justifying Paternalistic Behavior

In order to justify paternalistic behavior, it is necessary, not sufficient, that the moral rule violation prevent so much more evil for the person than the evil, if any, caused by it, that it would be irrational for him not to choose having the rule violated with regard to himself. When this is not the case, then the paternalistic behavior cannot be justified. If, given all the facts, it would not be irrational for the person to choose suffering the evil prevented by the violation rather than having the moral rule violated with regard to himself, then no impartial rational person would publicly allow this kind of violation of the rule. Publicly allowing the violation of a moral rule with regard to a competent person without his consent, when it is rationally allowed for the person to prefer the evil suffered without the rule violation to the evil suffered with the rule violation would result in a far worse situation than if such a violation were not publicly allowed. It would allow others to break moral rules in order to achieve their rational ranking of evils even when the victim of the violation has a different rational ranking.

The only factors that are morally relevant in specifying a given kind of violation are the answers to the questions that are included in the list of morally relevant features. When considering paternalistic behavior, the only features that distinguish one kind of paternalistic behavior from another are answers to the following questions: (questions 7 and 8 do not seem relevant.)

1. What moral rules are being violated?
2. What evils are being (a) avoided? (b) prevented? (c) caused?
3. What are the relevant desires of the people affected by the violation?
4. What are the relevant rational beliefs of the people affected by the violation?
5. Does one have a duty to violate moral rules with regard to the person, and is one in a unique, or almost unique, position in this regard?
6. What goods are being promoted?

These features alone determine the circumstances we must take into account when we determine the kind of violation. What is then needed is to determine whether an impartial rational person could advocate that this kind of violation be publicly allowed. This is done by deciding whether the evil that would result from this kind of violation being publicly allowed outweighs the evil that would result from it not being publicly allowed. If all impartial rational persons would agree that the evil resulting from the violation being publicly allowed would be less than the evil resulting from it not being publicly allowed, the violation is strongly justified; if none would, it is unjustified. If impartial rational persons disagree, it is a weakly justified violation; such cases are the most troublesome.

Determining whether an impartial rational person could advocate that it be publicly allowed that everyone deceive in certain circumstances is decided by seeing whether any impartial rational person would consider the consequences of publicly allowing this kind of violation preferable to the consequences of it not being publicly allowed. The following example may make the point clearer. A young woman of about thirty-five has come in with pain in the stomach. After going through several tests, the doctor discovers that she is suffering from inoperable cancer, and that she has from three to six months to live. Her pain, however, has temporarily gone away, and she and her family—she has two children, ages 9 and 12—are planning to go on a long delayed two week vacation. The woman is highly educated, a college graduate, and repeatedly asks the doctor to tell her what is wrong with her. What should the doctor do?

The options are (1) tell her the truth now or (2) tell her that you are not yet sure but that you will know in about two weeks and let her know when she gets back from her vacation. Option (2) involves deceiving her, but will supposedly allow her and her family to enjoy themselves on their vacation before they have to face the awful truth. What should be done? Many doctors would pick option (2) because they believe that in this particular situation less evil would be suffered. Utilitarianism would support this answer. However, in the situation as I have described it, this is the wrong answer. It is wrong because no impartial rational person would publicly allow one person to deceive another in order to prevent unpleasant feelings when the person to be deceived has a rational desire to know the truth.

One way to avoid partiality when considering any example is to restate it in completely general terms, those terms that would be understood by all rational persons. Suppose someone ranks unpleasant feelings for several weeks as a greater evil than the evil involved in the loss of some opportunity to plan for the future. Should he be allowed to deceive those who may have a different rational ranking if his deception will result in their suffering what the deceiver regards as the lesser evil? Would any impartial rational person hold that it be publicly allowed to deceive in these circumstances, that is, would any rational person advocate that this kind of violation be publicly allowed? Once the case is made clear enough, no impartial rational person would advocate that such a violation be publicly allowed. For it amounts to publicly allowing deception in order to impose one's own ranking of evils on others who have an alternative rational ranking. Not only would publicly allowing deception in such circumstances result in everyone being more likely to suffer the evils they considered more serious, it also would clearly have the most disastrous consequences on one's trust in the words of others. Publicly allowing this kind of violation would have far worse consequences on any rational ranking than not publicly allowing it, so that no impartial rational person would advocate that such a violation be publicly allowed.

Another way to make this point clear is to change the example, while keeping the morally relevant features, those presented abstractly in the previous paragraph, the same. A doctor has bought a new medical stock that is sold over the counter, some version of Genentech, and has had it for several months. It is not listed in the paper and he has not been concerned about it, so he does not know how it has been doing. Since he is now going on a long delayed two week vacation and wants to know how his stock is doing, he calls the broker with whom he has been dealing. The broker knows that the stock has gone way down, but that this is typical of these kinds of stocks; they come out high, drop sharply the next couple of months and then slowly begin to work their way back up. This stock looks as if it has hit bottom and is just about ready to start coming back up. The broker has two options (1) tell the doctor what the stock is selling for now or (2) tell him that it is doing as expected and that she will talk to him about it in more detail when he returns from his vacation. The stock broker is inclined to choose option (2) because not only will it enable the doctor to enjoy his vacation without the anxiety caused by knowing how much he has lost on his investment, but also because there is some probability that the doctor will panic and sell the stock at what the stockbroker takes to be its lowest point. Most doctors will say that the stock broker should not deceive. Even more interesting, some say that it is not sufficient to simply say what the stock is selling at, the broker should also point out all the facts about how such stocks normally perform. Similarly, the doctor should not merely inform the woman that she has terminal cancer, he should explain the situation as clearly as possible and provide support.

The value of using a moral system is that it allows one to judge a situation with an impartiality that is almost impossible to achieve when one considers only the particular case. If one believes that no impartial rational person would publicly allow a violation of the rule prohibiting deception in order to prevent bad feelings when the person being deceived wants to know the truth, then it is not morally allowed to deceive in this kind of situation, even if one is a doctor. Publicly allowing such a violation means that everyone knows that it is allowed to deceive in this kind of situation and this, as discussed earlier, would have consequences far worse than the consequences if this kind of violation were not publicly allowed. To admit that no impartial rational persons would publicly allow it, but to maintain nonetheless that it is justifiable for oneself to deceive in this case is to make a special exception for oneself. This is to abandon the kind of impartiality that the moral rules require, it is to behave in an arrogant manner, regarding oneself as not subject to the same moral system which applies to more ordinary mortals.

Negative Utilitarianism

In discussing the justification of paternalism, it is very easy to fall into the error of supposing that all that we need do is compare evils prevented with evils caused and always decide in favor of the lesser evil. It is this kind of view, a relatively straightforward negative utilitarianism, which seems to be held by many doctors and may account for much of their paternalistic behavior. If one holds this view, then she thinks that if she is preventing more evil for the person than she is causing him, this is sufficient to justify violating a moral rule with regard to that person. Taking this straightforward negative utilitarian view, one can easily understand why paternalistic acts of deception done in order to prevent or postpone mental suffering, as in the case described above, are so common. Little if any evil seems to be caused, and mental suffering is prevented, at least for a time; thus it seems as if such acts are morally justified.

Although the foreseeable consequences of a particular act are not the only morally relevant considerations, they are, of course, very significant, for they help determine the kind of act involved. Negative utilitarianism is not an adequate ethical theory because it involves considering only the evils caused, avoided, and prevented by the particular violation (a negative rule utilitarian would include the effects on the rule) and perhaps comparing them with the evils caused, avoided, and prevented by a different violation. However, for violations of a moral rule, considering the consequences of the particular act and of alternative acts is not enough; the consequences of publicly allowing this kind of violation must be compared with the consequences of publicly allowing different kinds of violations. In many cases, comparing the consequences of different kinds of violations being publicly allowed will lead to the same moral judgment as comparing only the consequences of the particular act and its alternatives. This may explain why many physicians have taken the simpler comparison to be sufficient.

The inadequacy of utilitarianism can be seen by considering the following example: a medical student has not studied during the weeks preceding the state medical examinations she is about to take, but believes herself to be well qualified for the practice of medicine. Since passing the first time is important for her, she is thinking about cheating. If she cheats in order to increase her chances of qualifying sooner for the practice of medicine she will prevent the unpleasant feelings to herself and her parents which would accompany failure. She has good reasons to believe that her cheating will not cause harm to anyone; the exam is not graded on a curve and she is sure that no one will find out so that the rule against cheating will not be weakened. If, as seems to be the case, the evils prevented by the violation are greater than the evils caused, a simple negative utilitarian view would regard the violation as morally justified.

Publicly allowing cheating for the purpose of decreasing unpleasant feelings whenever one has good reason to believe that no one will be hurt by the cheating will have serious consequences. Since everyone knows that such cheating is allowed it will destroy the value of those tests on which we rely, in part, to determine who is qualified for medical practice. Some individuals, who may believe themselves qualified when in fact they are not, will cheat and thereby pass. The effect of less qualified people becoming doctors is an increased risk of the population's suffering greater evils, such as pain and disability. Publicly allowing cheating involves holding that the activity in which the cheating occurs should be abolished, for it results in more evil suffered than evil prevented. If one holds the activity is worthwhile, that the evil prevented (or good promoted) more than compensates for the evil caused, then one cannot publicly allow cheating simply in order to prevent the suffering caused to those who would fail without cheating. Use of this more complex balancing leads to the conclusion that such acts of cheating are not morally justified. The long-range evils associated with this kind of violation being publicly allowed so far outweigh the unpleasant feelings that would be prevented that publicly allowing it would be irrational; no impartial rational person could advocate that it be publicly allowed.

Another Example

A fifty-year-old patient in a rehabilitation ward is recovering from the effects of a stroke. A major part of his treatment consists of daily visits to the physical therapy unit, where he is given repetitive exercises to increase the strength and mobility of his partially paralyzed left arm and leg. He is initially cooperative with his physical therapist, but soon becomes bored with the monotony of the daily sessions and frustrated by his failure to adequately move his partially paralyzed limbs and by his very slow progress. He tells his therapist that he does not wish to attend the remaining three weeks of daily sessions. The therapist's experience is that if such patients stop the sessions early, they do not receive the full therapeutic benefit possible and may suffer for the remainder of their lives from a significantly more disabled arm and leg than would be the case if they exercised now in this critical, early post-stroke period. Accordingly, she first emphasizes these facts in order to persuade him to continue exercising. When that is not effective, she becomes rather stern and scolds and chides him for two days. He then relents and begins exercising again, but it is necessary for the therapist to chastise him almost daily to obtain his continued participation over the ensuing three weeks.

The therapist's scolding and chiding is paternalistic behavior: she is causing the patient some psychological pain and discomfort without his consent for what she believes to be his benefit. She further believes that the patient is competent to give or refuse valid consent to physical therapy. She could claim that the relatively minor amount of evil she is inflicting by chiding him is much less than the evil he will experience by being significantly more disabled than necessary for the rest of his life. The therapist could claim that either the patient does not have adequate rational beliefs or that his ranking of the relevant evils is irrational. Accepting the therapist's claims leads to a description of her violation as inflicting a mild degree of suffering on the patient (through her chiding and his resumed exercising) by imposing her rational ranking of evils on a patient, whose ranking is (or would be if he had the facts) irrational. An impartial rational person could advocate that this kind of violation be publicly allowed, although some impartial rational persons might not do so. On this very limited description of the case this violation is only weakly justified. When dealing with a real case more details about the degree of added disability the patient will suffer, how much psychological pain is actually involved, etc., would be requested before a decision would be made.

This case involves the balancing of evils which, while significant, are not a matter of life and death. The amount of evil associated with the possibility of the stroke victim's needlessly greater lifelong disability seems just significant enough, primarily because of its permanence—and the unpleasantness of three weeks of exercising even together with the unpleasantness caused by the scolding, seems mild enough, primarily because of their short duration—that it seems irrational to prefer the former to the latter. Causing these mild evils by scolding thus seems to be a case of justified paternalism, although some impartial rational persons might not advocate that it be publicly allowed. Some kinds of paternalistic intervention would not be justified in this case. It would be unjustified to inflict intense physical pain on him to force him to exercise. The amount of evil associated with the possibility of his increased disability is not great enough so that one could advocate that such a violation be publicly allowed.

Philosophically, the most interesting alternative to consider is the possibility of lying to him. Suppose the therapist told him that unless he continued to exercise for three more weeks he would regress and never be able to walk again but that if he did exercise she could guarantee his being able to walk. Suppose further that she knew that, in fact, he was almost certainly going to be able to walk in any event, but that, as described above, physical therapy would very likely decrease his ultimate level of disability. If the therapist did lie in this way, it might prove quite effective in quickly remotivating the stroke victim to exercise daily without the need for the therapist to chastise him at all. In fact, such a deception might cause the patient less total suffering than daily chiding would, if he now perceived the exercising as something he wanted to do, because through doing it he was guaranteed to eliminate the possibility of being unable to walk. Using a simple negative utilitarian method of calculation, it might seem that if chastisement were justifiable paternalism, lying would be even more strongly justifiable.

The patient's desire to discontinue physical therapy is (or would be if he knew the facts) irrational, so that this is not a case of lying in order to impose one person's rational ranking of the evils on another person with a different rational ranking, but rather lying in order to substitute a rational ranking for an irrational one. Could an impartial rational person publicly allow this kind of violation of the rule prohibiting deception? The morally relevant features determine this kind of act to be deception which causes a temporary (three weeks) mild discomfort (due to physical therapy) in order to prevent the possibility of a permanent (up to twenty or thirty years) though moderate increase of physical disability.

Determining the kind of violation that the therapist would commit by lying shows that lying is not morally justifiable. No impartial rational person would publicly allow lying in a situation where trust is extremely important e.g., between a doctor, nurse, or therapist and a patient, even in order to prevent an evil just significant enough that it is irrational not to avoid it, viz., the possibility of a permanent moderate increase in one's disability. The erosion of trust that would follow from this kind of violation being publicly allowed would have such significant evil consequences, e.g., legitimate warnings may come to be disregarded, that even preventing a significant number of persons from suffering a permanent moderate increase in disability is not enough to counterbalance these consequences. It is this kind of case, where the present moral system gives a different answer than that presented by negative utilitarianism, that creates the most difficulty and requires the most careful analysis. Particularly troubling is the fact that if the increase in disability is great enough, deception might be publicly allowed. This makes it sound as if at some point negative utilitarianism gives the right answer. However, what is really happening is that at some point, the kind of act becomes one that an impartial rational person can advocate be publicly allowed.

The conclusion of the previous paragraph gains more force when the irrationality of believing in unlimited knowledge is remembered and one realizes that it is never certain that lying will produce the desired result. In this case lying may cause significant anxiety for the patient, and if he talks to other patients even more anxiety may result. If the patient finds out that he has been deceived, which cannot be completely ruled out, bad consequences are inevitable. One must make moral judgments using only what is known at the time the decision must be made; this point gains even greater force when one realizes that one must consider the consequences of publicly allowing such violations. Further, one must recognize that lying may not be the only method whereby one can get the stroke victim to continue his treatment. It may be possible to get him to continue with no violations of a moral rule. If some violation is necessary, all impartial rational persons would advocate that chiding and scolding, though itself a violation of a moral rule, be publicly allowed as preferable to lying, even though it might cause more suffering in the particular case.

Given equal chances of success, most people presented with these alternative methods of getting the patient to continue treatment regard chiding and scolding as morally preferable to lying, and most regard lying as completely morally unacceptable. If one uses a simple negative utilitarian theory, this result cannot be accounted for, since in this particular case it is extremely plausible that lying results in no more and most probably less overall suffering than chiding and scolding. If one applies the method of justification provided by the present moral system, these moral intuitions are accounted for quite easily. First, count as the only relevant differences between the two kinds of violations the different moral rules violated: causing pain (the unpleasantness caused by the scolding) versus deception (lying about consequences of stopping treatment); and the amount of evil caused by the two different violations: assume slightly less for lying. This determines the two kinds of violation. If this were all that were involved in making a moral judgment then lying would be judged morally preferable to scolding. Second, determine what would be the consequences of publicly allowing these two kinds of violations. At this level it is clear that publicly allowing lying would have much worse consequences than publicly allowing scolding. This determines which violation an impartial rational person would prefer to publicly allow. The result accords with the moral intuitions that one actually finds.

The above case is typical of a multitude of everyday situations in medicine in which doctors, nurses, and other health care workers act or are tempted to act paternalistically toward patients. Consider the problems presented by the patient with emphysema who continues to smoke, by the alcoholic with liver damage who refuses to enter any treatment program, or by the diabetic or hypertensive patient who exacerbates his disease by paying little heed to dietary precautions. Each of these patients is apt to stimulate a desire for paternalistic acts by a variety of health care professionals (as well as members of his own family). Before acting, it is important to get as much information as possible, e.g., the probability and severity of the evil that will be prevented by the treatment, in order to determine which kinds of paternalistic acts are justifiable and which are not.

When doctors and other health care professionals realize that the moral system that applies to everyone else applies to them, then they realize that if they violate the moral rules when they would not publicly allow such violations, they are acting arrogantly. Of course this does not stop all of them from acting in this way, but at least they realize what they are doing. My experience with doctors is that they do not want to behave arrogantly, that they are genuinely perplexed by some of the moral problems that have arisen because of the new medical technology. The most troubling moral problems are those that arise in dealing with patients who want to die. Is it ever morally justifiable to kill such patients? Is it ever morally justifiable to allow them to die? For such patients is there any morally significant difference between killing them and allowing them to die? A philosophically useful distinction between active and passive euthanasia should help one answer these questions.

Active Versus Passive Euthanasia

The distinction between active and passive euthanasia is an important one for doctors. Active euthanasia is prohibited by the American Medical Association while passive euthanasia is allowed, even though there is some dispute as to the proper way to make the distinction between active and passive euthanasia. I am going to limit my discussion here to competent patients whose decision to die is rational, that is, for whom continuing to live involves so much pain and suffering for themselves and often their loved ones as well, that it is rational for them to choose to die although, of course, it is also rational to choose to continue to live. In many situations it is rational to choose either of two incompatible alternatives. What is the morally right way to deal with such patients?

I am now concerned with deciding what a doctor should do when he has a competent patient who has made a rational choice to die. Some say that it is morally acceptable for the doctor to do nothing, that is, not to initiate any treatment, that this is passive euthanasia and is morally allowed. On this account, it is not morally acceptable to do something that results in the patient's death; injecting the patient with an overdose of morphine and turning off the respirator are both examples of *doing* something and hence are active euthanasia. Others say that the distinction between acts and omissions is not adequate. They say that it is the distinction between ordinary and extraordinary care that is important. It is not acting or omitting which is important; it is the character of what is being done or not done that is important. If being on a respirator is extraordinary care then either not starting it or stopping it counts as passive euthanasia and is morally acceptable, but providing food and fluids, even when done by mechanical means, is ordinary care, and either not starting or stopping is active euthanasia and is not morally allowed.

How can one decide between these two ways of distinguishing active from passive euthanasia? And even if one can, why should the distinction be of any moral significance? I am going to show how using the moral system suggests a way to make a distinction between active and passive euthanasia that does have moral significance. I take the distinction between active and passive euthanasia to be the same as the distinction between killing and allowing to die. The distinction between active and passive euthanasia arises for both competent patients and for incompetent ones; in what follows I shall concentrate on the distinction as it applies to competent patients, what is technically known as "voluntary euthanasia." I do this for two reasons: first, the distinction as it applies to incompetent patients is parasitic on the distinction as it applies to competent patients, and second, the application of the moral system to competent patients is much more straightforward.

Passive euthanasia differs from active euthanasia in that the former consists in abiding by a competent patient's informed rational refusal of life sustaining treatment whereas the latter consists in acquiescing to a competent patient's informed rational request for a treatment that will kill him. In deciding whether an action or failure to act counts as active or passive euthanasia the first question is: What moral rule is being broken by the physician's action or failure to act? In active euthanasia, the rule that the physician breaks is "Don't Kill." In passive euthanasia, he does not break any moral rule. Since the results of both active and passive euthanasia are the same, the patient dies, something like this has to be the case if there is to be sufficient moral difference between active and passive euthanasia to make it morally justifiable to engage in passive euthanasia and not in active euthanasia.

The Distinction Between Starting and Stopping Treatment

Consider two competent terminally ill patients alike in all respects except that one has just been put on a respirator while the other is about to be. After considering their future prospects, which are quite bleak, they both give informed rational refusals of respirator care: the former directing that he be taken off, the latter that he not be put on. If a competent adequately informed patient rationally refuses treatment, then it would be an unjustified paternalistic act to treat him without consent. That treatment has already been started on one patient but not yet started on the other makes no morally significant difference between their rational refusals. It would be equally unjustified to overrule either, even though it is psychologically much more difficult for a physician to take a patient off a respirator than not to put him on. Clear recognition of the moral equivalence of abiding by a rational valid refusal to continue respirator treatment and a similar refusal not to start it may, in fact, lessen the psychological burden on the physician.

On the level of practice, many doctors suspect that there is no morally significant difference between not starting treatment and discontinuing it, but given the misleading identification of passive euthanasia with omissions and active euthanasia with actions, it is not surprising that there has been significant confusion concerning the matter. This has sometimes had serious practical consequences. Some physicians feel compelled to make the critical decision about treating or not treating prior to putting a patient on a respirator, because they believe that once the patient is on the respirator it would count as active euthanasia, killing, to take him off. This may sometimes result in decisions being made in haste and without sufficient information. Patients who might benefit from being put on a respirator may not be put on because of the high probability that they will become respirator dependent until they eventually die. Recognition that taking a patient who refuses treatment off a respirator counts as passive euthanasia allows the physician to postpone the critical decision until he has had sufficient time to determine all the relevant information.

Stopping Food and Fluids as Passive Euthanasia

Mistakenly classifying the removal of "ordinary" care, such as feeding, as active euthanasia and counting only the removal of "extraordinary" care, such as a respirator, as passive causes some problems for the medical profession. Given that active euthanasia is not acceptable to the American Medical Association, classifying stopping feeding and hydration as active conflicts with the growing consensus that stopping feeding and hydration at the request of a competent patient is morally acceptable medical practice. Considerable confusion exists because there is no adequate theoretical explanation for classifying stopping feeding as passive rather than active euthanasia. On the present analysis of "passive," it is quite clear why stopping feeding and hydration counts as passive when the patient or his surrogate has given a rational valid refusal. A competent patient can refuse feeding, like any other treatment, and if that refusal is informed and rational, then it is not morally justifiable to feed him against his will.

I recognize the tremendous symbolic character of stopping feeding. I am aware that if parents do not feed their children and the children die, that counts as starving the children; it is killing, not letting die. In the situation under discussion this is not the case; here a rational valid refusal by a competent patient, or his surrogate decision maker, is decisive. When such a patient refuses to be fed, it is not the doctor's duty to feed anyway; on the contrary, the doctor is morally required not to feed. This is true even if the feeding is not done by tubes but in a more natural fashion. The physician is not morally required, though he is not morally prohibited either, to acquiesce to the patient's request to make his refusal of treatment more comfortable, e.g., to give pain medication or even to allow the patient to remain in the hospital, if the patient refuses food and fluids—this was the issue in the Bouvier case—or any other life-sustaining treatment. However, if it is clear that the patient will go ahead with his refusal, the moral ideal of relieving pain encourages doing what one can to ease the pain of dying.

The physician is not morally permitted to force feed a competent patient who has made a rational valid refusal to eat and does not request medical assistance. If this means the patient will die, then the physician has not killed him. It is true that seeking to prevent death is following a moral ideal and following this moral ideal normally needs no justification, for most people want to live. In the tragic case where it is rational to want to die, and a person has made this rational choice, it is disconcerting but correct that it is not morally justifiable to seek to prevent his death. To do so in these cases is to deprive a person of his freedom, and almost always to cause him to suffer significant pain. It is to impose one's own rational ranking of the evils on a person with a different rational ranking. Whatever the motivation for this paternalistic action, it is an arrogant action and cannot be morally justified.

What Is a Doctor's Duty?

Is it a doctor's duty to save her patient's life? If it is then it may be that failure to treat the patient does count as killing. Does a doctor have a duty to overrule an informed rational decision of a competent patient? How could anyone have such a duty? If people say that they want to be left alone, and they know the consequences of being left alone, and it is rational to want those consequences, then one should leave them alone. Not to do so is to unjustifiably violate the rule against depriving of freedom. No impartial rational person would advocate that people be publicly allowed to violate the rule against depriving of freedom when the person being deprived of freedom has a rational desire not to be so deprived, even if that means the person will die. Of course, for one to have a rational desire to want to die, it must be the case that continuing to live involves suffering significant evils without compensating goods.

When a competent patient rationally decides on no more treatment, it is not morally allowed to treat him. It makes no difference whether he does not want treatment started, or wants it stopped, whether it is the removal of the respirator or of antibiotics or of food and fluids. If he wants it stopped and that is a rational decision, the doctor has no moral choice but to go along with the rational refusal of treatment. This is not a conclusion which applies only to cases involving the death of a patient; that death will result if the patient is not treated does not change the conclusion although it makes it a more serious matter. This is why abiding by a competent patient's rational refusal of treatment is properly called "passive" euthanasia. It is not killing; it is not even clear that it is "allowing to die," for the doctor does not have a moral option to interfere. It is unjustified paternalism for a doctor to overrule a competent patient's rationally allowable refusal of treatment, even with regard to life-sustaining treatment.

Notice that the terms "ordinary" and "extraordinary," "starting" and "stopping," "act" and "omission," do not appear at all in explaining why passive euthanasia is morally acceptable. They are not morally significant. The moral rule involved in deciding whether or not to abide by a competent patient's informed rational refusal is not "Don't kill," but "Don't deprive of freedom." In the circumstances under discussion, no impartial rational person would advocate that a violation of this latter rule be publicly allowed. Given the account presented above we can see that when talking about voluntary euthanasia, "passive" refers to the doctor's acting (or refraining from action) when this is required by a rational valid *refusal* of a competent patient. "Active" means acting when this is not required by such a refusal, e.g., acting on a request for positive treatment by a patient. Suppose the patient asks the physician to inject him with some drug that will kill him. That is active euthanasia. It is a violation of the rule against killing.

Impartial rational persons can disagree on whether or not to publicly allow this kind of violation of the moral rule against killing because they have different views on the effects that publicly allowing this kind of violation would have (the morally decisive feature). Some may hold that given the limited knowledge of persons, the consequences of having this kind of violation publicly allowed would result in too many people being wrongly killed. Others may hold that the amount of extreme pain and suffering that would be prevented by publicly allowing this kind of violation would outweigh the very small number of wrongful deaths. Personally, I would not advocate that this kind of violation be publicly allowed, for given the understanding of passive euthanasia that I have provided, it seems to me that what is gained by publicly allowing active euthanasia does not compensate for the loss of force of the rule prohibiting killing. It is morally acceptable for physicians to administer pain medication to ease the pain of dying due to the refusal of treatment, and this does not violate the rule against killing.

It is the doctor's role vis-a-vis the patient that determines whether the euthanasia counts as active or passive: if a competent patient rationally refuses treatment, whatever the doctor does, e.g., turns off the respirator, or doesn't do, e.g., does not attempt resuscitation, counts as passive. If a competent patient rationally requests that the doctor treat him, e.g., give him an overdose of morphine, it is active. Passive euthanasia, when competent patients make such an informed and rational request, is not merely morally acceptable, it is unjustified paternalism to interfere. Active euthanasia may be morally acceptable; it involves a weakly justified violation of the rule prohibiting killing. Some impartial rational persons would advocate that a person be publicly allowed to violate the rule against killing with regard to a competent person who has a rational desire to be killed; however, some impartial rational persons would advocate that this not be publicly allowed.

Just as it is not morally permissible for physicians to force feed a competent patient who has made a rationally valid refusal to eat, it is also not morally permissible to feed and hydrate such a patient when he becomes incompetent. The patient's prior rational refusal continues to be decisive. The practical problem that physicians face is that most irreversibly incompetent, terminally ill patients, even those who have filled out Living Wills requesting no "extraordinary" treatment, have not explicitly expressed their wishes about whether feeding and hydration should also be stopped. All persons, but especially terminally ill patients, should be encouraged to explicitly state their wishes on this matter.

Living Wills should be amended appropriately, and surrogate decision makers, e.g., those who have been given durable power of attorney, should discuss these matters with patients while they are still competent.

The standard ways of distinguishing between active and passive euthanasia, act versus omission, and removal of ordinary versus removal of extraordinary care, do not have any clear moral significance. I have used the moral system to show how the physician-patient relationship enables one to make a morally significant distinction between active and passive euthanasia. Passive euthanasia is defined as the physician's abiding by the rational valid refusal of life-sustaining treatment of a patient or his surrogate decision-maker. It is obeying the moral rule against depriving a person of freedom. Understanding passive euthanasia in this way makes it clear why, everything else being equal, there is no morally significant difference between discontinuing a treatment and not starting it, e.g., taking a patient off a respirator versus not putting him on in the first place. It also makes clear why stopping the feeding and hydration of some patients is not merely morally permissible but morally required. Patients may make a rational valid refusal of food and fluids just as they may of other kinds of life support, and what patients rationally refuse when competent holds its force when they become incompetent.

The Value of a Universal Moral System

Basing the distinction between active and passive euthanasia on the universally recognized moral force of a rational valid refusal provides a clear understanding of the moral significance of this distinction. This way of making the distinction, which is grounded in the moral rule prohibiting the depriving of freedom, preserves for patients the control over their lives that has sometimes been unjustifiably taken from them. It also eases the burden on doctors who no longer are forced to make use of ad hoc and confused distinctions in which they justifiably have little faith. On a more abstract level it may show the usefulness of demanding that any morally significant distinction in medicine, e.g., between active and passive euthanasia, be justified by relating it to a universal moral system.

Some hold that there is, or can be, no universal moral system, only systems that apply to particular fields. Some who attempt to justify punishment think that the moral system that is appropriate for them to use cannot be the same one that should be used when doing medical ethics. However, one of the most important features of good work in applied ethics is that it shows how what may look like an acceptable solution to a moral problem in one field is not adequate because applying that same solution to another field comes up with a clearly unacceptable solution. It was only when physicians saw that there was no special moral system just for them that any progress was made in medical ethics.

Another virtue of having a universal moral system is that it enables one to organize a vast array of particular moral intuitions and thus to discover if they are all consistent. When we make moral decisions in individual cases without checking them against a universal system, we sometimes make different decisions in cases where all the morally relevant facts are the same. We may do this because we are swayed by morally irrelevant features, e.g., our friend is the one being punished, or simply because we did not see that the cases were morally similar. If we find a universal moral system that does, in fact, yield the answers that we would give in all of the clear cases, then that system can be used to help deal with the difficult problems in which we have no clear idea about what moral decision to make.

The goal of morality is to minimize the amount of evil suffered by persons. Committing an unjustified violation of a moral rule almost always increases the amount of evil suffered. However, some violations of a moral rule are justified, viz., those that an impartial rational person can advocate be publicly allowed. The primary practical function of a moral system is to help one determine which violations of the moral rules are justified. In order to do this one must determine whether or not an impartial rational person could advocate that such a violation be publicly allowed. This involves understanding what is meant by "rational" and "impartial," knowing that morality is a public system that applies to all rational persons, and knowing what counts as the same kind of violation, which involves knowing the morally relevant features of the act. When one knows all of this, it should be possible to redescribe a moral problem that occurs in business, medicine, government, or any other activity of rational persons in terms that all rational persons will understand. When this is done the same moral system should apply to all of these problems.

Summarizing the Moral Guide

To act morally is to act in the way that an impartial rational person can advocate be publicly allowed when the action is covered by either a moral rule or a moral ideal. It is very easy to forget this final qualification and to equate moral action with any action that an impartial rational person can advocate be publicly allowed. There is no great harm in this; acting as an impartial rational person can advocate be publicly allowed does rule out immoral action. However, ignoring the qualification tends to blur the distinction between acting morally and acting according to personal or utilitarian ideals. This tends to obscure the important fact that morality is primarily concerned with the minimization of evil, not with self-realization or the maximization of good. It is only for those who have duties in a political situation that the promotion of good sometimes justifies violations of the moral rules.

The Golden Rule, "Do unto others as you would have them do unto you," though it provides a guide that closely resembles the moral guide, is not identical with it. In fact, taken literally, it provides incorrect moral advice. It tells police and judges, at least those who have normal human desires, not to arrest or sentence criminals. Nor is there any simple way in which to modify it so that it does always provide the right moral advice in a complex situation. Even incorporating into the Golden Rule the concept of what an impartial rational person would advocate does not provide a completely adequate moral guide. "Do unto others as an impartial rational person would advocate they do unto you," though it eliminates many objections to the Golden Rule, still encourages one to do more than the moral guide. Changing it to the negative, "Do not do unto others what an impartial rational person would advocate they not do unto you," may be equivalent to the guide provided by the moral rules, but it leaves out those actions encouraged by the moral ideals. If one thinks of politics as involving more than morality, as involving not only the moral ideals, but also acting on the utilitarian ideals, then the Golden Rule, in its positive modification, can be regarded as the political guide to life.

The Ten Commandments are also inadequate as a complete moral system. These commandments leave out any mention of moral ideals; they incorporate only what is morally required. Also, as mentioned previously, they do not distinguish between moral rules or commandments and purely religious ones; the commandment to keep the Sabbath day to sanctify it is not distinguished from the commandments not to kill or steal. Even worse, the commandments seem to condone the clearly immoral practice of slavery. The commandment to keep the Sabbath includes the following passage: "But the seventh day is the Sabbath of the Lord thy God: in it thou shalt not do any work, thou, nor thy son, nor thy daughter, nor thy manservant, nor thy maidservant, nor thine ox, nor thine ass, nor any of thy cattle, nor thy stranger that is within thy gates; that thy manservant and thy maidservant may rest as well as thou." (Deuteronomy V:14) Manservants and maidservants are what we would call slaves. Granted that this passage recommends more humane treatment of slaves than was customary at the time, we still cannot take these commandments as providing a universally valid account of morality.

The moral guide can perhaps be best summarized in that ancient command, "Eschew evil; do good," where this is understood as meaning "Obey the moral rules; follow the moral ideals." It is unfortunate that the most familiar moral injunctions have to be modified or interpreted before they provide an adequate summary of the moral guide to life. I should have liked to be able to present an account of morality simple enough to be compressed into a saying as forceful as the more familiar moral injunctions. The best I can think of is "Always be just; be kind when you can." To which religion would add "And let the kindness be loving-kindness." Far more forceful is the patently derivative "What doth morality require of thee but to do justly and love mercy?" It is not mere coincidence that the familiar moral injunctions come so close to expressing the view of morality described in this book, for I do not consider myself as having presented a new morality, but simply as describing with more precision the nature of the morality which has been preached by all of the great moral and religious teachers of humankind.

The importance of presenting a precise account of morality lies primarily in the effect it may have on people's behavior. Although I am unable to hold that if one knows what is morally right he will always do it, I do think that many persons of good will will do what is morally wrong because they are unclear about the nature of morality. I fully agree with Hobbes's remark quoted at the beginning of this book, "The utility of moral and civil philosophy is to be estimated, not so much by the commodities we have by knowing these sciences, as by the calamities we receive from not knowing them."

Philosophical understanding, such as that provided by this book, is not enough. People must come to care for all other persons. Yet it is extremely hard to come to care for all other persons if it is clear that they do not care for you. To the deprived citizens of a country it is clear that other persons do not care for them. To show them that other persons do care, government must actively seek to eliminate all deprivation. It is also necessary for the natural compassion of humankind to be broadened and deepened. People must learn to care for others who are suffering regardless of their country, race, or religious beliefs. This is a task for art and religion. They, and not philosophy, have the power to increase a person's compassion and to widen its scope. More important, this compassion must yield a concern for humankind which is active even apart from the compassion that generates it. Parents and teachers, indeed all those who are responsible for the teaching of children, have a crucial role, for if children do not learn to care for others while they are young, it may be impossible to teach them when they are older. I have shown what morality is. Others are needed to teach people to follow it.

NOTES

Chapter 1

1. For further clarification of this concept, see "Voluntary Abilities" by T. Duggan and B. Gert, *American Philosophical Quarterly*, April, 1967, pp. 127-135 (reprinted in *The Nature of Human Action*, edited by Myles Brand); and "Free Will as the Ability to Will" by B. Gert and T. Duggan. *Nous*, 13, 1979, pp. 197-217 (reprinted in *Moral Responsibility*, edited by John Fisher). See also Chapter 6, Volitional Disabilities, in *Philosophy in Medicine* by Charles M. Culver and Bernard Gert, 1982, Oxford University Press.

Chapter 3

1. For a more detailed account of punishment, see "Moral Theory and Applied Ethics" by Bernard Gert in *The Monist*, October, 1984, Volume 67, Number 4, pp. 532-548.
2. For a more detailed account of malady, see Chapter 5 of *Philosophy in Medicine* by Charles M. Culver and Bernard Gert, 1982, Oxford University Press.

Chapter 13

1. 1965, New York, Random House, Abridged edition. All references to this work are to this edition.
2. 1971, Cambridge, Massachusetts, Harvard University Press. All references to this work are to this edition.
3. See the *Diagnostic and Statistical Manual of Mental Disorders* 1987 (Third Edition Revised), generally known as DSM-IIIR, published by the American Psychiatric Association, for a fuller account of mental disorders, esp. pp. xxii-xxiii.
4. See *Grounding for the Metaphysics of Morals*, pp. 426ff. Standard reference.

5. Baier uses the phrase "contrary to reason" to include all the ways of acting that I call "irrational." He uses "irrational" for a very strong way of acting contrary to reason.
6. 1971, Oxford, Oxford University Press, p. 282.
7. Op. cit., pp. 75ff.
8. *The Journal of Philosophy*, Volume LXXVII, Number 9, September, 1980, pp. 528ff.
9. Op. cit., p. 76.
10. Rawls, in the Dewey lectures, seems to be retreating from the theory of morality as impartial rationality. In these lectures he makes the rational subordinate to the reasonable in the original position. More importantly, he now seems to claim to be able to derive only the principles of justice and this only for those who already live in a democracy.
11. *Mill On Liberty: A Defence*, 1983, London, Routledge & Kegan Paul. Gray uses different terms, but my idea for this distinction comes from him.
12. John Stuart Mill, *Utilitarianism, Liberty, and Representative Government*, 1951, New York, E. P. Dutton & Co., p. 3.
13. Op. cit., p. 60.
14. I am grateful to the National Endowment for the Humanities and the National Science Foundation for the Sustained Development Award, grant number RII-8018088 AO3, which provided me with the time to work on this chapter. They are not responsible in any way for the views contained in it. I am also grateful for the criticisms and suggestions of Larry Stern, Bob Ladenson, Dan Clouser, Lynn McFall, Tim Duggan, Bob Fogelin and Walter Sinnott-Armstrong, who are only slightly more responsible.

INDEX

307